NEW YORK REVIEW BOOKS
CLASSICS

INHUMAN LAND

JÓZEF CZAPSKI (1896–1993), a painter and writer, and an eyewitness to the turbulent history of the twentieth century, was born into an aristocratic family in Prague and grew up in Poland under czarist domination. After receiving his baccalaureate in Saint Petersburg, he went on to study law at Imperial University and was present during the February Revolution of 1917. Briefly a cavalry officer in World War I, decorated for bravery in the Polish-Bolshevik War, Czapski went on to attend the Academy of Fine Arts in Kraków and then moved to Paris to paint. He spent seven years in Paris, moving in social circles that included friends of Proust and Bonnard, and it was only in 1931 that he returned to Warsaw, and began exhibiting his work and writing art criticism. When Germany invaded Poland in September 1939, Czapski was mobilized as a reserve officer. Captured by the Germans, he was handed over to the Soviets as a prisoner of war, though for reasons that remain mysterious he was not among the twenty-two thousand Polish officers who were summarily executed by the Soviet secret police. Czapski described his experiences in the Soviet Union in several books: *Memories of Starobilsk* (forthcoming from NYRB), *Inhuman Land*, and *Lost Time* (available from NYRB), the last of which reconstructs a lecture he gave to his fellow prisoners about Proust's *In Search of Lost Time*. Unwilling to live in postwar communist Poland, Czapski set up a studio outside of Paris. His essays appeared in *Kultura*, the leading intellectual journal of the Polish emigration that he helped establish; his painting underwent a great final flowering in the 1980s. Czapski died, nearly blind, at ninety-six. *Almost Nothing: The 20th-Century Art and Life of Józef Czapski*, a biography of Czapski by Eric Karpeles, was published by New York Review Books.

ANTONIA LLOYD-JONES is the 2018 winner of the Transatlantyk Award for the most outstanding promoter of Polish literature abroad. She has translated works by several of Poland's leading contemporary novelists and writers of reportage, as well as crime fiction, poetry, and children's books. She is a mentor for the Emerging Translator Mentorship Programme and former co-chair of the Translators Association of the United Kingdom.

TIMOTHY SNYDER is the Richard C. Levin Professor of History at Yale and a permanent fellow of the Institute for Human Sciences in Vienna. He is the author of several works of European history, including *Bloodlands*, winner of the American Academy of Arts and Letters Literature Award, the Hannah Arendt Prize, and the Leipzig Book Prize. His most recent books are *On Tyranny* and *The Road to Unfreedom*.

INHUMAN LAND

Searching for the Truth in Soviet Russia
1941–1942

JÓZEF CZAPSKI

Translated from the Polish by
ANTONIA LLOYD-JONES

Introduction by
TIMOTHY SNYDER

NEW YORK REVIEW BOOKS

New York

THIS IS A NEW YORK REVIEW BOOK
PUBLISHED BY THE NEW YORK REVIEW OF BOOKS
435 Hudson Street, New York, NY 10014
www.nyrb.com

Originally published in the Polish language as *Na nieludzkiej ziemi*
This translation is published by arrangement with Społeczny Instytut Wydawniczy ZNAK
Sp. z o.o., Kraków, Poland

PUBLICATION SUBSIDIZED BY THE POLISH BOOK INSTITUTE

BOOK INSTITUTE

THE ©POLAND TRANSLATION PROGRAM

©POLAND

All the illustrations are used here by kind permission of the National Museum in Kraków
(Józef Czapski Archive at the Princes Czartoryski Library), apart from: page 370, by kind
permission of the National Digital Archive (from the Tadeusz Szumański Photographic Archive), and page 444, CPA agency collection, by kind permission of Stanisław Mancewicz.

Library of Congress Cataloging-in-Publication Data
Names: Czapski, Józef, 1896–1993, author. | Lloyd-Jones, Antonia, translator.
Title: Inhuman land : Searching for the Truth in Soviet Russa, 1941–1942 / by Józef
    Czapski ; translated by Antonia Lloyd-Jones.
Other titles: Na nieludzkiej ziemi. English
Description: New York : New York Review Books, [2018] | Series: New York Review Books
    classics | Translation of: Na nieludzkiej ziemi. | Includes bibliographical references.
Identifiers: LCCN 2018024072 (print) | LCCN 2018040660 (ebook) | ISBN
    9781681372570 (epub) | ISBN 9781681372563 | ISBN 9781681372563 (alk. paper)
Subjects: LCSH: Czapski, Józef, 1896–1993. | World War, 1939–1945—Prisoners and
    prisons, Russian. | World War, 1939–1945—Personal narratives, Polish. | Prisoners of
    war—Poland—Biography. | Prisoners of war—Soviet Union—Biography. | LCGFT:
    Autobiographies.
Classification: LCC D805.R9 (ebook) | LCC D805.R9 C8513 2018 (print) | DDC
    940.54/7247092 [B]—dc23
LC record available at https://lccn.loc.gov/2018024072

ISBN 978-1-68137-256-3
Available as an electronic book; ISBN 978-1-68137-257-0
Printed in the United States of America on acid-free paper.
10 9 8 7 6 5 4 3 2 1

CONTENTS

PART TWO: THE FIGHT

INTRODUCTION

JÓZEF Czapski was a gifted child of a fading European aristocracy, a lifelong admirer of Russian thought, and perhaps the greatest Polish painter of the twentieth century—though during most of it he lived in obscurity in France. He was an introvert with the skills of an extrovert, able to speak to almost anyone about almost anything, who wanted only to compose his landscapes, portraits, and still lifes in peace. *Inhuman Land*, his recollection of the Second World War, is the work of a person who faced impossible demands with grace. One evening in Paris, decades after the events recounted in this book, Czapski attended a dinner party. When, unusually for him, he began to tell stories from the war, a French scholar gaped: "I had no idea what life could be!"*

That evening, the Frenchman listened. One must attend closely to Czapski. He was very humble. His style is descriptive rather than declarative, and he draws no conclusions. He gives voice to people and vitality to situations, which means that he withdraws himself. In this memoir, he tells us almost nothing about his life as an artist in interwar Paris and Warsaw, and very little about his confinement in Soviet concentration camps at the beginning of the Second World War.

Czapski was settling down in the late 1930s, with an atelier in Warsaw and a room near his friend Ludwik Hering in the suburbs.

*Michał (Michel) Heller, "Człowiek przeszłości i przyszłości," *Zeszyty Literackie*, no. 44 (2003): 93. In 1985, Jacques Cousteau called Czapski "the most astonishing man, in my opinion, whom one can meet today."

Just when it seemed he had found his way into life, he was summoned to war.

When Nazi Germany invaded Poland on September 1, 1939, Czapski, then forty-three, was mobilized as a reserve officer of the Polish Army. The Soviet Union invaded Poland on September 17, falling upon retreating Polish forces from the rear. Czapski was captured by the Red Army near the village of Chmielek and sent to a camp in a former cloister in Starobilsk, in what is now the Luhansk region of eastern Ukraine. About six months later, in April 1940, Czapski and a few of his fellow prisoners from Starobilsk were transferred to a camp at Gryazovets, about five hundred kilometers north of Moscow, where they met other Polish officers coming from camps at Kozelsk and Ostashkov.

Czapski, like Poland, was a victim of the Nazi-Soviet alliance known as the Molotov-Ribbentrop pact. In Gryazovets, Czapski and his comrades knew little about the course of the war, or about Poland under Soviet and German occupation. In late 1939 the eastern half of Poland was annexed by the Soviet Union, while Nazi Germany annexed some of the Polish lands it conquered and transformed the rest into a colony called the General Government. The prisoners placed their hopes in Poland's allies, Britain and France. But in June 1940, France was defeated and British forces were driven from the Continent.

The prisoners' fates changed a year later, when Hitler betrayed Stalin. The action of *Inhuman Land* begins after the German invasion of the Soviet Union in June 1941. As German forces raced towards Moscow, Stalin applied an Orwellian "amnesty" to his Polish prisoners of war: he had imprisoned them for fighting his Nazi ally, and now released them to fight his Nazi enemy. By the terms of an agreement between the Soviet Union and the Polish government-in-exile in London, a Polish army would be formed from released Gulag inmates. Czapski, who was released from Gryazovets in September 1941, would be at the center of its creation.*

---

*This was the Sikorski-Maisky agreement of July 1941. See Gabriel Gorodetsky, ed.,

Tens of thousands of other men also made their way from far-flung Soviet concentration camps to makeshift Polish bases, first in the Orenburg region of southern Russia, and then near Tashkent, in Uzbekistan. Czapski's job was to receive and register these fellow survivors, very often sick and starving, as they arrived in the bases in autumn 1941. Czapski writes about typhus, tuberculosis, dysentery, and hunger, with a precision born of experience. The surviving men formed the Anders Army, named for its commander, General Władysław Anders. It crossed the Soviet border to Iran in spring 1942, and then journeyed through Iraq, Palestine, Egypt, and finally to Italy, where, as the Polish Second Corps, it fought the Germans. It was these Polish soldiers who charged the bombed ruins of the monastery of Monte Cassino in May 1944 in one of the most daring Allied offensives of the war. In Italy survivors of the Gulag helped inflict a defeat on the defenders of the Reich. In *Inhuman Land*, Czapski tells the story of how this came about.[*]

The Anders Army achieved all this with a much smaller complement of trained officers than had been anticipated. In late 1941 and early 1942, Czapski and his colleagues trained some seventy thousand soldiers—but of the ten thousand officers known to be in Soviet captivity, about eight thousand never appeared. The missing men had all been held in three camps: Starobilsk (where Czapski had spent half a year), Kozelsk, and Ostashkov. Czapski was ordered to assemble a list of the missing officers and to speak to Soviet authorities about their whereabouts. When he met with NKVD chiefs and Gulag officials in winter 1941–42 in Moscow and Orenburg, he assumed that his comrades had been sent to some especially distant camp.[†]

The Maisky Diaries, Tatiana Sorokina and Oliver Ready, trans. (New Haven, CT: Yale University Press), 2015.

[*]See Norman Davies, *Trail of Hope: The Anders Army, An Odyssey Across Three Continents* (Oxford: Osprey Publishing), 2015.

[†]Among the murdered was one woman, the pilot Janina Lewandowska (née Dowbor-Muśnicka). She was the daughter of one of the commanders of a Polish army, discussed below, that Czapski joined in 1917.

Czapski could not imagine then what we now know to be true: The missing eight thousand officers were all dead, murdered at Stalin's orders, their skulls shattered from behind by bullets, their piled remains buried secretly at Katyn, Kharkiv, and Tver. In March 1940, Lavrenty Beria, the director of the Soviet secret state police (NKVD), received Stalin's written approval to shoot the prisoners of Starobilsk, Ostashkov, and Kozelsk. They were mostly officers, and the officers mostly from the reserves: educated men, professionals, and intellectuals; physicians, veterinarians, scientists, lawyers, teachers, artists. After a quick review of their files, 97 percent of these people were sentenced to death. Czapski and 394 other prisoners from the three camps were spared and sent to Gryazovets, some because a foreign power had intervened on their behalf, others because they were Soviet informers.*

In April 1940, the Polish prisoners at Kozelsk were transported to the edge of the Katyn forest, taken inside an NKVD summer resort, and shot by NKVD men: 4,410 prisoners were murdered in this way. At Ostashkov a band played as the prisoners departed for an NKVD prison at Tver, where each prisoner was bound and led to a soundproof cell. Two NKVD men held each prisoner's arms as a third shot the prisoner from behind: 6,314 prisoners were murdered in this way. The men interned at Starobilsk were taken to the NKVD prison at Kharkiv, led one by one to a dark room without windows, and shot: 3,739 prisoners were murdered in this way. Since the prisoners of the three camps had been allowed to correspond, the NKVD could locate their homes. Right after the executions, the family members of the victims, 60,667 people resident in the eastern Polish lands under Soviet control, were deported to the Gulag. The children and the wives and the parents of the murdered men were told that they were being sent to join their fathers and husbands and sons.†

---

*Czapski seems to have been spared because of the intervention of German diplomats. This was mysterious to him and remains so. One of the informers, Zygmunt Berling, was given the command of a second Polish army formed on Soviet soil, this one under Soviet control, which was allowed to fight on the eastern front and to reach Poland.

†More than 8,000 of the murdered were officers and more than 6,000 were police-

This mass murder, remembered as the Katyn massacre, is what Czapski escaped, although he did not know this at the time. He bore witness to the aftermath as best he could. Is it worth pursuing the truth even when it is unattainable? The answer that Czapski offered by writing this book the way that he did was in the affirmative. By the time he completed it, the death pit at Katyn had been discovered. Yet his book is about what he found while he was searching, and in that sense its major subject is an ethic. It is one that Czapski himself was far too modest to spell out: the attempt to see the world as a basic form of moral activity, one which disables evil forms of politics and enables good ones. Up until that point in his life, Czapski had been chiefly engaged in teaching himself to see. This account of the war reveals what he had learned, and what we can learn from him during our own trials with the truth.

Józef Maria Emeryk Franciszek Ignacy Czapski was born in Prague in 1896 to an aristocratic family whose estate was just south of Minsk, in the Russian Empire. He was descended from people who regarded themselves as Poles and Germans on his father's side and Czechs and Austrians on his mother's side—and from administrators of empire, Romanov and Habsburg, on each side. The local peasantry spoke Belarusian, as did the servants. Czapski's father, Jerzy Hutten-Czapski, spoke Polish to the children, although he had only learned the language properly himself at university—his own mother was a Baltic German Protestant who corresponded in English, French, and German, while his father had aspired to raise "Greeks and Romans."

---

men. Fulfilling Beria's quotas, the NKVD also murdered at the same time more than 7,000 Polish citizens who were not in those three camps but were in prison or had been arrested in April 1940. Thus the total death toll for the Katyn massacre (a name which is used as a shorthand for murders at five different sites) is correctly given as about 22,000. See Anna M. Cienciala, Natalia S. Lebedeva, and Wojciech Materski, eds., *Katyn: A Crime Without Punishment* (New Haven, CT: Yale University Press), 2007, and my *Bloodlands: Europe Between Hitler and Stalin* (New York: Basic Books), 2010.

Czapski's mother, Josepha, came from a German-speaking family, the Thun und Hohensteins, brought to Bohemia by the Habsburgs to displace Czech nobles, but she regarded herself as Czech and as having changed her nationality from Czech to Polish when she married her Polish husband. In her marriage she was known as Józefa Czapska. She spoke German with him and to her older children but Polish to the younger ones. She did teach the children to sing Czech patriotic songs and dressed them for public outings in Czech folk costumes—politically inoffensive in the Russian Empire. Czapski was the fifth child of seven and the elder of two sons. His mother died when he was seven. He was educated at home in French, German, and Polish, and then in Petersburg, the imperial capital, in Russian.

These Czapskis belonged to the wealthier element of the Polish nobility, which had survived and even prospered under imperial rule. Poland had not existed as an independent state since 1795, when it had been partitioned among the Habsburg monarchy, Russian Empire, and Prussia. Czapski's family was at home in that imperial world, and though he was raised as a Pole, he was certainly not taught to wish for Polish independence. As he was coming of age, the First World War was making an independent Poland thinkable. The three partitioning powers were at war, the German and Habsburg empires on one side, the Russian on the other. The mind of young Józef Czapski was elsewhere.

In 1917, as Russia passed through a February Revolution that promised law and rights and an October Revolution that promised class struggle, Czapski was a Christian pacifist living in Petersburg with a liberal uncle.* As an acolyte of Lev Tolstoy, Czapski believed that heaven could be brought to earth if men did not resist evil with force. In September 1917, he volunteered for a Polish army within Russia but was shocked to see a fellow officer abuse a Belarusian peasant. He told his superior officers that he had joined the army out

---

*This was Alexander von Meyendorff, the parliamentary deputy, diplomat, and legal scholar, a major influence on Czapski and a memorable figure in his own right.

of conformism and cowardice, and left it to help found a pacifist commune in Petersburg. His uncle and other connections looked out for him, but even so he spent his time searching for food in the hungry city. When this youthful venture came to nothing, Czapski departed revolutionary Russia for Warsaw in May 1918, planning to enroll as an art student in the fall. A new Poland was forming around him, but he did not identify strongly with it, and still believed that Christianity forbade the violence that many of his generation saw as necessary to create a state and establish and defend its borders. One fine day, strolling down the street eating cherries, Czapski suddenly found himself thinking about two comrades in the army who had supported his principled decision not to fight. Both of them had since been killed in action. Czapski volunteered again for the Polish Army, asking for an assignment where he would not have to kill. Such a task was quickly found.

Polish officers from the three empires were gathering in Warsaw. Among them was the man who had been Czapski's immediate superior in the Polish Army in Russia. He received Czapski cordially, ignoring his prior desertion, and found him the appropriate assignment. Five commanders of that Polish army in Russia had decided, after the October Revolution, that they would be most useful fighting with the French against Germany. As they made their way across far northern Russia, hoping to reach France by sea, they had lost touch with Warsaw. Czapski's assignment was to find them. And so in October 1918, Czapski was sent back to revolutionary Petersburg, his possessions in a basket and bribe money in his wallet, to learn what had become of these men. After a good deal of meandering, he found his way to an influential Bolshevik, Elena Stasova, who told him that the officers had been apprehended by Bolshevik forces and executed.*

One day that autumn, as Czapski was walking through Petersburg,

---

*Maria Czapska, *Czas odmieniony* (Kraków: Znak, 2014), 307–20. The city where these events took place was called St. Petersburg from its founding until 1914, Petrograd from 1914 to 1924, Leningrad from 1924 through 1991, and then again St. Petersburg. I call it Petersburg for the sake of simplicity.

he chanced to see a nameplate reading "Merezhkovsky" at the entrance to a building, guessed that it belonged to the symbolist poet and religious thinker of that name, and rang the bell. When Dmitry Merezhkovsky opened the door, Czapski unburdened himself: he was a pacifist at war, he told this complete stranger, and he did not know how to live. Merezhkovsky invited him in and called to his wife, the poet Zinaida Gippius: "Zina! Come! This is interesting!" Merezhkovsky told Czapski that the path to heaven was muddy, that God most valued those who besmirched themselves while trying to do right.*

Czapski returned to Warsaw with his news about the death of the five officers, and then enlisted as a regular soldier. Poland had been founded as an independent state while he was on his way to Petersburg, and its borders were uncertain on all sides. The most important conflict in 1919 was with a Bolshevik Russia that was seeking to spread its revolution through Poland to Germany and Europe. Czapski was promoted to the rank of officer and decorated for his courage in the Polish-Bolshevik War of 1919. Extremely tall and a good rider, he cut a fine figure in an engagement with Semyon Budyonny's famous Red Cavalry. One of Budyonny's men shouted as Czapski raced forward: "Grab that son of a bitch!" His men liked to remember that moment. Czapski himself recalled one of his soldiers lying in the grass and puzzling over the meaning of war: "And all this for the motherfucking homeland." That too became a saying among his troops.†

As Merezhkovsky had advised, Czapski made contact with the world and, in his own way, entered politics. Poland won the Polish-Bolshevik War, though the peace signed with the Bolsheviks in 1920 left the Czapski family estate on the Soviet side of the border. Czapski had dreamed neither of a communist Russia nor of an independent

---

*The career of Ivan Ilyin, today an influential thinker in Russia, began with a different sort of rejection of Tolstoyan pacifism. See my *The Road to Unfreedom: Russia, Europe, America* (New York: Tim Duggan Books, 2018).

†The first quotation is from Wojciech Karpiński, *Portret Czapskiego* (Warsaw: Zeszyty Literackie, 2007), 10; the second, like all remaining unannotated quotations of Czapski's, are from this edition of *Inhuman Land*.

Poland, but he now found himself a young man with experience of both, skilled at crossing borders of various kinds. His father, Jerzy, seems to have lost his authority with his children along with his property. Czapski, in any event, was open to new influences. He was one of those rare people who knew how to love older people when he was young (and younger people when he was old).

When Merezhkovsky and Gippius decided to flee Bolshevik Russia, Czapski helped smuggle them into Poland in early 1920. The couple was joined in their escape by their friend and collaborator, the journalist and political thinker Dmitry Filosofov. These Russians thought of Poland as a messianic country that should save Europe from Bolshevism; Czapski for his part saw in them citizens of a "Third Russia," neither czarist nor communist, a possible future.* Filosofov became an adviser to the commander of the Polish armed forces, Józef Piłsudski. In Warsaw Czapski visited Filosofov every week: "I was like a son to him."† In the 1920s and '30s, guided by Filosofov, Czapski continued to read (and write about) Russian poets, novelists, and philosophers.

What Czapski wanted to do was paint. Once he returned from the battlefield of the Polish-Bolshevik War, he enrolled again as an art student, this time in Kraków, where he studied for three years. In 1924 he led a Paris Committee of young Polish painters (Artur Nacht, Zygmunt Waliszewski, Dorota Seydenmann, Jan Cybis, Hanna Rudzka-Cybisowa, Seweryn Boraczok, and others) on a venture to Paris that lasted the better part of a decade. His sister Maria joined them. Czapski had no money, since his family had lost everything after the revolution, but he did have languages and breeding and poise and charm, his artist friends, and now his sister, who looked after him even as she wrote her own books. He shone in salons, drew for Coco Chanel, talked with Gertrude Stein, listened to jazz, and sang Negro spirituals. He worked hard at his painting, had his first exhibition,

*See Andrzej Nowak, *Polska i trzy Rosje* (Kraków: Arcana, 2001).
†Józef Czapski and Piotr Kłoczowski, *Świat w moich oczach* (Ząbki: Wydawnictwo Księży Pallotynów, 2001), 128.

wrote a history of impressionism, and planned books about Russian literature.*

While ill with typhus, Czapski read Proust's *À la recherche du temps perdu*. Czapski appreciated Proust's powers of concentration and recollection; he also admired Proust as a witness who sacrificed his health for his work. Above all, Czapski understood Proust, and literature generally, as a source of techniques and references that could be applied universally. When in 1939 Czapski went to war again and in 1941 found himself looking for officers a second time, he tried to connect his Soviet experiences to the Russia of his youth and the European art and literature he studied as an adult. At Gryazovets, in the guise of French lessons, Czapski lectured to his fellow prisoners on Proust. He did so from memory, treating a concentration camp as Proust had treated his cork-walled room, as a site enabling what both men called "*mémoire involontaire*." His lectures were a triumph of culture over politics and thought over circumstance that would be hard to surpass. They included a pertinent expression of Czapski's wonder at Proust: "It's he, and he alone in this crowd, who will make them all come to life again."†

The original edition of *Inhuman Land* begins when Czapski is released from Gryazovets and concludes when he departs the Soviet Union for Iran.‡ In his journeys through the Soviet Union, Czapski recorded what scholarship would later confirm: deportations of peasants in the early 1930s; deportations of nations in the late 1930s. He

*Czapski's recollections of Paris are scattered among several sources. On Stein, see his *Tumult i widma* (Kraków: Znak, 1997), 123. On spirituals, see Felicja Krance, "Józio," *Zeszyty Literackie*, no. 44 (2003): 86. On national tensions among the painters, see Paweł Bem, "Ten uroczy Ukrainiec Boraczok," *Zeszyty Literackie*, no. 131 (2015).

†Happily, they have just been published in English: Józef Czapski, *Lost Time: Lectures on Proust in a Soviet Prison Camp*, Eric Karpeles, trans. (New York: New York Review Books, 2018). The French edition is *Proust contre la déchéance* (Montricher: Noir sur Blanc, 1987).

‡This edition includes the chapters that Czapski later added for the German edition, which brings the action through Monte Cassino and includes his reflections on Germany.

describes the displaced Ukrainians, Koreans, and others whom he saw, records what they told him, captures the sadness of human faces. He felt unequal to the task, wishing for "a new Tolstoy or Proust," someone who could convey "the things that would suddenly give the game away in the course of ordinary, everyday life—a small gesture or a memorable glance. It wasn't the difficult conditions or the hunger—all that was less awful than the suppression of humanity, the mute look in the eyes of people among whom just about everybody had lost at least one of their closest relatives to the camps in the north."

Czapski could almost always reach people if he could speak to them in person, but his meetings with NKVD men—disguising their complicity in the mass murder of his friends, representing a Stalinist Soviet Union that was reeling under German attack during a freezing winter—posed challenges insurmountable even for him. He noted a difference between the early revolutionaries he had met in 1918 and the officials with whom he spoke in 1941 and 1942: both killed but the latter also lied. Throughout *Inhuman Land*, Czapski consistently tries to speak with Soviet citizens—his hosts in the apartments where he is billeted, his companions on train journeys, nurses in hospitals—with mixed success. There was no missing the contrast between the vibrant and unpredictable conversations of the Russian intellectuals he knew and the repetitive propaganda or depressing silence of Soviet public spaces. Even so, he produced an unsurpassed document of everyday Stalinism.

Czapski began his search with the hope that he would hear again the voices of Poles he knew at Starobilsk. He ended by giving a voice to the Soviet citizens whom he met along the way.

A touching scene in *Inhuman Land* is Czapski's encounter with a Jewish stranger in a Moscow hotel in February 1942. He is about to leave the Soviet capital, having failed to learn anything from Soviet officials, and feels crushed by the indifference of his surroundings. The Jew asks him politely if he is from Poland, and Czapski impulsively invites this stranger to his room. There they look at a photograph of the Old Town of Warsaw, in ruins after German bombing. The Jew bursts into tears. Czapski himself weeps, and is grateful: "the poor

Jew's red, tearstained eyes saved me from total loss of faith and bitter despair."

We tend to separate Stalinism and Nazism in our minds, but in the middle of the war in the middle of Europe tens of millions of people experienced both. Ludwik Hering, for example, saw his friend Czapski depart to fight the Germans, only to learn that he had been taken prisoner by the Soviets. Hering's brother died in Auschwitz, after which Hering himself was arrested by Soviet NKVD officers who understood his name to be "Göring." He could not defend himself under Soviet arrest because he had lost his documents when under German arrest. Variations of this sort of experience were the rule.

The history of Soviets and Poles and Jews and Germans was entangled in ways that Czapski's book helps to clarify. The Jews most likely to survive German killing operations were those who had fallen victim to Soviet repressions. The largest group of Jewish survivors of the Holocaust in Poland were people who had been deported in 1940 from annexed eastern Poland to camps or settlements in Siberia or Kazakhstan. Czapski helped such Jews enlist in the Polish army, even when this was not appropriate on military grounds. Among the Polish Jews who joined were Zionists, who subsequently left the army in Palestine. Menachem Begin, a future prime minister of Israel and the founder of the party that rules the country today, was discharged from the Polish armed forces in Palestine.*

Warsaw was a major Jewish city, home to more Jews than Palestine before the Second World War. Czapski was at Gryazovets when Warsaw Jews were placed in ghettos, in Iran during the transports to Treblinka known as the Grosse Aktion, and in Iraq during the Warsaw Ghetto Uprising. Though Czapski was not a witness to the events that we know as the Holocaust, he did learn of them. His sister Maria lived in Warsaw during the war, helping a social activist of Jewish origin write her memoirs. She also visited Janusz Korczak,

*For details, see my *Black Earth: The Holocaust as History and Warning* (New York: Tim Duggan Books, 2015).

a pedagogue she and her brother both admired, in the Warsaw Ghetto—before he was murdered in Treblinka along with his fellow teachers and the children under their care. She wrote to Czapski of the murder of the family of Dorota Seydenmann, one of his artist friends in Paris.*

For Czapski, the Polish interwar republic, broken in 1939 by the German and Soviet invasions, was supposed to have been a homeland for all. He came to Polish identity himself through action, and Poland was for him a nation of citizens rather than a group of ethnic kindred. When Poland's first president was assassinated by a nationalist fanatic in 1922 amidst roiling public hatred of Jews, Czapski founded a student committee to protest nationalism and anti-Semitism. In the 1930s, his Russian mentor Filosofov was an outspoken defender of Poland's Jews. Czapski understood his Paris Committee of artists as a microcosm of a better and more cosmopolitan Poland, and remained friends with its artists as they returned to Warsaw.†

During the German occupation, Dorota Seydenmann was sheltered by Hanna Rudzka-Cybisowa, one of the artists of the committee. Seydenmann left when Rudzka-Cybisowa was denounced, so as not to endanger her, and then was murdered. Artur Nacht, the second Jew of the Paris Committee, wrote to Czapski in Starobilsk, before he was sent to the Lwów ghetto. Nacht escaped and survived to paint again after the war. The Holocaust is not a subject of the chapters of *Inhuman Land* that narrate the years 1941 through 1943, but the attentive reader will find the allusions.

After the war, living in political exile in France, Czapski learned more of what had happened to Warsaw Jews. Ludwik Hering, the

---

*I owe some of this information to Mikołaj Nowak-Rogoziński, who is writing a book about Czapski during the war. Maria later wrote of the Holocaust as a crime that "weighs on all of humanity and all of us still living." She fled Poland in 1945 and joined her brother in France.

†On Filosofov, see Piotr Mitzner, "Rosyjski goj w międzywojennej Warszawie," *Nigdy Więcej*, no. 22 (2016). On the assassination, see Paul Brykczynski, *Primed for Violence: Murder, Antisemitism, and Democratic Politics in Interwar Poland* (Madison: University of Wisconsin Press, 2018).

friend he had left behind in Warsaw in 1939, was troubled by Polish reactions to Jewish suffering: he painted a carousel of happy Poles enjoying themselves as the ghetto burned behind them.* Though Czapski had parted with Hering when the Second World War began and would not see him again for more than thirty years, the two men kept up an extraordinary correspondence. During the German occupation of Warsaw, Hering worked as a night watchman in a tannery that bordered upon the ghetto. He observed Jewish children as they left the ghetto, hunted for food, and returned. He knew that their greatest fear was the Polish street children. He helped several Jews to escape, in some cases literally giving them the clothes off his back. In 1945 and 1946 he published two stories about the Holocaust, recording what he had seen (if not what he had done), and then never published again. Czapski pleaded with Hering to write more, and was reading his friend's work as he completed *Inhuman Land*.†

Hering's story "Ślady" ("traces," "footsteps") is a close description of the children of the ghetto and their daily search for food beyond its walls. Czapski's similarly entitled chapter, "Śladami" ("in the traces," "in the footsteps") describes the face of a hungry Russian woman crossing herself before slowly eating a single small tomato. Having read that chapter, Hering wrote to Czapski of a starving Jewish woman who sees a tomato vine through a hole in the ghetto wall and smiles. The theme of helpless public loneliness was shared by the two men before, during, and after the war. Czapski had long been preoccupied with the image of "the Jewish woman in the third-class cabin." After the war, when he returned to painting, it became "the African woman at the train station."‡

---

*The image is best known from Czesław Miłosz's poem "Campo dei Fiori."
†Hering was at the time raising his niece to be a painter; for her recollections, see Ludmiła Murawska-Péju, "Nachwort," in Ludwik Hering, *Spuren: Drei Erzählungen* (Berlin: FotoTapeta, 2011), 99–103. Czapski's main labor of the immediate postwar years was the establishment of the journal *Kultura*. For a sense of its influence, see my *The Reconstruction of Nations: Poland, Ukraine, Lithuania, Belarus, 1569–1999* (New Haven, CT: Yale University Press, 2003).
‡For the stories of Hering in German translation, see the previous note. For the

By the time he wrote *Inhuman Land*, Czapski was no longer a pacifist. The good was truth rather than peace: truth could reveal injustice; truth opened some possibility for the virtue of humanity. The two men discussed Hering's stories as "antihuman." The last words of Hering's "Ślady," following a description of the ghetto uprising and the indifference of Poles, leave little room for hope: "Fine snowflakes fall fast and thick. The sky, the earth, and the ruins of the ghetto tremble like printed words on a piece of paper that is coming apart." There is a finality here, a reduction to black and white. Despite Czapski's pleas, Hering stopped writing after "Ślady" was published in 1946.

For Czapski, words were like colors, to be kept in motion, in a search that did not end. The two men saw different wars and were of different characters. Hering was a perfectionist who liked to advise others. Czapski was ecumenical and industrious and liked to work alone. They loved and encouraged each other. When Czapski completed *Inhuman Land* in 1947, Hering was happy. When Czapski returned to painting in 1949, Hering was happier still.

In communist Poland, as in the Soviet Union, it was illegal to write about the Katyn massacre. Under communism, Czapski's name was on a special list of those not permitted to publish under any circumstances. Today Poland is sovereign, the truth about Katyn is known, and Czapski is receiving some of the attention he deserves. Some Polish politicians now err in the opposite direction, suggesting that an air accident that killed Poles traveling to commemorate Katyn in 2010 confirmed the eternal martyrdom of the Polish nation. Czapski's position about Polish suffering was different: rather than treating the victimhood of other Poles as an authorization for falsehood, he turned

letters, see Józef Czapski and Ludwik Hering, *Listy 1939–1982*, vol. 1 (Gdańsk: Fundacja Terytoria Książki, 2016). On the lonely figure, see "Wyrwane strone," *Zeszyty Literackie*, no. 45 (1994): 23. Writing to Hering from the United States in 1950, Czapski called the predicament of blacks "our Jewish question."

his own suffering into a search for the truth about those who suffered more than he. He quoted Proust: "Perhaps a great artist serves his fatherland—but can only do so by seeing truth, which means forgetting everything else, including the fatherland."*

Despite his experiences in the Soviet Union, Czapski in his postwar French emigration kept on exploring Russia through literature and kept on making Russian friends. The historian Michel Heller, the host of that dinner party with the astonished Frenchman, put it this way: "Russian was not for him the language of the executioners and the torturers, but the language of Tolstoy and Dostoyevsky, of Rozanov and Merezhkovsky, of Akhmatova and Solzhenitsyn." This was clear to the Russians who knew him during and after the war. In Tashkent in 1943, Czapski met the Russian poets Anna Akhmatova and Lydia Chukovskaya, and left an impression on both. Akhmatova devoted to Czapski a breathless poem that begins with the words "That night, we drove each other mad." Four decades after they had spent a night talking on a balcony, Chukovskaya asked Aleksandr Solzhenitsyn to tell Czapski that she dreamed of reading *Inhuman Land*. Even the distrustful Solzhenitsyn took to Czapski right away.†

One of the tasks in today's Russia is to connect the twenty-first century with the nineteenth without ignoring or falsifying the Soviet history that came between. For this, mediators will be needed, and Czapski is a precious one.

The truth about the Soviet Union that Czapski sought was a lonely cause, even in the West. Were Americans and West Europeans to remember that the war began as a defense of Poland, they would find it harder to qualify the outcome as a victory. Stalin began the war as Hitler's ally and annexed half of Poland; he ended the war as Churchill, Roosevelt, and de Gaulle's ally and annexed half of Poland. Were Americans and West Europeans to face the facts of Soviet repression

---

*Józef Czapski, "Złote gwoździe," *Zeszyty Literackie*, no. 45 (1994): 50.
†"В ту ночь мы сошли друг от друга с ума." It is possible that the poem had another *destinataire*. See Piotr Mitzner, "Wyspa Taszkient," *Zeszyty Literackie*, no. 165 (2018): 94–106.

in 1939–1941, they would have to accept that the war was an alliance with one totalitarian power against another, not a triumph of democracy. To see the truth about Katyn is also to realize that the Western allies endorsed Stalinist lies about mass murder. The issue closed only with the release of Soviet documents in 1990—fifty years after the murder of Czapski's comrades but three years before Czapski's death.*

This is the first translation of *Inhuman Land* from the Polish original into English, seven decades after Czapski completed his book. As new strains of untruth undermine the institutions that we take for granted, his example of truth-seeking serves us still.

—TIMOTHY SNYDER

---

*On the American and British lines on Katyn, see Jolanta Jasina, "Katyń 1940—Smoleńsk 2010," master's thesis, Yale University, 2011. Stanisław Andrzejewski, a Polish prisoner of war who escaped Soviet captivity, established the modern sense of the word "kleptocracy": rule by thieves, an enabling condition of today's untruths. See Oliver Bullough, "The Dark Side of Globalization," *Journal of Democracy* 29 no. 1 (2018): 26.

TRANSLATOR'S NOTE

SEVERAL editions of *Inhuman Land* have been published in Polish and in translation since the book was first issued in 1949. For this translation I used the edition published in 2001 by Wydawnictwo Znak (Kraków), which includes (as well as two other essays: "Memoirs of Starobilsk" and "The Truth About Katyn") the complete, unabridged original Polish text of *Inhuman Land*—part one in the edition you have before you. The illustrations included in this publication are from the most recent Polish edition, published by Wydawnictwo Znak in 2017.

The earlier English translation, originally published in 1951 by Chatto & Windus as *The Inhuman Land*, was translated by Gerard Hopkins from the abridged French translation that appeared in 1949 (translated by M.-A. Bohomolec). It excludes many personal anecdotes and references to Polish poetry, among other material. My sincere thanks to Boris Dralyuk for his help with the poetry translations in this book, which have greatly benefited from his sensitive skill.

Twenty years after the original Polish publication, Czapski was approached with an offer to publish the book in German and asked if he would write an afterword to explain facts that would be unfamiliar to the German reader. The result was six new chapters, which appeared in subsequent translated editions of the book (including the French and English editions of 1978 and 1987 respectively), and also in some émigré Polish-language editions, as part two. For my translation of part two, I used the 1969 edition published in London by Polska Fundacja Kulturalna.

INHUMAN LAND

For those who now lie suffering on wooden planks
With eyes wide open in an inhuman land.

—STANISŁAW BALIŃSKI

PART ONE
Inhuman Land

15 XI 40

w pospiechu
medwocityłen Józio

Self-portrait drawn by Józef Czapski in the prisoner-of-war camp at Gryazovets, which he then sent to his sister, Leopoldyna Łubieńska. The note on the drawings says: "15 XI 40 In a hurry to catch the post. Your Józio."

FROM THE AUTHOR

I WROTE this book in a wide range of situations and at long intervals between 1942 and 1947.

Some parts were written almost entirely on the basis of notes I made on the spot, in the Soviet Union (in 1941–42). Others are based on memories, and though produced at a distance in time from the events they describe, much earlier memoirs have also been added to them.

The more progress I made with the book, the more I felt that I was not free to write what I wanted but needed to write what I must. If not a report, a memoir is a blend of experiences and reactions; its composition is not just shaped by the period of time it describes but by one's entire life. And to be complete, a book of memoirs carries the silt of its own life with it, as well as a wealth of earlier memories of people who have passed on, and times that will never return.

Originally from White Russia, I completed my schooling in Saint Petersburg. Soon after the October Revolution I went to that city twice more, in 1918 and 1919, when it was called Petrograd. As I was writing about the final year that I spent in the Soviet Union (1941–42) and about my search for thousands of missing comrades, I cast my mind back to my earlier travels within Russia at the start of the Soviet regime; in those days too I was looking for missing people. The reader might find this accumulation of experiences from extremely different years set far apart in time tiring, but I was unable and unwilling, purely for the sake of rigid chronology, to mangle facts that seemed to me to connect and blend together in an organic way.

The more I wrote, I felt a rising rather than a waning awareness that Poland and Russia are tragically opposed, in our ideologies and our historical journeys. My sense of a lethal threat to Poland increased.

This book does not provide any conclusions or syntheses but is merely one Pole's account of his experiences, observations, and thoughts recorded during a year in the Soviet Union.

1. SET FREE

TWENTY-three months behind the wire: at Starobilsk in Ukraine, Pavlishchev Bor near Kaluga, and Gryazovets near Vologda.

The final days before departure were a time of excitement. In cooperation with the Bolsheviks, our senior officers compiled lists of those due to leave, dividing us all up by railcar. We were to travel in two large convoys; nobody knew with whom and in which convoy he would end up, nor did we know which one would take us where— all we did know was that we were going to some place in the south, apparently on the Volga, where the army was to be formed.* Just a couple of days earlier General Anders had been to our camp for a few hours, following his release from the Lubyanka prison and his appointment by General Sikorski as commander of the Polish Army to be created on Soviet territory.

He arrived by plane, visited our camp with an entourage of smiling NKVD officers, and conducted a review of the Gryazovets prisoners of war.

On a sunny, misty, already-autumnal day smelling of wet earth, he inspected our ranks, dressed as we were in threadbare uniforms that with some trouble we had brought to a passable state. He walked on a cane with a slight limp (we knew he had been seriously wounded in September 1939 and then dragged from prison to prison in Lwów,

*Signed on July 30, 1941, less than two months after the outbreak of the German-Soviet war, the Sikorski-Maisky agreement established the provisions for creating a Polish Army within the territory of the Soviet Union, including Polish soldiers whom the Soviets had taken captive, arrested, and deported since September 1939.

Kiev, and Moscow), his complexion was sallow, and his gaze extremely focused and attentive.

In the simplest words, which we found very moving, he called us all back to active service and ended his speech by saying: "We must forget our past injuries . . . and fight with all our strength against the common enemy, Hitler, alongside our allies, alongside the Red Army."

His words were clearly not to be argued with.

The day of our departure was gray and chilly; by now the camp's silver birches were rustling autumnally in the moist, windy air.

The whole day went by in anticipation. I bade farewell to the patch of land where I had spent the past year: our wooden huts, the large, thick-walled monastery building full of bunks, and the ruins of the seventeenth-century church blown up by the Bolsheviks; the small pond in which we laundered our underwear, and the clump of birches, silver poplars, and acacia trees where amid old broken gravestones inscribed in Cyrillic our debates and talks were held, attended by a handful of the liveliest, toughest officer cadets (how many of them, like the discus thrower Fiedoruk, or Hakiel, the violinist from Wilno, were killed in Italy!). Each morning in this same clump of trees we would run into an old Jew we all liked and respected, a timber merchant called Kleinemann (nobody knew why he had been deported and put here with us), saying his prayers in his black-and-white *tallit*. It was also the place where our dear, wise friend Father Kantak would spend hours on end walking up and down with his rosary in his hand.

We didn't set off until seven in the evening, at dusk. In the background, among the same camp poplars, birches, and acacias, stood a few of our fellow prisoners, watching us in despair: these were the Poles who turned out to have passed themselves off as Volksdeutsch. In the past few days Soviet command had divulged the statements they made, thanks to which they were expecting to be sent back to Poland. One of them hanged himself as soon as we had marched off beyond the wire in a long army column; the others must have been finished off by the Soviets, who were planning to move them to camps situated further north.

We set off in fours. On the way to the station, a journey of over four miles, it started to drizzle. The fine rain soon fell harder, as our muddy walk took us across miserable terrain, through poor villages consisting of black cabins made of immense logs. An old woman emerged from one of them: "*Gospod z vami, Boh z vami*—The Lord be with you, God be with you," she said. The same words were repeated to us in a whisper by another young woman on the street of a small town, which looked deserted, with no lights or traffic, and where the station was located.

We were walking at a soldierly pace, singing Polish military songs at the top of our voices, in an excellent mood despite the rain. We reached the station. We were ordered to go around the station buildings. We crossed a small, flooded meadow to the platform, where we were lined up in a column according to the numbers of the railcars to which we had been assigned and ordered to wait. By now it was pouring rain, and our mood was less enthusiastic.

Our commanders had believed the Bolsheviks, who had told them the railcars were already on their way from Vologda, but they had not arrived, and they wouldn't arrive until dawn. There was no question of billeting 1,700 of us in the local houses;* there wasn't room in the station building for more than a few dozen. Our commanders didn't show up, and so, with cold rain bucketing down on us, we stood and waited in fours until two or three in the morning.

---

*In June 1940, 400 Polish POWs were interned at the Gryazovets camp, most of them officers. They were the leftover prisoners, grouped together from three camps that were closed down in April and May 1940 (Kozelsk No. 1, containing about 4,500 officers and cadets; Starobilsk—about 3,900 officers and cadets; and Ostashkov—about 6,500 officers, soldiers and policemen). Apart from the 400 who were interned at Gryazovets, and about a dozen officers who had been sent to Moscow for interrogation and were later released, all the officers and the vast majority of the soldiers disappeared, and only 4,143 POWs from Kozelsk No. 1 were found with bullets in their skulls in pits in Katyń forest. Following Soviet annexation of Lithuania and Latvia, 1,300 Polish officers who had been interned in those countries were deported to the empty Kozelsk camp (Kozelsk No. 2), and then moved by the Soviet authorities to Gryazovets after the outbreak of the German-Soviet war. Thus at the time of our liberation there were about 1,700 of us in Gryazovets.

Right in front of me an officer lay down in a puddle, and categorically refused to get up. There were more and more shouts of: "Pass it on—fetch a doctor! Someone's fallen sick from car 115, car 118," and so on.

Several men fainted.

At about two in the morning discipline started to break down. At first men slipped away one at a time, in search of refuge from the rain, and then suddenly the entire column dispersed to seek shelter. The rain poured into every cranny, down my neck and into my boots; my entire body was soaked and my forage cap was like a sponge. Despite my own wretched state, I took note of some comical scenes, one of which featured two unlucky fellows pacing rapidly to and fro, desperately holding a sopping wet sheet overhead like a flapping sail.

I spent about half an hour standing under a narrow eave with a few comrades, until we pushed our way into an empty freight car on a sidetrack, where we waited it out until five. After scrambling into the dark interior, which was lit up by the occasional match (a match was a valuable object—there were very few, and most of them were soaked), I came upon Gniewosz. He was still a child in 1939 when he ran away to join the army, and two years in the camp had done nothing to mar the attitude of an extremely well-raised boy who was a diligent student and never made any complaint. His head was wrapped in a towel, and he had long, black strands of hair sticking out by his ears like side-locks, and small black eyes like beads in his very white face, almost that of a child. In the glow of the matches he looked like a student at a rabbinical school.

In the dark burrow of the freight car, stuffed with goodness knows what and whom, in his usual polite and friendly tone Gniewosz gave me an excellent piece of advice—to take my sweater out of my backpack and put it on under my wet shirt. With Gniewosz's help, I just about managed in the dark to extract my sweater from the bottom of my pack. I'd been wearing it almost nonstop for the past two years. It was wonderfully warm, made of Swedish wool; originally white with black spots, it was sent to me in the first few weeks by friends in Denmark, in the one and only parcel that had ever reached me.

Luckily it was only damp and did a lot to warm me up. Meanwhile we heard a loud splashing noise, as if someone had emptied a jug of water onto the ground: it was Kleinert, editor of the daily *Gazeta Polska*, pouring the water from his boots onto the floor and wringing out his puttees. As a result, we ended up wading in liquid mud. I was reminded of a passage from a book I had just read by a fellow prisoner at Gryazovets, a mountaineer called Wiktor Ostrowski, describing a night he spent up a Caucasian mountain called Dykh-Tau in a blizzard, on a narrow ledge above a precipice. This freight car was luxurious by comparison. At five, soaked to the skin, we transferred to the passenger cars, which had finally arrived.

And so after two years we regained our liberty. First came the thrill of marching along the muddy road, beyond the wire, through miserable fields and villages, past black, unpainted shacks. Then the overwhelming exhaustion and sorrow of a dark, shabby, dead little town in the mud and rain, and those endless hours getting chilled to the bone as we waited at the pitch-black station in the piercing cold and a continuous icy downpour. That's all that has stayed in my memory of my first few hours of freedom.

2. ACROSS RUSSIA

WE TRAVELED in convoy from the morning of September 3 until September 9, the date of our arrival in Totskoye, via Yaroslavl, Ivanovo-Voznesensk (we avoided Moscow), Arzamas, Syzran, Kuybyshev, and Buzuluk.

The journey was full of excitement—great crowds of people at the stations, everywhere Poles who had been released from prisons and camps, dressed in rags and shabby padded jackets, unshaven, their eyes burning with joy, a bit like drunks, all heading southeast from Arkhangelsk, the Kola Peninsula, and Vorkuta to join the Polish Army.

While standing in line for hot water at the station in Yaroslavl, I met my first compatriot who hadn't been a prisoner at Gryazovets, a stocky man of about forty-five in a faded brown overcoat, traveling from a camp that was also near Vologda. He had been deported from Mołodeczno, then in eastern Poland, and sentenced to three years in a labor camp.

"What for?" I asked.

"For being drunk and refusing to follow a militiaman. In Poland I'd have had a fine of…"—he pauses to think—"five zlotys at most. We had to work harder than horses, building a new railroad line. Each man had to dig up over three hundred cubic feet of earth per day, on fourteen ounces of bread—it was tough."

"Where are you going now?"

"To Saratov, to join the Polish Army. That's the only reason they let us go."

There was another encounter in Yaroslavl, when a number of Poles traveling from the Arkhangelsk area reported to the colonel with a request to be taken into our convoy. I remember two of their faces, one narrow, bird-like, aristocratic, and wrinkled, with a dark beard and dark, burning eyes. This was Lieutenant R., captured with the partisans in the Łomża forest. Three had been shot, and he had been deported to Arkhangelsk for hard labor. He was wearing a *fufayka*— a padded jacket of the kind everyone went about in here—worn to the last thread, faded into oblivion, the material so dirty that it had lost its color, and a hat with fur earflaps. There were several others with him, one of them a boy from Lublin with pale blue eyes, flaxen hair, a large, fat, upturned nose, and the smiling face of a child. The whole group was on its way to join the army, shifting from convoy to convoy to get there more quickly. We had a collection for them, and R. took all the money. "He looks after us like a father," said the boy from Lublin. Everyone was off to join the army, all wanting to get there right away.

Still in Yaroslavl, we had dinner at an army canteen—soup with blobs of fat, meat and buckwheat; that was all we could get our hands on, but it was the first dinner of the kind we'd had for two whole years.

We had polite conversations with the Red Army soldiers.

"Do you bear us a grudge for what we did to you in 1939?" asked one.

"Do you think we couldn't?"

"I'm sure you do, and we're very sorry."

On September 4 we spent all day long at stations packed with refugees and troops in Ivanovo-Voznesensk, with no dinner, but we were each given half a can of peas.

Next morning I came upon a boy from Lida. I'd have given him fourteen at most, but he claimed to be sixteen. He was little, very puny, with small gray eyes. He told me how he and his mother, father, brother, and sister had been deported to Arkhangelsk. There the family was split up; he had been sent to a camp, where he worked in the forest, now they had liberated the entire camp, but he had no idea where the rest of his family were.

The next day we crossed the Oka River and had dinner in Arzamas. In the Oka region the countryside changed; until now it had been poor and empty, but here it became fertile and beautiful, with large fields, lovely forests, and meadows in the distance. Yet further south the earth was blacker and blacker; there were fields of hemp, millet, and sunflowers, huge villages with plenty of straw-thatched roofs, and large churches with broken crosses, the metal already stripped from most of their cupolas. Only the "corsets" of the large cupolas stood out against the broad landscape stretching into the distance, so dark blue that it was black. The earth was as black as tar.

At the stations cucumbers and bilberries appeared, and we all made a dash for them. The occasional old woman showed up with a dozen eggs, or even bits of meat—six rubles apiece—all snapped up in a wild rush. Every railcar had its own fleet-footed "hunters" who raced for provisions at each station.

It all reminded me of the scenes I had witnessed twenty-three years earlier, in what was then Petrograd. It was Easter 1918, and in the run-up to the holiday all Petrograd was lying in wait at the stations from dawn onward for the rare dairymaids coming in from the countryside to sell their milk. People lined up there for hours, literally thousands of them. The more energetic and enterprising among them, including me, set out to meet the dairymaids at the first halt beyond the city, where in their thirst for milk, about a dozen citizens threw themselves on a single arriving dairymaid. It ended in a fight, all the milk was spilled on the ground, and the battered woman went away with nothing and in tears. At the time I traveled even further out of town and managed to get hold of a bottle of milk. When I came back and alighted at the station in Petrograd feeling triumphant, I stepped into an even bigger crowd than before, even more agitated as they waited in vain for the dairymaids. Suddenly an emaciated old woman in black came out of the crowd toward me, holding out her hand: "Give me a drop!" I can still remember the pleading look in her eyes and her begging tone of voice. I was taking the milk to a sick person, and that was my only explanation—without turning around or giving her any milk, I continued on my way.

Now, as I traveled across Russia twenty-three years on, I remembered that woman's imploring look as I gazed at the faces of my comrades, whose eyes were glittering as they waited with the same ravenous hunger for the thin pickings brought back by the railcar couriers, to be shared among them: a small piece of meat torn into tiny scraps, or a sip each from a glass of milk—things they had spent their nights dreaming about in the camps for the past two years as great good fortune.

At the stations the conversations were more and more candid—it was quite unbelievable. There was no sign of a *politruk*—a Soviet political instructor—and everyone was complaining of hunger, saying they had no bread, that they'd been forced to hand everything over to the state, that the population had only been issued ten ounces of bread, which they didn't always get, and that apart from this bread they had nothing—they hadn't seen sugar or meat for ages. A peasant with a big beard, in his prime, asked why we were willing to fight on the Soviet side, saying that he would never think of fighting for us but would prefer to fight against the "Red rogues." "We've had it up to here," he said, pointing at his beard. "A cow used to cost forty rubles, but now it costs three thousand. Our village has 180 cottages, and there are only two communists, but they have privileges, they never go short of anything."

At another station a peasant woman, who had sold us two eggs, told us that three hundred men from her village had set off for the war, but they had all hung crosses around their necks and said they would surrender to the Germans. She said it out loud, to foreigners, as if all of a sudden there were no more terror in the Soviet Union!

In Voznesensk two laborers came up to the railcar the cadets were in and asked them to sing, and while our men were chanting: "This is our fate, our lot in life . . . we know not where our grave shall be," one of them asked for a piece of paper, leaned over and wrote something down. As the train was leaving, he tossed the paper into the car. In a rough scrawl in incorrect Russian he'd written: "Brothers, save our nation, we're dying of hunger, are you really going to defend the Soviet Union?" I saw the note myself.

We kept hearing this antiwar tone, and even eager anticipation of the Germans. Somewhere near Syzran, by a small river there was a railroad worker standing outside a hut in a group of people, who watched us gloomily in silence; as we were often taken for Germans, I called to him from the very slowly moving train: "You probably think we're Germans, but we're Poles." To which he replied: "It's all the same to us if you're Germans or Poles." I said: "It's not all the same—you're at war with the Germans, and we Poles are now your allies." "What's the difference between a German, a Pole, or a Russian? They're all people," he replied gloomily.

Not far from Arzamas we heard the same tone of hostility toward the Soviets. I only managed to note down a small part of what I heard.

We stopped alongside a convoy of Soviet conscripts. Sitting there with no lights, gloomy and silent, occasionally they drawled: "The Volga, the Volga..." Many of them were well tanked up, but those fellows were gloomy too. One of them accosted Lieutenant W., saying: "Give us some water, give us some water, they're not giving us hot water, they're not giving us tobacco or food but they're telling us we've got to fight the Germans"—the same thing over and over. Along came their *politruk* or officer, so W. asked him to deal with the drunkard. "Move along, comrade, move along," said the *politruk* sheepishly. "Get lost, go f—— your mother!" the conscript shouted at him, forcing the *politruk* to back off. A little later the drunk noticed from a distance that the same Soviet officer was filling himself a bucket of hot water from the locomotive, and flew at him, swearing loudly that he wouldn't give it to others but was drinking it himself.

A small thing, but there were thousands of similar incidents.

Again I was reminded of the past, the beginning of the February 1917 revolution in Petrograd. I had had a similar impression at the time, as if the magic power of authority had suddenly disappeared, as if the shackles had fallen off. I remembered a fat policeman from the czarist Okhrana, trying to fade into the crowd on the Fontanka in 1917, flitting along close to the walls, and now in 1941 here was this *politruk* with flushed cheeks, dashing off between the railcars in terror, with no trace of his former confidence.

In the fall of 1941, those of us who had the opportunity to come into contact with the ordinary people, if only on trains or at stations, were struck by the wave of bitterness, hatred for the regime, and objection to the war that had surfaced everywhere in the few short months when the NKVD had relaxed its iron grip amid the chaos prompted by the pressure of the German offensive.

At a much later date, on a train to Moscow, a Communist Party member told me that in those months many people burned their party cards and there was a wave of sabotage. This loyal communist diehard took the same view of the situation as most of the Poles who'd been traveling right across Russia from the camps at the time: they reckoned the bonds were starting to break, and that in those days the Soviet regime was on the edge of collapse from the inside. Only when the Russians came to believe the initially incredible news of the inhuman, mindless cruelties committed by the Nazis on a mass scale did the mood change.

On September 6 we were forced to make countless stops because of blocked lines and stations. On one station platform a very young lady pushed her way through the crowd. She was a typical Polish blonde with a radiant, youthful complexion and smoothly combed golden hair, wearing a modest but clean and carefully ironed blouse. This girl positively shone amid the impoverished, ragged, unwashed crowd, their faces gray with exhaustion, dirt, and eternal neglect.

She emanated to a high degree the quality that for each of us immediately set apart Polish women, young or old, in Soviet Russia—a shade more reserve in the way they moved, the care they took with their clothing and hair; even when dressed in the meanest of rags they made an effort at elegance that showed taste. The young lady and her mother had been sent deep into Russia at the start of the war; our men crowded around her, because it was the first time in two years that they'd seen a young Polish girl. They questioned her rapturously, almost reverentially, about her fortunes and those of her relatives. It looked as if each man were bashfully trying to ask for permission to touch her hair or her hands, to find out for sure if this apparition were real.

Later on, we encountered other women traveling to Tashkent via Syzran from a camp in Mordovia, where there were several hundred wives of Polish officers and NCOs. One of them, weeping with emotion, approached Captain W., who was the officer on duty, and said: "A gentleman in uniform, it's impossible to refrain from greeting you." She was the wife of an NCO who'd been caught trying to sneak across the border and was sent to Mordovia, where there had been other camps like the one where she was interned.

We were coming into Ruzayevka. There our convoys were to be divided: the first was going to Saratov, and ours was headed for Chkalov.* We walked across a high bridge over the tracks to have dinner in some very crowded but clean cottage-canteens. On the walls there were some posters, one showing a soldier standing with a rifle, and a peasant woman in a headscarf behind him, telling him to "be a hero"; against the background of the stories and conversations we'd heard at the stations, it all seemed very "literary." We walked in extremely long crocodile file and met another group of our comrades on their way back from dinner, men from the first convoy with whom we were just about to part. In front of the wooden cottages and a long red poster with a slogan in white that said: "All our strength toward victory," I spent a long time saying goodbye to our friends, Imek Kohn, Józio Szpunar, and Sewer Ehrlich, with whom I'd kept company on a daily basis for the past year, having endless chats, working together, and enjoying friendship.

At one of the halts a train carrying evacuated civilians stopped alongside our convoy. It consisted of a few cars packed with boys who said they were seventeen or eighteen, but they were so small they looked like twelve- or thirteen-year-olds, homeless children (known in Russian as *bezprizorniye*). They were extremely indigent and dirty, in black calico rags; apart from a very few exceptions their faces were gaunt and ugly; all together they looked like a close-knit, enterprising gang. They refused to tell us anything, such as where they were from or who they were. When I gave one of them a pickle, he grabbed it greedily

*Now renamed Orenburg. —*Trans.*

and devoured it like an animal, without a word of thanks or so much as a glance. In another car further back there were some chattier boys who said they'd been traveling for several weeks from the direction of Gomel and that they'd been six miles from the front, digging trenches— these kids! They must have been some of the teenagers mobilized in the fall of 1940 who were meant to be trained as qualified workers.

Other cars were packed full of the poorest of the Jewish poor from small towns in the east. Here I shall describe the reaction of one of our men.

Through a small window three childish faces peeped into our car, not so much Jewish, but almost Chinese-looking, with flat faces and extremely subtle features, the most Oriental type of Jew possible. One of them ingratiated himself in a sweet, childlike way, smiled, and asked where we were going. "What's it to you, you lousy Jew?" replied a cavalryman with a bushy mustache who was one of our company, a National Democrat and landowner from the Congress Kingdom. A little later I saw the same otherwise benevolent fellow in a lively, warm conversation with the ultimate Jew, who had also ended up here. This man used to have a mill in the Kingdom in a town that was familiar to the National Democrat; from what I heard, they had plenty of friends in common. The Jew passed on news about everyone: who'd been murdered by the Germans, and which of the landowners of German origin had passed himself off as Volksdeutsch. The Jew-baiter was gabbling away, asking with kind concern about people called Abramek, Schwarz, and Goldberg; it wasn't strange that they were talking to each other, but that it was so natural and warm, with no hint of animosity or need to exercise self-control. Anti-Semitic slogans were irrelevant to them at this moment, for here was an old, almost family relationship. And suddenly I found the cavalryman with the bushy moustache amiable; the warmth in his voice and the Jew's eager, trusting undertone reminded me of my childhood in the remote Borderlands: at Easter we always paid a visit to old Lejba, the miller, who would treat us to *pejsachówka** vodka and walnuts in

---

*The colloquial name for strong Jewish plum vodka. —*Trans.*

honey. Lejba's face was white, covered in fine, Rembrandt-style wrinkles, and he had very red, unhealthy eyelids and a snow-white beard. We usually went there with our parish priest, the fiery, jolly, extremely kindhearted Father Zelba. Father Zelba never missed an opportunity to quote some passages from the Bible to old Lejba, testifying that the prophets had heralded Christ as the Messiah. Every time he did it, old Lejba would make a display of blocking his ears because, as he politely explained, he was forbidden to listen to such things. Lejba was very pious, and every Friday at dusk, as we were on our way home, through the curtainless window of his wooden cottage by the pond, we'd see his snow-white beard poised above a holy book lit by a seven-branched candlestick. Those were the old, "prehistoric" times, which gave Polish literature the pearls of Eliza Orzeszkowa's and Maria Konopnicka's short stories, writers who knew how to cast an affectionate eye on that closed world living in our midst.

After leaving Ruzayevka, we made a short stop and met an enormous convoy of two thousand people, from a party of ten thousand soldiers and cadets (as usual there were a few officers hidden among them) who were traveling from the Kola Peninsula, where they'd been building roads and airports on a daily ration of three ounces of bread. Some of them were from Kozelsk No. 2, and some had already worked in the Arkhangelsk forest for thirteen months before being transported by ship to Kola, where they had had to build roads and barracks for themselves to live in; meanwhile they spent their nights in the snow. Emaciated but elated, they jumped off the train with shouts of joy, calling out the names of the fellow officers they'd left behind in Kozelsk. It was such a lively atmosphere, so enthusiastic and indomitable, that one almost forgot about the hell these people had been through.

According to Saint Teresa of Avila, the time of grace that follows a period of total spiritual drought, a "dark night of the soul," is so out of proportion to the suffering that came before that one regrets not having suffered more to deserve such happiness.

At that moment in the train many of us half-consciously experienced the same thing on a different, more earthly plane.

The page had turned so suddenly, and in the eyes of these people, meeting for the first time, Poland had acted with brilliance, strength, and faith, and had remained unaffected; their feeling of Polish unity and fraternity was so tangible, and the happiness they felt on meeting people whose individual existence had been unknown to them a short while ago was so strong that they lost all the mental scars and wrinkles that had been covering them for years. All at once their sense of "diminution," of an inertia that in captivity they had ceaselessly had to combat to stop it from engulfing them simply fell away.

Like a recurring melody, some scraps of a poem by Słowacki kept running through my mind, though I couldn't remember more than this:

> ... for now the time is nigh ...
> O Lord, Thou shalt not remove Poland from the cross
> until ... it falls down dead.

We believed in the future, that our cause would lead to victory, and that Poland's strength was not just undiminished but tremendously augmented, and all our past tribulations disappeared in the light of our happiness.

Whenever we feel overcome by discouragement, bitterness, or lack of faith we should remember rare moments like that one.

A few hours after leaving Ruzayevka another large convoy overtook us; it was part of the force of twelve thousand private soldiers from the prisoner-of-war camp at Starobilsk, also on their way to join the Polish Army. Our trains stopped alongside each other in a field for twenty minutes. That was when we first heard the stories, many more versions of which were to reach us later with further details, about the fortunes of all the captive private soldiers who'd been building highways and airports at Brody, Jarmolińce, and Równe, after being herded 60–120 miles on foot at the outbreak of war by various routes;

the weaker men who couldn't keep up were shot or beaten to death. One on top of another they poured it all out to us, as if to relatives, to brothers, though it was the first time we had ever met. One of them confirmed that in the mass of people herded on his route alone several thousand had been shot dead. Details and names of the victims came pouring out, with descriptions of the terrible march, or rather the countless marches on the different routes from Wilejka, Brody, Jarmolińce, and so on, with the Germans at their heels. Then they had been packed into open freight cars and transported for days on end, in pouring rain, with a daily ration of six ounces of bread and no water, all the way to Starobilsk.

Speaking all at once, they told us what they saw in Małopolska (southeast Poland): how entire families were deported in subzero temperatures, how the deportees were crowded onto trains until the cars were full to bursting; and how the children who died on board had to be thrown from small windows onto the tracks, because burying them was forbidden. Two people told me of this; later I heard it again from several other eyewitnesses.

This was also the first time I was told how Ukrainian attitudes had changed toward the Soviets after a few months of Soviet occupation, especially among those who had formerly been well disposed toward them.

And so, with the German army breathing down their necks, herded and prodded along the way, a few days before the signing of the Polish-Soviet pact our fellow soldiers had been transferred to Starobilsk, and a week later they were sent off to join the newly forming Polish Army. Now the very same Soviet authorities escorted those prisoners whom they had failed to stab or shoot to death to the station with military honors and a brass band!

One of the older men in the convoy, an amiable corporal from Grodno, handed me a poem that he had just written in the railcar:

> They undid our shackles of Soviet steel
> That we had been wearing for two years in all
> But now they were smashed to smithereens

Thanks to our great leader General Sikorski,
Who's out of the country
A Polish hero of the rarest sort,
Under his command our freedom was restored.

. . . .

He did his level best and more
To tear us free of the lion's jaws.

. . . .

They marched us from Poland just weeks ago
At bayonet point, row upon row,
They treated us with cruelty and deceit
Stabbing to death the men who fell at their feet
But now they regard us in a different light
Now they're joining us, as allies in the fight,
We follow the White Eagle, they follow their Red flag,
Shoulder to shoulder, with one accord,
All the wrongs they did us are ignored.

"Written on September 5, 1941, in memory of Platoon Sergeant Stanisławow, by Corporal E. Kisiel." The signature was barely legible in a sea of flourishes.

When I showed interest, he offered me the poem, saying he had plenty of others but had sent them all to his wife.

This time, not just a handful of aristocrats had been deported, as in 1863. These people, now on their way to join the army, had endured appalling moral and physical suffering for Poland; they had directly experienced the charming treatment meted out by foreign governments. How cruelly Poland's history was being democratized.

I was reminded of an anecdote from 1920, when the Poles defeated the invading Soviets. In July and August, reinforcements headed to the front to join the Krechowce Uhlan regiment, most of whom were youths from the countryside who'd hardly had any training, farm boys straight from the plow. In August the defeated Soviet army withdrew in panic, and we covered over forty miles a day, chasing at their heels.

Once when we had exhausted our strength, and had stopped for a ten-minute rest, one of these newly recruited Uhlans, a young village boy, lay stretched out on the grass, plainly thinking hard; he started muttering to himself, not resentfully or regretfully, but as if he'd made a discovery: "And all this for the motherfucking homeland."

This remark became common parlance among us in the regiment.

Perhaps that same Uhlan from 1920 was now in the convoy of "amnestied" soldiers, held prisoner for two long years by the Soviets for the crime of fighting against Hitler in defense of Poland.

On September 7 we went all day without a proper meal. We were given canned food, and of course we bought whatever was available, such as milk and cucumbers. A vast number of our men were starting to fall sick. Not until we reached Syzran at three in the morning were we given dinner.

The only difference between the stations, all of which were extremely ugly and dirty, was the number of posters on display, the age of the red cloth they were hung on, and the portraits shown. Here there was a whole gallery of propaganda slogans, and portraits ten times larger than life, a whole constellation of Soviet leaders hung on pieces of red cloth. For the first time we could buy white rolls, second-rate black gingerbread that was uncooked in the middle, but gingerbread for all that; of course the demand exceeded the quantity available, but our car got quite a lot, and finally some relatively recent newspapers as well. We read that there was fighting on all fronts, and that the Germans had tried to bombard a destroyer. That was all.

That day we also talked to some pale-faced lads at one of the stations—the sallow complexion familiar from Gryazovets. Father Kantak had that look after months on end in the Lubyanka, and so did General Anders and Colonel Pstrokoński when they visited our camp straight after being released from prison.

These boys told us how between one and two thousand people had been arrested at Wilejka for all sorts of "crimes," from belonging to the Camp of National Unity (OZN) to having been members of the secret Polish Military Organization (POW). At least a dozen people from the Oszmiana area had been sentenced to death for owning revolvers and radio transmitters; the rest had been given six, eight, or ten years in jail. Many of them had remained in jail without sentence until the second day of the German-Soviet war, so narrowly confined that they could hardly move. From the second day of the war onward they had been forced to march some 120 miles; anyone who couldn't keep up was shot.

Exiled to Ryazan, they had no idea how the war was progressing. They hadn't heard about the Polish-Soviet pact. "We got our first piece of news from a scrap of newspaper," one of them told me. "We found it in the privy, so we washed and dried it and read it." All of a sudden, on November 4, they'd been sent off: the young men who had signed up were sent straight to the army, and other, older ones (the age range among the prisoners was from fifteen to seventy!) to Chkalov to be laborers.

We were endlessly horrified by these pieces of information; on the day we left the camp we had no idea about the scale of the deportations or how they had been carried out. A skeptic might say that what they were telling us was bound to be full of inaccuracies, and some nonsense too, and I'm sure that's true. In those first accounts the figures may have been vague, perhaps overestimated in places, though later, more precise statements proved that at the time nobody had any concept of how great the total number of deportations and murders actually was; each of us was only aware of the small scrap he had seen for himself, but everything we heard in those first few days of freedom was so consistent, so full of minor, material details and facts, and told in such a lively way, so spontaneously, without a hint of preparation or any conscious planning, that the truth of these stories was blindingly obvious, beyond doubt.

On September 8 we crossed the Volga. There was an endless wait before "the longest bridge in Europe," at what was probably its dirtiest, most wretched railroad stop. There were lots of cottages knocked together from planks, as there used to be in our poorest ghettoes. There were no trees at all, and most of the cottages had no garden plots, though there were a few new ones made of stone, which looked quite modern but were sticky with dirt, repulsive and probably unfinished: for instance, one of them was entirely inhabited, though upstairs there was a balcony door, but no trace of the balcony apart from a mark on the wall—perhaps it had fallen off? The dry hillsides were covered with burned, reddish grass. And we were only about seven miles from the big city of Syzran. We could see chimney after chimney in the distance, and tall church towers overlooking the most beautiful view—the fabulous, wide Volga, which forks just here, with large, extremely clean sandbanks, and islands covered in conifers and deciduous trees, as was the riverbank on the other side. We departed at last. The bridge really was impressive, and beyond it lay another world; for a while there were more trees, and undulating terrain, but all this was clearly the channel of the Volga during floods, because then came slightly higher ground, with more cottages and wooden cabins, but no trees, and then bare steppe covered with sparse reddish vegetation.

It was the first fine day of the journey, warm and sunny, not too hot. By the time we reached a stop called Buzunchuk it felt as if we were a very long way from the front.

That day we reached Kuybyshev; we dined there, and then sat waiting to depart until half past one at night. More and more men were sick after buying raw food or a canned Japanese product with the lovely German name "Drei Perlen"; after eating this delicacy my neighbor blacked out twice, was in severe pain, and plainly had food poisoning. The first time he fell off the bunk headfirst onto the carriage floor, and the second time he fell headfirst from the carriage onto the platform. I thought there'd be nothing to pick up.

On our last day on the train it was wonderfully warm and sunny, a hot southern fall, and at each station there were plenty of watermelons, cucumbers, and even milk.

In two years in the camps we'd had no fruit at all, and no milk. I could remember the only exceptions I'd experienced: twice in Gryazovets we were sold a quarter of a watermelon each at a high price, and twice I drank a glass of milk in the hospital—that was all. So despite the senior officers' warnings and strict orders not to, we'd been eating the watermelons and drinking the milk wherever possible; by the final day a vast percentage of us were violently sick, and two men were feared to have dysentery. On top of that, a few of our comrades had managed to drink themselves unconscious—they hadn't seen alcohol for two years either, so a glass of vodka had a lightning-quick effect.

After seven days on the move we reached the tiny little station at Totskoye as night fell; it was dark by the time we walked a few miles to a Soviet army summer camp on the bare steppe.

Travel weary and stunned by all the new impressions, as yet we had no idea about the conditions awaiting us or the difficulties involved in organizing an army. As we'd come from the north, for the first few days after our arrival the climate gave us the illusion that a southern idyll awaited us.

3. A SOUTHERN IDYLL

TOTSKOYE. The camp, three miles from the station of the same name, on the Kuybyshev-to-Chkalov line, was a summer training ground for the Orenburg Cossacks.

The steppe was bare, apart from the trees growing along the winding little river Samarka, with the camp located on a sheer cliff above it.

There were some tents, and a few summer cottages knocked together from thin planks, with no stoves—that was all.

Here, to these few wooden structures and too few tents on the bare steppe, hundreds of people began to pour in, from Komi, Arkhangelsk, and Vorkuta, from Kola, from all over Siberia and from Karaganda.

Our Gryazovets convoy comprised the first officer corps for the units that were being formed. Here General Tokarzewski's Sixth Infantry Division came into being, as did the Army Reserve Center, to which I was assigned.

Each day fifty, two hundred, or five hundred men were brought in from the station; I remember a day when 1,500 former convicts arrived. And what a state they were in! Wearing torn padded jackets, ragged clothes, mostly without shoes, just the strangest footwear fashioned from bits of cloth and string, they were human wrecks, ruined by hard labor, starvation, and a journey of up to a month without enough food.

The lovely, hot southern fall ended a few days after our arrival. Chilly weather set in, and as usual, "not in living memory" had the cold come on so quickly in these parts—there was heavy rainfall, followed two weeks later by sleet, while a gale blew constantly from the steppe.

There were still occasional short spells of sunshine and cloudless sky, when the rust-colored steppe dried out, but the nights were already below freezing.

From mid-October until January when our units left Totskoye, the frost took such a grip that there wasn't a single day of thaw; in December and January the temperature dropped to −67°F.

Establishing an army in these conditions, out of physically wrecked material, was a major feat, one many of us thought beyond our strength. The circumstances in which it was accomplished are hard to imagine.

There was a total lack of weaponry; for the Sixth Division, for example, comprising more than ten thousand men, there were one hundred light automatic rifles and nothing else. The very low number of boilers meant that hot meals had to be cooked not at a fixed time, but nonstop, twenty-four hours a day; the almost total lack of boilers for laundry, the lack of soap, and the lack of underwear in the first period made it impossible to restore the ragged, louse-infested soldiers to a reasonable state of cleanliness.

British equipment finally began to arrive at the end of November; before then only a small part of the troops had been provided with uniforms, Latvian and Estonian ones. Some of these were parade uniforms, the whole works, richly adorned with fancy white braid. Set against the steppe, the mud, the tumbledown huts and the rags, these uniforms introduced a bitter note of farce.

There was so little footwear (for both officers and private soldiers) that on their way out the drivers borrowed shoes from men who were off duty at the time.

There were tremendous problems with transport (in late September the Sixth Division in Totskoye had twenty-two vehicles, four of which were out of action), totally inadequate domestic equipment, and the lack of the most essential tools, such as saws and axes, was particularly acutely felt when the weather worsened. At this point we began to improvise stoves using the bricks paving the walkways between the tents of the Cossacks' camp, as well as bricks that the

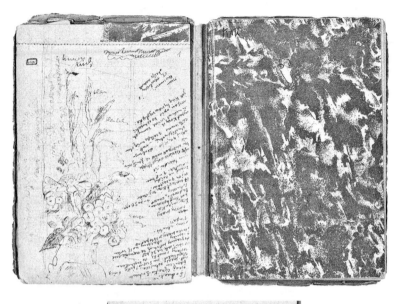

"According to Father [Zdzisław] Peszkowski this notebook is from Gryazovets, and later [Czapski] used it at Totskoye"—added by Janusz Przewłocki on a page of the notebook.

soldiers fired on the spot, and sheet metal. Firewood was brought in from a forest about five to seven miles away, at first on carts pulled by the men, or carried by whole units on their backs.*

From the first everyone was caught up in a whirl of work, thousands of things to do, so there was no question of any lack of involvement— we were up to our ears in it from dawn to dusk, and there was very little chance of noting down any impressions or observations.

As soon as I arrived I was given orders to set up a "Welfare Office," the aim of which was to provide and gather information and address complaints and questions from the incoming wave of officers and soldiers at the Rallying Point, through which all new arrivals had to pass.

These people knew nothing except that they had been released from the camps to join the army. My task was to provide them with information about the general situation, and to give some instructions on how to behave.

I remember one band of new arrivals on the steppe, powdered with snow, where they heard their first news of how Poland was fighting the invaders, that we had taken part in fighting in France and at Narvik in 1940; that our navy was in action, that in the Battle of Britain, the deadly fight for London, Polish airmen had shot down 219 German planes, thus one in seven of all the enemy planes destroyed over London at the time. These Polish soldiers, who had suffered defeat in September 1939 and then been abused in the camps for two years by Soviet propaganda, which had done its best to prove that Poland and the Polish Army had ceased to exist for good and all, were stunned by this news.

I ended every speech with confirmation of our alliance with the Soviets. On the orders of my superiors, I demanded their loyalty and comradeship toward the Red Army and asked them to forget the recent past. This bit always got a reluctant reception, but the soldiers'

---

*In a book called *Lwów Division* issued by the Sixth Division in Palestine there is a chapter entitled "First organizational steps," which best reflects the difficulties with which not just the Sixth Division but the entire Polish Army had to contend.

sense of discipline toward their Polish commanders was incredibly strong, and our leaders' authority was unassailable.

It only took a few days for the main role of the Welfare Office to become clear. We were assigned a hut made of thin planks; from the first instant a long line of people filled our "office" and continued in the rain outside, hardly ever disbanding except at night.

Three issues predominated.

The main concern of these miserable, frozen people in torn, soaking-wet padded jackets and with wet feet wrapped in rags was that their comrades who were still detained in the camps should be rescued and brought here to join the army.

Their second main concern was to find their families, deported to places all over Russia. They wanted to send them news about themselves.

We spent all day long writing out lists of names, recording the new arrivals' statements about the detainees who were still in the labor camps, and their families' possible whereabouts. We forwarded these lists to army general staff, and to the Polish embassy, which was being flooded with thousands of letters from deportees scattered across Soviet territory.

On the basis of these lists, sent from various places, including the ones we were sending from Totskoye, general staff and the embassy then applied to the Soviet authorities for the release of prisoners in ever more remote locations.

Only very scant news of the families reached us, and it took time to come; we posted the first lists of family names from Turkestan and Kazakhstan on the outside wall of our hut. Whatever the weather, there were always people standing in front of it, scrutinizing the rain-soaked list in search of the names of their relatives.

The third major concern was to question each new arrival for any news of the prisoners from Starobilsk No. 1, Kozelsk No. 1, and Ostash-kov. At the time we still believed they should be turning up here at any moment. But not only did they not appear, none of the hundreds of former prisoners arriving at our office from all over Russia was able to tell us anything about them. We simply couldn't understand it.

Ever since April and May 1940, when those three camps had been evacuated, all trace of the fifteen thousand men (including eight thousand officers) imprisoned there had vanished.

At the time it never entered our heads that such a huge number of prisoners of war could have been murdered, so we persisted in asking each man about them on a daily basis. When the first rumors came of their mass extermination in cold blood by the Bolshevik authorities, we refused to take them seriously.

For me, those few months of work at Totskoye, interrupted by a spell in the hospital and journeys to Buzuluk and Kuybyshev, meant gradual, daily immersion in a vast ocean of human misery, hearing how families had been torn apart, children had gone missing or had died of hunger, and how thousands of our comrades had disappeared in the tundra and the mines. The hardest thing to bear was our sense of helplessness; we didn't know if the lists we sent to Kuybyshev and Buzuluk or the demands for the people named on them to be released would have any effect, but we did know for sure that the thousands of dead would never come back to life, and that only a small fraction of those still rotting away in exile could be saved from death.

From the first days of my administrative work information began to reach me about entire convoys of prisoners who had frozen to death, and about the shooting of prisoners who had tried to rebel; according to a rumor that kept coming back to us, several thousand of our men had been drowned in the White Sea or the Arctic Ocean.

At the Welfare Office I very often had to deal with people who for some reason hadn't yet been accepted into any military unit. This was the flip side of the coin. Naturally, most of the people who came to see us were weak and feeble, incapable of physical work, not even capable of fighting against the mud and snow; they were being shifted into tents that were not properly dug in but had just been pitched on the bare steppe in the gale. There were lots of old men who couldn't possibly be incorporated into any military unit.

The rigid rules defining who was suitable for military service couldn't be applied without stretching them one way or another, for who among us was physically fit for the army at the time? But stretching the rules provided a wide range of freedom to commit abuses, apply favoritism, or settle scores. Meanwhile, the incoming human horde always contained a large percentage of old and sickly people, unfit for the army in any circumstances.

The Jewish question also came up in a drastic, unexpected form. Apart from the Jews who had been through the September campaign and the camps with us, who had proved their character and their loyalty to Poland, there was a vast crowd of penniless Jews from the eastern ghettoes, sent into exile not for fighting for Poland, or for any political transgression, but for stealing a wretched strip of cloth, a reel of thread, or a couple of herrings. Some convoys were 80 percent full of such Jews, for whom the army was the only route out of prison, nothing more.

The toughest trial in organizing the army, especially in such savage physical conditions, was how to distinguish the useful, well-motivated men from the unfortunate mass of weak and miserable wretches, indifferent to Polish concerns. There was all too wide a scope for mistakes to be made, unforgivable ones based on shallow generalizations and rash decisions. At the same time there was also an opportunity, through fair and humane treatment, to win over elements that were extremely alien or downright hostile to Polish statehood.

We tried to form work battalions to dig ditches. The feeblest people, whom no army unit could possibly accept, were assigned to these battalions. Crowded on the fringes of the camp, these wretched specimens were rotting away in the worst possible conditions, too weak to look after themselves. Some of them were living in a tumbledown barrack without windowpanes, and the rest in tents that they weren't even capable of pitching, let alone entrenching; the gale tore at them from every direction, while those old people sat huddled on the bare earth in nothing but rags, shivering with cold. I saw some in total desperation, weeping like children, their tears as big as peas. Because of the circumstances, these so-called work battalions, designed to gather up those who were unfit for the army or for whom lighter work was recommended, became a sort of penal camp into which anyone who was superfluous or for some reason inconvenient was packed away—quite a number of them pointlessly; some of them had managed to get hold of their exiled families' addresses and begged to be sent off to join them, seeing they were of no use to the army, but here again basic difficulties arose, and bureaucracy won the day.

For a person who had volunteered for the army to be discharged in a way that guaranteed he wouldn't be regarded as a deserter, either now in Soviet Russia or in Poland in the future, and to be issued with a document which the Soviets would regard as official, he had first of all to be provided with a certificate testifying that he had indeed volunteered. In order to be valid, this certificate had to have a round stamp, and there was no such stamp in all Totskoye; there was a big fuss between Buzuluk, where the Polish Army general staff was located, and Totskoye, over who had the right to issue this sort of certificate, Buzuluk or Totskoye. This fuss went on for weeks, while the people in the tents went on freezing.

It was these people who most often filled our office; they were in a shocking physical state, and when it came to being issued with underclothes or uniforms, which initially could only be supplied to a tiny proportion of the army, naturally they were put last in line. How very few of them we managed to help!

There was another attempt to find them something to do and a place to live, one that seemed comparatively realistic and humane. The area surrounding Totskoye included a number of collective farms, some relatively well off, but there was a lack of hands to do the work. We were always seeing unharvested potato fields and overgrown stacks of wheat from the train windows as we traveled to general staff in Buzuluk. A decision was taken to send the weaker men to do agricultural work at the collective farms, which would be lighter than military work. Winter was just around the corner, and temperatures several dozen degrees below freezing were a normal occurrence in these parts; these people had no chance of surviving it in tents on the bare steppe. My boss, Colonel Jacyn, who had taken charge of our post when its functions began to increase, made the arrangements.

As soon as the local collective farms heard that they could get workers, their agents came running every day, promising us the earth. With solid precision, determined, meticulous effort, and a humane attitude to every single man, the colonel concluded the contracts properly and did not let a single group go without a careful record and a plan for the continued care of these decommissioned soldiers.

I will never forget the scene as we bade farewell to two groups of these beggars who were on their way to the collective farms, most of them poor Jews. They walked to the station at dusk, in a cold downpour, dressed in nothing but rags, some leaning on sticks or long, snapped-off branches, one wrapped in an old quilt, most of them without shoes. The colonel made a heartfelt speech, saying that the Pole is not just a good soldier but must also gain the reputation of a good worker, and that they were just on leave from the Polish Army. The crowd responded warmly and gratefully, one after another asking him not to let them go but to continue to look after them; in these exclamations and requests there was a palpable impulse, the impulse of poor, doomed people who saw in Poland, in the Polish authorities, their only hope of salvation from destruction.

We received our first news of the people sent to the collective farms from two men who fled back to the camp. They told us there was nowhere to live at the farm; they had been made to stand outside at night in the pouring rain. Then they were told to unload several dozen tons of grain from a sort of granary, which was being reassigned as accommodation. Until they had unloaded it, they would be living under the open sky. (It was already the season of icy rain that fell for days on end.)

Was this deliberate ill will toward Poles? Not at all; it was the normal Soviet attitude toward human beings, to their own citizens too—extreme wastefulness and disregard for human life, and the same disregard for the tons of wheat we regularly saw at the stations along the way from Buzuluk to Totskoye. This wheat lay on the platform in the snow and rain, not even covered, though guarded by a soldier.

Through his envoys, through the central Soviet authorities in Buzuluk, and through general staff, Colonel Jacyn fought for the agreement to be kept and for the workers to be treated decently. He even dispatched cans of food to the ones who were worst off at the collective farms, but such aid can only have been a drop in the ocean.

My view of the army's efforts to organize an officer corps was from the weakest side, that of the nonfrontline officers, of whom I was one. As ever, there were some people of high caliber. There were many who put all their energy, intelligence, sense of responsibility, and heart into the organizational work, gave away everything they had and shared with everyone. (When the "amnesty" was declared, each of the officers released from Gryazovets was given from 2,000 to 10,000 rubles by the Soviet authorities, depending on rank; as a captain I was given 2,000—I don't know why... perhaps as a consolation prize.) As commander of the Main Rallying Point, Colonel Prokop oversaw the deployment of the new arrivals; I watched his tireless efforts, in the process of which he handed out everything he could, giving his own money, shirts and socks to the naked, barefoot newcomers. But there were others who were just as quick to dress up in their officer's privileges and concerns. Yesterday in tatters, today they were already looking down on their fellows who didn't yet have a posting or access to the officer's mess. There was a fat major who, despite repeated explanations, understood nothing I told him about the unbearable living conditions of the paupers in the labor camp next door to our office, while ardently agreeing that our own living conditions were dreadful. He could not imagine how different it was for us, fed at the officer's casino and with a roof over our heads. Full-time officers as we now were, our situation was miles above average for Totskoye.

However, even the "better" conditions were very tough for anyone old or sick.

Professor Stanisław Swianiewicz, an eminent economist of over sixty, shared an unlighted wooden cubbyhole with two other men, and he was relatively well accommodated. One time I saw this sickly man in the tumbledown privy, an image that has stuck in my memory. A winding stream ran around the camp, and on its steep bank there were a few houses, once surrounded by wooden fences that had since been smashed to bits, the boards torn off and used for firewood. There sat the professor, as low, steel-gray clouds flashed past and cold sleet fell, amid violent gusts of wind, on a hillock by the river, with a view of the frozen stream underfoot and the boundless steppe; there he sat, huddled on a filthy, wooden, ice-coated toilet, rubbing his ailing stomach, as the gale tore at his sparse locks of hair (he had gastrointestinal atony after many months of imprisonment in the Lubyanka, where he was only allowed to go to the toilet twice in every twenty-four hours, and then just for a couple of minutes at a fixed time). I waited for him as he made his way back to the room, his face a truly tragic sight. A year earlier he had fainted during roll call.

I was often struck by how coldly old people responded to the suffering of others, though once they had been sensitive and kindhearted. Our "surplus" strength dies away as, with age, it becomes harder to bear our own life. The selfishness of old age? How much harder it is to be "bountiful" when you have no strength left to cope with your own life as it rolls downhill.

There was one more attempt to solve the problem of the oldest and weakest, which was to send them further south. Everyone longed for Tashkent as if it were paradise, nothing but sunshine and grapevines.

Suddenly news came from army general staff that we could assign more than 200 people to a convoy destined for Tashkent. They could join a similar group traveling from Buzuluk.

I was ordered to make the selection, and managed to get the number increased to 370, equal to the number traveling from Buzuluk. How great the joy and gratitude! I included the professor too, the economist. How much hope that train to the south prompted, but how naive we still were—we had no doubt that, in agreement with our authorities, the Soviet authorities had organized some form of shelter there, where our weaker men would be able to survive the winter; we imagined that, come the spring, many of them would be able to play a useful role of some kind.

Imagine how hard it was for me to decide who was weaker, who was more in need of those "better" conditions, who to save sooner from the damp earth and the wet snow, from those flimsy tents where they were clustered.

I remember the happy departure of those few hundred people, the blessings and gratitude toward those who had put their names on the list for the journey to Tashkent.

However, that first expedition was a disaster. Not only had nothing been prepared for them in Tashkent, but, regarded as unimportant, the convoy took more than two weeks to get there, with no food organized for the travelers on the way. They had to sell everything off, swapping their priceless rags, scarves, and padded jackets at the stations for some low-fat sheep-milk cheeses or *lepioshki* (flatbread).

In the end, the convoy was not allowed to enter Tashkent but was instead detained at a stop along the way. Many people died of hunger, many were robbed by the local population of everything they possessed, a small number managed to struggle back to Totskoye, and the rest were sent by the Soviet authorities to the most famished collective farms in Turkestan.

Such was the story of the train into the unknown.

4. THE HOSPITAL

AT TOTSKOYE I had two short spells in the hospital, lasting a few days each. The first time, straight after arrival, the hospital was still in Soviet hands; the second time the staff was almost entirely Polish.

The hospital consisted of a largish wooden building by the little river, and a row of small cabins with one or two rooms in each.

I spent several hours outside the main building waiting to be admitted; from the moment of our arrival in Totskoye the hospital had been packed to bursting. A lovely fall sun shone. I sat on some wooden stools in a high fever. A young boy came up to me, almost a child, very thin, in a baggy black hospital gown. His head was too big for his long child's neck, like a poppy on its stalk. He started telling me his story with the total trust, so natural and so moving, that almost always appears when one Pole encounters another in their first weeks of freedom.

He was from Wilno and had been deported with his mother and little sister to Kazakhstan; he had run away from there with the aim of getting back to Wilno. He had managed to get all the way to the former Polish-Soviet border, by passing as just another *bez-prizorny*.

That border was carefully guarded until the German-Soviet war began, and that was where they caught him.

In September 1940, if I remember the date rightly, a decree was issued "On petty theft and hooliganism." Transgressions of this sort were from now on to be punished instantly by a kind of summary court, only one witness was enough, and the penalty could be years of forced labor. The boy from Wilno had accordingly been sentenced to several years' labor and deported to Kuybyshev.

In this way the Soviet government instantly acquired hundreds of thousands of unpaid laborers, which it badly needed, a workforce that made it possible to build and start up new military factories in Kuybyshev. These vast plants stretched for miles along the railroad tracks from Kuybyshev toward Chkalov. According to the boy's estimates, there were five hundred thousand to seven hundred thousand workers at the Kuybyshev factories who had ended up there the way he had. He had been there for almost a year, working hard and going hungry, alone among unfortunate convicts and petty thieves from all over the Soviet Union, from Russkies to Uzbeks, parted from his family, of whom he had no news, and from his country, and this at the most receptive and formative time of life. His spoken Polish was already badly corrupted with monstrous Russianisms and mistakes, but mentally, as his every gesture made clear, he had kept the subtle sensitivity of a child. I gave him some extra bread from my rucksack.

"Are you giving me this bread?" I remember his disproportionate gratitude; he must have been starving, but his reaction to my ordinary friendly gesture could only be emotional after a year of captivity among totally alien, ever-hungry people, for whom bread was the hardest thing to get hold of and their most precious treasure.

To qualify for the army he claimed to be seventeen, though he probably wasn't more than sixteen and was extremely emaciated.

A few months later, in extremely cold weather, I traveled to Kuybyshev in a warm, packed compartment within the "soft" carriage. The train crossed the snow-covered steppe, then went through a built-up area that continued for many miles; there were lots of factories, vast warehouses, and hundreds of low barracks, all buried in a dozen feet of snow under a gray sky, all with the familiar rows of barbed wire, and even with turrets, just the same as the ones at Gryazovets or Starobilsk, on which stood soldiers with rifles.

I stared out of the window. An aging NKVD man was traveling in the same carriage—he wore a badge on his chest that only distinguished Chekists have the right to wear—along with a young, amiable Soviet artillery lieutenant with a hemp-like shock of hair who was on his way to the front. The young man was talking to the older man with evident respect, as if addressing the hero of the now historical revolution, which he was off to defend with his own life. The older man was giving him advice in a friendly, benevolent way.

The young man gazed with pride at the factories behind the barbed wire. "Soviet power has achieved all this," he said to the old Chekist, rather timidly and rather pompously. And as I listened to these words, I thought about the thin boy from Totskoye with a head like a poppy on his skinny neck and what he had told me about these very places. Did it ever occur to the lieutenant for an instant that these factories were built on the back of modern slavery?

I was housed in one of the little huts, where none of the doctors or nurses took up much of our time. There were three diets to choose from: either milk, meaning milky soup three times a day with a pinch of boiled rice; or there was soup with a pinch of buckwheat three times a day; or normal soldier's food. That was the entire treatment. I lay in there with a small number of private soldiers, all of whom had been prisoners in Wilejka before being force-marched to Borisov, then imprisoned in Ryazan, and only released on September 4.

We spent the sunny hours swathed in black hospital gowns on the bank of earth in front of our hut, which was also where we ate our milk soup, as I listened almost nonstop to my companions' stories of what they had been through in the past two years; it was usually the thirty-year-old farmer Danek from near Wilno who did the talking. He was stocky, with a large head of fluffy fair hair. He gave a precise account, without exaggeration, while his companions added details or nodded in agreement. They all appeared to be straightforward people, incapable of making things up or showing off.

They had the unique charm that comes from the simplicity, kindness, and unadulterated humanity so typical of people from the Wilno area, an attitude to the world that is neither hasty nor nervous but friendly, goodhearted, and loyal to death. These were the sort of people Norwid meant when he yearned "for those whose yes means yes and whose no means no, without any light or shade."

And there is probably no other place in Europe where the Soviet plow has destroyed and trampled people as badly as in those very lands—truly innocent people.

Just from the way Danek told his story I'd have guessed he was from those parts.

"In prison in Wilejka," he said in his monotone, "there were at least two thousand of us, every one arrested by the Soviet authorities for all sorts of reasons, for belonging before the war to 'Strzelec' (the Riflemen's Association), to OZN (the Camp of National Unity), or even for having been in the POW (Polish Military Organization) before the previous war; any reason was good enough to lock up what they called 'the dubious.' In the Polish era there were from two hundred to two hundred and forty people in the same prison. So Stanisław and I," said Danek, pointing to his thin neighbor, his reticent pal in spectacles with a broken lens ingeniously glued together with paper, "spent more than a year in there. Some cells were packed so full that the prisoners had to take turns standing and sitting. The window vents had been knocked out, so even at the lowest temperatures the cells were unheated, so crowded and so stuffy that we all stripped almost naked; there was no air to breathe. And as for what they got up to! They were always taking someone out and beating or torturing him."

"Did they beat you up?" I asked.

"Of course," replied Danek, sitting on the wooden step of our hut, wrapped in his black gown. "Once they ordered me to do a hundred squats, then stripped me naked, punched me in the liver and ribs, and kicked my shins."

"I remember him coming back to the cell all swollen," added Stanisław.

"Plenty of the folks were swollen from beatings," added Danek, as if it were a maxim.

"Then at Wilejka the Soviets passed the death sentence on everyone from the Oszmiana district who'd been caught with revolvers and a radio transmitter. They shot them two days before the outbreak of the German-Soviet war."

"And what happened to you after that war broke out?" I asked.

"Immediately after they started taking us out in groups to force-march us to Borisov."

So I heard again, but now with names and details, the same facts I had hastily been told in the convoy on the way from Gryazovets to Totskoye by the men let out of prisons, about people being forced to march—from Jarmolińce and Brody on the one hand, and from Wilejka or Borisov on the other—and how anyone who couldn't keep up had been shot dead. Danek told me how a famous Wilno lawyer called Czernichow was shot along the way. He was a Jew who had very often defended communists at political trials.

"He was herded along with us," said Danek. "I was in prison with him too. He was always writing something (he said 'memoirs') on bits of paper, where and whenever he could get some, and he told me in confidence that he was noting down what he knew and saw here, that he had important friends in America, that it was for them, it just had to get to them... The Soviets weren't so dumb as to send those papers of his to America. They shot him on the way, because he was too weak to keep going. There was also a teacher, Paweł Marczewski. He'd run out of strength and couldn't keep going, but his son, a young fellow, helped him, the father leaned on him, but they were getting slower and slower, so one of the escort went up and shot the father in the head. Killed him instantly. And there he lay in a pool of blood. They pulled the son away, prodding him with bayonets to make him move along." Danek spoke with his head bowed low and his feet tucked under him, so I couldn't see his face as he went on to add: "They didn't just shoot, they stabbed too to make sure."

Many of those who weakened on the way were shot and bayoneted. Those who survived the journey were transported to Borisov in sealed railcars, packed in so tightly that once again they had to stand, and then to Ryazan, where they were kept in something no bigger than a village prison until September 4. Many of them had six, eight, or ten-year sentences, and many had been condemned to death.

A treasury clerk from Wilno, who was present during our conversation, had been forced to march with another group on June 24. He told us the same thing, providing a new list of those who had been shot or bayoneted; in my notebook I find the name Lipiński, a teacher and lieutenant who disappeared along the way and was probably shot. About twenty men, deemed too weak to complete the journey, were apparently shot at once on departure from Wilejka.

A student called Krupski, who had been badly tortured in prison, had disappeared at the point of setting off. Our hospital companions had heard that he was shot.*

The stories I heard from the thin boy from Wilno while I was waiting to be admitted, and these long conversations in the warm fall sunshine on the step outside our hospital hut were all that I gathered in my memory or jotted down in pencil during my first stay in the Totskoye hospital.

I found myself in that same hospital for the second time on September 30. Now I was put in the big block. There was snow outside, no stove in sight, and the cold was piercing. A sheet hanging in front of a large window blew about like a sail in the strong wind coming off the steppe.

We all lay under our blankets with our teeth chattering. If we poked a hand out it was soon frozen.

The building was full of people who were extremely unwell. On the day of my arrival three of them died; it was embarrassing to be occupying a hospital bed with nothing worse than flu or bronchitis. There were very few medicines at all and hardly any medical staff. For three days there hadn't been any light, and going to the overflowing privy at the other end of the building at night was a major expedition;

---

*According to data collected by Dr. Wieliczko, only two-thirds of those evacuated from Wilejka reached Ryazan, and 457 were unaccounted for. From one single evacuated cell containing fifty-four people, fourteen were killed, from another containing thirty, twelve were killed, from a third containing ninety-six, forty-one were killed, etc. (Dr. T. Wieliczko, *Wilejka*).

from behind the doors I could hear shouts and moans, people calling: "Nurse, nurse!" and getting no response.

To my left, an ailing soldier kept repeating the same thing over and over: "Am I a prisoner? Am I free? Are they going to kill me? What are they going to do to me?" He was a poor man from Równe with glassy, sickly green, terrified eyes and a crumpled face. "Will I see my wife and child again, will I see Równe?" he kept saying again and again, in constant fear that they were after him, that the Bolsheviks were just about to come and kill him.

To my right lay a very nice soldier with a quiet face who said nothing, not a word of complaint; he'd been there for a few weeks already, with severe pain in the bones and very swollen legs, probably suffering from bone tuberculosis.

Further off in the depths of the same ward there was a platoon sergeant, a polite, intelligent Jew who had survived all the camps and was now in a high fever, moaning and crying all night despite being unconscious. In the corner opposite was a man originally from Poznań, a former teacher in the eastern territory who had remained in his post for a long time and had only been deported a few months earlier. He told us how during the elections the most procommunist Ukrainian villages had written on sheets of paper: "We want Poland."

Dr. U. had been in Lwów until recently without being arrested and had only lately been deported from there. He described scenes from the life of "Soviet" Lwów to us.

One of the things he had seen was an anti-Polish movie being filmed on the street.

Old signboards had been put up, along with an old cigarette kiosk. A very long line was formed, as if waiting for sugar, and a fat Soviet actor in a Polish officer's uniform pushed everyone else aside to grab a huge packet of sugar without queuing. On another corner there was another set, made to look like a Soviet-style *gastronomia* (food store), with a very short line, where everybody was smiling and coming out with beautifully wrapped parcels.

He also told us how in the Soviet era there were lines outside the real *gastronomia*s for nights on end, and how some boys specialized in standing outside them all night as a substitute, and getting eight to ten rubles for this job.

In the same ice-cold ward there was a man called Abłamowicz lying on the floor in a draft. He was the son of a major and was suffering from diphtherial tonsillitis. In almost pure Kashubian, he whispered to his neighbor about Ivdel and Kolyma. There was another man lying on the floor beside him, whose face was covered by a blanket; as the window behind the billowing sheet let in a pale, cold light, I could hear his story from under the blanket: "I'm from Dubno, you see. I left two children there with no one to care for them, because my wife died."

"No one at all?" asked his neighbor.

"No one, it was like this, you see—they arrested me as soon as they came in. I was a clerk at the PKU (military administration), they held me for five days in a cellar; for five days they gave me nothing to eat or drink, not even water, and then let me go. When I got home, I didn't want my wife to know I'd been beaten up. I was covered in bruises, so when I had to get changed, I told her to leave the room. But she said: 'Undress in front of me.' I told her to leave again, but she kept on refusing. So when I took off my shirt and she saw the bruises, she fell to the floor and had her first heart attack. After all, I was just a humble clerk, I didn't belong to any party. In those few days my wife suddenly went gray—half her hair was white. And then she died. I had a pig and three sacks of flour, so I was able to get food for the children. Five months later a Jew denounced me, the Bolsheviks took me away again, and then they threw my children out of the house. Two weeks later my daughter, who was fourteen at the time and did everything in the house in her mother's place, came to the prison with a store-bought roll and a piece of store-bought sausage for me, so by then the children had nothing left. But those first days I spent in prison! I wasn't a nervous person, but I soon became one. The things I saw! They kept people in solitary in that cellar, they tortured and murdered. One time I looked through a keyhole and saw a soldier who had fired at them when they were taking the city. It was October and cold already but they kept him there in nothing but a shirt, with no drawers or pants, and his hands were tied behind his back with a piece of wire. He never stopped walking up and down. No, not walking but hopping on tiptoes—he clearly couldn't put weight on his heels, because they'd beaten him on them, and he never stopped shaking. He was badly beaten up and couldn't talk anymore—his tongue must have been twisted and all his teeth knocked out, so he just wailed. I saw them bring him a mug of coffee in the morning, but instead of giving it him to drink, they flung it in his face. And in that building they were always banging on metal to drown out the terrible wailing."

That day three more people died at the hospital.

A few days later I was transferred to one of the small huts. It was for tuberculosis sufferers, who lay there coughing up bacteria.

We lay on straw mattresses with pillows stuffed with dried plant stalks from the steppe; it was like lying on wire and splinters, but there was a stove, so it was nice and warm.

I found my hospital companions in a merry mood. I had only just lain down on the bed when I noticed a corporal lying very still.

"Has he got a lung disease too?" I asked.

"He hasn't got any lungs left," replied the consumptives, laughing. And after a pause: "He's dead, you know."

Next to him was the emaciated Corporal W., a man with a cadaverous face, large, watery eyes in deep sockets, the bones sticking out of his sunken cheeks, skin like parchment, and one hand missing, who instantly extracted the cigarettes from under the dead man's pillow. Less than a minute since we had confirmed his death, Corporal W. was trying to share his cigarettes with us.

None of us accepted any, so he took them all for himself. "What strange people you are," he said tetchily. "You sentimental saps, why be so sloppy? He lived and died, like anyone, so why not smoke his cigarettes?"

And the skeletal, jaundiced remains of the anonymous corporal were carried out under a sheet.

That day three more of them died.

When my temperature came down, I left the hospital as soon as I could and got back to work.

5. IN THEIR FOOTSTEPS

DAY AFTER day, in the hut where we lived and worked we heard an endless litany of stories, revelations, and reports from the north.

We walked in the footsteps of the new arrivals to our office—backward.

The monotony of the stories was striking, the adventures and sufferings so similar that they confirmed one another. We heard about the behavior of the Soviet authorities in Sosva, and analogous stories from Kola, and we heard about incidents at Oneglag that were just like those at Komi, while those at Jarmolińce and Brody confirmed the news from Wilejka.

Hastily we noted down the names and places of exile of hundreds of people whose release had to be demanded. There was no time to dig deeper, write down, or even memorize the particular adventures and experiences of each new arrival, outwardly so similar, yet never identical.

From the north news of mass deaths began to come through in all sorts of versions. They tended to confirm each other.

Lieutenant W. had learned from the NKVD chief in Ukhta, Komi Republic, that in February 1941, 1,650 Polish convicts and 110 Soviet escorting guards froze to death on a train; they were prisoners of war and included a large number of officers. Caught in a blizzard, the convoy got stuck in snowdrifts on the Kotlas-to-Vorkuta line and was only dug out a few days later. All the passengers had frozen to death; about a dozen were found about a mile away from the train, evidently having tried to escape and find help. They had battled through that short distance only to freeze to death in their turn.

The same lieutenant brought news about the shooting in Komi of 400 prisoners who had been evacuated from the Oneglags and the Kola Peninsula.

Other reports came in of several hundred prisoners freezing to death north of the Kozhva River and of an incident in which 750 people had perished near Ukhtizhemlag.

Beyond the Urals, entire parties of prisoners had died in the northern forests near the Sosva River (a tributary of the Ob), and also on the Yenisei.

Among the countless names of exiles that the new arrivals dictated to us, those of our fellow prisoners from Starobilsk, Kozelsk, or Ostashkov never came up, although by then we felt sure there could be hardly any camps in Russia from which we hadn't already had news. The one and only exception was Professor Stanisław Swianiewicz, then in one of the camps in Komi. We received at least ten reports about him from men who had been released from there, implying that he was seriously ill and that the Soviets were refusing to release him. We knew that earlier on he had been a prisoner of war in Kozelsk No. 1, one of the three prisoner-of-war camps from which we had no sign of life (with the exception of the 400 men concentrated in Gryazovets after May 1940). So where had the Kozelsk prisoners gone, we wondered.

Professor Swianiewicz was only released from Komi in July 1942, thanks to the repeated personal intervention of Ambassador Kot, and thus a year after the "amnesty"; as soon as he arrived in Totskoye he made the following statement: He had been taken away from Kozelsk No. 1 with a group of 300 officers in April 1940, to a station to the east of Smolensk; there he alone had been separated from the rest and kept apart, but through a small window he had been able to see what was happening to the others. Buses with darkened windows had driven up to the railcars, the officers had been made to board them, and then the buses had driven off into the wooded area around Smolensk. Professor Swianiewicz had been taken to Moscow for interrogation because of his academic work on the Soviet economy, and from there he was deported to Komi. How extremely exceptional this was, and that the professor had been excluded from the Katyn transport only at the very last moment could not possibly have been known in fall 1941 in Totskoye; the news that he was alive fueled our mistaken hopes that others had survived as well.

Thinking that here we had our first uncertain piece of evidence about the possible whereabouts of our fifteen thousand comrades from Kozelsk No. 1, Starobilsk No. 1, and Ostashkov, we naturally regarded the professor's statement as a discovery of the utmost importance.

An officer called Lieutenant R. arrived from Arkhangelsk. In the summer of 1940 he had met thirty officers in uniform (and thus probably officers taken captive during the September campaign) in the vicinity of Arkhangelsk; they were on a forced march toward the sea, and when he asked where they were going, one of them shouted back: "Onto a ship to Franz Josef Land."

Another officer, Lieutenant F. (who later proved to be an unreliable informant), one of the first to arrive from Kolyma, claimed that apparently 630 prisoners from Kozelsk were working about 110 miles from Pestraya Dresva (in Kolyma). He hadn't seen them for himself, but a friend of his, whose arrival he expected any day, had apparently seen and talked to a cadet from Kozelsk, sent out by the rest to buy tobacco for the camp.

Captain Z., who arrived from Kolyma later on, also claimed to have seen a few officers from Starobilsk in Kolyma. But none of these bits of information gave us a single name identifiable to us or to any of our surviving comrades who had ended up in Totskoye as I had, via Gryazovets, or via the Moscow prisons.

Some other very imprecise or vague pieces of information seemed to confirm that we should be looking for them in the direction of the northern islands and Kolyma.

I should mention that in the early days we were also misled by the fact that the men who were imprisoned at Starobilsk after May 1940, after the first Starobilsk prisoner-of-war camp had been closed down, also described themselves as "Starobilsk officers." We had not yet fully realized that later on there was a Starobilsk No. 2 and a Starobilsk

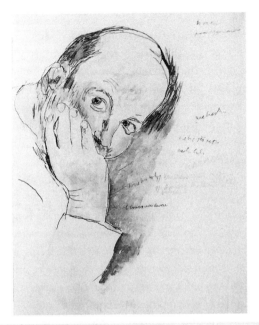

Two portraits of Adam Moszyński, Czapski's friend and fellow prisoner at the Gryazovets camp. *Above*: a watercolor from the first, now missing volume of Czapski's
Diary. *Below*: a drawing of the sleeping Moszyński from a later volume.

No. 3; there were women, civilians, and ordinary soldiers there, but also officers, except that these had been arrested on territory taken by the Soviets during the September campaign. The number of prisoners in Starobilsk, for instance, where in my time, the winter of 1939–40, there were about four thousand officers, had risen to twenty-two thousand in the winter of 1940–41. The central church alone, which when we were there was packed full with grain (to be transported to Germany, as we were told at the time), later housed three thousand prisoners, and thus three-quarters of the entire company from the 1939–40 period at Starobilsk.

We were also misled by the fate of those Starobilsk, Kozelsk, and Ostashkov prisoners who, before those camps were evacuated in April 1940, had been taken away to Moscow prisons for interrogation, and consequently, like Professor Swianiewicz, had avoided extermination.

The Bolsheviks so often referred to these very prisoners from those particular camps that perhaps they were consciously trying to confuse our calculations. And it was to foster confusion, among other things, that prisoners and POWs were, often against their will, shifted from place to place: very different groups of people were mixed together for no apparent reason, and those who were closely connected, even brothers, were split up. (Deported from Starobilsk, the Machlejd brothers were separated despite begging to leave together; both went missing without trace. The Jaroszyński brothers were also separated and went missing; Major Szuster was parted from his teenage son, who escaped alone and, via Gryazovets, ended up with us in the army.)

Gryazovets, where four hundred people from the three Starobilsk camps were put, once again mixing all civil states, political parties, and professions, may have partly been intended to cover up evidence of Katyn and to establish support for a future claim that the people in those camps could not have been massacred—after all, people from Kozelsk, Starobilsk, and Ostashkov had been found alive . . . at Gryazovets.

In the first few weeks at Totskoye we also heard rumors of the premeditated "liquidation" of the Polish officers.

The first version we heard was that some barges packed with army officers and policemen had sunk. These huge barges, each of which could carry up to four thousand people, had apparently sunk in the White Sea or the Arctic Ocean.

While laboring at a mine in Vorkuta, Captain N. had heard many reports of officers being deported to the northern islands and of three barges that had sunk. Others brought the same rumors from Vorkuta too. How much truth was there to them?

Much later on I finally got a report that seemed to confirm the rumors from Vorkuta, a detailed statement from Mrs. N., a nurse, about the sinking of three barges being pulled along by a tugboat on the Arctic Ocean. This information concurred to some extent with a report we received even later on from a Mrs. G. As the information in her report was the most precise of all, I shall quote the passage about the ships sinking without making changes:

In June 1941 I was traveling as a detainee to the camps in the Komi ASSR. From Arkhangelsk our convoy, numbering some four thousand men and women, was loaded onto barges, which were then pulled along by a tugboat. We were taken across the White Sea to the mouth of the River Pechora. During the voyage across the White Sea, as I was sitting on deck in tears, a young Russian came up to me, a soldier from the barge crew, and asked why I was crying. When I explained that I was crying because of my misfortune—because my husband, a reserve captain had been deported too, the soldier declared that our officers had already gone. When I asked where they were, he explained with a sneer that they had all been drowned, right here in the White Sea. As the conversation continued, I learned that this Russian had previously taken a convoy of our officers and police on two barges, numbering about seven thousand people. Somewhere out in the White Sea the tugboat pulling the barges had been uncoupled and both barges deliberately sunk. An older Russian from the barge crew was listening to our conversation, and after the young one had gone, he came up to me and confirmed that the whole story was true. This old fellow showed me great sympathy: weeping, he told me that he had witnessed the drowning of our officers and police. Before the barges were sunk the entire Soviet crew had moved onto the tugboat, but first they had made holes in the barges so the water would enter quickly. When I asked if anyone had been saved, I was told that everyone had gone to the bottom.

Nowadays, since the discovery of the Katyn graves, the committees and countercommittees, it has been conclusively confirmed that the remains of only 4,143 prisoners of war from Kozelsk No. 1 were found at Katyn, not 15,000 as the Germans had originally announced, and that they were murdered in April and May 1940. To this day the fate of the Ostashkov and Starobilsk prisoners has never been discovered, and the story of the drowned men does not seem entirely improbable.

And what about all the others, the tens of thousands of our private soldiers and officers who were deported from Polish terrain during the first occupation, and of whom all trace was lost—did they die of nothing but cold and hunger?

All this remains a mystery, but one thing now seems to be clear: the sort of massacre that took place at Katyn was not an exception. It did not just happen in the first stages of revolution, at a time when the lava of revolution was still fluid. Katyn was merely a small part of a broadly conceived plan, executed in cold blood.

But right then, in our role as caregivers at Totskoye, we were still incapable of accepting the idea that prisoners of war had been mass-murdered. Hearsay obscured those earliest rumors that our fellow officers had been exterminated, and we hoped that they were still alive in Franz Josef Land or Kolyma; at the time, those were the places we tried to rescue them from.

With these first pieces of information and rumors I headed off to army general staff in Buzuluk. At the time I thought that if General Anders and Ambassador Kot were to raise the matter immediately, it might still be possible to rescue at least some of our men from the far north before the winter.

For the first few weeks of our time in Totskoye I never left the camp grounds—nothing but wooden huts, tents, the steep cliff above the river, the boundless steppe, which we were too preoccupied to give a second glance, and a daily trip of a few miles back and forth to the officer's mess for dinner.

I set off for the station on foot with my colleague Platoon Sergeant Świątkowski. It was slightly below freezing, and there was total, windless silence. Dawn was only just breaking.

That first walk stayed in my memory—those few miles to the station. My companion was from Laski. He was one of the people who had built that strange community for the blind. I knew Laski from the days when it was an ugly, undeveloped, sandy plain outside Warsaw, edged with sparse woods. At the time the founders of Laski were just taking their first steps. Over twenty years, out of nothing a large foundation for the blind and a center for Catholic life and work in Poland had arisen from the sand. For Sergeant Świątkowski, Laski was more than a family home.

I had met him briefly in Poland and had come to know him better at the camp. At first he irritated me. It was like "the elephant and the Catholic question"—there was no topic that he didn't somehow try to connect with the issue of Catholicism. Just working with him or near him in Totskoye, I found out what his Catholicism involved: more than anything, an undying, Franciscan love for his neighbor. This sergeant with the thin, tired face, with bags under his eyes and a bad heart, always wearing an impossibly crumpled uniform, took on all the most laborious jobs, was always racing about the rallying point, escorting the weakest, most frozen, most louse-infested people to our hut, looking for something to wrap them in, while remaining extremely kind, not to say softhearted; in such cases he was persistent and relentless, capable of going to any lengths in order to relieve someone's suffering. Except that at dawn he always disappeared from our hut to run a couple of miles to an improvised chapel for Mass and then return to work with a new supply of strength and genuine sweetness. I don't know if anyone could possibly have nurtured the Laski tradition more consistently or keenly than he did in Totskoye.

As we crossed the alien steppe with our rucksacks, we talked about our loved ones and the days of our youth and we really felt as if the past few years didn't matter. How relative and variable our sense of age is. What triggers the sudden revival of our sense of joy at life, often appearing at the toughest times?

It was our first long walk, in fact our first walk at liberty for two whole years, along a few miles of rutted road with deep potholes in the frozen black mud. The day was still dawning, on either side of the road lay the white steppe, covered in snow or light frost, a totally silent landscape. At one point we walked across a small bridge. We could see the brown steppe dusted with snow, to the east some remote, undulating, bluish hills, a gray sky as smooth as porcelain, and in the foreground a little brook, where two fine gray geese with pink-and-orange beaks were splashing about, and in the distance a black string of women in large headdresses, like turbans, made of black headscarves. The marvelous precision of extremely subtle gray-brown, gray-blue, and white tones reminded me of an ink-wash painting by a Chinese master. This was my first impression of Asia.

While waiting at the station for a couple of hours, we listened to the stories of a duty officer and a military policeman.

This was where everyone disembarked on their way to our camp. The convoys of women and children being sent to the south passed through this station too; like an evil spell, the south drew everyone in, taking more people away from us than the northern frosts. The officer told us a minor detail. An impossibly overloaded train had made a brief stop at this station. Suddenly a man had started rapidly wiping the iced-up windowpane, then shortly after squeezed his way down the packed corridor to the exit, jumped off the train, gone straight up to the military policeman, taken off his hat, which had an eagle on it, and had kissed that eagle with extreme emotion. The train was already moving, so the stranger had only just managed to jump back on board.

There were many others like him, ready to defend their eagle against all attempts to change it, who proudly reported back to the Polish Army again.

At Totskoye station I also heard news of one of our officers, whom I had seen full of enthusiasm, hurrying to join the army; he had a fine, if not heroic past, and longed to be sent north again to save the rest of his comrades. But here he had been arrested and convicted by our authorities for the sale, together with his Russian lover, of valuable canned food, which he had been given to distribute at the station to hungry convoys passing through.

A few months later, at this same station we had our first sight of German prisoners of war. By then it was the middle of winter, and a huge convoy came slowly through the station on its way east. All civilians were ordered to leave the platform, but a few of us, who were in uniform, were allowed to remain.

Open railcars sailed by, secured with wire; the temperature was about −30°F, and each of those cars was packed with Germans in nothing but their shirts—not one of them had an overcoat. Each car was being guarded by a single Red Army soldier in a thick sheepskin coat, holding a rifle.

But on the day of our departure for Buzuluk there was still just a mild frost, and the crowded railcar was stuffy from the smoke of homegrown tobacco, known in these parts as *samosheyka* ("self-sow"). We spent a couple of hours in a packed compartment, traveling across the steppe and fields with overgrown, snow-dusted sheaves of still unharvested wheat; grain had been poured out on the platform at one of the stations and left to molder without a cover.

I remember that our traveling companions included a very old woman in beggarly rags. She huddled quietly by the window; at one point she brought one little tomato out of a small bag. She made a broad, Orthodox sign of the cross and, chewing for ages in silent concentration, very slowly ate it.

We reached Buzuluk, a poor, flat town, consisting mainly of small, one-story wooden houses. The road to the station ran straight ahead, with only the immense tower of a closed-down, lifeless church in sight.

Among the old, low-rise wooden houses with fences running between them stood a large, white, Empire-style building—the old, prerevolutionary Dvoryanskoye Sobranie, or meeting place for the local landowners, then, after the revolution, home to the Buzuluk Soviet, and now home to Polish Army general staff. Inside there was an impressive staircase, some large high-ceilinged rooms in which everyone was frozen to the bone, dozens of typewriters, and lots of rapid movement along all the corridors. There was a mess serving slightly better food. For those of us arriving here from Totskoye, it was almost like being in the capital, almost like luxury.

There were plenty of officers, friends from London, and even letters sent from there by relatives. There were Polish radio broadcasts from London, which we could listen to with impunity, including Big Ben striking at noon. These were intense impressions for every one of us, a link with the outside world, with freedom—proof that we were no longer cut off, not isolated from the rest of the world forever.

As soon as I arrived, I reported to the chief of staff in person, presenting the evidence we had gathered concerning the place of exile of our comrades from the three camps and other information provided by new arrivals.

The chief of staff was Colonel Okulicki. He had emerged from a Soviet prison, "amnestied" like everyone else; there they had knocked out all his teeth. He was stocky, with thick graying hair, and I found him to be a man of great energy and an affable, point-blank manner. Despite a huge workload, he received me at once and listened very attentively. This same colonel would be sent back to Poland in 1944, and his son would be killed at Monte Cassino. In Poland he would fight the Germans, and when the Soviet troops took over, "on their word of honor" the Soviet officers would treacherously lure him to a "conference," from where he would end up in the Lubyanka again, he would once again be convicted in Moscow at the "Trial of the Sixteen" and deported in an unknown direction.

But I am getting ahead of myself; in the phase when I first reported to "Niedźwiadek"—"Bear Cub"—as his pseudonym later was, he was in permanent, not to say friendly contact with the Soviets, deputizing in Buzuluk for General Anders, who had flown to Moscow. That same day Colonel Okulicki sent news of our comrades to Moscow by radio. I was given an order to write a precise report on the spot, including everything I knew about the Starobilsk, Kozelsk, and Ostashkov prisoners. At one of the HQ departments I dictated it to a friendly typist working on a shabby old typewriter. At dusk we had to break for an hour and a half to wait for the electricity to come on. What a different world it was already: young ladies, chitchat, some mild flirting, and even a box of chocolates from London or Moscow, and it all felt so natural, though at the time I was writing about Starobilsk, about the friends whose faces I could see before me, about Sołtan, who was "on bended knee" to go back to Poland (in those days Totskoye and Buzuluk counted as Poland too), about Chęciński, who if he had been with us would have been rushing about like mad by now, overwhelming us with ideas somehow related to his idée fixe—the Federation of Central Europe—and so the atmosphere at general staff seemed almost horrendous!

As soon as we enjoy slightly better conditions, even if they are far from the normal ones we were once used to, each day brings experiences and pleasures to blot out our bitter or painful memories. For every one of us at the time, not just being at liberty, not just the chance to commune with women after two years without seeing a single one, but a piece of cheese, some meat and potatoes, and a glass of vodka or a bottle of beer were great treats.

No man could live or smile if he were always reminiscing without ever erasing any of his memories.

That was when I met Lieutenant Zielicki, who was just back from Nakhodka Bay near Vladivostok. He told me a lot about Kolyma, a land most of us had never heard of, where we later spent a long time imagining our comrades to be.

Kolyma is a land populated by no one but prisoners and their guards. It is a network of camps and mines along the Kolyma River, the mouth of which is situated on the Arctic Ocean, between the Lena River and the Bering Strait. One basic rule applies, which was broken by the "amnestied" Poles: nobody ever comes back from

Kolyma, except as a total cripple. The prisoners there are relatively lightly guarded, because there can be no question of escape. The only route to the *materik*, or "mainland," as the people of Kolyma call the rest of the continent, is by ship. Between Kolyma and the populated territory to the north there are thousands of miles of tundra and mountains, which would be just as impossible to cross as getting off an island in the sea on foot. Should a prisoner survive to the end of his sentence, a new charge is normally brought against him, extending his sentence by a few years more. Naturally, there is no question of any correspondence with relatives—the isolation is total. There are however instances of a prisoner getting through his sentence without any new charges, and then he is at liberty to remain in Kolyma as a "free settler." As there is no other way to earn a living apart from the camps and mines where the exiles work, his only choice is to get a job at the same mine, though now he doesn't have to live in a barrack with the other prisoners but can have his own home.

This land is rich in copper, gold, silver, lead, and coal. The climate is extremely severe, the winter lasts for ten months, and there are no birds there at all. One of my comrades who came to us from Kolyma told me that by September the temperature could already be down to −22°F, and the snowdrifts were so big that they had to dig tunnels through them. All the exiles sail there on ships that go from Nakhodka Bay, between Sakhalin Island and Japan, across the Sea of Okhotsk to the port of Magadan on Nagayev Bay, or to another port situated five hundred miles further north of Pestraya Dresva. The prisoners are transported from there by automobile. A totally reliable informant, Captain Z., later vouchsafed to me that nowhere in Russia had he ever seen such excellent roads as in Kolyma. If a few thousand workmen were needed to clear the roads during a blizzard, a few thousand were sent out, and everything was all right. But in the Magadan region there is also a town inhabited by more than twelve thousand frostbitten cripples, with noses, hands, and feet missing, waiting to be sent back to the "mainland."

Captain Z., a famous horse breeder, also claimed that nowhere in Russia had he seen such beautiful horses (in this climate a horse is not able to live for more than three years), or such beautiful cars, which are used by the big potentates, the NKVD bosses who run the mines and the major camps, full of unpaid workers. Everyone told me about the enormous ships that transport the prisoners to the north. The man I spoke to on this occasion, Lieutenant Józef Zielicki, was from Borysław, and had ended up in a so-called *peresylny* (transit) camp at Nakhodka Bay in April 1941. He had come across some of our officers there, who had been transported earlier, in April and May 1940. He claimed to have met a colonel, commander of the state police academy; a regular army colonel of infantry; and engineer Szajna, also an officer. None of these three men had been sent to Kolyma purely because the medical commission regarded them as too physically debilitated. These officers told Lieutenant Zielicki that in April and May 1940 a few thousand Poles had been sent to the transit camp, among them some officers, and that they had been sent from there to Kolyma.

In 1941 Lieutenant Zielicki had loaded those huge cargo ships with sugar, salt, ball bearings, iron bars, machinery, and artificial fertilizer. The colossal ships regularly transported all this and up to 7,000 convicts.

A convoy that left on June 15, 1941, apparently contained 3,500 Poles, but there were no prisoners of war from September among them. All these statements were confirmed to me soon after by Major S., who had also been deported to Kolyma with a large number of Polish prisoners at the end of July 1941. He remained there until September of that year. He came back from Kolyma with 250 other Poles, and according to the data he had gathered, from 6,000 to 10,000 Poles were probably still there. But he hadn't come upon any trace of the officers from Starobilsk, Kozelsk, and Ostashkov.

Major S. told us that in one camp alone 70 percent of the unpaid laborers of Kolyma had died in the winter of 1940 to 1941, which shows how rapidly they were liable to perish. Scurvy and night blindness were so widespread there that in the units in which he worked, every single person was suffering from one of these ailments. Many were sick with both at the same time.

He was also the first reliable informant to confirm that convoys of Poles had been sailing to Kolyma via Nakhodka Bay from April 1940; this concurred with the dates when the camps at Starobilsk, Kozelsk and Ostashkov, were closed down. At the time I thought I was on the right track; our comrades had to be in Kolyma. But it was merely a coincidence.

Nonetheless, the rumor that there were six to ten thousand of our deportees in Kolyma in the summer of 1940 (the figure may be exaggerated) had not been explained. I heard it from several different sources. What was their actual number? Had they all perished?

After three days we came back from Buzuluk, full of impressions and optimism. We were on the trail of our missing men, and we could tell all our petitioners in Totskoye that in Moscow and Kuybyshev General Anders and Ambassador Kot were most energetically demanding the release of the people whose names were on the lists we were sending them, and that they should expect us to succeed in bringing all the survivors to join the army.

We spent hours and hours at the station waiting for our train; in those days they were running at random, and it was impossible to get a better idea of when the next one would come than within the next few hours. We took a good look at the station, with its hopelessly filthy waiting rooms packed with hungry people who'd been sitting there for whole days and nights on end; even at this small station, there were pictures on all the walls, portraits of the leaders and Civil War battle scenes.

I was impressed by how consistently the Bolsheviks disseminate and promote socialist realist art, the one and only aim of which is to glorify the heroes of the revolution and the revolutionary struggle in the most popular form possible. So-called *sotsyalny zakaz* ("social procurement") has led to the total suppression of any attempt at personal expression of your own experience in your own way; with the best will in the world, as I searched from Moscow to Ashgabat, I did not see a single picture that wasn't atrocious or hopelessly mediocre. What a tragic illustration, and to what a degree, for the arguments debated by Proudhon and Courbet of almost a hundred years ago—an illustration for Proudhon's book of 1865, *The Principle of Art and Its Social Purpose*, in which the great revolutionary, coming out in defense of realism, attacked the great realist Courbet, demanding that he should "paint only for the aim of the physical and moral perfection of our species," and that every artist should have a sense of what appeals to others and reproduce this alone, merely improving and enhancing it. Proudhon attacked artists from the social angle as the most servile race, the most lacking in discipline, corrupt and corrupting. Proudhon likewise "pulverized" Delacroix, the greatest Romantic painter of the nineteenth century. "I care little for your personal impressions," he wrote; Proudhon's principles were lofty and his intentions noble, but it was the same Soviet *sotsyalny zakaz* that in Russia, just as in Nazi Germany, destroyed everything in fine art that did not belong to the official aesthetic canon, or that was not wholly subordinate to the objectives of politics and the Party.

The station restaurant was closed, but we managed to sneak inside it along with a couple of lucky devils. All we could get there was warm water in extremely dirty glasses, and nothing else. We had some cheese and rusks from the officer's mess with us, so during our eight-hour wait we drank the warm water while nibbling the cheese and reminiscing about Laski, while the miserable crowd of starving people, jostling for space, gazed at us through the glazed doors, like fortune's chosen few, in the lap of luxury.

Our journey back to Totskoye was by night.

Bogdanek, a boy scout who helped with our work, met us in the doorway with the news that right there, just across the stream that ran near our accommodation, the military police had discovered the murder of a Russian boy who'd been grazing his cows. Someone had stuffed his mouth with cotton wool, strangled him with wire, and stolen a cow.

The boy's father was glaring at the Poles in fury, saying: *Prishli nam pomagat bandity!*—"The people who've come to help us are bandits!"

And so the famous "amnesty" even included murderers, who had crept into the Polish Army, but not our friends from Kozelsk, Starobilsk, and Ostashkov, who would have begged to join this army on bended knee, if they'd only had the chance.

6. BUZULUK

In MID-November, I was summoned to general staff in Buzuluk and to the embassy in Kuybyshev in connection with a couple of my reports and the material I had sent in about our missing comrades. Appointed manager of the unit whose purpose was to gather the names of the missing men and of other arrested comrades of ours who had not been released from the camps, I spent the winter of 1941 to 1942 based in Buzuluk, while taking trips to Chkalov (formerly Orenburg) and Moscow, with three stops in Kuybyshev.

In the final days of October we compiled the first alphabetical list of prisoners held in Starobilsk, Kozelsk, and Ostashkov; we drew on memory and on the lists we had made earlier, mainly in Gryazovets. At this point our list, including about four thousand names, was submitted to Stalin at the Kremlin by Generals Sikorski and Anders on December 4. A card index was then produced, which would be continually expanded, supplemented, and made more precise on the basis of newly arriving information.

I found myself in Buzuluk just when General Sikorski made his trip to the USSR. After going to see Stalin in Moscow, he visited Buzuluk and then one of our divisions that was being formed at Tatishchevo. Each Polish base received the man who was both prime minister and commander in chief with enthusiasm and emotion.

Sikorski was only at HQ for about two or three days. I was not present at any of his briefings and only saw him once, at a big banquet given in his honor by General Anders.

In the white Empire hall, where we worked during the day, three tables were set up that ran down the room lengthwise, linked by a fourth one running widthwise, at which the most honored guests were seated. General Sikorski and Ambassador Kot were there, and so was the Soviet deputy commissar for foreign affairs, Vyshinsky, who accompanied Sikorski here in Molotov's place; Colonel Svoboda, who was to create the Czech legion, was also there, as were some Russian writers, including Ilya Ehrenburg. Suddenly, meats and fish were available in large quantities in hungry Buzuluk, and every kind of alcoholic drink, all provided by the NKVD authorities. The tables were heavily laden with bottles and appetizers, and the staff who served us consisted of Russians only, also courtesy of the NKVD, who, before the dignitaries entered the room, locked the doors and conducted a thorough, hour-long inspection, looking inside every closet, tapping the walls and peering under the tables—because "Vyshinsky himself" was going to be in the room.

Sikorski was ill with a fever and only made a brief appearance, leaving after the soup. He had dark rings around his eyes, whose pale gray-blue color I always found striking. He looked tired, but as ever he had the manner of a general.

Before this banquet I had only seen him two or three times in the flesh. The first time was in the early part of 1922, just a few months after the assassination of President Narutowicz. I was a student at the Academy of Fine Arts, and in the wake of the president's death, several of my fellow students and I tried to start a movement to oppose the wave of nationalism and anti-Semitism. We wanted to band together in the name of law and order and to encourage solid cooperation with all minorities. I went to see Sikorski, who was then prime minister, with a letter of recommendation from his friend Professor Leopold Jaworski, the father of one of my colleagues. I was received at the Presidium of the Council of Ministers in Namiestnikowski Palace. Sikorski struck me as unexpectedly young and energetic; he was extremely courteous, and throughout the audience spoke almost incessantly on topics that had nothing to do with the purpose of my visit.

I must admit that I came away completely disenchanted and judged him accordingly with the innate cruelty of youth—for me he ceased to exist. Now I wonder why—was it by comparison to Piłsudski, whose every gesture I found surprising and fascinating?

Sikorski had given the impression of being inordinately self-satisfied. He showed none of the charm of utter simplicity, profundity, and humanity that Piłsudski had; certainly everything he said was intelligent and interesting, but it was marked by incredible self-absorption.

I could leave my post now, he told me, almost running about his office, I have gained recognition of the eastern borders, I don't care about power, etc., etc.

Sikorski had that stiff, artificial way of moving his lips that is typical of people who are self-absorbed, most visible in the corners of the mouth, in the opening and closing of the lips.

I next met him in 1930 at a dinner at the Hotel Chatham in Paris, where there were six of us in all. Sikorski's situation in Poland at the time prompted me to feel sympathy for the man, a general of outstanding merits who had been pushed out of the picture and was a virtual émigré. That evening Sikorski was in a tuxedo; his movements were brusque but they betrayed the qualities of a general. The talk at dinner was not very interesting. Sikorski was politely stiff, quite charmless, and spoke in generalities that were listened to with reverence. Only at one point did he say something that seemed to me to come from the bottom of his heart. When the talk turned to the subject of Marshal Piłsudski, he grimaced and said laconically: "Yes, but I'm sure to outlive him," his eyes shining with a flash of ice.

There was tenacity and incredible self-confidence in this remark.

Now I was seeing him for the third time. How much he had aged! His fair hair had gone very gray, and I found him far more likeable. Furrowed with wrinkles, his face looked much more natural.

I had close contact with him on two more occasions, once at Kirkuk, in Iraq, during a difficult hour-long conversation face-to-face, and once just before his departure for Gibraltar, at our diplomatic post in Cairo. These two meetings gave me an incomparably more human impression of him; his personal sensitivity and vanity seemed to have been extinguished or had been offset by the difficulties of the moment. The man whose face was always tense was paying for his own former attitude, paying with a huge and incessant effort, and with the greatest possible sense of responsibility. Now that he had the certainty of being Poland's leader, he performed the role to the full.

I will never forget his final words. He received me for a few minutes in Cairo before his flight took off, only a short time before the fatal crash. His face was strangely relaxed. It was the first time I felt I was talking to a tired, good man.

"You must admit that I have done well to come and see you—I've managed to smooth out a lot of problems and misunderstandings. It's crucial for all of us to work together and to do away with the discord."

In his pale, tired eyes and his wrinkled face there wasn't a shadow of artificiality or acting, just the sincerest possible concern for the thing that mattered to us all.

During the banquet at Buzuluk a figure of a rather different cut flashed past among the other guests, that of a solidly built, healthy-looking man with a pince-nez. He stayed until dawn and delivered a honey-coated speech about Polish-Soviet brotherhood. His face wore a brutal expression, and his solid head seemed to spring straight from his shoulders with no neck in between. He had a bald patch covered by a ginger "comb-over"—this was Andrei Vyshinsky, Molotov's deputy, the prosecutor at the Moscow trials, and the deputy commissar for foreign affairs.

The banquet went on for a long time. There was a copious supply of vodka, and each successive speech, invariably promoting Polish-Soviet brotherhood, was ever more vigorously and mindlessly applauded.

In these few winter months I had most of my encounters with Soviet citizens, and was able to make most of my scanty, yet interesting observations from the ground.

The Soviet government did what it could to keep us apart from the ordinary people. After great difficulties, we were allowed to occupy rooms in private homes in Buzuluk, but any sort of sincere conversation was rare, and dangerous for our hosts; moreover, news reached us from Turkestan that a large number of people from Buzuluk had been sent there after coming in contact with us during our stay in their town. They had been deported, just in case.

For some time I lived in a small, impossibly cold room in the apartment of an old woman who had once worked as a maid for a baronial family that had owned an estate near Buzuluk in the days of the czar.

She was reticent, cautious, and afraid. What did she have to hide? Perhaps that she was a believer who crossed herself and had a Bible and an icon; one time she secretly showed me a strange sheet of paper with a prayer in Cyrillic printed on it. She was keeping it safe for the time of her death. When a Russian Orthodox believer dies, their relatives lay this sort of paper on their face; it contains the prayer that the priest says over the dying. For believers cut off from the church, this substitutes for extreme unction and religious solace on one's deathbed.

After a few weeks I managed to gain the old woman's relative trust. Her name was Anna Stepanovna, and she was seventy-two, stocky, still vigorous, with wily, sparkling eyes hidden beneath drooping eyelids. She addressed me with the informal *ty* (like *tu* in French), told me off when my room was messy, and made the sign of the cross over me and said *Gospod s'taboyu* ("God be with you") as I went off to work. When from time to time I brought back a piece of meat or a can of food and asked her to cook dinner for me, she did it willingly and extremely painstakingly, though she wouldn't accept any instructions.

Nieuzhto nie znayu ("As if I don't know"), she would say disdainfully, and then, full of a sense of her own mysterious superiority, she would add in a whisper: *U baronov sluzhila*—"I worked for the barons."

During my stay in Buzuluk it was so cold that I barely poked my nose out of general staff or my little room a couple of streets away. Just once I accompanied my landlady to the market, held every Sunday.

I managed to buy a frozen lump of melted butter for fourteen rubles and ten eggs for four rubles each. That was a real bargain. My dear Anna Stepanovna recovered her youth there, diving into the crowd, ferreting about and haggling heatedly for a couple of eggs or carrots. It all took place in a large square in front of a church with two green cupolas and windows that were either broken or boarded up (I was told the church had been closed for many years) under a cream-colored, milky sky, very bright with tones of pale blue breaking through. Against the snow there was a crowd of people in gray sheepskin coats. Peasant farmers had come to this market from far away, with dozens of low sleds harnessed to small ponies, oxen, or even camels. The animals stood calmly, white hoarfrost forming on their thick coats. It was about −20°F. Almost every sled was loaded with large pumpkins and small amounts of carrots and onions; there was also frozen milk for sale, which was hacked up with an ax, as well as eggs and lean cheeses.

A gray crowd in gray patched sheepskins, with no colored head-scarves, not a single patch of color, standing against the bright snow under a milk-white sky—this is the only image of Buzuluk that I retained in my memory.

I did my best to question the locals about their religious attitudes. Until 1935 there had been one church left in a village almost two hundred miles from Buzuluk, where the locals used to travel once a year, but it had been closed too, and now there was no church anywhere within reach for the people here. When in connection with the German-Soviet war the Soviet newspapers started writing about religious freedom, people began to hope for a change of policy on religious matters. Out of the blue an Orthodox priest appeared and was housed with a local family; several people began to wonder whether the House of God might be reopened. But only a few days went by before the woman who owned the apartment where the priest was living was summoned and told to throw him out immediately; a large fine was imposed on her. She was barely able to defend herself; she was very poor and had two sons at the front, but she had to get rid of the priest at once.

When I left Buzuluk, Anna Stepanovna made the Orthodox sign of the cross over me and said once again: *Nu Gospod s'taboyu* ("God be with you"). There were tears in her eyes.

Two years later I toured Jerusalem, where I was taken to the Orthodox convent situated on the Mount of Olives. From there I had a view of the hills of Palestine and Transjordan in golden sunlight and among them in the white mist I could see part of the Dead Sea glittering. I went into the church; an Orthodox choir was singing and the nuns were gathering in front of the royal doors,* all in black, with black veils. Otherwise the church was entirely empty. I stopped beside one of the nuns, who reminded me of Anna Stepanovna in her impossibly cold apartment in snow-covered Buzuluk. I leaned forward and in a whisper I asked the nun to say a prayer for Anna Stepanovna, an Orthodox believer, who lived in Russia and hadn't been inside a church for many years, because there weren't any there. I looked into the nun's face—it was stern and aged, with fine wrinkles, and large black eyes that seemed to stare through me. She gave me no answer, so I repeated my words a second time, and once again there was the same impression of stony indifference. I thought she was deaf and asked if she could hear me. Suddenly she nodded and replied irritably: "Oh yes, I heard you."

A handful of very old nuns, a clean, bright church, the royal doors, the gold leaf, the smooth paintings that were not quite Byzantine, not quite Italian—it all made me think of that flimsy sheet of paper inscribed with a prayer in Cyrillic in distant Buzuluk.

I lived in another house in Buzuluk too, the home of a railroad worker. He had taken part in the revolution and was a die-hard loyalist. Old and taciturn, he had a meek, silent wife and a quiet only child. The man was self-taught and still studying—in his hands I saw not just Gorky but even Anatole France in Russian translation. The Russian Revolution had given him status. He was sincerely and consistently

* The central doors in the iconostasis. —*Trans.*

mistrustful and hostile toward us Poles. I failed to break through this aversion in any way. There could be no question of any form of conversation or honest debate—he had an argument for everything from *politgramota* (political literacy). He believed the Bolshevik dogma about the vileness, enmity, and stupidity of the *burzhuaznovo mira*— the bourgeois world. Together we listened to a speech made by General Sikorski in Moscow, which was broadcast on the radio a couple of times to all Russia. The old railroad worker listened to the Polish prime minister with evident distaste and made no comment.

I remember two other houses in Buzuluk. In one of them the wife of a painter from Leningrad was living, still a young woman. I don't know what she lived on. Her husband, a young painter suffering from a lung disease, had been deported to the far north for several years, but she had no idea what had happened to him, how long his sentence was, or for what offense. All she knew was that there was very little hope of ever seeing him again. Her tiny cubbyhole was hung with drawings and watercolors by her husband. From a distance they reminded me of the youthful drawings of Zygmunt Waliszewski when he came to join us in Kraków from Tiflis in 1920. In the unknown Russian painter's drawings I could see the same influences of Russian art, not yet Bolshevik—of the *Mir Iskusstva* (The World of Art) movement, of Sergei Sudeikin and even Alexander Yakovlev. There was a linear, affected manner, and some slightly artificial distortion, but there were also new ideas, bold color combinations, and decorative flair—there was definitely talent. I used to call in at one other house, home to some quiet, very sad people. Once, in the doorway, the mother of two small children told me in a whisper that the oldest— a very bright boy who stood out from the rest—had been sent from school to the far north. She had no idea why they had deported him. In the same house lived two young officers' wives who were perfectly happy; they had some new frocks and had been to see the world outside—meaning that they had spent a few months in Lwów and Stanisławów; they hadn't the words to express what a wonderful life was lived there.

As I write, I keep remembering more and more faces, more and more of what passed before my eyes. Once, in an office in Buzuluk where there were typists at their desks and officials running about, a woman working behind a thin partition suddenly addressed me. In a faltering voice, choking back tears, she said: "My husband was a railroad worker in Manchuria, but when the railroad passed into Soviet hands all the railroad workers and their families were deported to Soviet Russia and replaced by others. We were assigned here to Buzuluk, and my husband was even given a good job. But a few months later he was deported, I don't know where or why. I haven't had any news of him for several years." To be so incautious as to tell such things to a Pole with other people almost in sight she must have been driven to the limits of her endurance.

Nobody could possibly understand it—it would take a brilliant writer, a superb observer, a new Tolstoy or Proust, Russian or Polish, to describe the atmosphere that prevailed in Russia, at every moment, and the things that would suddenly give the game away in the course of ordinary, everyday life—a small gesture or a memorable glance. It wasn't the difficult conditions or the hunger—all that was less awful than the suppression of humanity, the mute look in the eyes of people among whom just about everybody had lost at least one of their closest relatives to the camps in the north.

I didn't know how many people were interned in the Soviet camps and prisons; one heard figures ranging from sixteen to thirty-five million, but a remark made by an examining magistrate was rather telling: when my acquaintance whom he was questioning told him that there were thirty million of us Poles, so it wouldn't be all that easy to eliminate us, he laughed and said: "Big deal—we've got more than that in the labor camps and prisons alone."

The impression that was made on me in December 1941, by those glances, hints, and scraps of confession, which I find so hard to describe, reminded me of another, identical one that I had gained years before.

In January 1919, I was on my way back to Poland from Russia after a three-month stay in Petrograd, sent there by my regiment in search of our imprisoned comrades. I was coming back through the so-called Ober Ost with a false passport and traveled on a Jewish sled from Białystok to Łapy (which was on the Polish border in those days). I dropped in at a small restaurant that was full of people eating and drinking, including a local gangster and his entourage, a petty noble in a *świtka* (a long traditional coat), peasants in sheepskin coats, and Jews—all Poland was there. The whole room was drinking vodka and talking—about politics, of course, criticizing everyone and everything loud and clear. According to the happy company, now one, now another political party consisted of nothing but blackguards, and they hurled insults at each other, which didn't spoil anyone's appetite or mood. This irresponsible litigiousness of ours, the critical remarks, the rowdiness and sense of security with which each person spoke his mind, literally shocked me after Russia, and it was as if I could suddenly breathe again after almost being asphyxiated.

Though this happened long ago, the contrast between the people in Soviet trains and trams—their silence, constant vigilance, and caution—and the people in that provincial Polish pub was so strong, and their behavior so spontaneous and joyful, that it has stayed in my memory to this day.

In 1935 I experienced the same contrast a second time, palpably and unmistakably, in the course of a conversation with a woman on a train.

I was traveling third class from Warsaw to Paris. I boarded a carriage running from Stołpce on the Soviet border to Paris. This woman was the only other passenger in the clean, comfortable, warm compartment. Getting on in years, instead of luggage she had a dreadful bag and a small, ugly, shaggy dog.

Her shoes were made of rawhide, and she had a dull, haggard complexion and the terrified eyes of a beaten dog. We started to talk, and she turned out to be German. It was the period when Hitler was getting everyone he could out of Russia. This woman had always lived in Russia, and like a large number of Germans was almost entirely assimilated there. She lived in a small Ukrainian town where she gave

German language lessons and worked at an institution for the deaf and dumb. She was on her way to Germany, a place with which she had almost no connection. Hitler did not exist for her; all she knew was that she was leaving Russia. Once we were in Poland, in the empty carriage, she told me about it in a whisper. It was nothing remarkable, just everyday fare for anyone who had ever been to Russia as more than just a tourist: she told me that when Kirov was assassinated, the next day hundreds and hundreds of people had been deported to an unknown destination, and that it was a fine trick for getting several hundred thousand laborers to work in forestry. Several dozen people had been taken from one of the factories, loaded onto open railcars and driven dozens of miles in severe frost. They were packed in so tight that there was only room to stand; most of them had no warm clothing, and when the railcars reached their destination they had to be carried out like wooden logs. Many had frozen to death. A young woman who was a good friend of hers had been deported along with these people. During the last war the young woman's father, a colonel, had been the garrison commander, or something of the kind, in the town where they lived. Somehow they had survived the revolution. The daughter earned a living by running a photographic studio, and the old father, who had been left in peace, had learned how to dry flowers and make beautiful frames for his daughter's photographs, by sticking the dried flowers onto cardboard under glass. The old man and his daughter made quite a good living, because every Red Army man in town wanted to have a photograph of himself in a decorative frame, and the daughter also earned extra wages teaching. These people had only one concern, which was for their origin to be forgotten, so they could live and work in peace. The day after the murder of Kirov they were both deported; all trace of them had been lost.

"As I was crossing the border, at the last moment they tried to take my dog away from me, saying he was a pedigree—I found him in the gutter as a puppy and took the food out of my own mouth to feed him, so I refused to give him up. Once across the Polish border, I was allowed to stay overnight at a nice clean Red Cross house, where I was given a room. A cleaning woman came in and started reviling the Polish government, saying they were bastards and thieves. I seized her by the hands: 'Woman, what are you saying? Be quiet, they'll kill you for that, they'll send you into exile!' But she couldn't understand what I meant."

She was the shadow of herself as she told me this story on the train, her eyes flashing with terror.

Every day I spent in Buzuluk in 1941 provided me with fresh confirmation of the truth and "banality" of my earlier impressions, and that in this respect nothing had changed for the better. Here in Russia, even after years in the camps, the Poles still couldn't "understand," they hadn't adapted.

For the Soviets, the Polish Army that was being organized in Russia, and the wave of Poles released from prisons and now streaming south, were to be treated with extreme wariness, suspicion, and repugnance by "right-thinking" people—these Poles moved differently, reacted differently, thought and spoke more frankly; this often made a powerful impression on the more sensitive Russians, who felt the need to take a deep breath, and an intense longing for life without fear.

"*Nasha zhizn ochen grubaya*—Our life is very crude, suddenly you arrive in our country, and we can see that there are still people who are free, so then it's hard for us to say goodbye to you," I was told by a Russian woman who was a great expert on the Soviet Union and a patriot too.

7. CHRISTMAS EVE

BUZULUK was also the place where I spent my first Christmas at liberty. General staff's entire "social" life centered on the broad corridors and the huge Empire-style hall, where the tables piled with our card indexes and lists were located. The tables and card indexes had to be carried out whenever there was a major briefing, a lecture, or a performance, all of which took place in that large space. Today, on Christmas Eve, they were being shunted off again. Everyone was in a mood of holiday madness. In the hall, as chilly as an icehouse, a small tree was being decorated. Apart from that, each unit would be holding its own Christmas Eve party in its own room, and all of them were doing their best to get an extra ration of vodka or to buy some on the black market. Even my virtuous railroad worker managed to get hold of a few bottles. Busiest of all were the ladies, making mayonnaise and preparing some disgustingly salty fish.

After a briefing by the commander in chief, who broke consecrated wafers with us all under the tree in the hall, they went off to their parties.

My unit had salty fish sandwiches, beetroot soup, sausage rolls, and some sort of beetroot salad—what a lot of work! Lots of talk, and naturally vodka from the word go, which instantly creates a warm and cozy atmosphere where it's very easy to say "let's make love."

That's how I'd have remembered the Christmas party, if not for one of the ladies. When things were pretty merry, she stood up and told us, awkwardly but with true emotion, how a year ago on Christmas Eve they had all been suffering, scattered in camps and famished collective farms, quite sure that we had all been shot dead, and how happy they were now that we were all together in the Polish Army. Her simple words could not be properly heard—the deep feeling was drowned out by drunken clamor.

After the more or less boozy unit parties, Midnight Mass was celebrated in the big hall, amid the Empire columns and electric lamps. Plenty of those in attendance were under the influence; worse yet, the soldier serving as altar boy was very unsteady on his feet and appeared to be making a hash of his national duty. But there were also people who went up for holy communion, whose faces showed that they were deep in prayer, so not everyone had spent Christmas Eve indulging in vodka-fueled debauchery. Perhaps my view of this particular Christmas Eve is biased by my own chilly response? All I could think about were the two Christmas Eves I had spent in captivity, the first in Starobilsk, memorable and fraternal, in communion with my closest friends from Poland, whose arrival in Buzuluk we still awaited in vain; the second in Gryazovets, in a sparser company by then, but it was just as profound and pure as the one before. On that occasion there was a consecrated wafer, sent from Poland, which, as a sacred object, we shared out between us until it was reduced to crumbs; Father Kantak had made a speech, and there were even some presents—one of the professors gave each of us a little picture with a suitable poem and a drawing. This third Christmas in exile, in Buzuluk, seemed to me unworthy of the previous two, rowdy and devoid of meaning.

But there was a significant moment that evening, when I talked to Eugeniusz Lubomirski. He was still in the ranks at the time. After attending Midnight Mass, I met him coming down the wide staircase at general staff, looking remarkably young for his forty-something years. We had been at school together. When I first knew him, he only studied as much as was necessary, spending all his time singing songs from Viennese operettas and playing tennis with a passion, though in fact his real interest was girls. I always took him to be an amiable playboy, nothing more. Then we lost sight of each other. He spent a few years in the United States, then came back to Poland, where he ran a large factory with great verve and success. I had come upon him by chance before the war. His pockets were stuffed with money, and he was as fat as a barrel, looking like a "bourgeois" from a Soviet propaganda poster. Now he had been through two years in prison and the northern camps. In jail in Lwów and Kiev he had been beaten up, locked in an unheated privy around the clock at −4°F in nothing but his drawers, made to keep walking for twenty-four hours nonstop until his legs were black and swollen like tree trunks, and then suddenly ushered into an elegant drawing room, where a smart Soviet general had offered to send him home to Kraków on one minor condition, which was that he should provide them with information about ... the Ukrainians. "We know you love your wife very much—in ten days you can be with her in Kraków. You're a patriot, so we're not asking you to inform on the Poles but on the Ukrainians—what harm can it do you? You don't have to agree to this offer, but if you don't, you'll never see your wife again." (This was in the days of the Nazi-Soviet pact).

Lubomirski refused, and was immediately deported from Kiev, not to Kraków but to the far north.

He had withstood the prisons and camps in the north extremely well, sleeping not even on floorboards but on logs nailed together to form bunks. During his two years of torment he had recovered the same physical form he had had twenty years earlier—not only had he lost weight but there was something remarkably youthful about his movements and his entire demeanor.

Yet on the staircase at general staff on Christmas Eve he seemed dejected. He talked calmly about the army and about the conduct of some of our officers: "They seem determined to arouse Bolshevik sentiments in the army. They take every opportunity to set themselves apart from the private soldiers (at least when it comes to distributing the vodka), they hurry to reestablish their own privileges, and the senior officers have mistresses, who throw their weight around at general staff. Our commanders are too soft on the officers. The Bolsheviks see it all, and believe me, they're pleased. I heard so much criticism of the Poles throughout two years in prison, and not all of it was wrong. If there's the same mood among the young," he stressed, "then I can't see how things will ever improve." (Listening to Lubomirski, I thought of the cadets from Gryazovets, who were spending that Christmas Eve with their line units in tents on the frozen steppe.)

"And how on earth can one organize an army here!" Lubomirski continued. "General Panfilov"—the Soviet general attached to our army—"told me in Moscow that it takes three years of training to drill a tank division, and we're fooling ourselves if we think we'll be ready in April. In fact the Bolsheviks are deliberately denying us weapons in the hope that we'll be totally demoralized by all the waiting.

"I did a lot of talking to the British in Moscow. They're not nearly as enthusiastic about us as some of our colleagues imagine. They regard us as a nation that has splendid bursts of energy, but that's incapable of any systematic effort. 'What are we going to do with you after the war?' one of them said to me, who didn't believe our army could learn the difficult art of modern-day warfare. I assure you, if we cease to be useful to the British, they're quite capable of wriggling out of all their obligations toward us.

"Look how thoughtless we are: who do you think attends the motor mechanics courses Kamieński is giving? Hardly any of the young men, just seniors—Colonel Sz., Captain Ch. Those talks should be compulsory for our youth. A motorized army has to have thousands and thousands of drivers, doesn't it? So where are we to get them from?"

I told him the views of another pessimist, Father Kantak, who had made similar gloomy predictions to me but had ended by adding: "If the Lord God led out of slavery the Jewish nation, who caused Him so much trouble, perhaps He will lead us out of it too, although we're doing everything we can to bring about our own downfall."

Lubomirski's harsh judgment contained no hint of conceit or stubborn superiority; instead there was sadness, perhaps of resignation, and the anxiety of an alert intelligence.

We moved to a hard bench opposite the broad staircase. How different my interlocutor seemed to me from the jolly, frivolous boy of twenty years ago.

"How do you come to see it all so clearly?" I asked.

"I went through some very tough times in New York, where I spent the night on park benches, and I learned a great deal there—the years I spent in the West were not in vain. Nothing teaches you as much about life as living in countries where neither money nor a name will do, and you can only gain a foothold through your own hard work."

Looking back now from the distance of a few years, I can see as I write this that that night on the staircase at general staff in Buzuluk he wasn't right about everything. Despite the Englishman's lack of faith, despite the skepticism of General Panfilov, the expert on tank divisions, and despite the tremendous obstacles ahead that neither of us could yet have imagined, the Polish Army did learn "the difficult art of modern warfare." During the Italian campaign, it was the Polish Army that provided those "thousands and thousands of drivers" of whom Lubomirski spoke, the same young men whom in Buzuluk it has been impossible to force to join those theoretical courses; as soon as they could sit behind the wheel and not just study driving from graphs, they took to their vehicles with a passion. But at the time, my conversation with Lubomirski, and the contrast between Christmas in captivity and at liberty led me to the gloomy conclusion that we all lacked the grit, that only blows and misfortune would make us shape up, while any change for the better was likely to go to our heads. The individualism we were so proud of was a poor thing and hardly self-sacrificing. How could we stand up to the blindly obedient followers of one or another political creed, one or another dictatorship, nurtured by totalitarian states, Nazi or Soviet, with the vodka-soaked "let's make love" attitude that I'd observed today, which we brought to our petty interests, always doing business on a "hail-fellow-well-met" basis, always dependent on the personal touch to get anything done? Everything that meant so much on the spiritual plane, our countless victims, our deported and murdered families, was a trump card against us for our enemies on the material plane. For countries where revolution had trained people to be ruthless, to be blindly obedient, to carry out orders in cold blood and in defiance of all that humanity holds dear, where it had trained them to denounce others, so that a husband was duty bound to denounce his wife, and a son his father, where the school textbooks for the lowest grades were full of stories glorifying denunciation—what was the meaning of our sacrifices? What did the courage of all those thousands of Poles mean? Courage in the face of doom, in the face of defeat, hopeless and ultimate, in a world where only force mattered, where only power mattered, and humanity meant nothing.

I left general staff well after midnight, and as I walked down the snowy, alien streets of Buzuluk, I frantically searched my most treasured memories for an argument in favor of our right to live in the modern world, in favor of the Polish spirit that every Pole could feel, even if he couldn't put it into words, and for which so many had died and were dying.

If what Cyprian Norwid says is true, that the word is "a testament to the act," what does it mean? What else is heralded by the spirit of Polish poetry, which is almost unknown outside Poland, but which "adorns our brow in vain"? What about the works of Adam Mickiewicz, a tragic pilgrim dying of cholera on the outskirts of Constantinople, whom George Sand compared to the Jewish prophets and whom Isidore-Lucien Ducasse Comte de Lautréamont, father of the Surrealists, very often cited as his master? Or of Juliusz Słowacki, émigré and consumptive ghost, whose poetry Marshal Piłsudski always carried, and whom Georgy Chicherin, Soviet commissar for foreign affairs and connoisseur of literature, called the precursor of Nietzsche, reciting his work at diplomatic receptions and claiming that in all world literature he had never met a poet of such panache? Or of Norwid (dismissed as a conceited fellow of limited talent by his publisher Tadeusz Pini), who from generation to generation reveals ever more of himself to us and goes ever deeper, becoming part of our bloodstream—Norwid, who died in Paris in an old people's home, and is being discovered today by the English and the Italians, both of whom are translating his work and regard him as one of the greatest, maybe the greatest poet of the nineteenth century? That night, as I walked the dark streets of Buzuluk, I could not yet see how Słowacki's *My Testament*, known to every Polish child, or his poem *When the Poles Truly Arise* would be tragically brought to life on the cobblestones of martyred Warsaw, where during the Uprising children and old people were to die "like stones tossed onto the ramparts" in the belief that it must be so, and in defiance of any cold-blooded consideration of political reason.

But in everyday life how much contemptible stupidity and shallowness there is, I thought! There's quite enough of that in any country, but in Poland the gap between *Dichtung und Wahrheit** is probably even wider—between reality and dream.

Take for instance the defenseless women here at general staff in Buzuluk, crowded together on bare bunks, their husbands missing. Meanwhile the men already have permanent jobs with salaries and are hungry for the company of women. The "social" and financial difference between a staff officer, who has a private house and a batman, and a colonel's wife or a young female student, women who have come here from a collective farm, crowded into the cold hall, is greater and more acute than the difference in the past between "the young master" and a poor seamstress. It's the same old story in the shadow of patriotism and grand words; the men take advantage of their better salaries and positions to blow off as much steam as they can. Watching these people and observing myself, I found that we had not improved in the slightest. It was enough for those women who had come from the brick factories, from remote exile, to be a little better dressed and fed, enough for those haggard men in torn padded jackets, those "heroes and martyrs," whether in inverted commas or not, suffering from scurvy, who had come from Kolyma or Vorkuta, to put on uniforms and eat a square meal, and at once out came the same old cheap trash, the flirting, the vodka, the lack of thought or intelligence, all the usual baloney and boundless conceit.

Lieutenant N., for instance—just one of very many! He had been in Vorkuta, transported on the death barges of the Pechora River, and now here he was, a blustering, genial fellow from the borderlands, tanked up on Christmas Eve, holding forth about how we were going

---

*"Poetry and truth," from the title of Goethe's autobiography, *Aus meinem Leben: Dichtung und Wahrheit* (From my Life: Poetry and Truth, 1811–1833). —*Trans.*

to butcher the German women and children (just so much ranting, because in fact he would never have harmed a single woman or child), and making vulgar anti-Semitic allusions in reply to the noble speech of a colonel of Jewish origin.

In vain did I keep telling myself that my pessimism and bitterness were the result of my own weakness and my own well-concealed faults and mistakes, in vain did I keep repeating a line from Norwid, which my sister had sent me in a letter from Poland while I was at the camp:

> Beware despair, which is loss of awareness,
> Or failure to recall that God is near.

That Christmas Eve, I felt flooded with bitterness and lack of faith; my missing friends from Starobilsk were constantly before my eyes, possibly murdered, though at the time I was still deluding myself that they were alive. I could still see Adaś Sołtan, dreaming of insane heroism as he pored over Sienkiewicz's *Trilogy*; Tomek Chęciński the federalist; old Dr. Kempner, the ardently patriotic Pole with the big Jewish nose who had shared his last rubles with me; Dadej, who had set up a hospital for the poorest children in Poland; or the bitter sorrow of Kłopotowski, sick with galloping consumption, desperate to stay alive and badly missing his son, who had eyes "like gemstones"—right then I could feel them all, from the most excellent to the quite average, like a stake in my heart. Every last one of them had given his entire measure of greatness through suffering and by now perhaps certain death. A cold and piercing wind blew snow into my eyes like sand. The bitter words of Father Cieński, who had heard thousands of confessions, came back to me: "People don't change—you can tell in advance how they're going to behave in any given situation."

In the dark, snow-choked streets of alien Buzuluk, some very old memories came back, as if to my aid. I had already spent years wondering about the space dividing our everyday life from the world of our poetry, whose austere grace had often enlightened us at the most unexpected moments. More than twenty years before that Christmas in Buzuluk, I had spoken about this very topic with a friend, sixteen-year-old Jacek Puszet, in the Planty Park in Kraków.

In those days we were both students at the Academy of Fine Arts. Years later, in September 1939 I ran into him, literally starving to death, on the terrible roads packed with refugees. I dragged him off to my platoon, dressed him in a uniform, and to the very last he carried out the duties of a private soldier with intelligence and passion. He was the last close friend from "back then" to whom I bade farewell when the Bolsheviks came to arrest us, letting the private soldiers go free, God knows why.

Jacek was a sculptor. One day I'd like to have the chance to write more about this man, who shocked, annoyed and moved people from childhood on. I have never known anyone who cared less about the opinion of others—it simply didn't occur to him that it might count for something; he went about looking ragged and dirty, spent months carving one and the same sculpture, while hauling heavy objects or building stoves for his female friends—whatever needed doing he did it, with the same fervor and strange detachment all at once. The first time I ever heard the following line by Norwid was from him, as little more than a child, chanting them under his breath as he worked his clay:

O shadow, why are you leaving, your hands broken against
    armor...

He once turned up at the Kraków Academy in a pair of long white drawers, with his head entirely shaven except for a long topknot that fell over his brow; he explained to me that he'd seen a similar costume and hairstyle in an old Ukrainian wood carving, that this sort of topknot is called an *oseledets*, and that this was how the Ukrainians used to dress and style their hair a few centuries earlier. In those days he was going through a period of pro-Ukrainian passion. When I scolded him for making a spectacle of himself, and said I was ashamed to go about the town with him, he regarded me as a fool and stopped associating with me for a good long time.

Of the sculptors I have known in Poland, I cannot remember a single one who had such a strong sense of the sculpted form. In those days, twenty years ago, he was particularly interested in animals. His synthetic sculptures of cats and birds were worthy of Brancusi, whom in any case he adored, but as well as that some of his later heads of women and nudes show just as much sensitivity and just as close an eye for form as works by the best contemporary French artists.

In 1923 Jacek went off to France. His family, though in difficult financial circumstances, rented a studio for him right by the Place d'Alésia. He had the perfect conditions for work. But not much time had passed before he found an old Pole under a bridge, wearing a battered snuff-colored summer coat and a faded bowler hat. He invited him to live in his studio, and then he discovered a Chilean poet, also in need, and put him up as well, translating Wyspiański's *The Wedding* for him, which apparently the Chilean found enthralling. He also took in a large stray dog. His mother came to visit and bought him a warm winter overcoat, but a few days later he was walking about in the cold with his teeth chattering—he had given the coat away to someone. He had an ancient, squinting concierge who looked like a hen with rheumy eyes and lived in a dreadful dark cubbyhole at the entrance to the courtyard where his studio was located. Jacek spoke French well and treated every last person not just politely but fraternally, so he immediately charmed the old woman, but his guests at the studio derailed her affection for him, and when he gave the coat away she was horrified. "Along comes some ragamuffin, and just imagine, off he goes in Monsieur Jacek's brand-new overcoat!"

I too was in Paris at the time. I was spending the spring in Châtillon, about twenty miles from the city, where I had a studio and a panoramic view of Paris. Suddenly Jacek started making frequent visits with his beloved dog. He always left just as he had arrived—unannounced.

"Don't think I've come here to see you," he said to me one day, "it's just that my dog needs exercise."

It was the year when Stefan Żeromski published his patriotic comedy *My Quail Has Fled*. Jacek read it, packed up his belongings, and a couple of days later went back to Poland; he'd had enough of Paris.

A few months later I told the old concierge and the woman who owned the studio on rue d'Alésia, Madame Lapersonne (both of whom regarded us with unspeakable disdain as that band of penniless Poles, *les saltimbanques*—the "buskers") about Jacek's fortunes. I had learned that on returning home he had been called up for military service. "At least he'll have regular meals in the army and won't go hungry," I added.

"*Pensez donc!*" bristled the ladies. "Do you really think so? Even in the army he'll find a way to give his soup away to someone else." There was genuine outrage in their voices. (A few years ago the old concierge died, and in the miserable straw mattress in her dark cubbyhole a large sum of money was found).

That's what Jacek was like. And so twenty years before that Christmas Eve in Buzuluk I was walking about the Planty with him. As I gazed at the throng of students in fraternity caps, office workers, Jews in gabardines, nannies with baby carriages, and pensioners dozing on benches between the university and Grodzka Street, I was flooded, as now in Buzuluk, with lack of faith in man's capacity to make any radical change.

"And how naive Słowacki was," I said to Jacek bitterly, "to believe that '...*you bread-eaters shall turn into angels*...'—just look at the crowd!"

"You know what," he replied after a pause for thought, "if only one of us were to turn into an angel, we'd all become slightly different."

As I climbed into my icy bed in my chilly little room on that third Christmas Eve in exile (I could hear Anna Stepanovna already snoring on the other side of the wall), I gratefully remembered what Jacek had said to me that day in the sunny Planty Park.

8. INHUMAN LAND

THE CHRISTMAS holidays were over. Our tables and card indexes were carried back into the large, chilly hall at Polish Army general staff in Buzuluk, and the work began again—constant bustle and tapping away at the typewriters.

More Poles released from prisons and camps were still arriving in Buzuluk, just as they had in Totskoye, but in lesser numbers, mainly individuals or small groups.

On December 28, a Lieutenant Sołczyński came to see us in the hall. He hadn't come from the north, like most of them, or from the east or the south, like the people from Kolyma or Turkestan, but from the west, from Artyomovsk near Starobilsk, via Stalingrad. At this point nobody else had come from there.

By now the sight of cadaverous prisoners of war in padded jackets no longer made any impression on us. We were very used to it, but the officer who entered our bright Empire-style hall that day was not "cadaverous" in the normal way. Small in height, with a big round head on a skinny neck, Lieutenant Sołczyński really did look like a skeleton in a ragged jacket. He had small features, a paper-white complexion, deep eye sockets under a very high forehead, and totally sunken cheeks—it wasn't the head of a living man but a skull, still alive for some incomprehensible reason, lit by a pair of bright eyes.

Lieutenant Sołczyński, of the Seventy-Seventh Infantry Regiment, was thirty-one years old, a student in his fourth year at the Warsaw Polytechnic. The thing we found most surprising was that some of us had known him briefly in Starobilsk, in January 1940.

In any case, my initial hope that he would be able to give us news of our Starobilsk companions from 1939 to 1940 was immediately shattered. He had indeed been in Starobilsk in January 1940, but only for three days, when he and twelve other men were brought in together. At the time they had given us our first real information on what the Soviet occupation was like, despite the fact that the thirteen new arrivals had been separated from us at once. Three days later they were taken away from the camp in an unknown direction, and for unknown reasons.

Now, arriving in Buzuluk, he was in a strange sort of deathbed state of elation. He told us a great deal about his experiences and his recent wanderings and kept coming back to one single topic: the half-dead companions whom he had left behind in Stalingrad, begging us to go to their aid and rescue immediately. Even having reached us in this state, at the very end of his strength, he had a burning need to share what he had been through; precisely, feverishly, as if afraid of forgetting something, or of failing to add some detail, he told us everything—people he had never met before, as if we were his long-lost brothers, whom after all those cruel torments he had finally managed to reach on the point of death.

I wrote down his story on the spot.

LIEUTENANT SOŁCZYŃSKI'S STORY

"Wounded at the front, in Halicz I was taken in by a railroad worker I didn't know, who nursed me at his apartment. Someone reported my presence to the Bolsheviks. I was arrested and taken to the prison in Stanisławów. I was locked in a cell with twelve other men, with whom I did not part ways for the next two years, through all the prisons, and right through my time in Artyomovsk. Most of these men had been captured trying to steal across the border; we were all in the military except for three civilians—Stanisław Burzyński, an agricultural engineer, Józef Bronikowski from Stanisławów, and Józef Mencel, a landowner and well-known horse breeder from just outside Stanisławów.

"Everyone else was in the army—Captain Antoni Pawlikowski,

Lieutenant Oskar Schab, both from the Artillery Training Center in Wesoła, Warsaw, Lieutenant Stanisław Rusznica from Stanisławów, Second Lieutenant Józef Szostak, a student at the Mining Academy in Kraków, Lieutenant Bronisław Garbowski, Cadet Jerzy Cepak from the signal corps, Cadet Bolesław Wisz, Master Sergeant Tadeusz Kotynia, and Second Lieutenant Podłużny, a lawyer from Halicz.

"From Stanisławów we were deported via Lwów, Kiev, Stalino, Donbas, Kharkov, and Voroshilovgrad. After several weeks on the move, we arrived in Starobilsk, sent there by the prosecutor in Stanisławów. But the camp commandant did not feel obliged to honor the prosecutor's decision and refused to accept us. As a result we were packed into the *stołypinka* (a prison railcar) again and sent back to Stanisławów. A battle of jurisdictions began. In his dispute with the commandant at Starobilsk, the Stanisławów prosecutor decided to stick to his guns, and on March 23 he sent us back to Starobilsk again. But we only got as far as Artyomovsk, about eighty miles from Starobilsk, where we were detained and locked in a cell.

"From then on, until October 12, 1941, and thus for a period of eighteen months, we remained in Artyomovsk, in tough conditions. We were imprisoned in a cell measuring ten foot by ten foot—twenty-six people, squatting one on another, mainly Poles. During this time we weren't allowed a single newspaper, and we knew nothing about events in the world outside. The only way to get any information was to pull scraps of newspaper out of the excrement in the privy, which we were allowed to visit just twice a day. By cleaning them, we discovered bits of news.

"A year later, when the German-Soviet war began, nobody told us about it, but the guard in the corridor was doubled, and every night there was a blackout, so we guessed. When we asked the warder if they were at war with Germany, he replied angrily: 'It took us three days to beat you, we'll beat the Germans in five.'

"On August 2 the local prosecutor, from the Voroshilovgrad district, came to see us. He inspected our cell and questioned everyone in turn, asking what we were in there for. I lost my temper and said to him: 'I fought against your friends the Germans; that's why I'm in here.'

"'The Germans were never our friends,' retorted the prosecutor. 'You were sold by Beck* and that's why you're in here.'

"Only in September did we learn from a scrap of newspaper about the formation of the Polish Army, and that Kot was ambassador. From day to day we waited for something to change. We simply imagined that the rapid advance of the German army might be making our evacuation impossible. We had no idea that the Russians would leave everything behind in Artyomovsk but take the prisoners with them.

"One day we were escorted out, a thousand men, lined up in fours, given two pounds of bread each, one fish each, and told to march off.

"We left the prison. We were guarded by the 107th Escort Regiment on foot, on horses, and with dogs. There were also eighty women among us, including a blonde Polish woman from Lwów with a wrinkled face, a prostitute apparently.

"As we walked down the streets of Artyomovsk, we met with plenty of sympathy. People threw us bread, including white rolls. From either side of the road at least a dozen women ran up, weeping, trying to get past the cordon of guards because they had relatives among the prisoners. The guards beat them back with their rifle butts. So we marched without stopping until six in the evening over very difficult, muddy terrain. At six we were bunched together on a hill and allowed to sit down. We weren't given anything to eat or drink. One of the Russian prisoners asked for water.

"'Here's your water!' replied the mounted escort and began to slash at him with his saber. We weren't given a drop to drink that day, nor the next day either; what's more, one of the convoy commanders had made it clear to us at the start that if he managed to get 5 percent of us through to our destination alive, that would be more than adequate. I was extremely thirsty. I took a bit of bread, and chewed it, but I couldn't swallow it for over ten minutes for lack of saliva. My spittle had gone strangely white and very thick.

"The escort used dogs from the first day; they weren't let off their

*Józef Beck was the Polish foreign minister, who in the 1930s had concluded non-aggression pacts with both Germany and the Soviet Union. —*Trans.*

leashes or they'd have bitten us, but they were brought close to anyone who slowed down or refused to walk any further. As the dog tore at the lagging prisoner's pants, and then bit him, the prisoner mustered the last of his strength and kept walking.

"After marching without a break from 10 a.m. to 6 p.m. there was a halt, and we sat outside with no food or water, crowded together, until six in the morning in piercing cold, and from three o'clock in rain. Then we set off again.

"We still weren't given any water. I couldn't get the rest of my bread down my throat, so hunger and mad thirst were causing me to decline so badly that I started falling behind the column. The mud was so thick that you ended up carrying a few pounds of it smeared on your legs and feet. Black spots began to dance before my eyes. At some point, on an uphill stretch, I collapsed.

"I lay there totally exhausted.

"When I finally got up and staggered another few yards, Second Lieutenant Podłużny came up and gave me a few sugar lumps, the iron rations he had kept in store. That sugar was my salvation. The black spots vanished, and with Podłużny's help, leaning on his arm, I started to walk again. He saved my life.

"Most of the Russians who were on the march with us belonged to two categories of prisoner. The majority were bandits, so-called *zhuliki*. They formed close-knit, ruthless gangs and terrorized all the other prisoners. On only the second day of the march they attacked several of their companions and robbed them of all they had. That day my last piece of bread was torn from my hands.

"The second category were the so-called *progulshchiki*; many of them were serving sentences that would end in a week or two. Most had been arrested for being a quarter or half an hour late for work; one had only two more days to serve. They were told they would be released upon arrival at our destination, and they were being herded well over four hundred miles, all the way to Stalingrad. I don't suppose many of them survived.

"At ten o'clock it started to snow. It was a great joy for us to grab handfuls of snow and at least quench our thirst a little! That day we walked nearly twenty miles. We were put up for the night at a collective farm, in a junior school and in several neighboring buildings. There we learned that a similar convoy from Artyomovsk jail had been through two days ahead of us, also consisting of about one thousand prisoners.

"There were from sixty to seventy of us in the room where I stayed, which was only twenty by twenty-three feet in size. In the bigger room next door there were about a hundred. Once again we weren't given anything to eat or drink. Only ten of us were allowed out to relieve themselves, so everyone else did their business in the room, by the door, producing a heap of slurry above ankle height.

"That night, from the thirteenth to the fourteenth of October, the first Polish member of the convoy died in our room. He was a Jew, who died of a heart attack. A Russian prisoner was also shot and wounded after he tried to hide in the attic. The next day he was tossed on a cart that went with the convoy to the next halt; flung off again, he crawled into a barrack where the next evening he died. As we were leaving on the morning of the fourteenth, we were finally brought a couple of buckets of water, which were taken into the bigger room. A wild fight for it immediately broke out, and not a single bucket was carried into our room.

"On the evening of October 14 we reached Dyubaltsev, a large railroad junction. Once again we spent the night in a school. Next morning at eight o'clock we were allowed to go outside and wash with snow. One of the NKVD men took a handful of refuse from a pail— consisting of bits of liver and other meat scraps—and threw it into our room. Once again, there was a fight. One of the Ukrainians, a large fellow, grabbed the biggest scrap of meat and tried instantly swallowing it. In his efforts to seize it from him, another prisoner tore his lip badly in two places at each corner of his mouth.

"At 11 a.m. on October 15 we were ordered to go outside into the icy yard. They were going to distribute bread there. A winter sun was shining, and the majority went outside. A few Poles remained, and a few Ukrainians. I was keeping company with Captain Pawlikowski and Lieutenant Schab. I got up to go out, and so did they. Suddenly

I had a premonition, so I sat on the ground and said I wasn't going. Twice Lieutenant Grabowski, who was the commander of our Polish group, came back to tell me not to make his job any harder but to come out and get some bread.

"I knew that in a short while they'd make me go outside, put me in line, let the dogs go, and force me to walk again.

"I saw through the window that each man was getting seven ounces of bread, but I didn't move. Once most of the men had gone outside, the supervisors came and started to beat the remaining prisoners with their rifle butts to make them go. When I refused to get up, one of them grabbed me by the collar and dragged me a good ten yards into the corridor. I hit my head on the doorsill, bit my lip, and started to bleed from the mouth. When he saw the blood, the guard merely said: 'He's sure to croak,' pushed me in the chest, and left me there. There were others lying motionless in the corridor and other rooms, just like me, helpless and resigned to anything. In fact I was actually feeling better than before, and if I insisted on not moving, it was because I had a strange inner certainty that it was the only way to stay alive. And if I hadn't insisted, but had been herded off like the others, I would never have survived.

"The column duly set off. Eight escorts were left to guard the thirty-two remaining prisoners, among whom there were fourteen Poles.

"At one o'clock we heard distant sounds of artillery fire. We thought it was light artillery from the front and that maybe the Germans were moving on, so perhaps they would stop driving us forward now. But it was just antiaircraft fire.

"That evening a vehicle arrived, carrying fish for the convoy. It took away four Russians and two Poles, who let themselves be persuaded to rejoin the rest on the promise of seven ounces of bread and a piece of fish. As far I remember, one of these Poles was called Czeczot."

"Czeczot," I said in amazement. "What did he look like?"

Lieutenant Sołczyński's description confirmed that it was the same young Lieutenant Czeczot, fair, slender, and likeable, with whom I had been transported when Starobilsk No. 1 was closed down eighteen months earlier. At the time he and I had spent seven days together, lying on the cramped top bunk of our *stolypinka* compartment (there was no question of sitting up—we could only lie down). I had been warned that he was in touch with the Bolsheviks and might be an informer. I didn't really believe it at the time. He was intelligent, he came from a modest landowning family in the Wilno area, the product of a fine public-spirited tradition, but he seemed to have been seriously radicalized. He had a thick copy of *Comments*, written by Lenin in the margins of the books he read on international capitalism. In the days we spent lying "in the attic" of our compartment, in furious heat, we did a good deal of talking. He vividly described the peasants with whom he had spent a lot of time, and his youthful travels about the woods and marshes. To our surprise he was disembarked a few stations before us. Once at liberty I found out that he had been sent back to Starobilsk. At the time Starobilsk was packed to bursting with more than twenty thousand political prisoners, men and women, in so-called Starobilsk No. 2. But Czeczot was housed in special, much more comfortable conditions. I imagine the Bolsheviks were expecting to make him into "their man"; perhaps he had sincere leanings toward communism or had shown a lack of character at some point, or had simply broken down. Now I learned about his further fortunes from Lieutenant Sołczyński. Studying Lenin, and one or another, more-or-less sincere or calculated game with the Bolsheviks had not been of any help to that dear, lost boy. Like so many others, herded along in a bestial manner, he too must have perished on that cruel march.

"Once those few prisoners had been taken away, there were twenty-six of us left at Dyubaltsev, including twelve Poles. That evening we were given seven ounces of bread, and that was the last ration until Stalingrad. The guards told us they had nothing for us, because the rations were with the column, which had gone toward Likhaya. We were driven to the station, put on board a freight car, which was locked shut, and that evening we set off. But we only traveled a very short way each day, about seven miles. The tracks were in a dreadful state, and there weren't enough locomotives. Of my former company of thirteen, Mencel, Bronikowski and Kotynia were with me. We were joined on this journey by Colonel Ludwik Miłkowski, who was a retired doctor and became a close friend of ours, a dentist from Lwów, the headmaster of a school in Ostróg Ostrowski, military police sergeant Witold Kasiński from Łuck, and a Polish studies scholar from the Tadeusz Rejtan high school in Warsaw.

"Miłkowski, an extremely amiable old gentleman, had been the head doctor at Corps District Command (DOK) in Lwów, at the time when the commander of DOK was General Sikorski. He was still corresponding with him in 1939. This sixty-four-year-old man was married with two sons, of whom he talked with great affection.

"We traveled on, either in closed freight cars or in wire-fenced open flatcars. Once we were put in a railcar packed with barrels of pickles. We made a hole in one of the barrels and fed up on those pickles. We weren't given any bread at all. We also ate raw maize from the fields, which people threw to us. We spent five or six days waiting at the station at Likhaya, where once again the local people showed us great sympathy, tossing us maize, and on one occasion some rusks as well. Along the way the escorts let us get water. The only reason we survived was because they stole for us. They had been given orders to get us to our destination alive, but they had no rations to feed us on. In fact I'm not so sure it was entirely necessary for all of us to arrive alive. One time one of the guards got drunk, and he and his pals started firing at the railcar where we were shut inside. One of the bullets hit a Polish farmer in the head, killing him on the spot. He was a pleasant man, a settler, patriot and peasant activist who had spent some years in America. Mencel kept naively repeating: 'There will have to be an inquiry into this.' And they left us with the corpse all night; in the morning they took it away, and that was the end of it.

"After a few days in Likhaya the *zhuliki* who went to fetch water (which we Poles weren't allowed to do) managed to steal some wheat and rye. They magnanimously gave us some raw grain to chew, and we wolfed it down—hunger had taken its effect on us.

"We hadn't had anything hot to eat since leaving Artyomovsk, and to make matters worse, the grain and pickles caused us all to suffer from dysentery. Everyone, without exception. Not far from Stalingrad three men died of it in my presence—that model of kindness, Dr. Tomaszek from Stanisławów, Szulc, the senior conductor and highly reputable voluntary worker, and Sergeant Kasiński from Łuck. Dr. Tomaszek explained to us that going without hot food or warm water for more than a month had caused acute colitis.

"Not until November 22 were we taken out of the railcar and transferred to a barrack located seven miles from the city.

"The next afternoon a group of the men from Artyomovsk, with whom we had parted ways in Dyubaltsev, arrived from a station some sixty miles from Stalingrad. They were incapable of walking any further.

"The first words spoken to me by one of the new arrivals, a Russian whom I had got to know on our journey together, were these: 'You're lucky. All your people have perished.'

"And as each man arrived he repeated the same thing—that all the Poles had died on the way, and not a single one was still alive. We refused to believe it. The next day the rest of the convoy arrived. About three hundred prisoners were packed into a barrack some fifty by seventy feet square, with four rows of bunk beds. A total of two neighboring barracks were assigned to all the new arrivals. They did not look human. Of the two original groups, each consisting of one thousand people, there were no more than five hundred and fifty, on top of which, in our barrack alone, on average from ten to fifteen died daily."

Sołczyński fell silent for quite a while, as if looking for the right words, and then in the same rather feverish, but very businesslike way, he continued his account:

"None of them had shoes, just rags wrapped around their feet. The temperature was already four degrees below by then, and their eyes were so sunken that they were hardly visible. Their faces were covered in stubble, they had holes instead of cheeks, and like all of us, they hadn't washed for over a month. Once they had been quartered, a dreadful stench pervaded the room; most of them had frostbitten feet with horribly stinking wounds—the flesh was rotting.

"On the first day I tried looking for the Poles. There was only one, a young tank soldier from Białystok who appeared to have lost his wits; he had no shoes, his feet were frostbitten, and he couldn't stop trembling. When I asked him about the others, his only answer was to keep repeating; 'I'm cold, I'm cold.'

"I asked everyone about our companions and kept being told the same thing: 'They all perished.'

"I asked literally dozens of people, and here's what I managed to surmise from the answers that confirmed each other.

"Most of them had died during the march across the steppes between the Don and Volga Rivers. One evening, around October 25, the entire column had reached a place out on the steppe almost fifty miles from the nearest collective farm. The guards had called a halt for the utterly exhausted prisoners, all of whom were kept for five days and five nights in a large pen for cows, with no roof, and in a barn, which in those parts they call a *sarai*—with no food, and at minus four degrees. The prisoners smashed up the pen and made bonfires. The *zhuliki* sat around the fire in a close, compact crowd, pushing away the weaker people, including the Poles. And since, in spite of everything, the Poles generally still had more clothing, the *zhuliki* tore it off them, leaving them in their shirts and drawers.

"On the snow at this croft Lieutenant Stanisław Rusznica died, an infantry officer from my original thirteen. And so did Captain Antoni Pawlikowski, whose unusual zip-up ski pants I saw on one of the prisoners.

"On the sixth day of their stop at the *sarai*, somehow they had procured some horse meat and cooked a meal for the prisoners, amounting to one cup of meat and buckwheat per person, before ordering them to march onward. Sixty people had insisted they could go no further, among them the Poles. Those sixty were put in a group, and then the convoy commander went up to them; he did not order them to join the rest but merely told them to go fetch themselves some water from a nearby well. Those who headed off to get water were told to join the column and were forced to get moving, with the dogs at their heels as usual. The fourteen men who hadn't moved (including platoon sergeant Drożdziuk) were told to strip naked in the snow and to go behind a nearby cottage. One of the Ukrainians gave me a detailed account of how immediately after that he heard fourteen shots. Nobody witnessed the executions, but a quarter of an hour later the same Ukrainian saw other prisoners fighting over the clothing of the men who had been taken behind the cottage.

"Then the company moved onward. More and more people had fallen by the way. That was when Second Lieutenant Podłużny died, the man who had saved my life by giving me his supply of sugar. I can see him now, as if he were standing right here. He had fair, wavy hair and a kind face; he was the son of a peasant farmer with a few acres of land and had worked his way through university by tutoring; now he was a legal trainee in Halicz and his parents had been deported deep inside Russia. Cadet Wisz also died at this point, and so did Cadet Cepak. I have no information on the death of Second Lieutenant Schaba. The one who held out longest was Lieutenant Tadeusz Garbowski, for whom the guards and their commander had a liking because he could speak Russian well.

"But he too perished after crossing the Don, about seventy miles from Stalingrad.

"During the week after the survivors from both convoys had arrived, the guards checked the records and called out names every day. There was no register of the dead, no statistics; whenever they called out the name of someone who had died, the prisoners themselves usually replied: 'Goner,' or 'Stayed at the *sarai*.'

"In the first two weeks of our time in the barrack we were each given ten ounces of bread a day, and also two or three buckets of water.

"The bread was usually distributed outside; we were lined up and each man was given a piece. We Poles ate it immediately, before re-entering the barrack, because anyone who went back inside holding his bread was robbed of it on the way by the stronger men. It was very hard to swallow the bread that quickly, but we made it easier by dampening it with snow.

"One day the guards did not make us go outside but distributed the bread in the barrack. We were ordered to sit on the bunks with our legs hanging down. The guards came around with sacks of bread, distributing it to each man. There was a naked prisoner lying on the floor in the passage, in the process of dying. He had already been stripped naked by others, his eyes were closed, and he was moving his arms and legs in a strangely fluent way. One of the guards said: 'He doesn't need any bread, he's going to croak anyway,' and then plainly hesitated, wondering who should get the bread. About a dozen prisoners leaped toward that piece of bread in a flash, treading and trampling on the dying man in a dreadful way; half an hour later he died.

"There was an endless fight for the water. The sick men moaned and begged for it, giving away their bread in exchange. We managed by gathering snow on rags during the morning clean-up (when we were taken outside and the corpses were removed), and we ate the snow in the barrack. The smarter fellows had a whole system, which involved sprinkling snow on rags, from which the water trickled drop by drop, and then selling this liquefied snow for bread. A few days later this became harder, because all the snow close to the barrack had been gathered.

"There were severe frosts at the time; one day, as I came outside, I noticed some strange tree stumps by a house. 'What's that strange purplish tree?' I said to Kotynia. 'It must have been stripped of its bark, and its boughs are twisted.' We went closer and found that they weren't boughs at all—they were the frozen limbs of naked bodies sticking out of the snow. The guards would grab them by the legs, drag them through the snow and throw them in the nearest pit. From then on we sought our snow in another spot, not where the corpses had been tossed.

"Every night we heard the wheezing of the weaker or dying men as they were smothered by their neighbors, who then tore the clothing off them to sell for bread.

"I've already told you about the one Pole who had survived, the tank soldier from Białystok. Two days after the column arrived from the steppe, when we went outside during the morning clean-up, our tank soldier failed to show up. But we saw his overcoat on the back of one of the men from his bunk. Like many others, he had probably been smothered by his neighbors and stripped bare.

"Every day at least a dozen naked corpses were carried out of the barrack. The only Poles remaining were the handful of men who had made the journey with me from Dyubaltsev in the railcars.

"But one by one, they too were starting to die. The first of the Poles to die in the barrack was the best, Dr. Tomaszek. By now he was utterly exhausted by dysentery, and charcoal couldn't help him. After him Kasiński died, his neighbor on the bunk; he sobbed as he lay dying, begging us to save him, because he had a young wife whom he longed to see again. Now I'm sorry that two days before he died I scolded him, but he was tossing about so much in the cramped space that he almost smothered Dr. Tomaszek, who was quietly dying next to him. Then it was Szulc's turn. Two hours before he died he asked me for some water. I had just found out from a scrap of newspaper that Sikorski was in Moscow, so I told Szulc, who was always passionately interested in every bit of Polish news, but now he just shrugged.

"Mencel and Bronikowski were seriously sick. Our handful of Poles was rapidly dwindling.

"I never saw a single corpse being carried out in any clothes at all. They were all stripped bare before they were removed.

"After a few days in the barrack all of us Poles 'moved in' together. At first we lay on an upper bunk, but a few days later we had to go underneath, because Mencel no longer had the strength to clamber up there. We lay packed in like dogs, in a space at most twenty inches high between the floor and the boards of the bunk above us. Kotynia and I were the strongest, so we were positioned at the edges, to be able to defend us—whenever the other prisoners tried tearing off our clothes we kicked out. We put Mencel, Bronikowski, and Miłkowski in the middle, but before then, the *zhuliki* had subjected Miłkowski to a special game. His cavalryman's riding boots made of excellent leather had been stolen from him. In those conditions they were extremely valuable, so they were sold to a guard, while Miłkowski went barefoot. But it didn't stop there—every day the *zhuliki* stole clothing from him, and two hours later they came back again, to sell him his own clothes for a portion of bread, only to steal them again the next day.

"Once we had put him in between us, under the bunks, the *zhuliki*'s game was at an end. I shan't forget one of the very last conversations I had with Miłkowski, when he told me about his children, and thanked me for looking after him. Suddenly he seized my hand and kissed it—the hand of a young pup like me!" (It was harder and harder for him to tell this story—I could see the tears choking him.) "So I was moved, and I burst into tears, and kissed him on the hand too.

"I was very attached to Mencel too. He was married to a Ukrainian peasant, they had eight small children and he loved his family very much. He was always talking about them. But he didn't just talk about his wife and children—this keen breeder often talked about his horses. Amid all that torment he was always telling us about them, what wonderful, clever animals they were, and how you couldn't compare them to people. During my last few days in the barrack he reached the end of his strength. For five days he had been incontinent. At this point I had a very memorable conversation with him. He asked me to go and see his wife when I got home, and to tell her to have the children brought up as Poles in the Catholic faith. I listened to what he was saying, but I didn't think I'd be able to keep my word. I wanted to die, I longed for death, though unfortunately for me"— at this point he hesitated—"or maybe fortunately, I have a very strong heart, but I told him I wouldn't survive, that I was sure to die.

"'No, you'll survive, you're younger,' said Mencel.

"As for me, from December 1 I lost my appetite. I couldn't even eat the bread they gave me, and I couldn't swallow the salty fish. I had a temperature of over a hundred degrees, I was suffering from lung disease, and I had mouth ulcers that made it impossible for me to swallow. From December 1 they started calling out prisoners' names, and if the person in question were still alive, they went on to say: '*Sobiraityes s vieshchami*—Gather up your things.'

"On December 11, I heard my name followed by *sobiraityes s viesh-*

chami. I leaped up, not even managing to say goodbye properly. Kotynia just called after me: 'Don't forget us!'

"They took me to an office, gave me four and a half pounds of bread, two pounds of fish, and forty-five rubles, and said I was free.

"On my way out I fell over twice out of weakness, then I mustered a bit of strength. One of the guards showed me how to reach a tram stop two miles away, from where I was to take the tram to Stalingrad. The journey wasn't at all easy—I was overwhelmed by my first impressions as I approached the tram, and I hadn't the strength to lift my feet onto the step.

"'*Nu starik, skariey*—Come on, old man, hurry up,' said the woman selling tickets. I asked her how old she thought I was. She said fifty, but I'm thirty-one, and people always used to joke before the war that I looked eighteen. I spent five days at the station waiting for a train until December 16, when I managed to tag along with a newly conscripted company including lots of Jews from Romania and Poland, so I was given some bread. Then I traveled by every possible means, on open railcars, where I thought I would freeze to death, and once I even in a passenger car. It was very crowded, and they packed me into it, pushing me from behind, so I lost the remains of my strength and fell over. A militiaman burst out laughing, and in a fit of rage I told him not to laugh. 'It's your fault I'm like this.' And then the whole carriage fell silent. I reached the embassy in Kuybyshev, and from there I was sent to Buzuluk. I dragged myself here with the very last of my strength," Lieutenant Sołczyński ended his story, "because I wanted to die in your company. It's not about the bread you're giving me or money, I just wanted to see at least one man who would show me compassion . . . and not die among those people, those jackals!"

His voice faltered: "Please believe me—I'm not hysterical, I'm just feeling rather . . . emotional."

That day the army commander received Lieutenant Sołczyński, who talked of nothing but the friends he had left behind.

The general immediately dictated two urgent telegrams to the NKVD in Moscow and the NKVD chief in Stalingrad.

A few days after Sołczyński's release from Stalingrad Sergeant Kotynia was also released, and he too reached the army.

No answer came to General Anders's telegrams, either from Moscow or from Stalingrad. Of the thirteen men with whom Lieutenant Sołczyński had been imprisoned since 1939, and of the eighty Poles with whom he traveled from Artyomovsk, Sergeant Kotynia was the only survivor. All the rest perished.

9. THE GULAG

OUR CARD index of missing persons continued to grow rapidly, as lists of names came pouring in to us from all directions—hundreds of names, and requests to search for people or to demand their release.

After entering each name in the card index, we sent the lists to the embassy. General Anders sent personal letters and telegrams to senior NKVD officials and camp commandants, but it was a stroke of luck if one missing deportee out of a thousand were found, or if one telegram out of a hundred brought a result.

We were haunted by the small, white, as if bloodless face of Lieutenant Sołczyński, and his minute, almost child-sized person, which had suddenly wobbled its way into our cold Empire hall like a living corpse in rags. We were haunted by the memory of his stories about our comrades dying so close by, in the Stalingrad camps, and the stories of others like him who had managed to make their way to army general staff, bringing us the exact same news of our comrades dying in all corners of Russia, even though by then most of the convoys were heading south, and not to Buzuluk, Totskoye, or Tatishchevo, all of which were packed to bursting.

Maybe personal messages to the command centers, or maybe personal contact, direct pressure on representatives of the highest ranks of the NKVD will produce more results, I thought.

It was crucial to take instant advantage of Polish-Soviet military cooperation to save those who were missing or dying. Otherwise it would be too late.

Thanks to the indiscretion of a certain Bolshevik, I found out that the Gulag head office had been transferred from Moscow to Chkalov, formerly Orenburg. I decided to go there in the new year, 1942.

General Anders, to whom as recently as December 4 Stalin had vowed in the presence of General Sikorski and Molotov that he would *lomat'* ("break") any camp commandants causing difficulties in handing over Poles, wrote an official letter appointing me his plenipotentiary for matters concerning "prisoners of war not yet returned," and also two messages addressed to the head of the Gulag and the NKVD chief in Chkalov. "By order of Comrade Stalin . . . ," he categorically demanded in both letters the immediate release of all prisoners of war and deportees who were still being unlawfully detained.

I went to Chkalov without even knowing for certain that the Gulag head office was actually there. I arrived at our representation at night. It was run from a hotel in the station building. I even managed to get a dirty little room, thanks to the efforts of my colleagues from the post, so I didn't have to sleep in the packed waiting room, like everyone else who had just arrived, or on the louse-infested floor of the hotel's one and only little reception room, where there were some fifteen Soviet soldiers lying like sardines.

At the time Chkalov was a site of great significance for us. Most of the convoys from all over Siberia and even from the north of European Russia came through there, so the city was full, not just with men fit for the army, but also women, children, and old people, dying of starvation, typhus, and dysentery. Some of the people fit for auxiliary service were being sent from Chkalov to Tatishchevo, Totskoye, or Buzuluk, and the rest were going south toward Turkestan, where new Polish centers were only just starting to be organized.

Through the agency of the Polish representation, these convoys were receiving medical aid, British canned food, and Soviet bread. This aid was just a drop in the ocean of human indigence, but the very fact that there were a few Polish faces at the station, including a male or female doctor on call from dawn till dusk, and often throughout the night, to visit those convoys, gave those crowds the hopeful thought that they were traveling toward their own people, that someone remembered them, and that they were no longer a herd of slaves, deprived of all rights. This crossroads was also the first point of arrival for news of our men being brought in from all over Soviet Russia, whether from the Urals, Kolyma, or Altai Krai.

In the late morning I went into the city. There was a large square, a wide street, a main road, and a few new cooperative houses. In the frosty mist the snow glistened and creaked, made smooth by sled runners, and a low red sun hung over the city.

A venerable camel with frost on its coat stood harnessed to a low sled. Its pensive, beautiful black eyes were blinking, and it had a frosted beard; next to it some small soldiers with sacks on their backs were scrambling aboard some large trucks. More and more flat, slant-eyed faces flashed past me in the street, reminding me that the river that runs around this city is the geographical border of Europe and Asia.

I wasn't entirely sure how to find Gulag head office; after some hesitation I decided to go and see the commandant, whose office was at the other end of the city in a fortress on a high riverbank. The streets I walked along were poor and shabby, but among the ugly tenements there were plenty of detached houses, neglected, but in an attractive, classical Russian style, from the early nineteenth century.

Orenburg, once the biggest center for barter trade with the East, was famous for valuable furs, precious stones, and silks. Now it radiated indigence and decay.

I reached the fortress, a curiously designed building with numerous annexes; far below me ran the frozen white strip of the river, beyond it a small wood, and further on, as boundless as the sea, the snowy steppe without a single habitation—Asia.

During my search for thousands of missing comrades, I came upon evidence of earlier Polish defeats and misfortune. It was to Kazan and Orenburg that the Bar Confederates (who rose against the Russian empire) were exiled in 1768. In 1771, the Russian statesman Prince Nikolai Repnin estimated them at sixteen thousand. Grouped in concentration camps in Lithuania, they were sent off by *kibitka*—a covered sled—or force-marched via Kiev, Smolensk, Oryol, and Tula to Kazan, Orenburg, and on to Siberia. In 1774 only two thousand of them returned to Lithuania, though later some individual groups also managed to make their own way back, mainly by taking advantage of rebellion and riots. There were various categories to which the amnesty declared by Catherine the Great in 1773 did not apply, including the "transgressors" who in 1773 had plotted against the Russian garrison in Kraków in collaboration with the students, nor did it apply to exiles working in the silver mines, or those handed over by the dozen to be soldiers in Russian regiments. Nevertheless, when the Poles who were scattered about the battalions along the Ural River and further inside Siberia heard about the amnesty, they demanded their release. This "revolt" was cruelly suppressed. Ksawery Kozicki, for example, and five others were stripped bare, given eight hundred lashes each, and then their nostrils were slit, a gallows was branded on their brows, and they were put in manacles and sent deep into Siberia. Even the empress took an interest in these tortures and deigned to find out the reason why the Poles had been so severely punished. The response of the "deputy king" of Siberia, General Chicherin, was literally: "They wanted to go back to their homeland."

When the Pugachev rebellion broke out, and the governor of Orenburg heard that hordes of Cossacks were going over to his side, that a nearby fortress had been captured and its commandant flayed alive, he issued his first command in defense of the city. The second point in this command went as follows: "Dispatch all the Polish confederates to be found in Orenburg, under strict guard, to the remote Troitsky fortress at the foot of the Urals." Even the death of Alexander Bibikov, who stifled the rebellion, was ascribed to the confederates. In his historical work on the rebellion, Pushkin claims that Antoni Pułaski, brother of Kazimierz Pułaski, the hero of the American war of independence, went over to Pugachev's side but left it a few days later, "outraged by his bestial savagery." And Pugachev was joined by "vagrants and bandits," incited, according to Pushkin, "by Polish confederates."

All this was getting mixed up in my head with hundreds of bits of news about today's exiles and today's imprisoned Poles.

Courteously received under the same, usually "hand painted," large portrait of Stalin in a worker's jacket, I was given assurance that there was no Gulag office here, and that I must have been misled. Refusing to give up, I entered various other offices on my way back, always to ask the same question. Quite by chance a caretaker gave me the address of the Gulag office without a second thought. I hurried off at once.

I entered a modest house with no sign, climbed some stone steps into a cold vestibule, and went up a narrow staircase to the third floor. There, behind a door well padded with horsehair and oilcloth, I found a large, warm apartment—the office of General Nasedkin, head of the Gulag, responsible for the life and death of at least twenty million people. It was very warm, and the secretary was well dressed, busy distributing NKVD rations, including foreign preserves, bottles of alcohol, and I thought I even saw some chocolate. I didn't have to wait long: I showed the letter and was soon ushered into the general's office.

General Nasedkin was extremely plump, in a uniform made of decent cloth, and received me with a polite smile on his smooth, clean-shaven face. He reminded me of the typical general of the czarist era. On the desk in front of him lay General Anders's letter, with a subtly stamped white eagle. Several packs of this paper had been sent to us from London; in Russia we had forgotten paper of this quality existed.

The first line of the letter, "By order of Stalin . . . ," and the surprise of my unexpected visit made it easier for me to initiate the conversation. Above the general hung a large map of all Russia, at which I cast a hungry eye, as subtly as I could. It showed the locations of all the prison camps on it, with the biggest clusters marked by large stars, others by smaller ones, and various circles, large and small. I managed to note that the biggest constellations were on the Kola Peninsula, in Komi and Kolyma. Besides that, there was another star of the biggest size in the vicinity of Yakutsk and Verkhoyansk; this latter city is the coldest in Siberia, as I had been told, at "the coldest extremity." The star for Verkhoyansk was the same size as the one marking Magadan. I already knew that Magadan was the biggest cargo port for Kolyma. I knew that most of the hundreds of thousands of prisoners deported to work in the Kolyma mines and to build airports had gone through this port.

I explained the entire matter of the three camps to Nasedkin. He stroked his well-shaven chin with a fat hand, looking as if he really didn't know a thing about this case. As I gazed at him, against the background of the constellations marking the camps, I realized how petty this matter must have seemed to him. He told me that in spring 1940, the period when the camps in question were closed down, he was not yet head of the Gulag, and that he had no recollection of these people having ended up under his authority, as he was not in charge of any prisoners of war, but just ran *robochiye, trudoviye lagera*—labor camps, for people who had been convicted for some offense or other.

"Even if the Polish officers were there," he told me, "they would be working for me not as officers but as convicts who had committed a crime."

I did my best to strike a convincing "Soviet" tone, saying as politely as I could that a refusal to hand over prisoners of war in spite of Stalin's orders "reeked of sabotage." The General picked up the telephone receiver and called an office in his charge, to say that *po prikazaniu tovarishcha Stalina*—on the orders of Comrade Stalin—they had to provide clarification of whether any these prisoners of war were in the camps under his authority.

I tried to sound out whether we shouldn't be looking for our comrades in Franz Josef Land. I had heard various reports about deportations to Novaya Zemlya and Franz Josef Land at the time, but always third-hand. The general promised me that nobody had been sent to that island. But he added cautiously that if there were any camps there, they could be prisoner-of-war camps in the strict sense of the word, and thus not under his command.

I also wanted to take advantage of my visit to clarify the fate of various comrades who, according to rumors that had reached us by a very circuitous route, were still alive. I was thinking among others of Dr. Henryk Levittoux, an eminent Warsaw surgeon who had been with me in Starobilsk and had gone missing along with all my other friends from that camp. News of him had just reached me via America and London, saying that he was to be found in Verkhoyansk. He was being eagerly sought by his brother Jerzy, who was killed a couple of years later, during the Allied attack on the coast of France, when he was head of general staff for First Armored Division. General Nasedkin promised to send a telegram to Verkhoyansk, and in my presence gave orders to that effect, which merely confirmed that there might also be Polish camps in Verkhoyansk, although nobody had come to us from there.

I never received any answer about Dr. Levittoux, or about the other Poles whose names I mentioned on that occasion.

Bidding me farewell and warmly offering me his chubby hand to shake, the general invited me to come back tomorrow, counting on being able to tell me something specific by then.

That same day I went to see the NKVD commandant for the Chkalov region, Colonel Bzyrov. I had a letter of recommendation from General Anders addressed to him too. I was given an appointment for eleven o'clock that night. I arrived punctually. From every cross street a sharp, frosty wind was blowing snowy powder down the sidewalk and roadway. Outside the huge NKVD building stood a shiny black luxury limousine. Through some heated corridors I came to a small secretarial office, and then I was admitted to the chief's large, elegant one. To my amazement I was admitted through a ... closet. Standing in the secretarial office was an ordinary closet, with three door panels, each topped with small glass windows. The little door in the middle was opened for me. Behind the closet there was a hole in the wall, and that was the way into the office.

When on my return I told the then head of general staff, Colonel Okulicki, about this unusual closet, he laughed and said: "Why are you so surprised? It's quite normal—in Moscow I too was often sent for interrogation through a closet." To this day I have been unable to find out what the point of it was. Some claim that the closets contain a device to check whether the person squeezing through it is carrying a hidden weapon.

I only waited a short while in the grand office before a young, affable military man came in at a springy step, through a normal door on the opposite side of the room. This was Colonel Bzyrov. With him, as was usual in such cases, came an inseparable comrade. It was warm in there, with the inevitable portrait of Stalin on the wall and a fluffy carpet on the floor. There were two sleek phones with handles and buttons made of bone in various colors. After reading the letter, Bzyrov received me in an almost friendly manner, like one of his own. I didn't want to arouse suspicion in any way and did my best to talk about the reason for my journey in a fairly detached tone, though I did stress that the fate of these people was not just of interest to General Anders but to Stalin himself. Bzyrov told me that I would not learn anything from anyone but the central authorities, and then only at the highest level. He advised me to go and see Merkulov and Fedotov. He listed in order of rank the then heads of the NKVD (Beria, Merkulov, Fedotov, Reichman, and Zhukov). I started to talk about Novaya Zemlya and Franz Josef Land. Bzyrov wasn't at all surprised. He went up to a large map of Soviet Russia, jumped on a stool, and showed me the routes by which the biggest convoys of workers were sent to the north. He pointed out a port called Dudinka, on the mouth of the Yenisey River. The largest parties were sent from there to islands in the Arctic Ocean. In the NKVD commandant's nice warm drawing room it all sounded like nation-building, entirely natural. Bzyrov even felt free enough to express his own surmise, which was that the prisoners of war who had not yet been released were probably right there, in the very far north (or perhaps he already knew of their fate and was deliberately putting me on a false track?).

Late at night, I walked back through the lifeless streets to the dirty hotel, hopping over sleeping travelers who lay in a row, packed together like sardines. One of our officers assigned to this post was waiting to give me the latest piece of news: our representative, Colonel G., had just returned from Aktyubinsk, where he had met two Belarusian peasants, recently resettled there. They had been deported to the far north in 1940, taken to Arkhangelsk, put on board a ship, and transported to a very remote island where it was permanently dark for several months at a time. Apparently, some barracks on this island housed a few thousand Polish officers, workers in the mines. After the outbreak of the Soviet-German war these peasants had been put back on the ship and returned to Arkhangelsk. From the description given by these two illiterate, simple people, we thought it might have been Franz Josef Land. Once again I thought I had received a new, providential confirmation of my suppositions, and a new argument to offer in my final conversation with General Nasedkin.

The next day I went straight to the Gulag office.

I was given a totally different reception from the day before. The general had probably had a telling-off from Kuybyshev for daring to talk to me at all. His face was stony, with no trace of yesterday's benevolence. He suggested that I should give him the lists of officers and soldiers who hadn't come back (I had four and a half thousand names with me), and he would send them to NKVD headquarters in Kuybyshev; only from there could I have an answer. I refused, preferring to take the lists there in person, if that was really going to be necessary; in any case, the vast majority of those names had already been handed to Stalin by General Sikorski and General Anders, and our embassy had delivered subsequent lists to the Soviet authorities.

Although Nasedkin did not betray the slightest desire to prolong our conversation, I returned once again to the question of Novaya Zemlya and Franz Josef Land, because I had fresh information implying that my compatriots must be there.

Nasedkin's reaction was different from the day before. Fixing his small gray eyes on a corner of the rug in front of his desk, he told me that the possibility of the northern camp units under his command having sent some small groups of laborers to those islands could not be ruled out.

"But there is no question of thousands of people being sent there, as you're suggesting," he concluded, with a rather sour look on his face. I failed to extract any other information from him.

As I was leaving the house where General Nasedkin had his office, on the stone steps in the ice-cold vestibule I came upon a beggar who was barely managing to stay upright. His body was bare apart from a torn, faded, dirty gray padded jacket and similar pants, so badly ripped that his shins were visible through the holes. He was also wearing a classic Soviet cap with furry earflaps. He was young, with an elongated, bloodless face coated in down that hadn't been shaved for some time. He asked for a bit of bread or money. Released from a distant camp, he was one of those prisoners who had been sentenced to hard labor for three, five, or eight years, and who in this period were being released if they had already served a couple of years and if their conduct in the camps had been impeccable. People were needed at the time to work on collective farms and to join the army. He had come from a far corner of Siberia but had been detained in Chkalov and not allowed to go further. Had his village already been captured by the Germans, or maybe it was just within the zone at the front? In any case he was stranded in Chkalov without means, condemned to die of starvation in an alien city. He asked for help with strange resignation; on his papery face with its subtle features I could not detect the slightest hint not just of rebellion, but of any great will to live. His pale eyes and well-defined mouth wore an expression of total impotence, a sort of sleepy defenselessness.

Perhaps he was already missing his northern camp.

That same day I made my way back to Buzuluk.

10. THE MANSION OF MISERY

TIME WAS running out.

Equipped with more letters addressed to the NKVD top brass, Generals Reichman and Zhukov, who had been specially entrusted with responsibility for the formation of the Polish Army, I set off for Kuybyshev and Moscow.

Apart from an official and insistent demand to make sure that Stalin's promise was fulfilled, these letters contained a handwritten postscript in which the commander in chief of the Polish Army in the USSR appealed to both generals, not by citing articles of the law but as fellow humans. He expressed his faith that, knowing how well disposed they were to Polish matters, as well as to him personally,* they would solve the mystery of the missing men; he was counting on them to understand the great significance of this issue for the morale of the army now being formed in the USSR.

I had military documents to take me to Moscow, but I traveled via Kuybyshev, because at the time the top NKVD officials were partly based in Kuybyshev, to where almost the entire apparatus and archives had been evacuated.

*

*Generals Reichman and Zhukov were commissioned on behalf of the NKVD to cooperate and assist in the organization of the Polish Army, and in the initial period they changed instantly from oppressors to guardians. Through a series of gestures they tried to express sympathy for the army, as well as friendship and respect for General Anders.

It was the second time I had been to the Polish embassy in Kuybyshev. The first time I had gone there was from Totskoye, via general staff in Buzuluk, summoned by a short note from Ambassador Kot, who had received one of my reports on Starobilsk.

The ambassador had a phenomenal memory for names, figures, and dates, and very few people were as knowledgeable about the missing men as he was. He had already brought the matter up with Stalin in October or November and had then doggedly returned to it in almost every conversation with the deputy commissar for foreign affairs, Vyshinsky. I now no longer recall each person whom I saw during my three visits to the embassy, but I still have a general memory of meeting a series of interesting and even remarkable people there. At the embassy there was a mixture of people who had been sent from Britain and various others who had only recently removed their louse-infested padded jackets; some had literally arrived the day before from camps and prisons. It made for a special atmosphere.

This prerevolutionary detached villa was densely populated with people who in Poland would have had a hard time sitting at the same table, because they came from different social worlds and belonged to rival political groupings that were at loggerheads. Now they were all eagerly buckling down to work for the common cause. Everyone imaginable was there, besides the professional diplomats and foreign ministry officials: the socialist Freyd, the peasant activist Wilk, "Regnis" (Bernard Singer), the journalist from *Nasz Przegląd* (Our Review), Eustachy Sapieha, former minister of foreign affairs and our long-term ambassador in London, Professor Stanisław Kościałkowski, the historian from Wilno, two members of the executive of the Second International—Henryk Ehrlich and Wiktor Alter—and writers, journalists, and critics such as Ksawery Pruszyński, Teodor Parnicki, and Wiktor Weintraub; the superb, communist-leaning poet and former prisoner in the Lubyanka Władysław Broniewski, and the National Democracy party activist from Wilno, Kodź.

All the threads ran together in the hands of Professor Kot. His small room was permanently packed, and his time fully occupied with conferences and audiences. He ate his meals in there, each time with a different guest or embassy employee. He regularly suffered from insomnia, so he played patience until late at night, and we brought him all the French books we could find at the local second-hand stalls. Any old nineteenth-century romantic novel would do, because it gave him some relaxation after the day's work and sometimes helped him to get to sleep.

During my first trip from ice-cold Totskoye I found out there was to be a Chopin concert that evening, performed by a past winner of the Warsaw competition, Lev Oborin. I went along with Ksawery Pruszyński. For the first time since 1939 I found myself in a large, warm, crowded concert hall. People were packed into the boxes, the seats, and the aisles, most of them with rough-hewn, Kalmyk features. Suddenly amid the crowd I noticed an odd figure: a very distinguished elderly gentleman in a black tailcoat and pince-nez, with a small white beard and tired, thoughtful eyes.

"Look," I said to Pruszyński, "the Bolsheviks can't have done all the aristocrats in—surely he's a Volkonsky, a Galitsyn, or a Sheremetyev?"

Pruszyński laughed and said: "That's Ehrlich, president of the Bund in Poland."

I met Ehrlich and his companion Alter the next day at the embassy. For several days in a row we had breakfast together, and dinner at the Grand Hotel, where some of the officials from the evacuated embassies were living; the most privileged of the privileged in starving Kuybyshev had the right to dine there too. The food was filling, the tablecloths were clean, and waiters glided across the carpets—there was even dancing. Both leaders of the Bund,* the Jewish socialist party, they had been arrested by the NKVD in October 1939 in Kowel along with the socialist member of parliament Mieczysław Mastek. As prominent anti-Nazi activists who were wanted by the Germans, they had gone

---

* The Jewish social democratic party known as the Bund was established in Congress Poland (the Russian partition) in the late nineteenth century. The overwhelming majority of leaders of this party were absorbed into the Menshevik cadres, while in independent Poland it cooperated with the Polish Socialist Party, though with regard to the various Polish governments it very often took a more oppositional stance than the Polish socialists.

there from Warsaw in search of asylum within the Soviet zone of occupation. They had been released in August 1941 along with the rest of us, and now they had come from Moscow to Kuybyshev, where they had been assigned a room at the one and only Intourist hotel.

When I encountered them there, Ehrlich, an extremely cultured man with a shadow of skepticism in his eyes, rather reticent and sad, was waiting for a transfer to London, where he had already been assigned a place as the representative of Poland's Jewish population on the National Council. It was even said that General Sikorski, who was in Moscow at the time, would be taking him back to London with him in his airplane. Meanwhile Alter, a man of great character with an explosive temper and lots of energy, was also due to leave any day, but to go east to one of the Siberian oblasts, as the Polish embassy's delegate for the Polish deportees in the region.

During the dinners and breakfasts we had together, Alter did most of the talking. What struck me about this tall, broad-shouldered man with very black eyes that always sparkled with animation was his remarkable intelligence, and his air of total detachment from personal issues; he talked a lot, with passion, about politics, science, and new theories in physics and chemistry. Both men were distinguished by something that immediately placed them above petty strife and petty human suspicions. Both these members of the International, who placed so much emphasis on their Jewish nationality, were also characterized by a deep connection with Polish culture and excellent Polish.

Before the 1914 war, as a young man Alter had been exiled to Siberia by the czarist regime; he had escaped via Riga to Belgium, where he graduated from the polytechnic and spent the rest of that war in Britain. Arrested in Kowel and thrown in the Lubyanka during this last war, he had written *A Critique of Newton's Theory*, managing to obtain paper for this work by going on hunger strike. (Moreover, he had been forced to write in Russian, though he hadn't used the language for twenty years).

Ehrlich and Alter were not just leaders of the Jewish Bund and the mainsprings in Jewish anti-Nazi activities, they were also members of the executive of the Second International. The reason why they had been arrested in 1939 was obvious. The Jewish social democrats had major influence in the part of Poland that had been occupied by the Soviets, where there were huge concentrations of Jews in the cities. Well-known as independent and incorruptible anti-Nazi activists, Ehrlich and Alter had extensive connections among the world's socialists. During the German-Soviet alliance they were at the very least inconvenient. The absurd plebiscite staged at the time in the eastern borderlands did not need any such witnesses either.

Both men were arrested in 1939, and they had to be accused of something. The charges laid against them and the reasons given for their indictment changed repeatedly; first they were accused of cooperation with the Polish government, then of involvement in a Polish offensive aimed at smuggling Bund activists into Russia for a terrorist campaign, on the basis of statements by two men called Rafes and Baltiklis-Gutman, who had left the Bund some years earlier to join the Communist Party. But when Alter and Ehrlich insisted on confronting their accusers to prove these absurd charges, they were told that for "technical" reasons it was impossible, because Rafes and Gutman had been imprisoned in the USSR and were now dead.

Alter and Ehrlich were sentenced to death. They did not lodge an appeal or request a reprieve. But the sentence was not carried out; a couple of months later they were given another sentence, once again condemning them to death. They couldn't understand how a person could be sentenced to death twice, but their fellow prisoners explained it to them: the first sentence was designed to terrify the prisoners and to extract at least some made-up revelations for the price of a reprieve. After all, hundreds of prisoners invented anything at all in the hope of their death sentence being commuted to ten or fifteen years' hard labor, which was in any case a death sentence too. But Alter and Ehrlich hadn't lodged an appeal or made any revelations, so they had been sentenced a second time; only the German attack on Russia and the pact between Stalin and Sikorski had then saved them.

In 1940–41, flung from one cell to the next, they saw and heard a lot. They later told a small circle of their closest associates about the heated debates held in prison by socialists and communists of various shades, from Trotskyists to Bukharinists. There in the Lubyanka they came into contact with prisoners of great interest to them, including people who had taken part in the trials of 1936, 1937, and 1938; there they heard confidences on the way the trials of the Bukharinists and Mensheviks were structured, talked to heroes of the civil war who had been swept up by the trial of Tukhachevsky, and also to people who had composed entire crime novels about themselves to avoid torture or to save their families. They also saw old comrades who had been waiting years for their indictment in the prisons of the Lubyanka.

Alter and Ehrlich were among the first to be released at the insistence of the Polish government in August 1941. The Soviet authorities had not only let them go but had attended to them with great care— they were given luxury hotel rooms, a car was placed at their disposal, and NKVD colonel Volkovisky was permanently at their service; more than that, a dozen of their comrades were released without having to wait their turn, and were brought back from remote corners of the USSR to Moscow, which at the time was a closed city. Later on, along with the embassies, Alter and Ehrlich had been evacuated with honors to Kuybyshev.

All this courtesy toward them, all this consideration was explained by the fact that the Soviets were counting on them to bring the Second and Third International together in a united front to defend the Soviets. Both of them had loyally agreed to this idea and immediately after their release had got down to work. They saw Hitler as the most dangerous enemy and believed that crushing the Nazis with joint forces could create a different political climate, even in Russia.

In Kuybyshev Alter and Ehrlich visited the British ambassador, Stafford Cripps, and informed him about the talks they had held with the aim of combining the efforts of the Second and Third International. Had this put the NKVD on their guard? Both men were determined to keep quiet about the past, and never spoke about the way they had been interrogated, or what they had been through in prison, but the Soviets were evidently not going to trust them. Having witnesses of this kind abroad was too great a risk. Perhaps the plan for Ehrlich's imminent departure to London with Sikorski speeded up the decisions that were made in their connection?

Only a couple of days after I left Kuybyshev, on the day when the Polish-Soviet pact was ceremonially signed at the Kremlin, in the room where in 1939 the Soviet-German alliance had been signed (nobody had taken the trouble to remove the photographs hanging in there that immortalized that "historic moment"), when the Polish national anthem was played at the Moscow Opera, and General Anders was received by Stalin and filmed from all sides, Alter and Ehrlich, those two prominent citizens of the Polish Republic and representatives of its embassy, after long and successful negotiations with officials from the Second and Third International on the need for a joint struggle against Nazism, made their way to the Grand Hotel restaurant. At twelve thirty that night an Intourist employee approached them and asked Alter to come to the telephone. Moments later Alter called Ehrlich over. They immediately left the hotel in the company of an unknown man. Their return was awaited with increasing anxiety. Thirteen hours later the embassy was asked to intervene and instantly referred the matter to Narkomindel (the Ministry of Foreign Affairs). Not until December 5 did Narkomindel inform embassy representatives that Alter and Ehrlich had been rearrested, because the NKVD had compromising material on them.

The days went by, without any news of the Bund representatives. A wave of protests began: from the embassy, which sent notes proclaiming an abuse of elementary legal principles, from our government in London, and from socialist and workers' organizations in Britain and America. In a conversation between Ambassador Kot and Vyshinsky, the deputy commissar categorically declared that Alter and Ehrlich were working for the Germans. When Kot tried to present the absurdity of accusing two relentless anti-Nazi activists, socialists and Jews, of working for Hitler, Vyshinsky replied: "Trotsky was a German agent too."

The interventions did not stop. The American and British press both ran articles protesting the arrests, in response to which the TASS agency issued the news that Alter and Ehrlich had not been rearrested, and that the Soviet authorities had no idea of their whereabouts. For a year the Soviets turned a deaf ear to the protests and questions that came pouring in from all over the world or gave evasive answers.

Not until fifteen months after their arrest, on February 23, 1943, did the Soviet ambassador to the United States, Maxim Litvinov, send American representatives of the Federation of Labor a letter from Molotov on the Alter and Ehrlich case, which contained the information that they had been arrested for agitating in favor of separate peace with Germany, and had both been executed by the Soviet authorities.

A period of Soviet victories was chosen to announce this news; against that sort of backdrop, the extermination of two men was just a trifle! Gone were the days of fighting for Dreyfus, gone were the days when the voice of a man like Zola or Tolstoy could move people's consciences or had any sort of influence on the rulings of judges and prosecutors.

The decision to eliminate Ehrlich and Alter, members of the executive of the Second International, could not have been made without the knowledge of Stalin himself, for the lethally endangered Soviets had placed too much hope in the campaign being conducted by Ehrlich and Alter. At the notion that this execution could provoke nasty repercussions in Western public opinion, Stalin had probably smiled to himself and thought—just as he was to say on a similar occasion about the people of the West: *"Nichevo, vsyo proglotyat—* Never mind, they'll swallow anything."

My second visit to Kuybyshev was en route to Moscow, as neither Zhukov nor Reichman, to whom I was carrying letters of recommendation, were to be found in Kuybyshev.

Ambassador Kot was the first person to pour cold water on my plans, saying: "Go if you want, but it won't do you any good."

Communication with Moscow was still extremely difficult. Through the embassy I obtained extra stamps and guarantees from Narkomindel.

Apart from the difficulty of obtaining permission to enter Moscow, apart from the railroad lines being overloaded with military convoys and all the stations being packed with evacuees and refugees from the west, it was the season of the most extreme frosts and heavy snowfall. The tracks were buried and the trains were at a standstill for many days on end.

My train was supposed to leave at night. To be on the safe side, I took my baggage to the station and left it in the vast waiting room, behind a thin wooden partition where our post had an operational desk. There was an NCO sitting there, in a space barely large enough for a table and two chairs. This was where the officers in charge of all the Polish convoys arriving from the north came to report, and from here they were sent on to Totskoye, Tatishchevo, and at a later date toward Tashkent. They were also issued with ration cards for bread and canned food.

I spent three days and nights waiting for the train, which was due to set off at any moment. I spent the days at the embassy or the hotel, and the nights sitting in the huge waiting room, behind our "Polish partition."

The temperature in the city center was approaching −45°F. Every time it looked as if the train might have had a chance of moving, I was summoned by our post. Then I would race a mile or so to the station. I have no memory of feeling the cold too acutely—there wasn't a breath of wind. I just had to be careful not to let my nose or ears get frostbitten. It was quite normal for a complete stranger to warn you: *"Vash nos byely!*—Your nose is white!" Then you had to rub it with snow immediately, otherwise it was sure to be frostbitten.

I do have one rather remarkable memory of those three days and two nights of waiting. I spent most of the daylight hours with Teodor Parnicki, the writer, who was sick at the time, in his room at the Grand Hotel. He knew a vast quantity of Polish and Russian poetry by heart, above all Słowacki, but also Blok, Bely, Tuwim, and Lechoń, right through to Wittlin's translation of Homer.

The room had old, yellowed wallpaper, and there was a miserable electric lamp hanging from the ceiling. An old waiter, whom we could just as well have met in one of Chekhov's short stories, brought our dinner to the room, laying a dirty cloth on a wobbly little table covered with a raspberry-pink, fringed rag of moth-eaten plush. The ailing Parnicki was lying on crumpled sheets, looking yellow and unshaven, as he declaimed a mixture of the most beautiful Polish and Russian poems, for hours on end. What harmony there was in that republic of poets! How the airy, musical language of Bely and Blok toned in with Słowacki, how Tuwim touched upon Pushkin and Blok. I used to leave that room late at night as if drunk, as if spellbound by poetry, repeating the winged lines I had just heard, lines that even in that place could get through to us and make us happy.

My footsteps echoed in the deserted streets, lifeless in the freezing fog. Only very rarely a man with a rifle or an army truck went past among the snowdrifts.

> My aim is for the supple tongue
> To say all that the head is thinking.

Those words are still ringing in my ears, soft, drawn out, in a mildly Lvovian accent, just as Parnicki uttered them.

> Sometimes as soft as a nymph's complaint
> Sometimes as fine as the speech of angels.

As for those nights at the station—the way into it was through a large square cluttered with trucks. Then you had to go around a wooden fence and slither along a steep, icy path that led to the large waiting room. Here you had to squeeze past long lines of people waiting for tickets not for hours but for days (there were always a couple of smaller lines of more or less privileged people, depending on their function, or on the kind of travel documents they had), then you had to walk or rather hop across the large room. The entire floor was littered with hundreds of people, in an extremely emaciated state, waiting goodness knows how many days for transport. In the greenish, foggy, sticky light of weak bulbs, in air full of damp from steaming bodies and wet, tattered clothing, the main thing on view were the unnaturally vast, full-length portraits of Lenin, Stalin, and other leaders. On the floor lay the thin stumps of legs, miserable, puffy faces, and heaps of ragged human figures in padded jackets over their naked chests. The entire waiting room was filled with the roar of a superb radio. A brilliant orchestra, broadcast from Moscow, was playing Strauss waltzes with truly Viennese panache. Meanwhile screaming and quarrelling kept erupting in the waiting room, the howling of a woman who may have been robbed or may have been a lunatic.

After forcing my way through, hopping over the sleepers, treading on them and inadvertently waking them, I would finally reach our partition.

The officers in charge of an increasing influx of Polish convoys kept coming to report to the NCO on duty: a convoy from Arkhangelsk, from Gorky or from Kotlas. How much vigor, how much joy and passion these people still retained, despite tough years of inhuman deprivation and many weeks traveling in packed freight cars, where they had to fight at every station for a piece of bread, and where children and old people were dying by the dozen of diarrhea and typhus.

Two of these officers, a broad-shouldered sergeant from the First Krechowce Uhlan Regiment and a lieutenant from Wilno, entered our area and though they had never seen us before hugged us like brothers, with tears of joy in their eyes.

On one of these nights I saw some trucks crossing the station square that were loaded, as if with timber, with the corpses of people who had frozen to death in the trains, now being driven off for burial. These were the corpses of people who, following their release from labor camps* at the time of the German attack on Moscow, had been forced to travel for weeks, with hardly any clothing, quite often in *open* railcars, on trains that stood for days at a time on snow-covered tracks in cruel frosts.

---

*I mentioned them at the end of the chapter entitled "The Gulag."

I spent both nights in a chair behind the partition. I'm good at sleeping in a chair when I'm very tired, but for the sleepless hours at the station, of which there were plenty, I brought along some books from Professor Kot's library—*Karikari* by Ludovic Halévy, who wrote the libretto for *La Belle Hélène*, and Gautier's *Le Capitaine Fracasse*.

The first book was a set of light sketches from Parisian life in 1890, describing the boulevards, premières, aristocratic salons, magnificent cocottes, grooms, and fashion houses. To my shame I realized that I found these stories highly absorbing. While living in Paris, I had never had any desire to read the book, but here among the crowds dying of hunger I read it with pleasure. After two nights in that chair, I found Théophile Gautier's *Le Capitaine Fracasse* very hard to read. In a different literary class, Gautier is in no hurry to entertain his reader quickly and easily. The precise and penetrating way in which he describes the "Château de la misère," without cutting any corners, made a strange impression when read in a real "mansion of misery" at Kuybyshev station.

I had always found it impossible to understand how Leonardo and the other Renaissance artists could have been so creative in an era of cruel tortures, of destruction and plague that wiped out entire cities. But now here I was, not only listening in rapture to Parnicki declaiming poetry but eagerly reading light, fragrant novellas, Halévy's "baubles," while the dismal background, the corpses being removed, and the woman howling failed to stifle my hunger for light fiction, which was not so much an escape from surrounding reality for me but just a way of *dulling* it. I was also suffering from a hunger for books, any book; those who have never been deprived of reading matter for months on end can have no idea what it is like.

At the time, the British military mission was divided into two sections. The head of mission, General MacFarlane, and part of his staff were based in Moscow, while the rest were in Kuybyshev, and were due to go back to Moscow. On learning that I was waiting at the station, one of the British officers organized an invitation for me to join the mission's railcar, so on the third night I was no longer sitting at the station but had a place in a first-class sleeping car of prewar Belgian manufacture.

I traveled in a compartment for two, on a comfortable folding bed upholstered with turquoise plush; there was red mahogany paneling, a washbasin, mirrors, and some secession-style decorative features, as well as a large window through which one could peacefully and comfortably look out at the world from the warm railcar. My traveling companion was a friendly British air force sergeant. Just before leaving Kuybyshev we were brought some large bags of white bread and fresh sausage.

The journey lasted for three or four days. We spent long hours standing at stations or in the open fields. After two years in the camp I found everything extremely interesting. I spent several days with nobody but the British—not knowing English, I could only talk to one of them, who spoke a bit of French. But communing with the British after those years of "camp" contact with Russians not only gave me pleasure but moved me.

The British behaved in the most natural way imaginable, which in itself was extremely unnatural in Russia: they were well raised and treated me without suspicion, as an officer from an allied army, the army of a nation they respected. The instinctive courtesy of each of my traveling companions (most of them airmen), the friendliness and readiness to be of service, all made a very strong impression on me, stronger than the "mansion of misery"—the Kuybyshev waiting room. I couldn't help thinking of something Norwid wrote in a letter to Bohdan Zaleski: "Some people have no idea that courtesy has cost mankind centuries of hard work."

Naturally, the British shaved meticulously every day and wore smartly pressed uniforms. Every day, as soon as he had washed and shaved, my companion—who showed me a photograph of his dear wife and child, taken in his garden at home somewhere in Wales—spent a good half hour crumbling rusks and pounding them in canned milk to achieve something resembling his ritual bowl of porridge.

Along the way, at Morshansk, dinner was made for our carriage.

Everyone had been told to vacate the restaurant for the passengers. We walked through the waiting room, which had also been cleared of a swarm of people to make a wide passage for us. I can still see the smartly pressed, clean-shaven British officers, walking along with indifferent expressions on their faces (what could be more natural than a light supper at the station?), as if quite unaware of what was going on at the station or of the starving crowd in padded jackets and sheepskins, staring "all eyes" at us, as the Russians say.

The dinner was tasty and relatively substantial. We were served by young ladies with flushed cheeks, in white *silk* blouses and curled hair. There had evidently been an order from above to receive the British in style.

Sitting at table, being served by the confused young ladies, and thinking of the crowd packed into the next room, just like the one that had filled the Kuybyshev waiting room, I felt I knew too much of what was going on behind the scenes of this feast to be able to consume it with such British phlegm. As Germany was busy invading Russia, with the crowd of people jammed into every corner staring at us as if in total disbelief, the perspiring young ladies, blushes framed by wavy locks, were a sort of "Potemkin village," provincial theater carefully rehearsed for the British.

We reached Moscow at dusk. There were cars waiting for the British, who politely took me to the National, one of the two hotels assigned at the time to foreigners. It had a beautiful view of the stone walls of the Kremlin and its bizarre towers and churches.

11. MOSCOW

I HAD REACHED my destination. I deposited my things in my hotel room and went down to the dining room, which had small tables laid with snow-white cloths and elegant menus, as in all the world's grand hotels. Practiced, obliging waiters shimmered across the carpet.

Outside the large, carefully curtained windows (there was a blackout in force in Moscow), stood the gray, castellated walls of the Kremlin.

A couple of tables away from me sat a gold-braided British naval admiral, strangely young-looking, and a couple of British senior officers. A jovial British airman who had beaten me at chess on the train came to sit at my table. Apart from that, the place was empty.

My one previous impression of Moscow came back to mind. It dated back to June 1940. Evacuated from Starobilsk in May of that year in the direction of Smolensk (it was the time of the Katyn massacres), in June several hundred of us had suddenly been "shunted" to a site near Vologda. We were traveling in *stolypinki*, prison railcars. We could only see the world through the thick bars of the small door leading into the corridor, and also through a chink above the boarded window of our compartment. Only those lying on the top, third level of benches had access to that chink—if a few planks close to the ceiling can be called a bench. I was lying on one of these.

Our escort consisted of probably the most stony-faced Soviets I ever chanced to encounter.

We were packed sixteen to a compartment. One of my companions had a fit of madness, and another had a serious heart attack. Fed on small, silvery, impossibly salty herrings and water, generally only allowed out to the WC twice a day (we had to roar to be let out more often), we had no idea where we were being taken. After a couple of days' journey with long stops, the train halted on the outskirts of Moscow. We spent ages on the Moscow River, being shifted onto different tracks from dusk until night.

Through the providential chink above the boarded window I caught sight of a church with a tall bell tower. The shape of its windows, the slender columns and small golden cupolas offered a mixture of the Renaissance and the Orient. After a year behind wire, I was enchanted by the light architectural lace in the blue silence of a moonlit night.

Finally we moved onward. That day we had been provided with our first newspapers since leaving the camp, which with palpable satisfaction enthusiastically described the defeat of France and the successes of the German armies. The same newspaper included a lengthy review of the first symphony concert to be given in Moscow at a new, apparently fabulous concert hall, with glowing praise for Eisenstein and his excellent production of *Parsifal*.

Then our prison train glided through the city; for the first time in ten months I saw arc lights, large buildings, and thousands of windows lit up by electricity, not red and flickering as at our camps but the normal kind we were used to from "prehistoric" times in prewar Poland. And so, between my first and second year in the camps, through a chink in the *stolypinka*, moving as silently as a ghost, I spent several minutes gazing at Moscow—a great big capital city, *la Rome du prolétariat*, as Georges Sorel called it.

Now, in 1942, as I sat in the dining room at the National hotel below the Kremlin walls, with a friendly airman and a British admiral at the next table, as one of a few privileged foreigners and allies, I couldn't help feeling reckless optimism—the goal of my journey seemed close and attainable. Was it just the contrasting memory of the *stolypinka* in 1940 that prompted my optimism? Other experiences I'd had twenty-three years ago, though tragic, also seemed to argue in favor of the hope that my comrades were still alive, and that I would at least be able to discover the truth about their fate.

As I ascended the soft carpeted stairs on my way back to my warm bedroom at the National, I recalled the analogous expedition I'd made in 1918, though that time I had only been looking for five missing Polish soldiers, not fifteen thousand as I was now.

In November 1918, three days after Piłsudski's return from a German prison in Magdeburg, I made my way from Warsaw to Petrograd, hidden among a crowd of Russian prisoners of war returning from Germany, already involved in the revolution. Two months later I managed to confirm that the five officers and private soldiers I was looking for had been shot dead at Povenets, a small place on the Murman coast. But at the time the lava of revolution was pouring across Russia. Tens of thousands of people were shot, thousands of counterrevolutionaries as well as thousands of incidental people who weren't enemies of the revolution at all. The Soviet state was only just being formed and had no effective authority in charge, because a vast percentage of the intelligentsia and bureaucracy was fighting against the Bolshevik Revolution or trying to sabotage it. The Soviet government had already left for Moscow by then. "The northern commune," as the Petrograd region was called at the time, was being run by a triumvirate consisting of Trotsky, Stasova, and Zinoviev. In Petrograd I found our only representatives, the "Closing Down Committee," already under lock and key.

After banging on lots of doors, after being given false information by profiteering swindlers wrongfully preying on other people's misfortune, I managed to reach one of the three members of the triumvirate, Elena Stasova, "the conscience of the Russian Revolution," as she was called at the time. This ascetic woman with smoothly combed gray hair, wire-rimmed glasses on a large nose, and a torn, shabby sweater ran things from a tiny cell of a room at the Smolny Institute, where she sat under portraits of Marx and Lenin, with two telephones on her desk. She found the time to receive an unknown Pole and undertook to get information for me about the missing men. Through her I found out about the place and circumstances of my colleagues' execution and the reasons for their death.

Now, in February 1942, as a deputy for the unreleased prisoners of war, I had a perfect right to believe I was starting from an easier position. In late fall 1918, when I was received by Stasova, our representatives were in prison, and the Polish-Soviet war was imminent, but now we were in the honeymoon period of the Sikorski-Maisky agreement, and we Poles were allies.

In 1918 the revolutionary elements were running riot, but now you only had to look at the people's faces on the trains, at the stations, or in the street, at the dirty Soviet flags, no longer red but faded to purplish-gray that were hanging everywhere to see that Russia's revolutionary magic had faded long ago, just like the flags. It also seemed to me that in such a highly centralized state, with such an iron administrative apparatus, there should be a hundred times fewer possibilities for accidental or anarchic murders and trials. Nor did it concern just a few people, like the five Poles that other time, who had been trying to get from the First Krechowce Uhlan Regiment in eastern Poland to France via the Murman coast, but fifteen thousand officers and private soldiers. They had already fought against Hitler in September, they belonged to the allied Polish Army, and were bound to be regarded as a valuable resource, not just for us but for the Soviets too. I refused to believe that Russia was carrying out mass murders twenty-five years after the revolution. I was sure that in the present circumstances I was bound to have easier access to the head of the NKVD, Beria, than I had had to Stasova in 1918.

Such were my thoughts as I lay on my comfortable bed in the National hotel and switched off the genuine electric lamp with a stylish shade that stood on my night table.

On that first day of my visit to Moscow in 1942 there was one element I did not properly appreciate: what a mighty, hierarchical, and pitiless administration, isolated by armor-plating from the outside world, the Soviets had created since that earlier trip to Petrograd in 1918.

After all those nights at stations or on trains, I fell asleep in my nice clean bedclothes in a positive, hopeful mood.

The next morning, at breakfast in the same dining room with large windows and a view of the Kremlin, I was informed that I was being transferred to the Hotel Metropole; these two hotels, the Metropole and the National were the only ones where foreigners could stay. I packed up my modest luggage and went outside shouldering my backpack. In white snow and frosty fog I gazed with emotion at the walls of the Kremlin and the crazy architecture of St. Basil's Cathedral, the sight of which had already captivated me through the large dining-room windows.

Gigantesque madrépore, une cristallisation colossale, une grotte à stalactites retournés ("Vast coral array, crystal cave, colossal upturned stalactites"), writes Théophile Gautier of this church. I couldn't muster quite so much delight, just avid interest in the cupolas large and small, shaped like pineapples or pears, and the walls that were cut and hewn into every possible pattern, triangles, semicircles, and cones.

Ivan the Terrible built this church after his victory over the Kazan Tatars in 1557. Delighted by its beauty, he had the chief architect brought to him and asked if he would be capable of building another, even finer one. The architect replied in the affirmative. To prevent him from creating a masterpiece equal or similar to St. Basil's, the czar had his eyes put out.

Right by the National there were some modern buildings of more than ten stories high, the Hotel Moscow and the headquarters of Sovnarkom. At the time, the Sovnarkom building was camouflaged with long black, green, and gray streaks to protect it from air raids. Cutting across the outlines of the windows, cornices, and roof in flowing lines and blotches, these painted streaks gave the massive, heavy building a surprising, fantastical look. It reminded me of the drawing and the colors of an early Cubist painting by Braque or Juan Gris.

As I regarded this wartime masquerade, I thought of 1918 again and the great state edifices in Petrograd; to mark the first anniversary of the revolution they had been draped from head to foot in huge propaganda banners in the Futurist style. These long sheets of cloth either fluttered and flapped or hung sadly, crumpled and dripping in the fog and rain. Incomprehensible to the man in the street, it was an expression of the alliance between the revolution and some extreme trends in art, an alliance that had completely vanished now that any artistic innovation was suppressed.

The mighty Sovnarkom edifice, painted in stripes and streaks, the vast, modern Hotel Moscow, the immediate area surrounding these buildings, and the wide-open squares, purged of dirty old cottages and covered markets, all impressed me with their size and grandeur.

But before I had had a chance to admire the Sovnarkom building, two young soldier boys in pointed caps with earflaps demanded to see my documents. I'm not sure they knew how to read. They stared at those papers of mine with serious expressions on their faces and immediately arrested me, escorting me at bayonet point to the city headquarters. I took it more seriously than necessary.

At the time, there wasn't a single Pole in Moscow in a uniform with insignia. *Kakoy u vas krab w galavye?*—"What's that crab on your head?" they asked ironically, pointing at the eagle on my cap. There were also very few British officers, because only part of the military mission was here, as the rest had been evacuated to Kuybyshev. All the Soviet soldiers and officers whom I saw in the street were wearing soft *valonki*—felt boots, while I was in black English boots and a green English overcoat, both of which looked like the German coats and boots that the Russians knew from photographs of prisoners of war published in the press. The whole city was obsessed with German spies dropped by parachute. Locked up at city headquarters, I presented my documents; to my amazement I was released after half an hour, thanks to those papers of mine. From there I finally reached the Metropole.

I was assigned a luxurious, permanently heated room, with dark-blue wallpaper, sapphire-blue plush armchairs, a table with a glass top, a couple of electric lamps, and a view of a large square. None of my future acquaintances living in this hotel had any doubt that the telephones contained bugging devices; we always covered them with a blanket as soon as the conversation moved on to sensitive topics.

My fellow guests in the almost empty hotel were a dozen or so foreign correspondents, mainly from English-speaking countries. We foreigners all met up a few times a day, along with one or two interpreters, in a small room set aside for our breakfast and dinner. In this smart but boring room the war correspondents had their coffee and buttered rolls. Cut off from the outside world, left to stew in their own juice, and seeing the same faces every day, they were desperately bored. They included the representative of a major British newspaper who had once toured Eastern Małopolska during the most acute friction between the Poles and the Ukrainians, and had sent pro-Ukrainian telegrams from Lwów, which had got him into trouble with the Polish security forces. This loud, amiable, portly man was now railing about how he knew nothing, couldn't go and see anything, and was entirely cut off from any firsthand information.

"I've sent a telegram demanding to be recalled from this post," he cried. "I refuse to be treated like a monkey in a cage—I'm only free to see what they show me, and that's very little."

One night, through the huge windowpanes I saw all the "caged monkeys" standing in the hotel lobby. They were patiently waiting for a representative of Soviet propaganda to take them to a meeting with a Russian priest; the entire Soviet press was trumpeting that he had been persecuted by the Germans, had escaped, and was now doing very well in the Soviet state, where religious freedom prevailed. At the time, religious tolerance was one of the slogans being hammered into the heads of foreign correspondents.

On the very first day I got down to the business that had brought me to Moscow.

Through General Anders's letters I had a means of direct contact with Generals Zhukov and Reichman, Beria and Merkulov's direct subordinates. In those days they were in charge of the entire security service in Soviet Russia, including all the camps and all the prisons, and they were regarded as the most remarkable and influential people in Stalin's immediate circle. Reichman and Zhukov were subordinate to them (via Kruglov), and on behalf of the NKVD they were "taking care" of the organization of the Polish Army.

I was also counting on the eventual help of the British and possibly of Ilya Ehrenburg, who was then the most popular Soviet war correspondent, and—after Alexei Tolstoy—the most famous of the contemporary Russian writers. His book *The Fall of Paris* had already been published by then, for which he had won the Stalin prize (worth 100,000 rubles).

I started by taking my letters to the Lubyanka, headquarters of the NKVD. I was not allowed to enter this great edifice (the entire complex included new buildings joined onto ones dating from before the revolution) but was sent to a house located much further away. There I went into a cold upstairs waiting room, where the floor was wet with snow brought in on people's boots. After some waiting, and after explaining through a tiny window who I was and why I had come, I was summoned by telephone up a dirty staircase to another waiting room, heated this time, where I had to explain the purpose of my visit again to a young, uniformed NKVD officer, the picture of health. The fact that General Sikorski and General Anders had been received by Stalin barely two months earlier, that the organization of the Polish Army was being publicized everywhere, and that there were photographs of General Anders in the illustrated newspapers was enough of an advertisement, so I imagined, to facilitate at least my initial steps. I was counting on the letters, which I had been ordered to hand in person to both generals, to open doors to them for me at the very least. But when I asked to hand them the letters in person, I was met with a smile bordering on amusement and a firm refusal from the young NKVD officer; the only thing I was free to do was to hand both letters to him and wait patiently for an answer. In this regard there could be no exceptions; no explanation I could possibly provide would be strong enough to rock his cast-iron orders.

The long, narrow waiting room, with old-fashioned bits of furniture, looked as if it hadn't been touched since the days of Nicholas I, and was one of the few places where I was able to observe the gray citizens of Moscow. A string of ageless women in battered capes, with the complexion of malnourished people that we knew so well, and also one old man stood there in silence. Humbly and patiently they waited for the rare moments when the little window at the back of the room opened, for formulaic answers to emerge in a few short words. From what I could overhear, they had come to ask about deportees and whether they were still alive. This string of people waiting plainly had special privileges; even though the convicts were more than likely to be close relatives of theirs, they had the right to live in Moscow, which was a great distinction in Russia, to ask questions about the fate of their loved ones and even to get answers. After all, very many people from all over Soviet Russia had told me that there was never any news of deportees, and that communicating with them was forbidden. But here one of the women, as she was walking past me on her way out of the room, said goodbye and then whispered under her breath: *Slava Bogu, zhiv*—"Thank God, he's alive." She left after a long wait, once a few words had been barked at her through the little window.

As I sat in the waiting room, I feverishly scoured my mind for any kind of alternate route that might get me to the top authorities, if the official route let me down. My view of the prevailing reality was completely clouded by my out-of-date recollections of the Bolsheviks of the initial period; thanks to the fact that they included plenty of original, highly remarkable individuals and not just blindly obedient pawns, through various chinks in the armor it was possible to reach them, and then find a common language on various topics. Once you had made human contact by this route, you could try to get an answer on other matters too. For instance, in 1918 Stasova had not been afraid to discuss the question of whether "existence defines consciousness" or to advise me to read the works of the Polish scholar Ludwik Krzywicki as soon as I got back to Poland, the sociologist whom she regarded as her mentor. An eminent official from the Commissariat for War, a man from Kraków called Fenigstein, who gave me direct information about the tragic fate of the colleagues I was looking for, then expounded to me at length the British plans for intervention on the Murman coast.

I had forgotten that nowadays the situation had entirely changed. In 1918 there was none of the present Soviet legislation, thanks to which there was no freedom of movement, not even inside the country—a place where the high-up functionaries actually supervised each other, where foreigners, including communists, were under constant vigilant control, and where crossing the border illegally was a crime for which hundreds of my acquaintances sneaking in from Nazi-occupied Poland had been punished with three-to-eight-year prison sentences. I had overestimated the fact that these days I was an ally, and that General Anders and the vast majority of Polish soldiers were determined to fight loyally alongside the Soviet army. The nightmare of the three missing camps, of my fifteen thousand comrades, among whom everyone had someone they knew, if not a close relative, was poisoning us all, taking away our faith in the possibility of cooperation. I was stubbornly counting on the Soviets to understand all this, on my plainly written memorandum, on eventual lateral pressure, and on the authority of General Anders; all these were trump cards to be played but ones I didn't have in 1918.

As soon as I left the NKVD waiting room I headed for the British mission; as the embassy had been bombed, at the time it was housed at the Yugoslav diplomatic post.

I was received at once with the greatest courtesy. I explained the purpose of my journey and was taken to see the head of mission. This was General MacFarlane, commander at Dunkirk, then in charge of defending one of the more endangered stretches of the British coast. Within hours of the outbreak of the German-Soviet war he had been transferred to Moscow.

The office was in semidarkness; on the large mahogany desk an electric lamp cast strong white light on papers, reports, and telegrams. From behind the desk a very tall, slim old gentleman stood up. His shoulders were so rounded as to look almost hunchbacked. Many years ago he had injured his spine falling off a horse while spear-hunting wild pigs in India. He had a thick, gray, old-fashioned mustache, a direct gaze and an engaging manner, with no trace of formality.

We sat down on the sofa. Fluent in French, the general heard me out attentively. He could not give me any help, apart from allowing me to work at the mission and deposit my papers there, which I preferred not to keep at the hotel. He warned me that getting to see the NKVD chiefs, Merkulov or Beria, was almost impossible and that he himself had to wait weeks for such meetings.

From this man, and from all his subordinates with whom I came into contact, though they could do little to help me, I was met with an immediate, disinterested response. I did not have to explain to any one of them that it was a matter of immense importance at the human level; through small gestures of courtesy, each of them did his best to show me how they felt about it.

Anticipating a sign from the Lubyanka, every day I went to the British mission, where I feverishly worked on my memorandum, which in a relatively succinct form was meant to explain the purpose of my journey, the evidence gathered so far, and the data on the missing men. From the British mission I was also allowed to send letters on the matter and copies of my memorandum to the Polish government in London, although in this period the quantity of materials sent off to London was extremely limited in view of the communication difficulties. Against the background of Soviet mistrust, my short-term arrest that morning, the time spent in NKVD waiting rooms, and the hostile sidelong glances in the street, I was extremely grateful for the friendly courtesy of the officers at the mission.

Invited a few days later for a Saturday lunch party, I heard Mac-Farlane and the other officers' accounts of Dunkirk, and of the past thirty months of the war. For me, after two years in the camps it was all new. Among others things it was the first time I had come across British officers expressing their deep resentment and downright anti-French feelings following the catastrophe of 1940.

"Just as our troops were being killed, as we were being forced to retreat to Dunkirk before the enemy attack from all sides, I saw French soldiers ripping out our phone wires to make themselves bootlaces," one of the officers told me. "At the moment when the disaster was at its worst, the local farmers were charging twenty-five francs for each glass of water to be served to Belgian and French refugees."

A kindly old major described London to me. Since the start of the war he had been at general staff in Egypt but had now been transferred to Moscow. He had just been to London on a special mission by plane for a single day. Very calmly and unemotionally he told me that entire districts had ceased to exist and it had been a shock to see it for himself.

"I could only follow the progress of the battle for London, where my closest relatives were, from the newspapers and bulletins in Cairo. Just across the wall from my mother's flat an entire house came down, and at the time," he said, dropping his gaze, "I was signing idiotic papers."

I found some of the British reactions unexpected, to say the least. At the time, there was fighting in progress for Singapore. The world press was blaring about the city's fabulous fortifications. A nice young officer, with the face of a young Churchill, invited me for a drink at the embassy. A couple of years earlier he had served in Singapore. When I asked him about the fortifications and the chances of defense, he let out a burst of casual laughter and said: "But Singapore has no such fortifications and is sure to fall any day now!"

I found these people to have not just strength of character and astonishing equilibrium but also a deep and unshakable confidence in ultimate victory.

During dinner in a room with dark wood paneling at the diplomatic post the presiding officer stood up (it was not General Mac-Farlane, though he was present at the table), raised his glass, and said: "Gentlemen—the King!" That laconic mark of respect for king and country, in ice-cold Moscow, made a stronger impression on me than I could ever have imagined.

That evening, the general took me back to the hotel in his car. We drove through the pitch-dark Moscow streets, where only the beams of floodlights sweeping the sky produced a little light. The conversation turned to personal matters. The general talked about his wife, from whom he had been far away since the start of the war. When he was put in command of the British coast, he had been able to find her accommodation nearby. But only a few days after her arrival, he had been transferred to Moscow.

I asked if he could bring his wife here.

"How could I?" he replied. "Every one of my officers might make the same request, but in these conditions I would have to refuse."

Of course he was complaining, but he was plainly very tired and finding it hard to be parted from his family; he wasn't at all ashamed and didn't try to hide this intimate, human side of his life from a stranger.

This is the heartfelt memory that I have retained of him.

In those first few days of my time in Moscow I also went to see Ilya Ehrenburg. I had read the short daily political propaganda articles that he had written when the German onslaught was coming close to Moscow. They stood out from almost every other article in the Soviet press, so hard to read, and full of recurring clichés that couldn't just be skipped—these weren't only in the press but in every conversation with a Soviet citizen. It was like listening to the same old gramophone record over and over again. Ehrenburg's articles had a freshness of view and some humanity, the sensibility of the common soldier or the Soviet officer who was fighting in the most savage conditions, the railroad worker who couldn't leave his engine for eighty hours at a stretch but just wetted his face with snow to stop himself from sinking into deep sleep. In Paris before the war, I had occasionally seen Ehrenburg in passing, in the cafés of Montparnasse. But I had only met him properly in Buzuluk in early December, two months before my trip to Moscow. He had been there in the entourage of the deputy foreign commissar, Vyshinsky, who accompanied General Sikorski on his visit to Polish Army general staff. I had talked to him quite a lot at the time, mainly about Paris, French writers, and art (Ehrenburg had been to Paris during the German occupation). He told me about the uncompromising attitude of numerous Catholic writers, stressing the merits of Mauriac. He told me how highly he rated French art, how in Soviet Russia he had fought in defense of French painting, and that he had a unique reproduction of a painting by Bonnard in his Moscow apartment. Being a painter by profession myself, I asked him about Soviet art, still deluding myself that there were some other artists besides the constellation of official stars whose propaganda kitsch or mediocre academic "compositions" I had seen at exhibitions in Paris and Warsaw. Ehrenburg had not concealed the fact that there was no real painting in Russia. He told me there were just a handful of artists of the genuine kind and that the only way for them to exist was as stage designers, which allowed them to do a little painting for themselves in the margins of their set design work. We also talked about Poland, of which he had warm memories, about the Poles, and about his enduring fondness for them, despite his many critical remarks. He seemed to me human and sincere.

So now I had a right to expect him to help me. But in a bright, luxurious room on the sixteenth floor of the Hotel Moscow, I instantly realized that if he really did want to help me, if he were to show me sympathy merely by the look on his face, or to give me real advice through just a short phrase, he would not be what he was in Russia, he wouldn't be living in the Hotel Moscow but would have long since been rotting away in the Siberian tundra, in the taiga of Kolyma or Komi, or the steppes of Karaganda. I can still see him, sitting in a low armchair, quite far away from me, answering me in a loud voice, as if assuming that here too the room was bugged. He said he didn't know or barely knew any of the dignitaries on whom this matter depended; he was surprised that I had been chosen for a mission of this kind, as I was *tolko kapitan*—just a captain, and said that a telegram from General Anders could be more effective than all my efforts in Moscow, because Anders was a general.

Outside a fine winter sun was shining. From here too I could see the Kremlin walls and church towers. Once again I recalled my extremely different conversation with Stasova and started to understand the road the Russian state had traveled since 1918.

I said goodbye to Ehrenburg and left with a sense of still being faced with the same stone wall that no human groan could penetrate, unless politically useful at the time. I left with a sense of hearts of stone, which no emotion can possibly move without the advance "blessing" of the highest authority.

After the British and Ehrenburg my last resort was to wait for an answer from the Lubyanka. For several days I waited, with rising impatience. Writing my memorandum occupied me for the first few days, and then I found a foreigner to type out the text for me in Russian. This old, blurred-looking man had lived in Moscow for many years. He was quiet and extremely painstaking in his work. At the start, he didn't know what sort of work he was to do for me. The memorandum filled him with unconcealed fear. There were several points that he cautiously but insistently advised me to change, to which I could not agree. He was shocked by the overt assertion that Stalin had not kept his promise. He felt this to be the height of impudence. He also insisted that I should modulate the sentence about rumors of ships and barges full of prisoners of war being sunk. He always spoke in a virtual whisper, almost cringing, whenever Stalin was mentioned.

Finally the text was ready and only had to be handed in.

One night I was awoken by a phone call from the Lubyanka; I was to present myself in the same waiting room as before at such-and-such a time the next day, and from there I would be taken to see General Reichman.

At the appointed hour I arrived at the familiar cold and dirty upstairs waiting room. There was a well-fed official waiting for me, in a tall cap made of gray karakul lambskin and the same sort of collar—he looked a bit like Chichikov from Gogol's *Dead Souls*. Once he had checked my papers, we drove past a number of houses and stopped at the main entrance of the central Lubyanka building. I was surprised by the unexpected elegance of the place—there were tall glass doors, a bright-red fluffy carpet, and an armed guard consisting of two tall soldiers in perfectly pressed ankle-length overcoats and pointed caps.

At the entrance, my papers were carefully checked, then came some corridors, an elevator, and more corridors. I was admitted to a modest little sitting room to wait my turn. Here to my amazement I found Major Khodas, the former Bolshevik commandant of our camp at Gryazovets, near Vologda, also waiting to be received.

Khodas had been the last in a series of commandants. My memories of him were not the worst. Indeed, he and his subordinates had tried in every way possible, through threats and promises, to force us to join the Red Army before the Sikorski-Maisky agreement had been adopted. But he had also allowed us to give lectures, which had been forbidden in Starobilsk, and when I insisted on being able to receive books about art that I needed for these lectures, he brought me from Moscow some shoddy color postcards featuring pictures by Shishkin from the Tretyakov Gallery. Shishkin was a poor, once very popular, naturalist painter of pine forests, active in the second half of the nineteenth century. Khodas brought me the postcards as the last word in art, thus implying that he wanted to be of service to me. I was grateful to him for that.

Now he was being received a quarter of an hour before me. Was it a coincidence? Or was he there to report on me? That was probably why he had been summoned. Then it was my turn.

The room had heavy drapes and a carpet. Reichman was thin and small in height, with an aristocratic face and manicured hands. He greeted me and showed me to a seat facing the window. Throughout the conversation a third person was present, also in an NKVD uniform, sitting in total silence by the drapes, against the light. Reichman seemed cold and extremely self-controlled. He received me properly but coolly. During the entire visit I was not aware of a single gesture or facial expression, nor did I hear a single word that was not calculated. The dry face of this relatively young, balding, fair-haired man did not show the slightest hint of any kind of emotional reaction.

I handed him my memorandum, in which I had set out the exact number of officers and private soldiers taken captive with weapons in hand and interned at Starobilsk and Ostashkov. I stated that at the point when it was closed down, in April 1940, Kozelsk had about 5,000 prisoners of war, of whom about 4,500 were officers of all ranks. (That was the approximate number of Katyn victims, according to calculations based on documents dating from 1945.) I went on to state that at the point when its closure began, Ostashkov had 6,670 people, including 380 officers, and Starobilsk had 3,920, of whom just a few dozen were cadets and civilians, while all the rest were officers. I added that of the total sum of 15,000 from all three camps, only about 400 had been found, grouped together from May 1940 at Pavlishchev-Bor, and then at Gryazovets near Vologda.

Reading very attentively, Reichman ran a well-sharpened pencil along each line, each word; meanwhile, following the trail of his pencil, I read over his shoulder:

"Since August 12, 1941, when the amnesty was announced for all Polish prisoners of war, almost six months have passed," I had written in the memorandum. "Polish officers and private soldiers released from the camps and prisons have been arriving to join the Polish Army in groups and individually. These men were arrested attempting to cross the border after September 1939 or were arrested in occupied Polish territory; but despite the amnesty, despite the categorical promise made to our ambassador Kot in October 1941 by Stalin himself to return our prisoners of war, despite the categorical order issued by Stalin in the presence of the commanders in chief of the Polish Army General Sikorski and General Anders on December 4, 1941, to find and release all the officers from Starobilsk, Kozelsk, and Ostashkov, not a single prisoner from these three camps has returned—apart from the above-mentioned group from Gryazovets and a few dozen who were imprisoned separately and then released in September 1941; not a single call for help has reached us from prisoners of war from the above-mentioned camps. Questioning thousands of people returning from camps and prisons has not provided us with any definite information concerning their present location but only secondhand rumors: that 6,000–12,000 officers and NCOs were sent to Kolyma, via Nakhodka Bay, in 1940; that there was a concentration of more than 5,000 officers in the mines of Franz Josef Land; that they were exiled to Novaya Zemlya, Kamchatka, and Chukhotka; that in the summer of 1940 some 630 officers were working 110 miles from Pestraya Dresva (Kolyma); that 150 prisoners of war from Kozelsk, in officers' uniforms, were seen to the north of the Sosva River near Gari (east of the Urals); that Polish prisoners of war, officers, were transported on huge barges (1,700–2,000 people on each one) to the northern islands, and that three of the barges sank in the Barents Sea. Not one of these rumors has been adequately confirmed, though the information about the northern islands and Kolyma seems the most probable."

How many versions were sifted through and rejected, how many wretches in torn jackets were questioned, investigated, and interviewed, in Kuybyshev, in our cold wooden hut in Totskoye, and in Chkalov, just to write those few sentences, I was thinking, while casting furtive glances at the text as Reichman dispassionately drew his pencil down the page.

"We know how precisely each prisoner of war was registered," I read on, following his pencil. "How each 'case' was kept in files including numerous written statements, verified photographs, and documents, we know how very carefully and precisely the NKVD carried out this work: as a result, none of us can possibly believe that the present location of fifteen thousand men, including 8,000 officers, could be unknown to the senior ranks of the NKVD. Surely Stalin's solemn promise and his categorical order to explain the fate of the former Polish prisoners of war give us reason to hope that we shall at least be told where our comrades are to be found and, if they have perished, how and where it happened."

I watched Reichman's face and movements; not a muscle twitched, as he calmly slid his sharpened pencil down the lines. The next bit was as precise a numerical statement as possible. The memorandum ended like this: "Based on these data, the total number of officers who have not returned from Starobilsk, Kozelsk, and Ostashkov is 8,300. All the officers in the Polish Army now being formed in Soviet Russia, totaling 2,300 on January 1, 1942, were imprisoned or interned in Lithuania, Latvia, and Estonia, but were not prisoners of war (with the exception of the 400 from Gryazovets mentioned earlier). As we are not in a position to define the total number of all those who have not returned with equal precision, we are only giving the number of prisoners of war interned in Kozelsk, Starobilsk, and Ostashkov, the majority of whom are officers, as we have been able to confirm this number with relative precision. In expanding our army in the south of the USSR, following the resolution adopted by Stalin and General Sikorski, we are increasingly aware of the lack of these people, without whom we are missing our best military experts, our best commanders. It goes without saying that the disappearance of these men is impeding our efforts to build our army's trust in the Soviet Union, which is crucial to the favorable development of mutual relations between the two allied armies in the fight against the common enemy."

Reichman finished reading, drawing the pencil over the lines as he read, without deleting or marking anything, to the very last.

Without looking me in the eyes, he drily declared that it was not his department and that he knew nothing about it, but that for General Anders he was prepared to investigate the matter (*navesti spravki*), and that I was to wait; in a few days' time, as soon as he found something out he would let me know.

Meanwhile the other man sat in the shadow of the drapes, tall, broad-shouldered, and mute.

I asked the general to facilitate an audience for me with Beria or Merkulov, and I added a few more comments and specifications, perhaps in too heated a tone, desperately and hopelessly wanting to infect him with the human side of the matter.

Reichman responded with the same ice-cold, laconic courtesy. He did not believe I would be able to see Merkulov or Beria; in any case, Merkulov was away. General Zhukov, to whom General Anders had written a second letter that I had handed in with the letter to Reichman, had also left for Turkestan on business concerning the Polish Army and it was impossible to say when he would be back.

The audience was at an end.

Although it was plain that I couldn't possibly extract anything from this stern NKVD official, I was reluctant to leave, because I had spent such a long time preparing for this conversation. But there was no hope of prolonging my visit. After a farewell bid with icy politesse, I walked out, my steps muffled by the carpet.

"I'm not familiar with the matter. It's not my department," General Reichman had said to me. But I knew a staff officer who had been through the Lubyanka, where he was interrogated by this same General Reichman. I knew that Reichman had spent a long time in charge of the Polish department at the Lubyanka, and that he couldn't be

ignorant of the fate of the fifteen thousand prisoners of war constitut-
ing the entire corpus of Polish officers and private soldiers captured
in September 1939 with weapons in their hands.

In the corridor I ran into Khodas, who was on his way out. We
left the Lubyanka and walked to Dzherzhinsky Square together. I
mentioned Gryazovets, invited him to lunch, and did my best to start
up a conversation. Perhaps here I would manage to grasp a thread or
find a clue.

But as Khodas went racing down the icy sidewalk, I could tell that
he wanted to flee from me as the devil flees holy water, and that he
would take the first opportunity to get away from me. He politely
but firmly refused, not just lunch, but any meeting at all, on the excuse
that he wasn't living in Moscow at present.

I went back to the Metropole. What was there left for me to do?
Nothing but wait for mercy, wait for Reichman's summons.

During those long days waiting for the call from the Lubyanka, I
found consolation in the bookstores, especially a few secondhand
ones, where I kept finding French books in the packages that were
brought in on a daily basis, as people sold off their libraries.

At the time, a pound of butter cost several dozen rubles in Moscow
and was impossible to obtain anyway, but for ten rubles I managed
to buy an 1868 edition of *Fleurs du mal* with a portrait of the author
and an introduction by Théophile Gautier. A few days later I even
found some Polish books, including an uncut copy of Mieczysław
Treter's book on Matejko, which I bought for our army library.

As I read it at the hotel, I remembered how we had fought against
Treter's* views, and our attacks on historical painting in Poland,
especially on Matejko. From a remote perspective, those battles seemed
almost an idyll.

I tenaciously searched for the work of Vasily Rozanov in all the
bookstores I could find, but there was no sign of him anywhere.

Rozanov had a major influence on Russian literature in the early
twentieth century and on émigré literature too. His *Solitaria* and *The*

*He died in a German prison.

Apocalypse of Our Time were translated into French and published by Plon, but naturally the translations did not do justice to Rozanov's brilliant word-formation, which Tuwim found a delight. It seems I was the only person in Poland to own a copy of his book *Tyomny lik* (The Dark Countenance: the Metaphysics of Christianity).

Less than two years after the Russian Revolution, this Russian Nietzsche and follower of pagan religions was starving to death when he was taken in by one of the last Orthodox monasteries, where he died. I discovered his books, brilliant and shocking for Christians and atheists, reactionaries and progressives alike, through Merezhkovsky in Petrograd in 1918. Ever since I had been reluctant to part with them.

In one of the Moscow bookstores I managed to get on friendly terms with a typical old bookseller, in a faded gabardine. I asked for Rozanov.

"Rozanov? But of course it's kept in storage—there's a very strict ban on selling him," he said gloomily. "How often I've tried to explain! Why don't they at least let us sell a few copies to the literary types or to the specialists, but no, there's no question, he's strictly banned."

And the old man fell silent, refraining from further comment.

As I tramped about the new and secondhand bookstores, I was amazed to find so many works in translation, even on the topic of painting, which was of the greatest interest to me. It's true that in the days of the czars Russia could already boast a large number of superb translations. But the growth of this sector in the Soviet period can also be ascribed to the fact that for many writers, including some of the best who refused to write to order, the only source of income was translation. When at a later date I urged a certain writer to translate some Polish poems, he replied bitterly that unfortunately he wasn't any good at translation.

"I swear to you that if I only knew how, I'd willingly translate. In our country it is just about the only safe and honest way for a writer to earn a living."

I had been able to read some of these translations in the camp, including Balzac's *The Peasants*, which had delighted Marx, and Flaubert's *Sentimental Education*, with minor annotations, intelligent introductions, and naturally the indispensable Marxist preface. At the same secondhand bookstores one of the things I found was a superb selection of the letters and writings of David. Of course David was a dictator of the arts during the French Revolution, a costume and set designer for the rallies of the day, and to some extent also a precursor of socialist realism; he more than anyone understood painting as a didactic tool for ennobling man, the propaganda of heroism and revolution. And what seems to us today to be pure pseudo-classicism was realism in the eyes of his contemporaries.

As well as David, I also chanced upon a translation of the letters of Winckelmann. This author of stiff pseudo-classical standards was of interest to the Bolsheviks, perhaps since breaking with the "putrid" art of the modern West they were seeking a genealogy for their own artistic theses. I also took away from Moscow a translation of Poussin's letters and a selection of letters by nineteenth and twentieth-century painters. I have never read an equally interesting and intelligent selection, either in Polish or in French.

I carried these books off to the hotel, and for hours on end I read and read until my eyes were sore.

Apart from books about painting, I looked for actual paintings. But all the major galleries, including the Shchukin, which was every painter's dream, with one of the richest collections of Gauguins and Van Goghs, were shut or had been evacuated. However, I did discover an exhibition of paintings in a freezing-cold hall, where there were artists' get-togethers and lectures on art. Most of the pictures were quite small, and it was roughly on a par with the feeble exhibitions put on at our Zachęta Gallery from 1920 to 1930. Landscapes, morality scenes, with distant echoes of the *Peredvizhniki* (The Itinerants), a Russian school of naturalists against whom the journal *Mir Isskustva* (World of Art) had already rolled out its heaviest cannon before 1900. This trend, related to the pre-Witkiewicz* trend in Poland, was for my generation so passé that it was only ever referred to in art criticism as a horror story.

---

*Naturally I am referring to Stanisław Witkiewicz.

Only a few of the artists exhibited in this room showed signs of a deeper heritage. There was a bit of timid impressionism at third hand, while one of the painters must have come under the influence of Cézanne; his canvases revealed a sense of a painter's intentions, or rather persistence, but there were absolutely no leanings toward the abstract and no postimpressionism. All the pictures, even the least awful, gave off a strange sense of sorrow and oppression. The painters, old and bearded, in spectacles and ancient, moth-eaten fur coats, were wandering about the cold hall, breathing out clouds of steam. By the entrance there were beautiful art books on sale from the prerevolutionary era. For tuppence halfpenny one could obtain luxury editions, which probably came from the remains of these people's libraries.

I dared not approach any of them in my Polish officer's uniform. Even through the most neutral conversation I could cause harm to one of these poor, apolitical painters, these survivors of a bygone world.

Roaming in the vicinity of my hotel, I came upon a Catholic church, the only one open in Moscow. Small and surrounded on all sides by the high walls of the Lubyanka, it stood in a snowy little square. It was built of dark stone, with low columns, perhaps in the first half of the nineteenth century, and was called the French church. Inside it had something of the *salon*, because there were paintings in gold frames, rugs trodden threadbare, and just one single novelty: a hideous picture of Saint Teresa with a bouquet of fake flowers. Mass was said by the only Catholic priest in Moscow, an American citizen with determined, military movements. Each morning the church was packed, mainly with women, and many of them went up to take communion. By the entrance a few old beggars timidly requested alms, ardently thanking and blessing for every donation. A procession of penniless women in worn-out, colorless overcoats scurried to and from this little church under the walls of the Lubyanka, in an alien, hostile world. I couldn't help thinking of a phrase of Norwid's: "It was like the cortege for an exiled king, the last ruler of his kind—the remnants of purple and gold and the retinue of followers were poor."

One time, just before leaving Moscow, I dropped in at an almost empty store where one could buy sketchpads with passable gray-and-yellow paper. The sales assistant was a young girl in a rabbit fur coat and a gray headscarf. On my way back from church, I was holding a small copy of the Bible, issued in London for the army and sent out to us. There was a small white cross stamped on its black oilcloth cover. I noticed that the girl was staring at the book with strange insistence, and suddenly she addressed me in a hushed tone: "I see you have a book with a cross—are you a believer? Because I am a believer too, sir. I used to know an old woman who was a nun. She did no harm to anyone. She was a saint. And she did nothing but pray. But a few years ago they exiled her to the far north and all trace of her was lost."

Just then someone else came into the store. The girl instantly broke off her story and told me the price of the sketchpads. A little later we were on our own again, and she frantically unbuttoned her coat, then extracted a little wooden Orthodox cross from under her blouse.

"She gave me this cross as a parting gift, and I'll keep it as long as I live," she said with tears in her eyes.

My attempts to evade loneliness also included long conversations with two of the journalists living at the same hotel, and with whom I often spent the evenings. They took advantage of Intourist's extra rations of goodies; as honored foreigners, now and then they were given the right to buy wine and fruit, so they entertained each other to modest feasts, spent hours sitting in their rooms, reading hundred-year-old French romances bought at the secondhand stores. I learned nothing about the Soviet Union from them. They may have known something but were just being careful. I also tried to get through to the diplomats. I had two excellent breakfasts, also in hotel rooms occupied by counselors. There I saw transient officers and representatives of smaller countries. I took away nothing from these meetings but a sense of their total uselessness. The talk was of food, anecdotes that had nothing to do with politics, and how greatly they missed the ballet since it had been evacuated from Moscow to Kuybyshev.

My permit to stay in Moscow was close to expiring, twelve days had gone by, and there had been no news from Reichman.

One night I went to bed early and fell asleep. Suddenly the telephone rang: it was only midnight. Awoken from deep sleep, I thought it was eight in the morning. Who was calling? General Reichman. He told me he had called me three times and was surprised the hotel administration could have failed to let me know (?); he wanted to see me in person, but unfortunately tomorrow morning he was leaving, and there wouldn't be time. All this was said in an extremely friendly tone, engaging, warm even. He went on to say that he had inquired into my case and had been informed that all the materials concerning the Polish prisoners of war had been passed from the NKVD to the NKID (the People's Commissariat for Foreign Affairs); he advised me to go back to Kuybyshev and to approach Comrade Vyshinsky or Comrade Novikov there.

"Has anyone already approached them?" he asked naively.

Fully awake by now, I could see the whole thing. Reichman had chosen the easiest pretence to fob me off without offending General Anders, who at the time was of concern to him. I don't doubt for an instant that he was lying when he said he had called three times before. The management of one of the two hotels where foreigners were allowed to stay, half empty and packed with NKVD men, would have immediately let me know about a telephone call from such an important person.

I felt the final thread snapping in my hand as I replied to the general that our ambassador had approached those gentlemen on this matter not once, but *eight* times, that in November and December Stalin had promised to release the missing men, that I had put all this in the memorandum I had given him, which he had read in my presence. To which Reichman replied that he had heard that a very large number prisoners of war had been pouring in to join the army from various places lately, from Irkutsk for instance.

"I know all about that," I replied, "but none of them are those men, not the same arrests, not the same camps."

"Oh, indeed," he said, "what a pity I'm not well enough up on the matter to be able to offer any pointers."

He went on to explain that the entire NKVD administration had left for Kuybyshev, and that he hadn't been able to present the matter to his seniors, because Comrades Merkulov and Zhukov still weren't back. He added that he had instructed Comrade Khlopov, to whom I had had to present my papers at the NKID, to extend my permit to stay in Moscow, where "naturally" I could remain as long as I wished. However, he advised me to return to Kuybyshev and to get in touch with Vyshinsky—and that was all he had to say. I still tried to explain the total fruitlessness of our talks with Vyshinsky, but Reichman cut off the conversation, which had actually been much longer than the one at the Lubyanka and was maintained to the end in an almost cordial tone.

I was once again alone with a silent telephone on the glass top of an elegant little table, amid the blue plush armchairs. The cut-off phone call nullified not just the purpose of my journey to Moscow but also the months and months I had spent preparing for it.

I had gained no news at all and still had no idea if my comrades were alive or where they were. There were no more doors for me to knock on in Moscow in the hope of them being opened to me. As for Reichman, I was sure he was refusing to say anything simply because he knew something that he could not tell me.

The story of his sudden departure and the nocturnal call that woke me up gave him nothing but pluses, and me nothing but minuses. I hadn't even been given the time to prepare an answer, so all I could do was accept the verdict and leave not just empty-handed but also with a sense of having been given to understand "don't poke your nose into matters we're not going to tell you about anyway."

I decided to leave Moscow.

I spent the next two days getting ready for my departure and waiting for a seat on the train. At the NKID Khlopov was exceedingly polite and had clearly had orders from Reichman; he sent me to the Intourist stores, where I was supplied for the journey according to such-and-such a category of privileged foreigner. The storehouse was full of the most delectable provisions: smoked fish, sausage, and condensed milk. I was given a couple of bottles of good wine, some white bread, sausages, and canned food. At the hotel I was given the news that a seat had been reserved for me in the "soft" carriage. I'd be leaving in two days.

With no more phone calls or anything at all to wait for, I spent those final gray, windy, frosty days trailing about the city, sunk in gloomy thoughts. The multistory modern buildings, most of them banal and ugly, rose alongside the charming eighteenth-century mansions. A raspberry-red one with white stucco was then the Gorky hospital, and the blue Palace of Science had been destroyed by air raids. I admired the modern profile of the great Lenin Library, a high-rise devoid of embellishment; from top to bottom this tall, solid block consisted of nothing but uninterrupted rows of windows of equal size. Around this structure, almost unreal in its geometry, the new library had been built, with less confrontational architecture, beautifully proportioned with sculptures and bluish-gray columns.

Every time I went to the British mission, next to a small yellow neoclassical mansion with white columns, I admired a vast Le Corbusier edifice—as far as I remember, it was the commissariat for light industry. It was a multistoried block set on light concrete pillars, almost floating in the air, with walls of glass, partly replaced at the time with yellow and pink brick because of the bombardments. But apart from the few old mansions and the few modern buildings that I am describing, most of the streets, recently widened, and running across the city, seemed to me rather hideous. Corinthian columns and stucco had been tacked onto new houses, and on the roof of a large cooperative there was a naturalist sculpture of a woman, two stories high, with her arms stretched skyward: she was meant to represent the Soviet slogan, *Zhit stalo veselei*—"Life has become jollier."

I was crushed by the enormity of Moscow and its atmosphere.

At every step I saw the expression of a brutal, unbending will; I saw thousands of human faces that were closed or hostile, and I felt the terrible disproportion in physical strength between us and this empire, which in recent years had killed off more Poles than in the whole of history to date. I still didn't believe our men had been murdered, I was deluding myself that they were in Kolyma or Franz Josef

Land, but now I had no idea what steps to take to discover their location. Wherever I went along these streets, as the wind blew gray snow down them, the "Bronze Horseman" from Pushkin's epic poem came chasing after me. No wonder that in the first version Pushkin was going to have a Polish exile as the hero of his epic—utterly ruined, he curses the Bronze Horseman, the statue of Peter the Great, and in revenge the Horseman chases the poor wretch down the empty stone streets of the imperial capital.

On the day of my departure I got back to the hotel, feeling frozen and depressed. Shortly before I had been accosted in the street by a passerby, who had fetched a policeman to check my identity; I had immediately been surrounded by a group of people with glowering, impatient expressions: they were expecting my papers to be out of order, then maybe they would finally be able to crush a spy or an enemy parachutist. But no, to their bitter disappointment my papers were in order.

I strode across the dark hotel vestibule, its windowpanes painted ultramarine. Standing in my path to the elevator was an old Jew in a shabby overcoat with a shabby yellow fur collar. He had tired eyes with red rings around them and a wrinkled face. He fixed his gaze on me. Still feeling the impression of the stares I had had in the street, I went straight past him, but suddenly I heard a quiet voice say: "Looking at you I feel like crying. That's a Polish uniform—are you a Polish officer? Because I'm Polish too, I'm from the Pińczów area, I was a landowner there. If I could see my country again before my demise, I would die without regret."

It occurred to me to give him a copy of *Polska*, a journal issued by our embassy in Kuybyshev. I asked him to come to my room. As we went up in the elevator together, the old man talked nonstop, without taking any notice of the attendant, as if making his confession, as if admitting something he couldn't tell anyone. He had a sense of guilt about Poland, for having left in 1915 and never gone back. As we walked down a long corridor, he continued to talk. In the room I handed him *Polska*, which was lying on the table. On the front page there was a picture of the ruins of Zamkowy Square at the heart of

Warsaw, Zygmunt's Column and the Gothic towers of St. John's Cathedral in the distance, through burned rafters, stones, and rubble. The old Jew cast an eye at the photograph, leaned against the armrest of his chair, let his head droop very low, and began to sob. Then he took the journal like a holy relic and left, almost without saying goodbye.

"Pass it on to other Poles, if you know any," I said.

"Oh yes, I know a doctor," he quickly replied, already in the doorway.

He was gone, and suddenly I too began to weep. After all this time waiting amid strange and hostile faces, after tramping about the stony city in the freezing wind, thinking gloomy thoughts about shrinking Poland, strangled and slaughtered, the poor Jew's red, tearstained eyes saved me from total loss of faith and bitter despair.

12. MOSCOW—KUYBYSHEV

IN 1941–42 I made many train journeys within Soviet Russia and was able to gain a good idea of the conversations and mood in three types of railcar, not shamefully called first, second, and third class but "soft with reservation," "soft without reservation," and "hard." The hard carriages also had two categories: "with" or "without reservation." I don't need to say that in railcars "without reservation," both hard and soft alike, one could hear and learn more unembellished facts than anywhere else. While the hard-with-reservation car already had a privileged clientele, the cream of Soviet society traveled in the soft-with-reservation. Each traveler had his own couchette, the railcars were well heated and friendly, though incredibly dirty female conductors threw out the "guests without reservation" who tried to push their way in, and they also made buckwheat soup for the passengers.

It was from the traveling officers, specialists in various branches, and NKVD men that I most often heard patriotic, steadfast, and servile remarks. On a journey from Moscow via Kuybyshev to Tashkent I came into close contact with this stratum, which had profited the most from the revolution, and which regarded the Soviet system as their personal achievement. To judge from the conversations I heard, it seemed that the vast majority of them really did believe in Stalin's infallibility and also that outside the Soviet Union there was nothing but "weeping and gnashing of the teeth." This class of people, who had managed to come through all the purges intact and had not yielded to any deviations, despite all the political tightrope-walking of the Soviets, certainly consisted of more than just debased humanity. In a similar way, the pre-1914 Moscow general's wife was not debased, of whom I was told that whenever the czarist regime was criticized in her presence, she immediately interrupted the conversation to say: "*Urra! Urra! Bozhe, tsarya khrani!*—Hurrah, hurrah, God save the czar! That's my entire politics."

It would be quite incorrect to assert that in those days the Soviet Union did not have support in any of the country's social strata that was not just prompted by terror, because it also had support inspired by blind faith, or even blind love. Despite the deportations, cruelties, and injustices, many people, even those who had been wronged, still believed in the "truth" of the Soviet Revolution.

The difference in living standards between the specialist officer and the ordinary soldier, between the senior official and the hungry peasant at some Chkalov collective farm, was not necessarily smaller than that between a banker and a worker in the "putrid" capitalist countries; but in interpersonal relations a certain obligatory manner, calling each other *tovarischch* ("Comrade"), addressing each other with the informal *ty* (like *tu* in French), was still in force, creating a sort of smoke screen that erased awareness of the deep social inequalities in the Soviet Union.

But some conversations and sudden confessions revealed to me that an outer shell of the most convincing enthusiasm could be hiding a person full of doubts, fearfully concealing that a loved one had been exiled to Kolyma, that another had been tortured during the Trotskyist trials, or that his father, taken away years ago, was a kulak, whom he was not free to acknowledge. Naturally, this sort of person was bound to advertise his servile sentiments and official optimism more loudly than others. I met plenty of people among the privileged strata whose every word was an ostentatious declaration of their blind devotion to today's government and today's system. They were united by a single feature: a total lack of criticism, or worse—a total incapacity to think for themselves.

In 1941 Ehrenburg had told me how under interrogation the German prisoners of war were terribly monotonous, apparently all giving exactly the same replies, all thinking in the same formulaic way. I have not verified this claim, but judging from first, superficial contact,

I think it could just as well apply to the "right-minded" citizens of the Soviet state. With them I experienced the same constant sense of monotony. It took a lot of patience, sympathy, or an odd moment, for my interlocutor to stop talking like a gramophone record.

A few weeks earlier, on my way to Chkalov, I had traveled third class, but with a reservation, in a railcar where each person had his own seat. Among my traveling companions, who gave random accounts of patriotic scenes of the indomitable bravery of the Soviet soldier, the lead in the conversation was taken by an old lady in spectacles with the kindly face of a granny. Quite stocky and brisk, she was simply dressed, with her white hair tied in a bun. She was the loudest person in the whole carriage, the most subservient and militant. As manager of a chocolate factory in Moscow, in 1939–40 she had often traveled to Lwów to nationalize and reorganize our chocolate factories there. As she hinted to me herself, she had to her credit some acts of bravery performed in Turkestan in the early years of the revolution, and a senior rank in the Party. In my presence she tried to be tactful about the Poles, in other words to hide her patent dislike of them. Just a year ago she had read about the villainy of the Poles in all the Soviet papers and how every Polish officer was a bloodthirsty fascist, and now here she was, traveling with one of these officers; lately she had read in the very same papers that the Poles were a noble allied nation, marching shoulder to shoulder, and so on. Only after a long and friendly conversation did she mention Lwów, of which she had just one memory: of her stay at the Hotel Georges, and how the Polish *damochki* ("little ladies") came there to sell her and her friends their hats and dresses. The only words she could remember in Polish were "*przed wojną to kosztowało*," meaning "before the war this cost." She kept repeating this phrase, pursing her lips, and squeakily mimicking the Polish ladies' accent and manner of speech. They must have seemed frivolous to her, twittering bourgeois women, justly punished by fate, from whom it was very cheap to buy various wonders. But it probably didn't occur to her that these women's husbands had either been killed or deported to the remote Soviet north, or maybe they were trying to cross the border at the time, to go on fighting against

Hitler, of whom in those days not a single bad word could be said in the Soviet press. In that cruel winter in Lwów, when the citizens chopped down the trees in the city squares to get a bit of firewood for the ice-cold apartments where their hungry children huddled, those frivolous *damochki*, mocked by the revolutionary chocolate factory manager, and most of whom would be deported into the depths of Russia in 1940, were probably performing wonders of resourcefulness, energy, and self-sacrifice to feed their families. Those *damochki* bore humiliation after humiliation, pushing their way into the Hotel Georges to sell the remains of their property for a pittance to the dignitaries from Moscow who were flooding Lwów at the time. The dear old lady had never once imagined that maybe those women deserved a second glance.

Suddenly a poor little soldier with a ragged coat and a bandaged arm burst into our compartment illegally. This village peasant from the army near Chkalov was going on two weeks' leave to cure his wound, which had barely healed in the hospital. He was in a wretched state. All my "patriotic" companions began to eject the intruder in unison. But after making a speech in honor of the heroes at the front, the kind manager insisted on keeping him in our compartment. We put him on an upper bunk and treated him to what we had. The extremely emaciated soldier, whose name was Vasily, had a pointed little head, hair as stiff as wire, and a yellow, pimply complexion. He looked a bit simpleminded. He didn't react at all to the patriotic oration but instantly lay down on the bunk and slept for a very long time. Once he was fully rested, we began to ask him questions: Where had he been and what had he seen? And here he gave us all a surprise, telling us not just strange but shocking things. This peasant from a miserable collective farm had not been given any basic propaganda education. With no moral judgment, he described how the peasants, whom the Soviet authorities had ordered to flee from the Germans, had refused and—even when removed by force—had run back to their cottages, toward the Germans, with their horses, carts, and livestock. He talked on, as if he couldn't hear the regrets which each of his listeners was eagerly trying to express. When one of them began to talk about German cruelties, our Vasily suddenly replied: "I don't much believe in those cruelties—I deliberately stayed on a few days in Kalinin after the Germans had taken it, and although I was in a Soviet soldier's uniform and had Soviet papers, nobody did me any harm." This remark caused extreme consternation. The chocolate factory manager saved the situation. In a very sharp tone she reviled the soldier, finishing her performance by squeakily but firmly uttering: "So do you have to check with the Germans whether the Soviet press is telling the truth? You've been reading the Soviet press for the past twenty years"—I doubt Vasily was as much as twenty years old—"and you still haven't learned to trust that it always tells the truth?"

In this particular instance the Soviet press and the chocolate factory manager were in fact right; somehow or other the poor little soldier had managed not to be wiped out by the Germans, but what stuck in my memory was this accent of faith from a woman who was ideological but not without intelligence, a specialist and probably professionally educated. For her, *Izvestiya* and *Pravda* really were the gospel.

The peasant cringed and fell silent; luckily he was wounded and very emaciated, so the patriotic passengers didn't eject him into the snow but from then on treated him like thin air.

Departing from Moscow, I boarded the railcar late in the evening. All the seats, apart from my own, were already occupied, four in each compartment. The passengers were talking loudly to get acquainted.

My fellow travelers were a Ukrainian captain, a Russian expert on flamethrowers, also from Leningrad, and a reticent railroad worker in a battered leather jacket.

I was received with distinct mistrust. The conversation died.

At least twenty-four hours went by before the law of attraction of people from different worlds condemned to several days' cohabitation kicked in; most of them replaced their former mistrust with sincere courtesy or even effusiveness. I soon lost the sense of being walled in and isolated that I had felt in Moscow and finally achieved some human contact, some friendly communication.

The train ran well for the first night. In the morning an orange sun awoke us, shining through the ice-coated windowpanes. We had all slept well; now we lowered the couchettes, and I took a seat by the window. It was very warm in the carriage despite the freezing temperature outside. We glided across vast fields of snow, past low villages with the half-destroyed cupolas of churches with broken crosses towering above them. I could feel lice crawling over me and caught one on the blanket covering my legs, while wondering to which of my neighbors or predecessors I was indebted.

The carriage was settling in. The two conductors, Masha and Tanya, were always on the move, both small with ample bosoms, both grimy and disheveled but amiable and energetic, repelling the soldier-heroes and tattered civilians with sacks who tried to push their way in; if necessary, they let their fists fly without much ado. Pushed off the steps, the entire reservation-less riffraff either remained at the station halts with their bundles or grabbed on to the rails of the without-reservation cars, where real hell prevailed.

In the conductors' compartment Masha and Tanya made us English tea from my supplies. The faces began to brighten. During the day Masha served us soup.

The heat in the carriage, the lack of activity, the hot tea and the soup, collecting rations of buckwheat or bread at the stations, treating each other to our provisions for the journey, and at the same time constantly getting further away from the threat of the front all contributed to a euphoric atmosphere. I was struck by the tone of "comradely" equality, where everyone was on informal terms with the conductors. Now and then each person uttered a similar patriotic remark.

I had time to observe the passengers in the entire railcar, who went in and out of each other's compartments. A heated game of dominoes was being played in one of them from dawn to dusk (as a substitute for cards, which were banned). This compartment attracted plenty of players as well as spectators.

In the next-door compartment there was a young man with an

intense face, wearing "American" thick-rimmed spectacles. He had clean hands, not coarsened by physical work. Throughout the entire journey, he never opened his mouth in my presence but remained plunged into a thick geology textbook. He had the typical face of a pensive intellectual. The rest of the travelers, whose conversations I was listening to nonstop, appeared to be the sort of people to whom it has not yet occurred that "it's easier to hang on a hook than to think," people who meekly believed that above them were leaders who thought for them and were always right, and that their duty was to serve, and only to think from A to B. I knew the Russian railroads, I knew Russia before the revolution, and I could tell what a vast difference there was between this mass of pea-brains and the Russians of the past, when in every backstreet, at every station, in every tavern or railcar you'd run into people, whether intellectual or illiterate, who thought about everything, including the ultimate questions. I shall never forget the young man I met on a peasant sled in the Pskov province who loved Tolstoy; or the old woman pondering questions of religion in a street in Petrograd; I shall never forget the squares of Saint Petersburg in 1917, filled during the northern white nights of June with many small groups of people passionately debating everything: the right to wage war and to pacifism, agricultural reform, the existence of God, how to conquer the world or make it happy, and what one should or shouldn't be allowed to possess. Where had all that diversity gone, all that exuberance and courage to think things right through, which had been so typical in prerevolutionary Russia and not just among the intelligentsia? Where had the sectarians gone, of whom there were some twenty-five million before the revolution? They were willing to go into penal servitude for their often-fantastical beliefs. Those who hadn't yet been exterminated were probably to be found in the labor camps, where they were "rendered harmless" and could not "infect" younger generations of captains, experts, and officials. For them, parroting newspaper articles was supposed to suffice, limiting oneself to thinking of nothing but one's own profession, one's own work in the strictly technical sense, and mechanically carrying out orders.

In our railcar, which had something of the style of a collective farm, as the bearer of a rich dowry of products from Intourist, I was a valuable member of the company and was soon treating my comrades to white bread and sausage.

The first person to break the ice of mistrust was the Ukrainian captain. He was young, with a round, open face, pale eyes, and very white teeth; friendly and obliging, he told me about his village near Kharkov and how to inject spirit alcohol into a ripening melon, causing it to ferment in there, with extremely tasty results. As the youngest and most agile of us all, now and then he managed to obtain provisions for us from the station food supply points, either bread or buckwheat, which we then handed to the conductor for the soup. Everything he obtained was shared with me in the first place. He was from a large peasant family and had a brother who was an engineer, two sisters who were teachers, and a third who was a doctor.

"My old mother often says: 'How can I not regard Stalin as a father, when all my children have gained an education of a kind they couldn't have had in my youth?'"

Although the captain took a liking to me, I could tell that he related to me as a nice-enough but undoubtedly backward person, with whom he should speak with caution. Can we really be surprised by this suspicion? As prisoners of war in Starobilsk, we were flooded with Russian communist journals, Polish ones too, published in disgracefully bad Polish in Lwów, Wilno, and Kiev, specially for our use. These papers were constantly comparing the occupation of Poland's eastern territories with the victories of Suvorov, and we were all described as cowardly fascist bandits. One particular story stuck in my memory: in eastern Małopolska, as a group of officers from the defeated Polish Army was retreating eastwards, they ran into a Hucul peasant, who had come down from the mountains looking for work because he was very hungry. He asked one of the officers to give him a bit of bread, upon which the officer and his fellows slit the peasant's belly, disemboweled him, and stuck a loaf of bread into his open abdomen...

They printed this sort of garbage every day in hundreds of versions, because at the time their job was to prove that every Polish officer was a rascal. How could the attentive but naïve readers of the Soviet papers—my fellow passengers—fail to remember these stories? "This Pole may seem polite, but what if he's also a cutthroat?" some of them must have been quietly thinking. All the more since my behavior may not have inspired trust—I was constantly writing things down in a notebook, and I had books that weren't in Russian, but Polish and French. On top of that, at every station without exception, whenever I went outside in my uniform, I ran into some Poles who were hurrying to join the army. My uniform was enough for any Pole in rags to address me like a brother or an old friend, and to ask about the army, where to go and how to get there. I did my best to give each of them some advice or point them in the right direction.

"How come you have good friends and acquaintances at every station?" my nice quartermaster comrade asked me in surprise. It was quite impossible for him to understand that I had never met them before and that they were simply Poles.

For the first twenty-four hours the train ran well; the wooden fences laid along the tracks for miles were buried in huge snowdrifts, like petrified waves. But gradually the train began to stop more often, until near Morshansk it came to a halt for an entire day and night. Then it moved a couple of miles and stopped again for another fifteen hours. Our train was number 22; there were two other trains with the same number standing just ahead of us, from the two previous days. We were told that there were snowdrifts from twenty to thirty-six feet high that had to be dug out before we could go any further. By now we were well settled into our railcars and had grown used to each other's company; we liked the soups, we were making jokes with the sweet conductors, and the dominoes were still occupying most of the passengers' attention.

But first of all I had to break through a second wall of mistrust and to leap across the opening sluice gates of patriotic clichés, across the comments taken wholesale from the newspapers. By now it was dangerous to try to evince a genuine story or to prompt my inter-locutor to express his own opinion, rather than one dressed in formulaic propaganda, because it smacked of individualism, or maybe even of the secret service, spying on behalf of a foreign power.

I was most intrigued by the reticent flamethrower specialist from Leningrad. He ate not just the soup we were served in the compartment but went off to the conductors' compartment to eat up the leftovers. An image of his face as I once caught sight of it through the windowpane has stayed in my memory. Late one evening, during one of our endless stops, I had gone outside; we were standing in an open field, the wind was blowing and the sky was full of stars. As I stood in the snow, I noticed the flame of the conductors' oil lamp through the compartment window, and there in the red glow of the lamplight I saw his prematurely aging face. He was polishing off a plate of soup, scraping it clean with his spoon. I remember his avid look, the insatiable speed with which he raised spoonful after spoonful to his lips, and the rapid way his Adam's apple bobbed up and down his scrawny neck.

There he sat without a word, with a dark, as if absent, expression in his eyes. He only broke his silence once and began to talk about Leningrad, hurriedly tossing out the words, suddenly stopping and then starting up again.

"No bombs are as terrible as the hunger there," he said. "From November to the beginning of January was the worst period! But the population didn't decrease at all, as you might suppose—it even increased during the siege, because they stopped evacuating people in August or September 1941, and others came pouring into the city from the entire local area, so what was there to feed them on? People were collapsing in the streets with hunger, emaciation, and cold. What was to be done with them? There was nothing to remove the bodies ... So they piled them up like timber, one on top of another. And those piles just lay there, on the street corners ..."

I couldn't get much more out of this man, huddled in his seat; his seemingly absent gaze only grew animated, or even lit up with a blaze of passion as he took a spoon in his hand, its veins hard and swollen, and began to eat.

In the opposite corner sat a man with his head shaved as bald as a billiard ball, smoking homegrown tobacco all day, and wearing a classic shabby leather jacket. He didn't say a word. I thought him the most mistrustful of all; he claimed to be a railroad worker. After almost four days of glaring at me, the moment came when he actually told me the longest and the most credible story.

It was the last night before our arrival into Kuybyshev. After dark, there was a loud crunch of brakes, the feeble light of the inferior lamp lit up the compartment, and the raised bench cast a long shadow.

Apart from a new guest who had replaced the quartermaster from Leningrad and was snoring on an upper bunk, there were just the two of us. Our compartment and the ones either side of it had emptied. Everyone had gone to watch the game of dominoes.

The man in the jacket was an old Party activist. He told me he was on his way to one of the railroad lines beyond the Urals to conduct a "purge" of dubious elements, with letters of authorization from Kaganovich himself, whom he had known personally for many years. His status as a Party worker since the time of the revolution gave him a certain weight and a sense of his own worth—more than that, self-confidence. He appeared to be self-educated. He told me that he had just been to the front outside Moscow on official business.

"Did you see many German prisoners of war?" I asked.

"Very few," he replied without hesitation. "Most of them are finished off on the spot. In one section I saw a few prisoners of war, young men. They were in light overcoats, with their heads wrapped in our old women's headscarves, and they were addlepated with cold. Can you imagine, they were from the Afrika Korps! Under interrogation they admitted that their division had been brought here straight from Pomerania, where they'd been through months of training in specially constructed barracks where the temperature was kept at 30°C , and they'd only been given a small glass of water per day. These divisions were being prepared for Africa, but they were sent to the Soviet front, where it was 30°C too, but thirty below, and what's more they didn't have any winter uniforms.

"Once they'd been interrogated, the unit commander told his Cossacks to take them three miles into the countryside. Half an hour later the Cossacks were back. 'How come you were so quick?' asked the commander. 'It wasn't worth the bother—we shot them on the way there,' replied the Cossacks. What could the colonel do? Our soldiers know what the Nazis do to their comrades.

"When I drove from Moscow to the front lines," the railroad worker continued, still rolling tobacco in his nicotine-stained fingers with dirty nails, "in terrain that our men had recaptured from the Germans, there were still plenty of German corpses lying on the snow. It was extremely cold and there was deep snow, so our village children were pouring water over the corpses, which instantly froze, and then they were using them instead of sleds. They were sliding down the slopes on them. *Oni iz nikh delali sebye salazki* ... They made toboggans out of them ..."

He told me all this without comment, and without a smile. The conversation continued. Everything he said was precise, without the help of any ideological literature. All of a sudden we moved on to the topic on which never a word was spoken in Russia—the trials and purges of 1935 to 1937, in which hundreds of thousands were murdered and tortured, people with whom all of today's older Party activists had worked and fought for years.

"I had a friend," my interlocutor began again after a short silence. "We founded and ran a newspaper together in the town of N. once they'd thrown the Whites out of there. He was the editor—and such a well-educated, real intellectual! He was a good worker, who spared no effort, and he was smart, he knew everything; he was ... a good colleague and a good friend.

"But after a couple of years it emerged that when the Whites were there he'd been with them, and he'd written something for them (I already knew about it, but the man had only seen the light a little later than we had). So there was a trial. By then I knew plenty of high-up people in Moscow, so I went and spoke in his defense. He wasn't deported, and he was even given permission to go on writing for our paper. But once he had served his time in jail, he stopped being the editor but wrote reports on the regional economy instead and lived on that. He was no longer in any danger. But the devil got into him, and in 1935 he wrote a book *po ekonomicheskoi chasti*—to do with economics. He placed a lot of promise in this book, he had high hopes for it. And it was published, but by the time it came out, there was a different policy in force, and boom! They said the book was bad, with various deviations. So there was another trial, and the old stuff came up again."

He spoke without moving, with his dark eyes lowered most of the time, but whenever he raised them, he looked me straight in the face, without a shadow of deception or ambiguity.

"I did everything I could to defend him; one time the prosecuting magistrate even asked me how dare I defend a counterrevolutionary? They wanted me to testify to something that wasn't true, saying that if I didn't appear as a witness there might be consequences for me. But I told them who I was, that I always spoke the truth, and that the man was innocent. They didn't touch me, but I couldn't defend him ... and he was deported. And that was that—we'd worked together since the revolution, I don't know if he is alive or where he is."

The man in the jacket spoke at length, and in detail, telling me how he had fought for the man, how he had vouched for him, and how he had been accused of involvement in a conspiracy to which he had never belonged.

He sat almost motionless, hunched, from time to time methodically rolling a cigarette. He spoke in an even tone, without sudden stops or stresses. He regarded himself as protected, perhaps by the name of Kaganovich. I sensed no shadow of moral appraisal of the actual purges. I imagine he didn't doubt that every enemy of the Soviet Revolution had to be crushed. But he clearly felt outraged by the eradication of loyal people, unjustly condemned as a result of fraud, cowardice, and denunciation by second-rate organs. It was stifling him, and he clearly had to get it out of his system.

This self-educated man spoke to the last in his own tongue, without a hint of the language of propaganda. Maybe for the very reason that in his conviction and throughout his past life he had closely adhered to the ruling apparatus, he could easily be true to himself, and did not need to hide behind a smokescreen of platitudes.

The train was approaching Kuybyshev, so our conversation came to an end, as did the game of dominoes, and all the passengers returned to their own compartments. We packed up our belongings and said goodbye. There was one more holdup before Kuybyshev, one more wait sitting on our suitcases. We finally pulled into the station at night.

After five whole days in the same compartment, there was no longer any trace of mistrust between us, we'd eaten the same soups, flirted with the same conductors, and done a lot of talking. Nowhere in Russia did I ever manage to topple the walls of silence as often as in the trains, where the clank and rattle, and the almost anonymous, casual nature of the encounters created a sense, maybe illusory, of less of a threat, less chance of being denounced.

It was sad for me to part with these people.

While staying at the embassy in Kuybyshev, I tried to get in touch with one of my fellow passengers, but it proved totally impossible, even though I had a specific excuse for doing so, to swap bags that been inadvertently confused. But these people were afraid of the embassy, and they were afraid of me, just as Khodas had been a few days earlier in Moscow.

In Kuybyshev it was windless and rapaciously cold. An army vehicle dropped me off at the embassy. Everyone was asleep, except for Ambassador Kot. He was stooping over a table in the drawing room, laying out the cards for patience. I dumped a bag of French books from the Moscow booksellers on him—a remedy for his insomnia— and told him about my failed mission until late into the night. He listened closely.

"I did tell you there was no point in going and that you wouldn't achieve anything," he said pensively.

Then I stopped in Kuybyshev for a few weeks. I needed to compare the lists of missing men that we had compiled in the army and the ones coming in to the embassy. I had to straighten out a series of inaccuracies and mistakes. Names repeated from memory, sometimes with one letter changed, or incorrect dates, were causing a lot of misunderstanding. For this work, which affected and concerned literally everyone (for who was not looking for missing loved ones?), I was given the most far-reaching, sincere help by the entire staff of the embassy. I stayed at the embassy all day, dictating lists and correcting names and dates. One of the people who helped me was a young man from Wilno with thick fair hair, newly released from a camp. He was just a child when he was deported from Wilno to Russia; he found the laborious, almost mechanical work boring and longed to be in the army or the air force.

Soon after, he took off for Britain, and there he died an airman's death.

When the day was over we walked down the freezing, deserted streets to the apartment that acted as a sort of hostel for embassy officials and transient guests. During my stay there were about ten of us in a large room with dirty, tattered wallpaper and a large tile stove. Ten iron beds and a few Vienna chairs were the only furniture.

At a time when we were usually all asleep, midnight at the earliest, Władysław Broniewski would come back to the "hotel" from a game of bridge or from drinking and would crash into the room with a lot of noise. Who didn't know him? He was a superb poet, in the past he was an officer in Piłsudski's Legions, had won a Virtuti Militari medal for bravery, and as a communist he had been in jail a couple of times in independent Poland.

In Starobilsk we had found out from the Soviet press that he had been imprisoned as a *zlostny natsionalist*—a "malicious nationalist," and as a "traitor" who had apparently corrupted the working class.

Only released from Moscow's Butyrki prison after the "amnesty," at the time he was stuck at our embassy, waiting for permission to leave for Britain, which the Soviet authorities were refusing to give him.

Whenever he came home for the night, Broniewski would switch on the only light bulb in the room, which shone in everyone's eyes. He would respond to the curses of those whom he awoke with such colorful expletives that his opponents immediately felt beaten and fell silent; he was furious if any of us dared to be asleep when he came back. Once he had got into bed, and those unaware of what was ahead of them were expecting to get back to sleep again, he would start to declaim poetry.

I remember one of those nights, when the recital dragged on until after four in the morning. Even the sleepiest, and those least sensitive to poetry had given up complaining. We all listened to him, prompting him and reminding him of one or another of his poems.

> From the Vistula or from the Tatras
> A frosty gust of nostalgia blows,
> When onto the Polish tents at night
> The Orenburg wind showers snow.

This poem was new at the time, and he often had to recite it to us, as well as this one from his time in prison in Lwów:

> I never felt a breeze as sweet
> As I did then, in prison; now, as I write these lines
> I remember a young soldier, and listening hard
> To the hush of spring... I hear these words:
> Convict, step back—step back from the bars...

Then came others: "Miła Street," communist and revolutionary ones, such as "Magnitogorsk, or a Conversation with Jan," and "Bakunin," and some woven from the purest nostalgia for streams that "flow among the weeping willows," and for the Vistula:

> when the leaves of birches
> not yet very green,
> still daunted...

Broniewski would pepper these nocturnal performances with poems by Norwid, Słowacki, Blok, and Mayakovsky, jokes and murderous improvised stanzas, which gained him the greatest popularity and the most virulent enemies.

Even those of our roommates who had never picked up a book of poetry in their lives surrendered to the charm of these recitals. There were really no objections to the nights of poetry.

The next day it would be hard to recognize the pugnacious, aggressive companion who had kept us spellbound all night in the quiet, rather sleepy, and seemingly shy soldier-poet.

One day when I came back to the "hotel" our room was still empty, except for a couple of fellows sleeping on their beds. As there was no space left against the walls, a new bed had been placed right in the middle, under the electric lamp. The man lying on it had the bony look of a roadside figure of Jesus, an emaciated but extremely sympathetic face with a small beard. The fellows who had come in earlier had not put out the light, and the old man kept nervously shielding his face from it in his sleep. I found out from the men who were getting ready for bed that he was Professor Kościałkowski from Wilno, and he had just arrived from Sosva, one of the gloomiest camps, far out in the tundra, between the Urals and the Ob River, where he had buried many of his friends. His wife had been deported somewhere else, and he didn't know if she was still alive, or where. He had just arrived, at the embassy, after several weeks' journey in freight cars packed with soldiers, deportees, typhus sufferers, women, and children.

I put out the light. Gradually all our roommates dropped off and total silence reigned.

Suddenly the one and only light bulb came on sharply above the old man's face. Broniewski had rolled into the room at a loud and all too vigorous pace, showering us in curses of the most "seven-story" kind, as the Russians say, for daring to fall asleep without waiting for him to treat us to his stories and poetry.

By a joint effort, we only just managed to put the poet to bed, and to protect the old man from a sleepless night, the first he had spent among his own people at liberty.

We usually got up at eight, but next morning I awoke at half past seven and saw the professor, kneeling by his bed, immobile, immersed in a long prayer. At eight he was washed, neatly dressed, and introduced himself to us all. The first words he addressed to us were to apologize for having surely woken us up, as he was in the habit of getting up at seven, and no doubt he must have disturbed our sleep. We looked at his kind, modest face and wondered whether he was saying this ironically, considering all the noise there had been at midnight, all the expletives, the light coming on, and the triumphal entry of the poet, who could have woken the dead.

But there was no trace of irony on the professor's face, merely sincere goodwill and concern about his roommates' sleep.

Just after arriving the professor fell sick, and for several days he did not get up but lay surrounded by our constellation of iron beds; he told us what his life had been like beyond the Arctic Circle, on the other side of the Urals, and how he had founded a philological study group there to save the Polish language. Because like Radoński in Starobilsk, the professor too had been horrified by the ease with which in particular circumstances we all started to contract, impoverish, and coarsen our vocabulary, how we littered it with random Russianisms and linguistic sloppiness. And he was also shocked by our stereotypical abuse of the word *cholera*, which in Polish means "dammit!" and which he himself uttered in a hesitant whisper.

This distinguished historian, who in his youth in the czarist era had been a keen organizer of underground schools in Wilno, was one of his beloved native city's most famous figures and knew it better than just about anyone. Despite the tough years in exile, his mind had not lost a single spark of its brilliance. Gentle, eager to be of service to everyone, immeasurably grateful for everything, and often deep in prayer, he enchanted us all. I have met few people in my life who had the same sort of inner light, such unconstrained, natural goodness. It never occurred to him to moralize or lecture us. But his mere presence meant that we all behaved better; even our poet came back to the bedroom on tiptoes and undressed ever so quietly in the dark to avoid waking the professor, who would be fast asleep like an innocent child.

Some two years later a little book reached me in Italy: *L'Iran et la Pologne* (Edition de la Société Polono-Iranienne). It was by Professor

Kościałkowski. While living in Tehran in 1943 he had done a thorough study of cultural and diplomatic relations between Poland and Iran, compiled a considerable bibliography on the topic, and obtained a list of translations from Persian into Polish, starting with *The Gulistan* by Saadi, written in 1610 (the first European version of this work).

The professor's accurate academic study ended with a few sentences in which I immediately recognized the tone of voice of our dear companion from those nights in Kuybyshev: *"Le sort couvre l'avenir, même l'heure la plus proche, d'un voile noir et jaloux devant les yeux de l'homme. Mais nous savons tout à fait surement et sans aucun doute qu'Ormuzd vaincra Ariman."**

---

* "Fate shields the future from the eyes of man, even the next hour to come, with a black veil. But we know with total certainty and without any doubt that Ohrmazd will conquer Ahriman."

13. IN THE STEPPE

DURING my travels to Kuybyshev, Moscow, and back again, the Polish Army had been redeployed to Turkestan.

Back in October, in Totskoye, we had all longed desperately to get away from the steppes on the Volga, where our units were stuck in a few windy barracks, in dugouts, single-layer, windswept summer tents that weren't deeply entrenched, in rainstorms and blizzards, and then violent cold. The northern part of Turkestan, where there were vineyards, peach orchards, and where, so we were told, there was *kishmish* (dried fruit) to be had for a very low price on the free market—we spent our nights dreaming of this place.

Our commanders' insistence and efforts to have the army transferred further south had brought no result. Stalin had only agreed to the move after General Sikorski's visit, and following a dramatic discussion in which, without mincing his words, Sikorski had brought up the conditions for forming the army in the Soviet Union, in the presence of Ambassador Kot and General Anders.*

The redeployment began in early January, when the temperature was −58°F. But the evacuation of five divisions had to be interrupted for a couple of weeks because of a severe outbreak of typhus among the troops.

At the beginning of March, when I traveled to Turkestan, the entire army, including general staff, was scattered about Uzbekistan, Tajikistan, Kyrgyzstan, and Kazakhstan, all the way to Stalinabad,

---

* The text of the conversation is given verbatim in General Anders's book *Bez ostatniego rozdziału* (No Final Chapter).

below the Pamir Mountains, all the way to Jalalabad towards the Chinese border, and all the way to Alma-Ata.

General staff was located in Yungiyul near Tashkent, and that was where I went after completing my work at the embassy in early March.

The route of my journey was through Chkalov, the Hunger (or Mirzachul) Steppe on the Aral Sea, Kyzylorda (formerly Perovsk), and Tashkent.

Once again I traveled comfortably, in a soft railcar with a reservation, through abandoned Buzuluk, through "our" Totskoye, where I had spent the first "idyll" of freedom.

As we passed through Totskoye station, there was no sign of the *Polyaki* anymore. There in the snowy wasteland stood the dirty, shabby gray station block, like so many others, with a few Soviet soldiers and civilians in faded padded jackets or sheepskins trailing about.

Apart from the son of a Lwów professor, who was on his way to join the army too and had his nose stuck in a book, a notebook, or newspapers from dawn till dusk, I have preserved a fairly vivid memory of just one other traveling companion, a Russian thirty-something-year-old railroad worker. He was very haggard and gaunt; he had been sent out by the Commissariat for Communications with a few thousand other railroad men for *lesozagatovki*—timber felling. After a stop-off in Chkalov, he was due to go across the Urals, to join his comrades there. Because of the lack of fuel for transport, teams of railroad workers were being sent off to the forests to fell timber, and so to provide a supply of it for the railroad hubs. Here was further testimony to the lack of enough laborers in Russia, and it explained something that we had at one time found incomprehensible, which was the priority given to political prisoners when terrain under threat of German occupation was evacuated. They were the first to be deported, even sooner than Party workers, because they were the workforce so sorely lacking in Russia. We should remember that this workforce, which Russia so badly needed, was used up at an incredibly rapid rate. On average 30 percent of the labor camp population would die over the winter. I heard that in Kolyma 70 percent of an entire labor camp perished in the course of a single winter.

So my railroad worker had evidently been sent to fell timber because there were too few political prisoners, and perhaps in the hope that the actual railroad workers would be more enthusiastic to do the work for their own branch of industry.

He spent the whole time lying on an upper bunk, mostly asleep. I have a dim memory of his face in the gloom of a winter evening, the first time we talked. I thankfully remember that never for a moment did I sense the usual Russian mistrust of foreigners in him. Semisupine, resting on an elbow, with his head lowered, he humbly told me real, vivid things, in his own voice and his own words. He spoke of the mass panic that had only been restrained in the second half of October 1941 and of how there had been moments when everyone realized that Moscow's fate—the fate of the Soviet Union as a whole—was hanging by a thread.

"People were burning their Party documents and destroying equipment," said the railroad worker, smoking green homegrown tobacco. "They were destroying material rather than carting it away, and they cut the phone wires, even the tram cables—such fine cables!" (His greatest regret was for the tram cables in one of the towns outside Moscow.) "If Stalin hadn't remained in Moscow then, if he hadn't made that speech on the radio, on the sixth of October, then all would probably have been lost. But Stalin remained, and then everything changed." The railroad worker spoke sincerely and with conviction; he had spent a couple of months in the capital that winter, and now he was on his way back from there.

"If you knew what the famine is like in Moscow! There were times when I'd have paid fifty rubles just to put anything in my mouth, but there was absolutely nothing to be had, not even for that sort of money."

As I listened to him, I thought with shame of the buttered rolls, chops, and sweet cream the foreign correspondents and I had been eating at the very same time in the smart dining rooms at the National and the Metropole. Although he complained about the famine and the endlessly miserable conditions, his grievance was docile, with no grudge towards anyone, apart from the Germans.

"Why do the Germans think they're better than everyone else, when they've been banging it into our heads for the past twenty years that it's all the same if you're a Russki, an Uzbek, or a Jew—what makes them any better?"

He admitted to being extremely fond of reading. He talked with delight about Dickens's *Nicholas Nickleby*.

"When I like a book, I can't tear myself away from it," he confessed in a whisper, almost ashamedly. "Do you know, I once read without stopping from eleven at night to seven in the morning; I went on reading until I'd finished the book. What a wonderful book it was!"

"What was it called?" I asked.

"I can't remember the title," he replied after a pause, "but it was a novel by Sir Walter Scott."

On entering the compartment, I found a small volume lying in the net above my seat, the size and shape of a prayer book, clearly left behind by one of my predecessors. The cheap paper had gone yellow, and it had a shoddy cardboard cover. It was a collection of poems by Andrei Bely, published about fifteen years earlier in Soviet Russia. From then on this little volume, of perhaps the most musical Russian poems I have ever known, was with me all the way to Iraq, where I lent it to a young Polish poet, who lost it in the desert. In this volume I discovered two poems that shook me at the time. The first was written in 1908, after the collapse of the 1905 revolution, in the years when there was a wave of depression and suicides in those Russian circles that believed in revolution. In this poem, "Despair," Bely sees no alternative for Russia but to disintegrate, to dissolve into thin air like a nightmare; though no translation can possibly render the music of the poem, it ends like this:

> There, where disease and death
> Have blazed their infernal path,
> Disappear into space, disappear,
> O Russia, my Russia, my dear!

But in the same collection, a few pages further on there was a poem written in 1917, "Russia," full of mad, ecstatic enthusiasm, again expressed in stanzas full of brilliance and unique resonance. In it Bely writes about the Russian Revolution as the coming of a New Jerusalem:

> Weep not: O bend your knees
> Towards the fiery blaze,
> The thunder of seraph songs,
> The streams of cosmic days.
>
> The rays of His speechless gaze
> Will warm, when Christ appears,
> The arid wastes of shame,
> The seas of endless tears.
>
> ....
>
> And you, element of thunder,
> Rage till I burn away:
> O Russia, Russia, Russia,
> Messiah of the coming day.*

Both Blok and Bely, the greatest Russian poets of the prerevolutionary era, were intoxicated by the revolution and believed in its miraculous, regenerative power.

Blok died totally disappointed and abandoned, in 1921. Bely lived for much longer; after a brief semiemigration he returned to Russia, but he never again achieved the poetic heights of the period before the revolution. He wrote his memoirs, worked on formal issues to do with poetry, and died in 1934, almost forgotten, on the sidelines, more and more alien to the world whose founding he had greeted

---

*Translated by Gerard Shelley (1891–1980), originally published in *Modern Poems from Russia* (London: G. Allen & Unwin, 1942), cited in *1917: Stories and Poems from the Russian Revolution*, ed. Boris Dralyuk (London: Pushkin Press, 2016).

with such enthusiasm.* How many times I have seen Russian life within the bracket of these two poems since then!

In Chkalov I said goodbye to the friendly railroad worker, and our train continued on its journey southeast, crossing the Ural River toward Tashkent.

It was Catherine the Great who renamed the ancient Yaik River the Ural, banning the use of the old name, and "punishing" the river because the Pugachev rebellion erupted on its banks.

In a similar way Stalin gave orders for the name of the city Ordzhonikidze to be changed back to Vladikavkaz, because during the last war its citizens had rebelled against Soviet power.

Through the dirty train windows I could see the banks of the river—icebound and deserted, small by comparison with the neighboring Volga—which, according to Pushkin, were once densely forested, with wild boar and tigers lurking in the rushes. Today not only are there no wild boar or tigers there, but I saw no trace of any forest either.

These sad shores were the scene for the first act of one of the most dramatic episodes in the struggle of the Kalmyks against Russia. On the steppes between the Volga and the Yaik (today's Ural) River, large tribes of Kalmyk herders once lived a peaceful nomadic existence. They had come from the Chinese borders in the early eighteenth century, seeking the protection of the white czar, and ever since they had served Russia loyally. But some of them, oppressed and cruelly exploited by czarist officials, decided to escape Russia and return to China, having made a secret agreement with the Chinese government. And suddenly in 1771, on thirty thousand *kibitka* wagons they crossed to the other side of the Yaik and headed toward their old homeland. The Russian government did its best to stop them, ordering the Yaik Cossacks to pursue them. But it was February, and without enough food, when their horses began to die of hunger, the Cossacks refused to continue

---

*As *Pravda* wrote about Bely on August 8, 1947: "leader of the symbolists, representative of reactionary obscurantists, a renegade in politics and art."

the pursuit and turned back. Only the Kyrgyz Cossacks and their khans attacked the Kalmyks, having old scores to settle with them, as well as being part of the regular Russian troops. The units ordered to pursue the Kalmyks also included a few exiled Polish Confederates, made to join the Russian army, who took advantage of this expedition to escape to their homeland. Over a year of constant fighting as they tried to defend their families from pillage, the Kalmyks kept moving toward China. In 1772 the Buryats reduced them to total despair by forcing them onto the spacious, sandy steppe, where hunger and thirst wiped out thousands of their people and cattle. When after incredible hardships they finally reached the Chinese border, a chain of Chinese sentries forbade them entry into China. They were only allowed to cross the border on one condition: yielding their independence.

The Kalmyks totally surrendered to the Chinese. Their commander, Ubashi, had left Russia with 30,000 kibitkas and 169,000 people of both sexes but entered China with no more than 70,000 followers. In one year, 100,000 of them had been lost to the sword, illness, and wild animals or had been captured and forced into slavery.

On the same Yaik River, in connection with their refusal to catch the Kalmyks, mutiny erupted among the Yaik Cossacks. A year later the Pugachev rebellion raged on this terrain, spreading slaughter and arson all the way to Kazan, which was captured by Pugachev,* and threatening Moscow; at one point it shook the foundations of the empire.

Even this highly dangerous rebellion was crushed too, and Pugachev was publicly quartered in a Moscow square (a packed crowd of Muscovites spent all night waiting for the spectacle, watching as the executioners sat on a high platform, drinking wine). The very name of Pugachev was condemned to oblivion on the highest orders. The order was so strict that when Pushkin was writing his history of the

---

*In his *Memoirs of Soplica* Henryk Rzewuski describes Kazan in that era as follows: "In Kazan we found so many of our people that if a man were to fall from the moon he might think he had landed in a Polish city, until he looked around and saw nothing but Orthodox churches, and no Catholic ones there." The large number of Poles were exiled Confederates.

rebellion on commission from Nicholas I, he found it very hard to extract any information from the old people who had witnessed those events—none of them yet dared to utter that dreadful name.

Since the days when 169,000 Kalmyks crossed this river on their flight to China, and since the days of the Pugachev rebellion, how many more revolts and massacres there have been, nowadays known as "pacifications."

After the revolution a Kalmyk Republic was found on the Caspian Sea, but in 1945 on Stalin's orders it vanished without trace from the map of the Soviet republics, while its entire Kalmyk population was shot or exiled to an unknown location for their hostile attitude to the Soviet Union during this war.

How many times, by exterminating whole tribes or wiping out whole nations or republics, from Novgorod under Ivan the Terrible to the Kalmyk, Crimean, and Chechen Republics under Stalin, by changing the names of rivers, or by changing their system, has Russia condemned its own past to dishonor or oblivion? But has anything ever changed for the better in the very fabric of those ruling Russia, have they become better, more sympathetic, more human?

From the Yaik-Ural River I traveled across boundless steppe, all the way from Sol-Iletsk to far, far beyond the Aral Sea I did not see a single tree, just the same snowy, even expanse like an ocean, with no buildings, no trees, and almost no people.

At the rare stations there was a handful of low mud huts with flat roofs buried under the snow, so small and with such heaps of snow surrounding them that at first glance they didn't look like human habitations but animal dens.

I arrived at the Aral Sea after four days on the train from Kuyby-shev. Here I saw the same low mud huts, tall stacks of salt covered with straw, and a few Kazakhs in fur caps and mainly sheepskins. One of them came right past our railcar, in a hare fur hat and some-thing like a chasuble made of heavy, lemon-yellow silk embroidered with various patterns. It positively shone against the background of mud huts and endless snow.

At one of the junctions a Kazakh woman went past us in a purple coat. These splashes of color were a novelty for me—I had grown unaccustomed to seeing them in Russia, where the crowd always wore such faded, threadbare clothes that one saw almost nothing but gray. Here everyone wore large russet-and-silver or black-and-silver fur hats, with large earflaps either side of the face.

As I gazed at the passers-by, Kazakhs—the steppe Kyrgyz, at their flat faces with strong cheekbones and lively, mobile, rather leporine eyes—I wondered why they seemed so familiar. What did they remind me of?

From deep in my memory a vivid image emerged of a painting by Józef Brandt in a heavy gilded frame that used to hang in my family home. Today's direct impressions of the East were like an overprint on top of that old, now rather faded memory: the steppe, Tatars chasing some Cossack horsemen who, loaded with booty, are fording a river amid long grass. Their horses are up to their bellies in water, and one of the Cossacks is holding a thick flagstaff. Against a sapphire-blue night sky and the red light of a distant glow, high above shines a slender crescent moon, and below the Tatars' curved swords. One of the Tatars is wearing a red coat, like the Kazakh woman whom I had just spotted at the station. I can still see this painting with the delighted eyes of childhood; for us it illustrated *With Fire and Sword* and was naturally a masterpiece. Nowadays I imagine its artistic value must have been quite low, but the portrayal of the people of the East was clearly apt, if I was now seeing exactly the same faces on the Aral Sea—thanks to Brandt they seemed warmly familiar.

As I crossed this terrain, passing the mute local people at quiet stations, I realized how little I knew about it. What could I say about this land of invasions and massacres, from Genghis Khan to the Russian czars and the Soviet powers?

It was the same steppe, with the same faces as centuries ago; at the stations, replacing toppled statues of the czar, there were wretched little monuments to the "prophets": Lenin and Stalin, usually a head, or a bust in imitation bronze on a whitewashed pillar. At some of the stations, for a huge sum of money one could buy *lepioshki*, or sheep's cheese. At every station there were Moscow newspapers in Russian on sale, and also local ones in the native language or printed in the Russian alphabet. Soviet reforms in this sphere had been made in stages: first the Arabic alphabet had been replaced with a specially modified Roman alphabet, after quelling the complaints of the population's "reactionary strata," who were used to the Arabic alphabet, but then the previous reformers were eliminated, and the Roman alphabet was replaced with Cyrillic.

Beyond the Aral Sea, the train ran almost parallel with the Syr-Darya River. This was one of the main routes of Russian expansion in the nineteenth century. In the second half of the nineteenth century the Russians took control of the Syr-Darya valley and captured Tashkent, now the capital of Uzbekistan. According to the new official history, and also to the memoirs, the distinct advantages of the Russian army meant one long cycle of slaughter and pogroms, sparing neither women nor children. The Russian elimination in this period of three independent Central Asian buffer states—Kokand, Khiva, and Bokhara—was to some extent a classic repetition of the partitions of Poland, using the same method of successive dismemberment of the approaches to the buffers, playing larger or smaller states off against each other, for "threatening the Empire," or even being "imperialist"; just as in Europe they had done this to Poland, so in Asia they had done it to Bokhara. All this constant fighting resulted in the biological destruction of the Asiatic nations, instant colonization, the forcible removal of the population from the richest irrigated terrain, and their replacement with Russians and Ukrainians.

Anti-Russian feelings in these countries were extremely strong. There's a Kyrgyz saying: "If you have a Russian friend, keep a stone up your sleeve." In Uzbekistan an ugly boy is called *urusbaj*—"like a Russki." How could those feelings possibly have changed now, since the most recent disappointed hopes, the latest waves of rebellion and Soviet suppression?

Most of my traveling companions were Russian officers, and Russian speech was constantly audible. They treated me with an attitude that was at the very least correct, and often courteous. Just once, at one of the stations a young officer passed our railcar, wearing a cap set at a rakish angle, a tightly belted *gymnastyorka* (or soldier's tunic), and an insolent look on his face.

"What's a Polish officer doing here?" he called in my direction. "Wouldn't you do better to fight on the spot instead of bolting all the way here? Get the hell back to where you came from—what are you shoving in here for?"

This was the only incident of this kind that I encountered on my journey. It was widely known that we were here in Russia after two years of "compulsory" internment in the camps. But I also heard of another incident when a Russian officer refused to offer his hand to a Polish officer, of whom all he knew was that he was a Pole.

"The Poles are enemies of the Soviets. I don't trust them," he had said. He had clearly failed to keep up with the political slalom according to which Soviet citizens were told for a short time to "love the heroic Poles"; meanwhile he was honestly drawing conclusions from what the Soviet press had been writing about Poland for the past few years.

Throughout the journey, traveling in the soft carriage, all the passengers I met were Russian, except for one Kyrgyz *politruk*. He was coming home from a two-year course for *politruki* in Moscow. He was bursting with political slogans, all of which explained everything in Stalinist terms, and he spoke incomprehensible Russian, swapping vowels and consonants that were clearly difficult for Kyrgyz pronunciation, as a child might do. Broad-shouldered and quite plump, he addressed me with a timid, extremely polite smile, wanting to make closer acquaintance. He talked about politics, constantly repeating that Stalin was a true prophet who foresaw everything. On his plump, flat face, in those sympathetic eyes shining like beads, I could read a childlike faith in Stalin-the-prophet. But maybe I was wrong. It's hard to guess what a man from the East is thinking in his own oppressed country. In those days I knew too little about the recent history of the Kyrgyz, and there were too many Soviet officers present for us to be able to tell each other much.

Naturally, for centuries Islam had been a focal point for anti-Russian movements. In the eighteenth century Russia had tried to destroy Islam through forced conversion to Christianity, but after the Bashkir rebellion (1754–55), and then the Pugachev rebellion (1773–75), it was ostensibly legalized. The mufti was appointed by the minister for internal affairs, and the only mullahs allowed to perform their duties were those who showed distinct "reliability and loyalty" to the czar.

All this appeared to have changed entirely since the revolution. Subordinated and stifled by the czar, Islam was now exploited by the Bolsheviks; in the beginning, the hatred of Mohammedan circles was played off against the czar. After the February revolution, in May 1917 an Islamic congress was established in Moscow, composed of national democrat elements. It demanded broad economic, national, and religious autonomy for the Muslims. A decree of the Provisional Government refusing individual subjugated ethnicities the right to absolute self-determination prompted deep dissatisfaction among the Islamic nations, which facilitated the campaign of the Bolsheviks, who demanded the most radical amendment to allow self-determination, "including separation." In this way the Bolsheviks exploited the ethnic minorities whom the democratic revolution had failed to win over. On December 16, 1917, an appeal signed by Lenin and Stalin was issued to the Islamic nations: "You are the sole masters of your own fate." In the same appeal, Lenin and Stalin delivered to the Muslims "the most sacred Osman's Koran," removed from Samarkand by the Russians. Lenin understood the need to treat "with particular care surviving national feelings in the longest oppressed countries"; one and the same Lenin also wrote: "we would be very poor revolutionaries if in the proletariat's great war of liberation for socialism we did not know how to exploit every national movement."

Here in the land I was now crossing, exchanging polite generalities with the Kyrgyz *politruk*, in 1916 a universal rebellion had erupted among the steppe Kyrgyz, whom the czarist government had mobilized for labor behind the front. As a result of this uprising thousands of people were shot: some three hundred thousand of them were Kyrgyz, just as in the days of Catherine the Great the victims had been the Kalmyks, emigrating to China.

At the start of the revolution the Kazakhs (as the steppe Kyrgyz were called) created the Alash Party. It declared Kazakhstan to be autonomous, under the name Alash-Orda, and also established co-operation with the Kazan Tatars, the Kalmyks, and the Bashkirs, and with Turkestan. The Bolsheviks were promoting total independence. The Alash-Orda government tried to establish cooperation with the Finnish directorate and demanded recognition for Kazakhstan's autonomy. But naturally the Russian White movement combated these ambitions for autonomy and threw the Kazakhs into the embrace of the communists, who were calling for the self-determination of nations. The Kazakhs fought against the White commander Kolchak under the leadership of Bolshevik Mikhail Frunze, who would go on to crush their later uprisings with total ruthlessness. The Soviets then declared the Kyrgyz Autonomous Soviet Socialist Republic (ASSR), the Turkestan ASSR, and a large number of top Russian communists, such as Kaganovich and Frunze, were on the revolutionary commit-tees in these countries. Kazakhstan went through many years of civil war, in which hundreds of thousands of Kazakhs perished, not just in battle but simply of hunger.* And then a Bolshevik called Tobolin declared at one of the central executive committees: "Being eco-nomically weak from the Marxist point of view, the Kazakhs have to die out anyway. So rather than combating famine, it is more im-portant for the revolution to maintain support for the fronts (in the civil war)."

The vast majority of the nation took an anti-Russian stance and organized insurgent units, which from 1925 operated against the Russians, both White and Red, throughout the territory. From 1925 to 1930 the Communist Party waged a constant battle against Kazakh nationalist tendencies; in this period about 100,000 Kazakhs were deported to the Far East and to Siberia.

*In his book *Turkestan pod vlastyu sovietov* (Turkestan Under Soviet Power, Paris 1935) Mustafa Shokay calculates the number of famine victims from the revolution to 1921 on the basis of Soviet sources at 1,114,000. *Pravda* (June 1920) wrote of "over a million Kazakhs" who died of hunger and fighting in the period of civil war and terror in Kazakhstan.

Such was the fate of the Kazakhs, also known as the steppe Kyrgyz.

What about the highland Kyrgyz? Some 260,000 Kyrgyz had already gone across to Mongolia or died fighting the Russians in the nineteenth century.

As among the steppe Kyrgyz, in 1916 an uprising erupted among the highlanders too. As a result of forced conscription, 450,000 highland Kyrgyz were either exterminated or ran away to China. The 1917 revolution was played out there among Russian immigrant elements. Revolutionary committees were formed consisting of former officials or criminals, who did not alter their attitude to the population. National self-awareness increased, moving in an anti-Russian, pan-Turkic direction. In December 1918, some two years of continuous anti-Bolshevik insurgency began. A Kyrgyz peasant army was formed under the command of Konstantin Monstrov. Red Russian troops crushed this uprising as cruelly as the czarist army had done. At this point more than 150,000 highland Kyrgyz were massacred, as kulaks and agents of imperialism.

Kyrgyz patriots within the Bolshevik Party tried to maintain separatist tendencies. In 1922, of 2,975 Party members there were 2,254 Kyrgyz, but the purge of 1923–24 eliminated 1,800 Kyrgyz communists for nationalism, of the entire total of 2,254!

Then the Kyrgyz grouped within the Basmachi troops, which had fought against czarist Russia in the past. These troops conducted a campaign of insurgency throughout the whole of Turkestan. Poles coming to join the army told me how they had passed through a vast number of villages that were totally ruined and deserted, from where the entire population had been deported for rebelling, and how there were vast graveyards in the mountains, the burial site of thousands of Basmachi, hacked to death by Budyonny's cavalry.

Only ten years earlier Guzar, the site of our army organizational center in 1942, had had 40,000 inhabitants. In 1942 it had only 4,500, following the pacification conducted in the region by Budyonny in 1936.

But then, as I sat in the train with the friendly Kyrgyz *politruk*, I didn't know the history of these lands, I hadn't yet heard my comrades' endless stories of how in every labor camp, from Vorkuta to Kolyma, and as far as the Lubyanka and Butyrki, they had met crowds of exiles from Central Asia—Kyrgyz, Uzbeks, Tajiks, and Kalmyks. The one and a half million Poles deported in 1939 were just the next stage in the policy of exterminating nations that refused to submit passively to Soviet dictatorship. For years this extermination had been ongoing most precisely and consistently, as if "without witnesses," in Turkestan.

I wonder if after returning to his country the Kyrgyz *politruk* remained in his post for long. Maybe he's now stuck in a camp in the north, condemned for "malicious nationalism."

While I was traveling to Tashkent, my friend Professor Aleksandrowicz was also on his way there by train, but from Bokhara. There was just one other passenger in his compartment, an Uzbek who spoke Russian well. The professor steered the conversation toward great moments in Asia's past and questioned his companion about Genghis Khan and Tamerlane. They happened to be near Samarkand, in Tamerlane's home territory. The Uzbek talked to the professor long into the night. He told him with great sincerity how after the Bolshevik Revolution the progressive Uzbek classes had got down to work. Large groups were sent to schools in Russia and even abroad, and many people thought a time of freedom had set in, which would provide an opportunity for the rapid development of their own culture, taking from the West whatever proved most advantageous for these countries. It was then that the Roman alphabet was adopted, with the required modifications. None of this first generation of intellectuals, educated at European universities, remained; the Soviet authorities had eliminated them all. Regarding this spontaneous drive for culture as nationalism, the Soviet government had started all over again, selecting and forming cadres consisting of people who were blindly servile to Moscow. Then in its turn the Roman alphabet was removed and replaced with the Russian one.

That was the reality of the Bolshevik call for the right to total self-determination, "including separation." If in the second half of the nineteenth century the czarist government conducted a policy in the Near East analogous to the one it had conducted a hundred years earlier toward Poland, at the time of the partitions, then I wonder whether nowadays in Soviet policy the reverse order was emerging. In his book,* which is a well of astonishing facts, figures, and quotations, Ryszard Wraga writes as follows on this topic: "We can see a pattern throughout the territory of the Soviet Union with regard to the successive exploitation of national elements in order to destroy nationalist movements. In the initial phase, outbreaks of national independence ambitions were destroyed on the basis of the idea that all the ethnic elements in the given country or nation were reactionary, imperialist, or capitalist factors. In the next phase, as federalism was implemented, they were destroyed by local revolutionary elements, the rural or proletarian poor, and by anarchist and all kinds of national separatist elements. In the third phase, in the transition from federation to union, all, even the most revolutionary and democratic anti-imperialist national elements who dared to insist on striving for autonomy or federal rights, were destroyed. In Central Asia this pattern was fully applied, with the first phase shortened to the minimum."

On my way to Tashkent in March 1942, I only guessed at all this, as I gazed at the quiet, as if mute, skulking figures of the local people, among the alien swarm of Russian officers, soldiers, and officials.

Somewhere near Kyzylorda it stopped snowing. Past Zhosaly the snow was completely gone. On both sides of the track the same boundless steppe stretched into the distance, no longer white but gray, just as deserted and treeless as ever. Only on the sixth day of the journey did we start to feel that we were going south, toward the spring. At one of the stations, whose name escapes me, we had to switch to another train. It was extremely overcrowded, without any

*Sowieckie Republiki Środkowo-Azjatyckie (The Central Asian Soviet Republics), Rome, 1946, 101.

reservations, and I couldn't even find room to stand in a compartment. I installed myself and my luggage by a door in the corridor, with a lot of other passengers. I was rewarded a hundredfold, because here I could watch the local inhabitants trying to get on board and look at a new country and new landscape.

It was warm, the sun was shining, and there was an odor of wet earth. The ground was undulating, the earth suddenly became russet, even red in places, and covered in withered grass. The hills on either side of the railroad track were gently rounded, and to the east, in a sunlit, faint touch of mist, a mountain range showed blue in the distance.

Next to me in the corridor stood a young Soviet NCO. We instantly became acquainted. He was a bit tipsy. He told me he was going on leave from the front and had been wounded. In the process he embellished his story with some improbable nonsense about his own heroism, including a claim that as an artilleryman he had in person shot down seventy-six German aircraft. This record number stuck in my memory. His eyes shone, not just with joy but also good fortune. His light wound was healing, he was on leave, thousands of miles from the front, and there was vodka. He declared his love of the Polish allies to me.

Meanwhile, Uzbeks kept pushing their way into the railcar, coming and going as much as possible, through the door and over the buffers. Women in colorful shawls, with countless tiny braids, necklaces made of coins, and silver bracelets. They had a matte brown complexion and very dark eyes. The men wore long handwoven coats and turbans. All the old ones were bearded, moving quietly and nimbly, with agile, rather catlike actions, clambering onto the buffers in total silence. The first impression of the race suggested a sort of dignity, a self-contained world with an ancient culture, cut off from us outsiders. They all carried little knotted parcels and sacks. The ones who failed to get inside the train rode on the steps, clinging on outside. An old Uzbek had installed himself against the railcar door that the artillery NCO and I were leaning against, gazing through the window; he was in a long brown robe, with a light-gray turban and a small sack under his arm. His bony, wrinkled face was ringed by a white beard, and he had the swarthy complexion of a man who lives in the fields, out in the sun. He was riding on the outer steps of the railcar, calmly curled up, clutching the handrails. When the conductor came along and demanded through the window to see his ticket, the Uzbek showed it to him. My companion, the hero from the front still in jolly holiday mood, gave the Uzbek a friendly smile. Then suddenly something occurred to him. Quick as a flash, for no reason, while the train was going at full speed along tracks winding downhill, he yanked the door open, and in an abrupt burst of rage began to kick the Uzbek in the chest, trying to toss him off the steps.

"*Uzbetska svoloch, pashol von!*" he cried—"Get lost, you Uzbek scum!"

The old man was very strong and clung to the iron handrail even tighter, refusing to let himself be pushed off. He didn't say a word in reaction, and his face hardly changed, just gaining a few more wrinkles around his squinting eyes. But the expression in those eyes was a sight to be seen.

With some difficulty I tried to pull the hero away from the Uzbek, dragging him by the coattails and explaining that he had no right to throw the man off, and that I had seen his ticket. Taking no notice of me, he went on kicking the old man. Red blotches came out on his face. Suddenly he turned to me, his eyes white with rage, and said: "Oh yes, so you like defending counterrevolutionaries, do you? Where's the NKVD officer here? I know these rascals well, they're all profiteers—just take a look in his bag, they're all taking rice to Tashkent, the swine!"

None of the passengers reacted to this incident with a single word or gesture, or even a change of facial expression.

The Russian writer Ivan Goncharov, author of *Oblomov*, made a journey to Japan in 1858, which he wrote about in a book called *The Frigate Pallas*. There he describes a scene he witnessed in China: a British officer was walking down the street of a Chinese city, languidly grabbing the pigtail of any Chinese who didn't immediately make way for him and pulling him into the gutter. At first surprised, the

Chinese would gaze after him, wearing "a smile of stifled indignation."
Goncharov, who contrasts this description in one of the later chapters
with the idyll of fraternity between a Cossack and a Korean, ends
the scene with the Englishman and the Chinese by writing: "I wonder who here is supposed to be teaching civilization to whom."

As I bade farewell to my "hero" amid the crowd of Uzbeks, Russian
soldiers, and officers, I remembered Goncharov.

14. YUNGIYUL I

On a dark night, in pouring rain I arrived at a station some ten miles from Tashkent. From there I walked to Yungiyul.

Yungiyul means "new road" in Uzbek. With a sack on my back, in deep, unbelievably slippery mud, I rambled for several miles, falling over and wading onward over the hills. Covered in mud, soaked to the skin, and furious, I finally reached our tents at around one o'clock. A merciful gendarme let me sleep on a table in one of the offices.

The big white general staff building stood in a large orchard, with a huge red-and-white flag on the roof. Right next to it were some small white cottages with verandas, where General Anders and a few of the senior officers were accommodated. The rest of the staff employees were in tents or in the nearest small town and villages.

At the edge of the orchard, on rounded, russet hills, by a yellow "Chinese" stream that skirted the orchard in a deep ravine, there were dozens of tents, pitched in exemplary style, wooden standards painted red and blue, a brand new pillbox with a sentry standing under it, and carefully laid-out paths. Every day at noon the division bugler played the Mariacki bugle call.

Across the river there were some small clay houses with almost flat roofs and tall fences, also made of clay, and some large Asiatic trees, quite like the poplars that grow on the Vistula.

A few days after occupying our staff building, while installing electrical cables our electricians discovered a series of bugging devices fitted into the ceilings of several of the rooms assigned to be our main offices. They had to be quietly eliminated, just like the analogous fittings we had found at general staff in Buzuluk. The NKVD authorities had to put on a brave face and accept the elimination of their laboriously installed secret surveillance system without complaint.

The orchard in which the general staff buildings stood was large and well tended, with several thousand old apple, cherry, peach, and apricot trees on a high bank of the Kurkuldyuk River, where the rolling hills sloped gently down to the water. The orchard was irrigated. At sunset, on hot spring and summer evenings, the whole place suddenly began to bubble gently, as the *aryk* (or ancient irrigation system) was activated, carrying water to every little tree; a few minutes later every single one was standing in water, and as the ground was hilly, this irrigation performed by the simplest means (little ditches or wooden troughs running above the paths) gave the impression of a miracle. To us it was as if the Uzbeks, ancient specialists in this art, even knew how to make the life-giving streams of water flow uphill.

The original owners of the orchard were two Uzbeks who had also founded a large preserved fruit factory and distributed their products all over Russia. Both of them were murdered during the revolution and the orchard had passed into state ownership.

When I arrived at general staff, the trees were still bare. In the first few weeks it poured with rain almost every day, the constant damp was a torment, and there was thick mud everywhere. At the same time the temperature was up to 60°F under a cloudy sky. The leafless trees had yet to finish their winter sleep. It was like the atmosphere in a bathhouse.

On fine days we could see a mountain range in the distance, its ridges stretching along the entire horizon to the north and southeast.

As soon as the gray sky cleared, it became strangely blue, acquiring a brighter color than I had ever seen before, vivid peacock-blue. Was it the contrast with the brown clay and the pink branches? Or was it really an unusual color, different from the sky in Poland, or in Italy, and totally different from the sky in Vologda and Gryazovets, where above the subtle green of the birch trees it was so pale blue as to look diluted, like watercolor?

My first strong impressions of this new country included the wealth and novelty of the human types to be encountered there. As well as the flat faces and high cheekbones of the Uzbek bearded men, and the strong, chiseled shapes of the Uzbek women, there were other faces, almost Chinese, with fine features, fragile, slender-boned figures with eyes as black as beads, numerous little braids, and great subtlety, mildly superior and aloof in their movements and expression.

To the very end I was never able to get a grip on the incredible mixture of ethnicities and types. Apart from Uzbeks, Turkmens, and Kazakhs, there were also numerous Koreans who had been resettled en masse from Manchuria to Uzbekistan for the rice harvest. Apart from that, there was a large number of Russian officials and factory workers (from the preserved fruit factories), and a lot of Ukrainians, mostly women with children, deported some dozen years earlier in the days when the collective farms were being introduced in Ukraine. The men, kulaks apparently numbering three or even five million, had been exiled to the far north, while the women and children had been driven into Central Asia. In the typical Uzbek villages, where all the cottages are made of raw clay, amid the bubbling aryks and lush greenery of the fruit trees, poplars and maize, nowadays you can find whitewashed, thatched cottages, as if transported from Ukraine.

I was given quarters along with a colleague about a mile from general staff, in one of these typically Ukrainian white thatched cottages. We had a clean room in the home of two single women. The older one was constantly at work, in a white apron over her large belly, and her still young daughter-in-law was thin and very active. A few graying blond locks protruded from under her headscarf, shielding a brow cut across by a deep furrow of constant care. They had one feature in common: both of them were always silent. I don't think we exchanged more than a few sentences in the first few weeks, apart from the most practical conversations to do with our accommodation. They were attentive, clean, always very busy and very sad. They had a cow and a patch of garden, and the younger one worked at a factory. I can still see the kind, pale eyes of the old Ukrainian woman, and I remember her as if I knew all about her, but in fact I know nothing.

Every day I went to work at general staff across a little bridge guarded by sentries who only let people with passes through, then across the orchard, amid the trees, at first bare, then covered with blossom. The wooden bridge had been slung across the mountain river Kurkuldyuk, whose dense, fast-running water was the color of milky coffee. This was the official access to general staff. But in my time I was told that for fifteen rubles the specialist Jews at the station would guide anyone wanting to reach general staff without a pass via side roads.

After submitting a detailed report of my journey to my superiors, I went back to the abandoned task I had started in Buzuluk, and thus to the card index of missing people. During my absence it had grown immensely on the basis of more and more letters from people looking for their relatives, and other information received. The work was being run by Mr. Bala, former mayor of a major city in Wielkopolska. I had already met him in Totskoye, during the first few weeks of the army's formation on the steppe. Mr. Bala had had to leave his home-town in September to escape a German arrest warrant; on his way to Lwów with his six-year-old son he had run into a skirmish between Soviet troops and a surrounded Polish unit. His son had been wounded in the head by a stray bullet, and all the father knew was that a Soviet colonel had put the child in his car and driven him to a nearby Polish field hospital. With no idea if his son was lightly or seriously injured, Mr. Bala had tried to reach the hospital to find out what had happened to him. But he hadn't been allowed to visit the child, and the next morning he was deported into the depths of Russia. Since then the most contradictory tales had reached him about his son, first that the Soviet colonel had been delighted by the charming child and had taken him with him, then that a month after the accident another prisoner he encountered had apparently seen the boy playing happily in the hospital garden—but neither letters nor inquiries had brought any result. Mr. Bala always carried a photograph of his son in his worn-out wallet, a lovely child with light eyes and fair hair in a sailor suit. This broad-shouldered man had grown thin and miserable. Worrying about his child was killing him, and you could see in his eyes that his mind was always preoccupied. He fulfilled the duties of a fifty-year-old soldier most conscientiously, never trying to wriggle out of them—morning exercises, gymnastics, and assembly. He once told me with a benevolent smile that as he was trying on his battledress he hadn't noticed a young officer, had failed to salute him, and was sternly rebuked.

"Don't you know what the army is? Where and when did you do your military service in Poland?"

The fifty-year-old mayor humbly replied that he hadn't served in the army since 1920, and that as a private soldier he had "only" taken part in the liberation of Wielkopolska from the Germans and in the 1920 campaign against the Bolsheviks. Then the young officer added in a confident tone: "I always knew the soldiers of 1920 weren't real soldiers."

It was in Totskoye that I had involved Mr. Bala in our work. Right from the start, from dawn till dusk he had slaved over the lists and files of names. Now he was no longer on his own. About a dozen energetic women, most of whom had missing relatives too, worked under his management, never sparing any time or effort.

But what did it matter? We had more and more cards, more and more precise information about those missing, and less and less hope that the Soviet authorities were willing to take an interest in these people's fate. Our telegrams and urgent demands for their return were daily bread for the Soviets, whose replies were rare and almost always negative. My commanders admitted that the original aim of this work was becoming less and less realistic and that there was less and less hope of saving those people.

Those first weeks in Yungiyul are associated in my memory with a sense of the fruitlessness of my work and a diminished will to live.

The long-desired south that we had yearned for on the snowy, violently cold steppes had many surprises in store for us. As far as physical resilience was concerned, the far north was much less of a threat to the health of the emaciated Polish masses than the south, where typhus, dysentery, and other diseases decimated our population. I had a hard time getting used to the new climate and the humidity. On top of that, my failure in Moscow, and my journey back to Poland in the opposite direction (we were as far from Warsaw as from Singapore) combined to produce a permanent feeling that ever since leaving actual Poland my entire life had been an illusion.

I remembered the Belarusian who had left the Minsk area with us after the Bolshevik invasion in 1918. He had even gotten himself a good job in Warsaw as a caretaker, but he could never find his place in the foreign city. Every month he went to see his sister, in her student room on Nowy Świat Street, and stood motionless in the corner, asking: "Well, missie, when are we going home?"

Months later, one day he came to see her, as if he had something very important to say, and once again he asked: "When are we going home?" Then, staring at the floor, he added: "Because the way I see it, the place where a man is born is the place where he should die."*

Maybe all our work, compiling those card indexes, and issuing all those futile demands, was just a way of deceiving ourselves and others, I thought bitterly.

In this mood all my efforts went into coming to work each morning, doing my shift, and going back to the cottage each evening. On top of that, every second afternoon, first in the block, then under the apple trees, the whole staff underwent military training. In this period the Germans were still advancing toward Stalingrad and into the Caucasus. There was talk of the possibility of a landing. So there were lectures on air raids, landings, air campaigns, artillery, and on assembling and disassembling machine guns. After a day of office work, in the stuffy air, I listened to those talks half asleep and to no avail. Only a talk about the defense of Moscow by an old Soviet general, and another one on the fighting at Narvik by General Szyszko-Bohusz, who took part in the Norwegian expedition, have stayed more vividly in my memory. There were also lectures within private circles, where people gathered and talked about everything. At one of the white cottages assigned to the senior officers I ended up at a talk by Father

---

*We once told this story to a sympathetic American woman, who came to Poland in 1920 with the American Red Cross mission. She was most indignant. "Nothing of the sort!" she said. "One should die in a completely different place from where one was born!"

Kamil Kantak on the Apocalypse. He kept coming back to the Jewish question, quoting the *Protocols of the Elders of Zion* as if it were the holy gospel and talking about the latest research by Russian scholars (on the basis of stories heard from an academic he had met in prison). I only remember one statement, that the sky was supposedly "hard"...

We were sitting on the cottage's white veranda, with the sun warming us through the leafless apple boughs. I listened to it all with an almost physical sense of alienation and inertia. None of it seemed remotely relevant to the present moment—it was all quite fruitless.

On the social front, who wasn't there at general staff? And as ever, it was the most colorful, noisy characters who attracted the most attention. There was a captain with graying hair and large blue eyes, who had only just arrived from Kolyma. Known for his good looks, as a womanizer and horse-lover, he was a Małopolska landowner. War, disaster, Kolyma—nothing had changed him.

During a conversation in our canteen, the captain said: "How idiotic, fancy having Kot as our ambassador!"

I cocked an ear—I thought there were some differences in political views coming. I asked him what he meant, to which he replied: "Kot, Kot, what sort of a name is that?"*

"As I'm sure you know, Professor Kot is a brilliant scholar," I replied.

"A scholar! What I'd like to know, sir, is whether this Kot knows which side to mount a horse." And he went into a long diatribe, full of admiration for his own wife, about how a horse had thrown her under its hooves, but thanks to her presence of mind, she had managed to escape this dangerous accident unharmed.

"I'd like to see Kot in a similar situation. I'm sure he wouldn't cope!"

Another time, in the same canteen I heard the captain's stentorian voice saying: "You know what, yesterday some chap called Fiołek or Florek gave a speech on the radio."

"Fiołek?" I asked. "Surely you mean Mikołajczyk?"

"Yes, that's the chap, Mikołajczyk. So this Mikołajczyk said that

---

Kot means "cat." —*Trans.*

the days of the landed estates are over, you should only have as much land as you can work yourself, and other such nonsense. But what I say is this: just let him try and take half an acre from me when we get home, and I swear I'll punch him in the gob!"

And this was said with such sacred conviction in those sky-blue eyes, as if nothing, absolutely nothing in the world had changed. What imperviousness! *Le XVIIe siècle empaillé dans un homme*, I thought to myself, paraphrasing a sentence from Lamartine's *Nouvelles Confidences*, a work I had come upon at a book stall in Tashkent.

These conversations and encounters with colleagues mainly took place in the canteen during meals. The canteen was entirely in Soviet hands (both the management and the staff). For lunch we were served mainly a bit of sausage—a great luxury in those circumstances, and as a starter a piece of herring, all of it on flat tin plates. As there were no glasses or mugs, we were sometimes brought tea to end the meal on the same tin plates, without being washed after the herring. The tea, which had to be consumed with a spoon, was accompanied by one red caramel candy, which substituted for sugar. For breakfast there was herring again, and then tea on the same flat plate the herring had been on. The lunch, as we soon learned, was better than on many Soviet officers' training courses in that country, and for the civilian Poles arriving from all over Russia it was like a dream come true. We continually divided our rations with the new arrivals, and there was always a long line of haggard newcomers waiting outside the kitchen during mealtimes.*

A few weeks later, into the same canteen for herrings and tea on a single plate came the poet Czuchnowski, known to be an active communist sympathizer in Małopolska. His face was sharp, birdlike, and emaciated. He had ended up in Soviet captivity, where he was beaten and tortured. Suspected of Trotskyism, he had had a far worse time than the landowning captain. After numerous demands for his release, he had managed to reach us. As soon as he left the hospital,

---

*The kitchen for private soldiers, which was under our management, served more generous, tastier rations.

where he was treated for a serious lung disease, he got down to work for us, writing cutting articles and delivering good lectures against Nazi ideology. For the Bolsheviks, this militant socialist was more inconvenient than the nice captain—a fine argument for their propaganda about "aristocratic, reactionary Poland."

There was always a crowd of people outside general staff waiting for passes, trying to get rations, or looking for work. Most of them were women in rags, often wearing strange foot wrappings instead of shoes. A shawl, some colorful piece of material, or a pair of heavy ski boots that had managed to survive the years in exile were reminders of bygone days. And so they waited for the verdict—getting access to general staff meant not only assuring your own existence but also a greater chance of saving your relatives, possibly from starving to death, by getting them to this one and only source of hope for all the Poles pouring in to us, as if arriving in the promised land.

With each passing day, although general staff was separated off, I knew more and more about what was happening further afield. In the same canteen, in the office, and in the corridors I kept running into friends and colleagues from all directions and all units. Colonel J. had come from Chok-Pak, where the Eighth Infantry Division had been formed, and told us that they were stationed amid high ridges four thousand feet above sea level, where for three days a week a *buran* blew—a highland gale strong enough to overturn the tents. Within next to no time, 124 men were dead. They buried them at dusk, without coffins, for lack of planks to make them.

A young woman in uniform arrived from the army organization center at Guzar. She confirmed that people were dropping like flies there, and that the main occupation for the sappers was to dig graves each evening, where they buried two or three corpses at a time, also without coffins. On her last day there 126 people had died. Arriving from all directions, they were already infected or louse-ridden, spreading typhus, and most of them died in quarantine.

Typhus victims were starting to be taken from general staff to the hospital as well. Malaria was also spreading for lack of preventative drugs.

I was constantly passing silent figures, all expecting something from us: the young girl in a battered but still very good Zakopane sheepskin coat, her feet wrapped in rags, with neatly combed raven-black hair, a slightly mad expression, and determined black eyes in a beautiful face with Renaissance Florentine features; or the woman I met on the way to the office, her thoroughbred face furrowed with wrinkles, her gray hair cropped, walking down the middle of the road in mud up to her ankles, wearing a tight, faded sapphire-blue sheath dress, which could have been made in Paris years ago, and huge Soviet boots made of barely tanned leather—with the figure and gestures of a young woman, the face of an old hag, and those boots under the "Parisian" dress she was almost like a parody of elegance.

As I was passing the front of general staff, I saw a gendarme escorting a fourteen-year-old boy; his face was flushed and tear-stained, with a look of terror in his pale eyes. His brother was in the army, his father had died in the north, and his mother was in Semipalatinsk, from where she had sent him to the army alone, in an effort to save his life by attaching himself to the Poles. He had a place at a newly founded school for Polish youth at Vrevsk, but had run away from quarantine, "because everyone in there is dying." On his way back from the delousing unit he had found live lice on his clothes. He had run off to general staff, where the gendarmes had caught him. Wiktor Ostrowski, manager of our photographic and film department at general staff, himself still suffering from scurvy wounds on his legs, went about furious, wearing the face of Savonarola. "No one is to lay a finger on the boy!" But what was to be done with him? The disinfection unit was closed now, but the boy hadn't been deloused, and that was how typhus was spreading left and right. We didn't know where to put him.

General staff had to be separated off. It was impossible to work amid this flood of wretched deportees without feeling a constant sense of privilege; it was like Gide's description of the sailors saving the passengers of a sinking ship on lifeboats and having to chop off the hands of those trying to cling to the lifeboats—one person more and the lifeboat would sink. And we, lowly employees of general staff, spent our time writing papers and were occasionally given some candy or a bit of jam that had to be carefully protected to keep the huge, whiskery cockroaches out of it. Meanwhile we complained about the monotonous food and often couldn't help forgetting about the indigence all around us.

Stuck in general staff among my card indexes, I felt cut off from the ranks, and all my news about them came thirdhand. The most positive work, the organizing and grouping of the young people, assembling the units and changing ragamuffins into soldiers—all that was happening in the field, out of my reach.

As I was waiting for a disinfected uniform at the delousing unit, I met five private soldiers who were under arrest. One of them sat cross-legged on a bench, thin, naked, unshaven, and angry, with the bitter look of a failed artful dodger. He kept complaining that they were being fed on water ("worse than in the camps"), that it was the cook's fault ("everyone knows him"), and that "the soldiers go hungry, while the civilians down six hundred dinners a day."

Then Mrs. Mycielska arrived, a woman from Wilno. Her husband had been deported and had died at a remote camp in Sosva. She was with her sixteen-year-old son and her seventeen-year-old daughter, who had disproportionately huge, clear eyes framed by dark lashes on the childlike face of a porcelain doll. The daughter had been seriously ill, I imagine with brucellosis, and the son had the nervous gestures of an adolescent. Uneducated for the past three years, he desperately wanted to study, but nothing had been organized yet. In each unit, the boys and girls were all but screaming: "Let us study!" But there were no schools here, no textbooks, nothing.

Mrs. Mycielska told me about a friend of hers who had remained in Altai Krai. After burying two daughters there who died of pneumonic plague, she had just one left. They were starving to death.

One of the hundreds of letters that poured into my missing persons office was signed by a name I recognized. Also from Altai Krai, it was from a woman writing to her brother: "If you're alive, I beg you, please help my four children, we're starving." Dated December, the letter had reached our office in March. The brother, a staff officer who had been seriously wounded in the eye, had last been seen in late September 1939. According to an unconfirmed rumor, he was in a camp hospital somewhere on the Finnish border. But our letters and telegrams inquiring about his case went entirely unanswered.

In the damp twilight I was on my way back to our cottage. I crossed the river and passed the sentries, and then, as on the preceding days, I came upon a wretched Jewish woman with dirty gray hair and a small child at her breast. She offered me wine and matches, and complained that she was hungry.

"I haven't seen bread for a long time."

She and her husband had been deported from the borderlands, but he had vanished for good, so now she was try to survive by trading. Some ten days later she disappeared; apparently the Soviet authorities had arrested her for illegal commerce and deported her again. I waded on through the yellow mud. Three open trucks splashed me, full to the brim with old Uzbeks; just their stony, shut-off faces flashed past me. They were being taken off to prison camps under a heavy escort of NKVD men and armed Soviet soldiers.

> O Russia, Russia, Russia,
> Messiah of the coming day!*

Looking at this "coming day" since 1939, all I could see was death, prison camps, and the degradation of mankind.

---

*See note on page 185.

15. YUNGIYUL II

IN THE same month, March 1942, there was a fierce struggle going on at the highest level for the very existence of our army in the Soviet Union. Our chief command suddenly received news from the commissariat of the Central Asian military district that from the twentieth day of the month we would only receive forty thousand rations of food,* when as recently as December Stalin had agreed to build up the army to ninety-two thousand; at the start of that same March we already had seventy-five thousand soldiers, and the army was still growing by the day. Despite orders to the contrary and more and more restrictions on the railroads, not a day went by without new parties of "recruits" reaching our units.

The sudden halving of the soldiers' rations put the army in a tragic situation.

Anders immediately sent a telegram requesting an audience with Stalin. In reply he received a telegram dated March 9, in which Stalin invited him to Moscow for a meeting, explaining that the size of the rations had been reduced because of nonreceipt of promised supplies of American grain, which was a result of the outbreak of war with Japan. "Nevertheless," wrote Stalin in his telegram, "with great difficulty I have fought to maintain today's level of provision for the Polish Army in the USSR until March 20. After this date it will be

---

* These rations were 40 percent of a British soldier's ration and were never adequate. Food that was not delivered to the relevant unit on the appointed day was never supplied at all, and was lost to that unit, counted as "state goods." The units constantly suffered from failure to supply the food due to them—buckwheat, meat, or bread, not to mention vegetables.

necessary to reduce the number of rations for the Polish Army to almost forty thousand."

A few days later Anders flew to Moscow and was received at the Kremlin on March 18. Stalin demanded a reduction in the size of the army from seven (the number established in December) to three divisions and one reserve regiment. The rest of the soldiers already enlisted were to return to work at the collective farms, mines, and forests.

Anders realized that this was the start of the elimination of the army in the form established in December during General Sikorski's trip to Moscow. Anders knew that if he went along with this decision, from one day to the next he would be condemning his soldiers to something that for many of them was worse than death—starvation as slave laborers. During the ninety-minute audience, he managed to achieve the dictator's consent for the evacuation to Iran of all those units that Russia was not in a position to feed.*

News of the partial evacuation from Russia stirred such a reaction among the Polish masses, who somehow or other found out about it the length and breadth of Russia. Nowadays even those of us who lived through it are incapable of taking the strength of this impression on board. The avalanche of Poles that came rolling southward from the remotest camps and collective farms in the north grew even bigger. In the famine-hit territories of Turkestan, where before the war cotton was the only crop sown at hundreds of collective farms and the people lived on grain supplied from central Russia, each of our divisions, each of our units grew to include masses of civilians, women, old people, and skeletal children. On the very last of their strength, they had managed to reach the Polish Army in the hope that of accompanying it out of Soviet Russia.

Yet in this humid, muddy Yungiyul March not only the mass of deportees besieging the steps of general staff, but many of us, the actual employees, had no idea that the ever optimistic General Anders,

---

*General Anders wrote about the struggle to maintain the size of the army and to evacuate it in his book, *No Final Chapter*.

From left: General Zygmunt Bohusz-Szyszko, Lieutenant Józef Zielicki, and Lieutenant Józef Czapski. The picture was taken at Yungiyul, Uzbekistan, USSR, in May or June 1942.

who gave everyone hope and courage, always smiling as he toured the units, was conducting such a persistent, shrewd, and fierce battle—no longer for the development of the army being formed but for its very existence. We had no idea that the spontaneous influx of new recruits, what we saw as the happy growth of the army and of the Polish centers around it was unsettling the Soviet authorities, going against their wishes and against Stalin's orders.

At the beginning of April I was summoned by General Anders and appointed head of army propaganda. What was the scope of the job? All the press and information work, issuing two bulletins, one for the exclusive use of the commanders, the other a general one for the army, editing and issuing the weekly *Orzeł Biały* (The White Eagle), and cultural contacts with the Russians. All the educational and propaganda work in the army was my professional responsibility too; at that point a youth department and all the schooling were also attached to the Propaganda Unit. On top of that, there was also creative arts propaganda, including photography, cinema, music, posters, variety shows, an embryonic theater, and orchestras.

This appointment came down on me like a ton of bricks. I was terrified by the diversity and scale of the task and by my lack of preparation for it. I had never done any social or team work before, apart from being involved with a group of artists, and thus the most individualistic types, as far as you can go from the standard form of organizational or social work.

But I was lucky, because work that had been so alien to me shortly before was now of passionate interest to me. The team I joined consisted mainly of people who were wildly ideological, and apart from that were very close to me intellectually, people of an entirely civilian background, scholars, journalists, and artists. Every day I learned something from my colleagues who were already well versed in this sort of work. This was the start of a two-year whirligig of work for me, in frequent, often daily contact with the commander in chief and his heads of staff. In these special circumstances my unit blew up every model of military routine, and there was a great deal to be learned from the propaganda apparatus of the Bolsheviks, which had an exemplary structure from the very top to the very bottom. Our "central propaganda apparatus" was crammed into two little rooms at general staff. It couldn't be said that the small gang of people taking care of it was particularly popular among most of the staff officers at the start; they were all intelligentsia, with not a single professional officer, and, horror of horrors, the lowest ranks, or none at all, were in the majority among the most energetic, university-educated activists.

It was obvious that covering such a wide range of activities straightaway was in the realm of fantasy, as the slender apparatus was only just starting to take shape, and the scope of the work had not yet been clearly established. It wasn't until May, at the first meeting of education officers, that I could present instructions signed by our head of staff defining our tasks and area of competence. For ninety-nine officers out of 100 it was a third-rate department, and within the units it was often the weakest element, the man they didn't know what to do with, who was assigned to be the propaganda or education officer. This was perhaps the most acute point of difference between us and the Soviet army, where the most valuable and capable men were selected as *politruki*. Nonetheless, "Propaganda" was blamed for every shortcoming in the area of work entrusted to us, and on some people's lips this word became virtually a term of abuse. If not for the help of the army commanders, who showed their understanding for this department, we could not have built up the entire apparatus that, despite all its deficiencies (some of which grew, unfortunately, as the range of our activities extended), did play its role in our travels all the way to Monte Cassino. Now as I remember all the Polish journals and publications, the brochures and propaganda articles in English, Hebrew, and Arabic, the photographic and film labs, the special lecture cars with loudspeakers sent off to the units during action, the vast schooling and education department, which in time broke away from Propaganda, became a real ministry of education for the Second Corps, and prepared thousands of boys for professional schools in Palestine and Egypt, and then in Italy, for their school certificate and university entrance; when I think of Aleksander Fredro's play *The Revenge* superbly performed for all units one murderously hot summer in Iraq, and Molière in Italy, it's hard for me to believe that the whole job started in those two little rooms at general staff in Yungiyul.

Often by half past six or seven I would be having breakfast with General Anders. The general would still be lying in bed, with a window open to the spring world; it was the only time of day when there wasn't a line of people waiting for an audience, when I could calmly set out my concerns to him and receive his instructions or his signature. I had known General Anders for many years, but only superficially. I had met him in the First Krechowce Uhlan Regiment in 1917 where he commanded a squadron. It was a period when a great deal separated me, a greenhorn officer, from what nurtured the best of my colleagues; I would debate the theory of "nonopposition to evil" and read a great deal of Tolstoy. Captain Anders was renowned as an officer of incredible courage, elegant and extremely courteous, with something hard and cold in his wide-set, large dark eyes; for me he represented an unattainable and rather alien type of sophisticated cavalry style. Now, twenty-something years on, I got to know him again, hard at work, and how very different he seemed. One particular characteristic stood out for me, which was the great attention he paid to everything, never ignoring apparently trivial matters, always listening carefully and never rushing. I don't think I ever heard him raise his voice or cease to be courteous where service matters were involved. On the contrary, he expressed criticism with even greater politeness, but with such a cold look in his eye that his interlocutor instantly knew what to think about it. Anders placed a great deal of trust in his colleagues, which gave each of us wide scope at work and a broad range of responsibility, without obliging us to keep looking over our shoulders. He was very cautious about making decisions, sometimes putting them off, out of unwillingness to strain relations with his subordinates. Nonetheless, it was to him that I owed consent to a series of necessary but sometimes unpopular orders or redeployments. When it came to helping people, he helped at every step, wherever he could, and never used too much work or "higher considerations" as an excuse to shirk a thousand matters of this kind.

His prudence, the slow pace of his decision-making, and then the great speed and persistence with which he took action once resolved on it were perhaps what most characterized General Anders's way of working.

During the first few months of my work in Propaganda, Anders was preoccupied, among other things, with evacuating the Polish Army and getting as many people out of Russia as possible. He already had Stalin's consent for the first evacuation but was concerned about the daily deliverance of further civilian convoys that could be taken out along with the troops to Persia. Here Anders, always so cautious, performed *faits accomplis*, often in defiance of the Russians, in defiance of the British in Persia, and even in defiance of the Polish embassy in Kuybyshev. The aim was: 1) to create realistic conditions for the organization of a modern Polish Army; and 2) to save people's lives. By now he no longer believed it would be possible to bring the Polish troops to a state of readiness for combat within the Soviet Union, where they had no hope of getting equipment or tanks or an air force, where in some units sticks were still substituting for rifles, where food rations had been cut by half, and where every other soldier had wounds caused by scurvy. More Polish soldiers died of typhus and dysentery in Turkestan alone than were killed in combat at Monte Cassino.

I only remember one occasion when General Anders lost his temper. At a breakfast meeting, one of the officers in his inner circle started trying to explain to him—and this was in late May or June—that the army should be kept in Russia.

"Don't talk nonsense," he bristled. "What sort of an army lets 18 percent of its men suffer from night blindness for lack of vitamin A, be undernourished, and go without guns? Can you imagine any other troops in such conditions, except as cannon fodder for the Bolsheviks?"

Anders already knew that the Soviets weren't going to let the Polish Army rebuild, but on the contrary, they'd cause it to shrink. He could see the people pouring in to the army by the thousand, all begging him in unison to free them from "captivity in the land of Egypt."

Joining the propaganda department is linked in my memory with Easter in Yungiyul, because I assumed my new post just before the holiday. One of my first tasks was to prepare an Easter edition of *The White Eagle*. On the front page we led with an article by Colonel Perkowicz in a decorative frame. Written in a tone of religious love and longing for the home country, it included the sentence: "The church bells are ringing out in Poznań, Kraków, Warsaw, Wilno and Lwów."

This sentence prompted my first visit from Captain Sokolovsky, a young Soviet officer, small and fair, with blue eyes and a little blond mustache. Of Polish origin, he came from Minsk and claimed to be a Pole. In 1920, as a high-school student he had crossed to the Soviet side and had remained in Soviet Russia ever since. He had been the censor for *Prawda Wileńska* (Wilno Truth, a Polish-language Soviet newspaper) during the first occupation of Wilno, and now he was the censor for *The White Eagle* and "guardian angel" of our propaganda department on behalf of the NKVD. Captain Sokolovsky categorically demanded that Wilno and Lwów be deleted, as their mention implied the future borders of Poland, a matter not yet resolved. We refused to budge an inch, but he wasn't going to either. Until finally the author of the article had the idea of adding Chicago and Curitiba (in Brazil), as the places with the largest numbers of Polish émigrés. Only then did Sokolovsky agree to the inclusion of Wilno and Lwów. And so the Easter issue of *The Eagle* went out to the army and to all Russia, where it was snapped up by the badly homesick Poles, hungry for their native language.

None of our readers guessed that there had already been a need for Curitiba to save the "church bells ringing in Wilno and Lwów."

Easter Week began. A memory of the Thursday mass has stuck in my mind. Early that morning, we walked down a potholed road of clay, not yet dry, between rows of apple trees. In the pale lilac sky, the disk of the moon was only just fading, still glowing amid the black branches of the old apple trees. We could see poplars and the white-washed walls of houses in the distance, as military men and poorly dressed civilians came in from all directions. Poplars, apple trees, and that road of clay... For a moment I yielded to the illusion that maybe this was the Kielce province? The village of Skalmierz, perhaps? Or Kazimierza Wielka? But then the landscape began to change. We entered a gorge between dome-shaped hills, their slopes already coated in greenery, with the "Chinese" river flowing at their foot, and clay, flat-roofed houses on the far bank. The hills were dotted with tents housing the guards unit, and in the gestures of the soldiers passing by, the arrangement of the tents, the flags painted red and blue above them, the brand-new pillbox, and the layout of the paths and fences I could sense a bright, joyful rhythm and military order.

The field altar stood in a valley, with a small crucifix shrouded in purple, a priest in a white chasuble and a large gold monstrance. A quiet, very quiet crowd of soldiers and compatriots had come from all over: women, old people, and children. Most of them went up for Holy Communion. Amid the silence the altar boy chanted: "Jesus Christ, dear Lord, O most patient Lamb." The crowd, shyly praying, took up this hymn with emotion.

There was still shade in the valley, but the sky was gradually clearing; above the rare, dark streaks of cloud it no longer looked lilac but pale-blue, green, milky, lemon-yellow in the east, and at a great height woolly white cloudlets floated in the spring sky—just like in Poland...

Then we went back to the staff building. In the pure air of the Asiatic spring a large red-and-white standard fluttered, and amid the Asiatic poplars and apple trees some of Norwid's simplest lines came insistently to mind:

> For the land where they gather a crust of bread
> From the ground out of pure respect
> For heaven's gifts,
> I am yearning, Lord...

For the land where it's a grave offense
To harm a stork's nest in a tree,
For they serve us all,
I am yearning, Lord ...

16. YUNGIYUL III

AS APRIL turned into May, violent heat came beating down on us. The thousands of trees in the orchard blossomed pink and white. In my office with its south-facing window the sun blazed mercilessly, and it took a lot of trouble and friends in high places to get a drape to cover it. In the stuffy canteen, pouring with sweat, we lapped up our tea from the plates. The fresher evenings were a lifesaver.

Our group became ever closer-knit, working with passion and joy. What about ranks? Was there a gulf between soldiers and officers? Not in Propaganda, where—to the later outrage of the British in Iraq—we even shared a canteen with the ordinary soldiers. Nor did the NKVD representatives in Yungiyul entirely understand why in the Propaganda Unit of the "bourgeois" Polish Army the division between officer and soldier was far less significant than in the Soviet army, where the ranks were increasingly separated from the mass of common soldiers.

Our group was a strange mixture, a strange alloy: a scout leader from Lwów who had survived thirty-nine days in a death cell in Butyrki prison, a mountain climber who had taken part in a major Polish expedition in the Andes, a musician from Wilno, a long-standing minister of foreign affairs, a procommunist peasant poet from Małopolska, badly tortured and beaten in the Soviet prisons, and so many others too... including Stefania, wife of a sergeant deported from Równe and lost without a trace, who cleaned our premises in Yungiyul, and then ran our kitchen in Baghdad, Naples, and Rome. She was always hard at work. Each morning she woke us up, and then bustled around all day; once when I urged her to take a rest, she refused, adding: "Better to be on the go from dawn till dusk—my worst day of the week is Sunday, I pine so badly on Sundays I think I'll die of homesickness."

Not despite, but thanks to the diversity of professions and views, and of what the Bolsheviks called *sotsproiskhozhdeniye* (social origin), our team, not easy to form, was all the richer and more active.

Sokolovsky had a tough job to do with us; his grandfather from Minsk had taken part in the 1863 Uprising, and as the grandson of an insurgent, the Soviet captain took offense when addressed in Russian. He clearly had a soft spot for Poland, in spite of which I was always having to force myself to address him in Polish, breaking off the Russian that came to me naturally when talking to him, so imbued was he with the Soviet-Russian spirit, so in tune with the revolutionary Bolshevik tradition, from Chernyshevsky to Stalin.

My predecessor had warned me loud and clear about Sokolovsky, whom he had kept at a distance, rarely letting him into the office, and never engaging him in any lengthy conversation. My own approach to him was completely different, and we soon came to like each other. This man really did believe in Soviet communism, and was so well trained to be totally obedient, not just in deeds but also in thoughts, that we couldn't blame him for doing his job heart and soul, since the only salvation he saw for Poland too was in the Soviets. But I often found it sad to look at that slender, energetic figure, with the fair mustache and pale eyes of a "young Wołodyjowski" wearing a round Russian cap, in blind subservience to Stalin.

His constant monitoring of every word in *The Eagle* was extremely tedious. He demanded the deletion of all allusions to Polish fighting against czarist Russia, not to mention the least shadow of criticism of Soviet power. He demanded the removal of an epigram by Gałczyński, which we had put in to have a go at our own bureaucrats:

> From clown to clown
> The papers go around...

Sokolovsky suspected this of being a deliberate allusion to Soviet bureaucracy, and he was so consistent that every one of these matters had to be brought to the head of staff. We saved the epigram by adding: "because of the head of staff's instruction to save paper in the Polish Army." In Sokolovksy's mind this was linked with an honest desire to cooperate with us. Thanks to his unique efforts we gained the opportunity to illustrate the journal, thanks to his persistent running around we got tip-offs, and we were able to include Matejko's painting *The Prussian Homage* on the anniversary of that homage. And *The Prussian Homage*—showing a Prussian duke swearing allegiance to a Polish king—in a Polish journal in the Soviet Union at that time was a feat and a sensation! Sokolovsky went the whole way, as long as he saw no "fundamental" obstacles. For he had much greater ambitions than merely making censorship amendments—he wanted to convert us to "the true faith." He was always bringing us books he'd bought in Tashkent, and even fresh strawberries from the countryside, and then he would launch into serious talks. He tried to marry up Maria Konopnicka's poetry, for which he had a sincere passion, with Chernyshevsky's *What Is to Be Done?*, suggesting a debate on the emancipation of Soviet woman on the basis of the writings of this Russian revolutionary. After a year or two in the camps and collective farms, our women were happy to eat up the strawberries he brought, but they didn't want to know about emancipation Soviet style. As he chomped on the strawberries, my Lvovian deputy never failed to remind Sokolovsky of some broken promise or story about the conduct of the Soviets in his native city.

Despite a personal liking for our guardian angel, more genuine contact with him was impossible; he had lost the capacity to consider the arguments of others or to think from the opposite point of view. For the Soviet citizen, the very idea of "thinking from the other side" is counterrevolutionary. How very often I have managed to interest a Frenchman in Poland by talking about it with total sincerity, without concealing any of its mistakes and shortcomings. In response, I have mainly met with the same sincerity and criticism of France from the French person. The result has been mutual trust and a genuine interest in what each of our native countries is really like, not the propaganda-embellished version. But you only had to tell Sokolovsky that the trams didn't run well in Poland, in the tiny village of Kłaj, for instance, for him to try to prove that the obvious reason for this was because Poland was not a communist country. On the slightest excuse he tried to extract elements of propaganda. But I can't think of a single Pole on whom these arguments would not have worked to the contrary. Whereas it was enough to defy Sokolovsky with examples that logically led to conclusions that did not follow the party line, for the "guardian angel" to lose his hearing on the instant.

But that was just small beer. Despite our pleasant, even very pleasant relations, despite the strawberries, whose flavor we could still taste on our lips, more and more issues came up that were not just unpleasant but threatening; they came as a surprise, though by now we should have had time to get used to anything.

When the tape snapped during the screening of a movie about the defense of Moscow at general staff, the NKVD regarded it as suspicious and demanded an immediate inquiry to find out whether our film technician was a saboteur. This amiable man, always hard at work, performed miracles to put on the film shows, despite appalling equipment and worn-out tapes that were always breaking. The matter was brought to General Anders, who laughed out loud at such a suspicion and categorically opposed an inquiry.

Another time Sokolovsky came to me with some "extremely confidential" advice (he had evidently been given orders from above) to dismiss a couple of colleagues with Jewish surnames from the propaganda department. Evidently, in Soviet terms we had exceeded some secret but obligatory *numerus clausus*. Indeed, among the editors of *The Eagle* and in a few other sections we had employees who were excellent Poles of Jewish origin. Sokolovsky must have been very surprised that I not only took no notice of this suggestion but regarded it as an obscenity.

On joining Propaganda, I found a wide-ranging plan for education and schoolwork within the army that had already been prepared by my deputy. At the time very few officers understood the importance of this department. Whenever we tried to talk about it, the usual response was: "We'll be off to the front in a few weeks' time, so only military exercises matter—we can talk about education back in Warsaw." With these generalities more than one commander, convinced he was acting patriotically, was killing an initiative coming from below; everywhere, in every single unit there were children pretending to be adults, and people sinking back into illiteracy who hadn't seen a book in Polish for several years. Wherever there was a commander to be found who understood the point, an ideological teacher or educator, embryonic schools and mini-schools immediately sprang up.

More and more children kept arriving on their own with letters saying: "We're done for, but please save our child." Each of these children stood up straight, trying to add a few years to their age, just to be accepted into the army. Schools, children's homes, and camps for the two youth organizations, the Junaki and the Orlęta,* were set up within the units—at Vrevsk, where there was some greenery and water, and at treeless Kermin, where during the savage summer heat (exceeding 158°F!) water was imported in insufficient quantity in metal barrels. For every single qualified teacher there were ten jobs needing to be filled immediately. Apart from the stalwarts, who were working themselves to death, there were some very unlikely educators, such as ex-policemen. On every patch there was a fierce struggle for the children, to improve their existence, and for schools to be set up immediately. We tried to have teachers and scout leaders transferred to the schools from the units. How hard it was! Of course valuable people weren't let go without violent resistance, strong pressure from above; even a university associate professor who was acting as an orderly was retained in this "post" at any price. But during this fight, whenever we tried to prove that the educator's posts had to be filled by professionals, we were constantly refused: "Calm down, calm down, gentlemen, nobody is irreplaceable." Quite often, at the pivotal points where the decisions were made, we came upon people who had already managed, even there, to make their own lives comfortable, including evening bridge, and preferred not to think.

From this period I have retained a grateful memory of the PSK

*Literally, "Young Blades" and "Eaglets." —*Trans.*

(Women's Auxiliary Service) Inspectorate. The inspectorate was headed by Bronisława Wysłouchowa. Widow of a well-known peasant activist, deported from Lwów, and tortured in the Lubyanka in 1940 and 1941, she was surrounded by a swarm of dedicated women. She and her coworkers wholeheartedly devoted themselves to the PSK, which played a positive and sincere role at every stage of Second Corps' travels and combat.

I went to see them about the Junaki; I was on my way back from seeing a cardboard cutout officer who did his job soullessly, hiding behind the usual slogan: "Nobody is irreplaceable," and responding to all criticism with: "That's an overstatement!" I had got nowhere. Driven to despair by all his "clever" answers, I dropped in at the PSK Inspectorate. The matter involved the immediate assignment of four nurses to the Junaki in Vrevsk, who were due to be transferred to lethally hot Kermin. Would I meet with the same sedate, sterile reaction here too?

I was received by Mrs. Marysia Olechnowicz. She had a broad face, with flushed cheeks and a direct, human look in her youthful gray eyes. She listened carefully, without gesturing or speaking, but in her eyes I could see that she was focusing her thoughts on how to help, how to multiply the as yet limited body of women joining the army. Where were four nurses to be found? Dozens of female nurses, teachers and caregivers were dying of emaciation, overwork, and typhus. For now she gave me a negative answer but promised to come to see the Junaki in person on Sunday and to bring a few girls to help. Why do I still recall this conversation at the PSK with such gratitude? Because I'm sure that only thanks to employees like Marysia, of whom there was a legion in the corps, were things achieved, and lives saved, even in those savage Soviet conditions.

By the end of April, army staff had summoned Professor Aleksandrowicz and Janina Pilatowa to work in Propaganda. The arrival of these two people marked the start of sensible, consistent work on the education and schooling section. Aleksandrowicz, an eminent scholar, former deputy minister of education in Poland, and one of the most cultivated people I have ever met, set about the task with Lithuanian persistence. Under his bushy eyebrows, his seemingly cold eyes paled with irritation whenever some bureaucratic formality stood in his way. Dr. Pilatowa, from Lwów, had already completed a major piece of work organizing Polish educational centers among the deported population in Kyrgyzstan. This small, fragile-looking woman showed iron determination in her work, despite resembling a little girl in a funny little flowery hat. We immediately realized that these two weren't going to stop at any difficulties. A vast amount of work had to be done in order to change, at least for a while, the attitude to education among most of our colleagues, who initially treated the whole effort with contempt, but by the time we reached Italy were taking pride in it as one of the great achievements of Second Corps.

The work of the propaganda department as a whole gave me an extremely great deal of joy. Neither the talk on the Apocalypse, nor the debate on the *Elders of Zion*, nor the extremely tedious lectures that passed as officer training at general staff, and not even our work on the card indexes—none of that had offered cultural nourishment; it had all shown up our helplessness, abstraction, and imprecision, our failure to reckon with reality, and the backwardness of many of the officers who somehow or other had latched on to general staff. Joining Propaganda gave me genuine opportunities to take action on important matters, to get right inside what was happening in the army. Thinking back on that work, I'm sure that in every section I came across nothing but highly enthusiastic people; despite the stones thrown under our feet by the Soviets, despite our own tedious routine and our bureaucracy they devoted all their strength to building this strange society, which as the Second Corps went on to pass the test in Italy.

17. CLOUDS AND PIGEONS

JUST AFTER joining the propaganda department I received a letter from Ambassador Kot instructing us to get in touch with the Russian writer Alexei Tolstoy in Tashkent.

The Polish embassy in Kuybyshev had given a dinner that winter in honor of Tolstoy, author of *Peter I*. The host was Professor Kot, who was a great expert on the sixteenth century in Poland; there were writers and journalists present, including Teodor Parnicki and Ksawery Pruszyński. The atmosphere at this party had been extremely pleasant, and the idea was to maintain these relations.

In that period, official, undebatable Soviet opinion regarded Tolstoy as the greatest of their contemporary writers. *Peter I* was distributed in millions of copies each year. Tolstoy was then working on a major drama about Ivan the Terrible. The aim of it was not to debunk but to eulogize Ivan the Terrible, making him into a tragic, noble defender of the people, and thus a forebear of Stalin. At the same time Tolstoy was writing articles for the newspapers that authoritatively expressed the patriotic policy direction of the time, praising the heroism of the Soviet army, and of the Soviet peoples, and the greatness of Alexander Nevsky, Kutuzov, and Suvorov.

"Even Alexander the Great, Julius Caesar, and Napoleon lost battles—but Suvorov never lost a single one," wrote Tolstoy in July 1942.

These brutal articles, written with great skill, like *lubochniye kartiny* (Russian popular sketches and prints), were packed with comments such as: "The Russian people are good and love kindness"; "The soul of the Red Army warrior is pure and severe."

It was said that Tolstoy was on friendly terms with Stalin, that he was a frequent guest at the Kremlin, and that he was also one of the richest men in Russia, a collector of paintings and antiques. Just after Wilno was occupied by Soviet troops, Tolstoy was said to have sent a special agent there to buy him the whole cellar of the Hotel Georges.

Some of the things he said at the party at the Polish embassy were repeated to me; two of his remarks about the Soviet intelligentsia stuck in my mind. The first defined his nationalist attitude: "The prerevolutionary Russian intelligentsia," he said, "apart from some very rare exceptions, did not go along with the Bolshevik Revolution, and the Soviet government was forced to replace it with the Jewish intelligentsia. By now we have our own intelligentsia," he went on proudly, "a Russian one, which we raised ourselves. As a result the percentage of Jews in managerial posts has declined."

Asked what the young Soviet intelligentsia was most interested in, after some thought Tolstoy replied: "Dostoevsky."

In the Soviet Union, Dostoevsky was, if not on the index, at any rate frowned upon. While Leo Tolstoy, Chekhov, or Gorky could be found in literally any library, the works of Dostoevsky were rare. The Bolsheviks couldn't forgive him for the religious drift, or the reactionary element—they couldn't swallow *The Devils* or *The House of the Dead*. Tolstoy had tried to explain his reply: "The young Soviet intelligentsia mainly focuses on psychological questions—they want to know what's going on inside their own minds. This is a new generation."

Tolstoy had come down to Tashkent for the spring. I asked General Anders to invite him to general staff. Anders was leaving for Britain, so he entrusted the task to his deputy, General Szyszko-Bohusz. I could only communicate with the Bolsheviks through Sokolovsky, which prolonged matters. Meanwhile I got hold of the first volume of *Peter I* and read it in spare moments. Towards evening, when it became a little fresher and I had finished my work, I would escape up the hill above the ravine. There I was surrounded by greenery. The quiet, bearded Uzbeks, in *tubeteiki*, meaning colorful embroidered skullcaps, and barefoot, bustled about in their gardens, while the irrigation systems bubbled away. As the sun set I would gaze at the garish green of the poplars against pink, woolly little clouds, while finding the reading uphill work. Though perhaps brilliant, this rich, dense, almost stifling form, this typical "applied art" contained none of the charm that I had always found in Russian literature, not just in Leo Tolstoy or Dostoevsky but in Rozanov, Blok, Bely, and a legion of others. *Peter I* had none of that quick-wittedness, that pain, that bold panache to a point of madness, to a point of self-destruction, but it was full of Russia's apotheosis, laid on with a trowel, and the author's sense of well-being in the wild, cruel atmosphere of those times, so close to the reality surrounding us. I put the book aside after reading only a chapter, and involuntarily some lines of Bely came to mind, painful to a point of blasphemy:

> Enough: wait no more, hope no more—
> Disband, my wretched race!
> Shatter and fall into space
> Year after torturous year.

Sokolovsky regarded our eventual communication with Tolstoy as no less than a historic event—the fact that the writer knew Stalin well impressed him beyond measure. He came with me on my first visit to Tolstoy.

Tolstoy was living in a nice white house with high windows, high ceilings, and a primitive, shady garden in the downtown area. It had a study, a large airy sitting room with a fabulous Bechstein (maybe from Lwów), a bedroom shaded from the sun, and even a bathroom.

He received us in his study, where there was a desk, plenty of books, and hanging on the bare walls a huge, multicolored wooden mask of a deity from the Mongol Republic, topped by a golden crown and decorated with rich red-and-gold carving.

Fat and burly, Tolstoy received us simply and extremely cordially. He immediately agreed to visit Yungiyul. His lively black eyes squinted behind large horn-rimmed spectacles; everything about him was large and sensual—a big nose, thick lips, and a tough, aggressive look on his face, which reminded me of a large, stuffed boar's head that had hung in my childhood home.

Tolstoy asked if he could bring his wife, who "has been in Paris, and is so interested in Poland."

Mr. and Mrs. Tolstoy's visit to our general staff took place in May. I went to fetch him (accompanied as ever by Sokolovsky) in General Anders's wonderful ZIS car (a personal gift from Stalin). Brimming with intelligence, Tolstoy spent the whole journey telling us colorful tales about the routes of Alexander the Great in this country, and even more about his pet obsession of the time, citing examples that refuted the German theory about the exclusively German origin of science and knowledge; he provided historical arguments that testified to the creative gifts of the Slavs and proved that the Germans were only talented as compilers.

"The German will not survive into the future, his mind is square, whereas the Russian is made for the future," he wrote at the time in one of his articles.

Everything he said, and the way he said it, was bursting with passion for life, and throughout the evening that was how he ate, talked about politics, listened to poetry, or gazed upon our huge blossoming orchard. The host of the evening, General Szyszko-Bohusz, had a perfect command of the Russian language, so the conversation went very smoothly. It was evening, and the heat had abated, so we visited the guards unit housed in tents on the hill above the Kurkuldyuk. Then came dinner. Tolstoy and the general did a lot of talking. Szyszko-Bohusz described his visit to Stalin, and what he had seen in Britain, while Tolstoy talked about Russia, the Kremlin, Paris, and even some Russian émigré writers (including Bunin) in a tone of sympathy. Mrs. Tolstoy, an attractive young singer (his third wife, apparently), in a colorful dress with a light printed scarf, danced with the adjutants (there was a band of course) and charmed the entire company.

Sokolovsky was invited too. He never left Tolstoy's side for an instant and drank in his every word. Of course his reason for sticking so close to Tolstoy could well have been an order to monitor our contact with the writer. For I had heard that as well as being showered with gold,

Tolstoy was also supervised, despite providing commendable proof of his loyalty to the regime: in the days of the Trotskyist trials, he and Ehrenburg had been the first to sign a declaration by the Soviet writers demanding death for low fascist dogs and traitors to the people.

After twelve, by which time the atmosphere was very warm, I brought out some poems by contemporary Polish poets Stanisław Baliński and Antoni Słonimski, and translated some of them off the cuff. Tolstoy went into raptures over Baliński's "Kolęda warszawska" ("Warsaw Carol"), his "Ojczyzna Szopena" ("Chopin's Homeland"), and some poems about Paris and France. I had to translate the texts into Russian, then read them slowly in Polish, while Tolstoy listened carefully and avidly. He reveled in the metaphors, the sounds of the poems, and the line "under a sky full of sun, clouds and pigeons," and asked me to repeat it a few times. Finally he suggested a project to translate and publish the poems in Russian. He invited me to his home, promising to introduce me to a publisher and some translators.

In May and June I saw him several times at his home in Tashkent. One time I attended a real Lucullan feast there, along with some generals. There were Turkestan wines with an extraordinary taste and smell (they had nothing in common with the poor, alcoholic wine available in the stores), there was shashlik prepared by a genuine Georgian chef, spiced with special aromatic herbs and baked in a special oven set up in a shady avenue in the garden, as well as some unusual vegetables, and various sweets. After dinner and a few toasts "to confound the Germans," in a lovely mezzo-soprano the writer's wife sang songs by Mussorgsky. Tolstoy's son was also present for the evening, small and stocky, resembling his father in his passionate vitality, which was perhaps Tolstoy's most striking feature. The boy talked naturally and trustingly about the famine and destruction affecting Leningrad, speaking with sincere anxiety about his mother, who had been left behind there, and about how he had tried to get her a *payok* (ration card) for the best canteen in the besieged city, the canteen for "Party workers."

Bidding me farewell, Tolstoy offered me a book in which he wrote a dedication, saying that the time was already nigh when he would visit me at my studio in Poland, and together we would watch the *strizhi* fly. We couldn't find the Polish name for these birds, but as far as I could tell he meant those large dark swallows* with long wings that flit so fast, turning arcs and sharp corners in the windows when it's about to rain.

The most interesting evening I spent with Tolstoy was devoted to the plan to translate some Polish poems written during this war. Suddenly detained, Sokolovsky was absent just this one time, so I was able stay at the writer's house until late at night without an escort.

Tolstoy had invited mostly translators, and a few Russian writers, including Anna Akhmatova, whom I had not met before. A well-known publisher called Tikhonov was also present, an old friend of Gorky, who came across as a modest, quiet man. Gorky's daughter-in-law was there too. At about ten in the evening we gathered in the large drawing room around a table with wine, superb *kishmish* (raisins), and other sweetmeats. The heat of the day had passed. It was fresh and breezy.

We established that Tikhonov was prepared to publish the volume, and that it would be divided into three parts: poems from occupied Poland (some of these had reached us via London), poems by Polish writers from London, and poems written within the Polish Army being formed in the Soviet Union. As at the evening in Yungiyul, here too I read the London poems off the cuff.

The atmosphere and the ardor of the Russians' reaction exceeded my boldest expectations. I can still see the tears in the large eyes of the silent Akhmatova, as I clumsily translated the final stanza of the "Warsaw Carol":

> And if you want Him born in the shadow
> Of Warsaw's smoking ruins,
> Better put the newborn
> Straight up on the cross.

---

*The Russian word *strizhi* (стрижи) actually means "swifts," but Czapski describes these birds in Polish as *jaskółki*, meaning "swallows." —*Trans.*

"The Ballad of Two Candles" and "Chopin's Homeland" (both by Baliński), and Słonimski's "Alarm for the City of Warsaw" made a shocking impression. I had to read them all in turn, poem after poem, and was not allowed to omit a single one. In the past, I had very often tried to attract foreigners to Polish poetry, especially French people, with a minimal result; never before had I sensed such receptivity among my audience, never had I managed to evoke such a lively, genuine frisson as among this surviving handful of Russian intellectuals.

Akhmatova agreed to take on the translation of the "Warsaw Carol," although she claimed never to have translated poetry before. Tolstoy loudly bemoaned that nobody in the Soviet Union wrote about Russia like that, complaining that the only poems being written about their homeland were "cold and artificial."

That evening I was struck by the vacuum that had arisen in Russia in the sphere of art after twenty-something years of supervised culture; what a hunger for genuine poetry prevailed there. The great tradition, from Derzhavin and Pushkin to Blok, right through to Mayakovsky and Yesenin, seemed to have been broken off, apart from a few survivors of the stature of Pasternak or Akhmatova. But profound, disinterested communication between Poles and Russians is possible, it occurred to me—how easy it was to penetrate each other's cultures, to infect each other with poetry, the sound of a poem, or to transmit the tiniest little tremor in each other's language.

Tolstoy scoffed that in Russia nobody knew a thing about Polish poetry, how in general Polish literature was "nothing but Przybyszewski!" He joked that it was thanks to Przybyszewski that he had learned to drink, and that nowadays it was hard for him to imagine what a literary event Przybyszewski had been in Russia in his youth. Tikhonov agreed, saying that as a young man he had once seen Przybyszewski in Saint Petersburg, playing Chopin wonderfully in the hall of a great restaurant, despite being completely drunk, while rambling on about "Chopin . . . the Bible . . . Nietzsche . . ."

"For the young," Tolstoy repeated, "drinking and discussing Przybyszewski was sheer ecstasy."

We spent the whole of that evening talking about literature, or rather I did, trying to show that Polish literature has far more to offer than just Przybyszewski. I talked about Słowacki and Norwid. When I started to translate Norwid's "Fatum" from memory:

> Like a wild beast Misfortune came to man
> And fixed its dreadful eyes upon him
> Waiting
> For him to turn aside ...

Tolstoy was so interested that he helped me to translate it into Russian, wrote it down, and kept it.

I had Norwid's letters with me and translated the one he wrote to Zamoyski in 1864 about patriotism, which describes it as "a creative force, and not a force for isolating oneself and pushing others away." He writes that our sense of nationality relies on the force of appropriation but not on the force of Puritan exclusivity.* Tolstoy went into raptures and insisted that I come back for an evening of Norwid, claiming that he had finally found an apt definition of patriotism.

That evening Tolstoy showed me a fine edition of a Russian translation of Bolesław Prus's novel *The Pharaoh*, fairly recently published by Tikhonov, who was there that evening. I asked why this particular book had been so beautifully published.

"I don't regard it as a very great book," replied Tikhonov. "Its portrayal of Egypt is operatic and artificial, but," he added in a whisper, dropping his gaze, "it's Stalin's favorite book."

As for Akhmatova, I had read her poetry many years earlier; I knew she was the wife of Nikolai Gumilyov, a Russian poet shot by the Bolsheviks in 1921, and also that she had a son, a student who had been arrested and exiled in 1938. The boy was in the eastern languages faculty and had dreamed of going to Central Asia; nobody knew where

---

* "That is why those fighting the Tatars shaved off their hair in Tatar style, and rode their horses in Tatar style. Latin, Italian, and Spanish were also spoken in Poland's most national eras. But not by a sect—by the nation."

he had been exiled to, or on what charge. Before the war there was talk of Norilsk, then there was a rumor that he'd been seen at Nakhodka Bay on the way to Kolyma. What was this woman doing, the mother of a convict, in the house of the regime's most devoted writer?

Then I was told that Stalin had praised one of Akhmatova's poems; as a result, she was not just tolerated but even protected. In 1946 she was violently attacked by the Communist Party Central Committee and Zhdanov for "refusing to walk in step with the people" and was banned from publishing her work. But then, in 1942, she was still in "the highest care"; apparently on Stalin's personal orders a special plane had been sent to Leningrad for her when the besieged city was suffering famine.

That evening Akhmatova was sitting under a lamp, wearing a modest dress, in between a sack and a light habit, made of very poor material; her slightly graying hair was smoothly combed and tied with a colored scarf. She must once have been very beautiful, with regular features, a classic oval face, and large gray eyes. She drank wine and spoke little, in a slightly strange tone, as if half joking, even about the saddest things. Once I had read out the Polish poetry, we asked her to recite some of her own for us. She agreed willingly.

She declaimed a few passages from her as-yet-unpublished "Leningrad Poem." All those present treated her with the greatest respect, giving me to understand that she was a great Russian poet. The verses she recited in a strange, singsong tone, as another Russian poet, Igor Severyanin, used to, contained none of the optimistic propaganda or praise for the Soviet Union and Soviet heroes that even Tolstoy sank to time and again, with his "stern and just" Soviet knights. But her "Leningrad Poem" was the only work that moved me and gave me a brief evocation of what the defense of the starving, devastated, heroic city must have been like.

Akhmatova's poem began with memories of youth: difficult metaphors, *commedia dell'arte*, peacocks, violets, lovers, and a maple tree with yellow leaves in the window of the former Sheremetyev Palace, and ended with Leningrad cold and hungry under bombardment, besieged Leningrad. I never forgot the lines about the hungry little boy who during the bombing, in early spring or late fall, brought her some *travinki* (blades of grass) that had grown between the cobblestones.*

I was eager to get to know her better, to see her on her own, and go further into her world, but I didn't dare. Once already an innocent visit that I had made to a woman, without Sokolovsky as my escort, had had very tragic consequences. I have retained a memory of Akhmatova as someone "special," with whom contact was difficult because of a certain affectation, or perhaps she just had a more singular manner. I felt as if I were communing with a wounded person trying to mask her wounds, defending herself with that affectation. Her poem—she then recited more of them—is linked with my memories of the Russian symbolists and sometimes of Rilke. Before 1914 Akhmatova had lived in Paris, where she was a friend of Modigliani. Many of his letters and drawings which she had kept were destroyed during the siege of Leningrad.

The evening at Tolstoy's went on until three or four in the morning. We spent a long time saying goodbye outside the writer's house, under the crowns of the spreading trees. Tolstoy was in full flow, talking about the old days, about Russian writers from before the revolution, and about Remizov, to whom, as he put it, he owed everything, as far as feeling for the Russian language was concerned. He mentioned Rozanov and his passionate sensuality, like that of old Karamazov. "I like to leave the bathhouse, get in my sled, and feel the frost nipping my face as I savor some sweet grapes," Rozanov had told the young Tolstoy.

Tolstoy told his stories artfully, and he had an excellent memory, but in talking about Rozanov, he only captured a single aspect of the writer, the one most closely related to himself, as if he hadn't noticed his tragic split personality.

---

*In fact when he talks about Akhmatova's "Leningrad Poem," Czapski means her famous "Poem Without a Hero," but here he is interpolating another poem she wrote while in Tashkent, dedicated to a young boy named Vova Smirnov, her neighbor, who was killed during the bombing of Leningrad, *"Postuchis' kulachkom—ya otkroyu."—Trans.*

We parted, promising to meet many more times. At dawn I reached the apartment at the edge of the city, where thanks to a helpful intermediary from Poland I had found a bed for the night.

A couple of people were already filling the room with loud snores.

The impression stirred by the poetry, and the wish to hurry up the translations and have them published in Russian prompted me to remain in Tashkent for another day. I got permission to occupy a room in the main hotel reserved for the commander in chief. I had with me a few cans of corned beef, some real tea, and even some sugar—all I needed to hold a feast, by local standards.

I invited some of the people who had been present at Tolstoy's house. They were going to bring a few of their friends, who also wanted to hear the Polish poetry. But at the last moment my plan failed to materialize. Akhmatova sent a message to say she was unwell, Yakhontov, one of the best known Soviet declaimers of poetry (who lived in the same hotel), suddenly had to go somewhere. I received the same sort of refusals from the other invited guests, who only the night before had so warmly agreed to come and see me. I suspected "diplomatic" illnesses—an official ban.

Evening came, and I was alone in the room, when suddenly a young woman came in. She introduced herself as a friend of Tolstoy, and she had been informed that I was going to read some poetry, but clearly the instruction cancelling the gathering behind my back had not reached her. Tall and slender, with fair hair as light as down, she had subtle, pedigree features and a strikingly natural manner. Seeing that she had come alone, she wanted to leave at once, but I made her stay. We sat on a narrow stone balcony overlooking the street, where there were two old poplar trees. We spent the evening together on that balcony.

Once again I experienced that rare, so very Russian, instant contact with someone whom I had never met before, and will probably never meet again.

I read the poetry just for her, translating it into Russian, then reading it in Polish, and again I felt the same acute, wonderful reaction. She didn't say a word but just kept asking for precision, for the sound of a word, for an exact rendition of the meaning in Russian. And then suddenly she said: "So you have already found ways to express what you have endured ... though we ... have not yet..." and fell silent. She dropped her gaze, and the corners of her mouth were trembling.

"You know what's happened to Leningrad. I'm from there, it's my city—now it's a heap of rubble. Do you know what it's like in a city where two million people have died as the result of bombing, cold and hunger? I have nowhere to return to now. Our young Soviet intelligentsia no longer exists—they've all perished, especially the Leningrad intelligentsia. After the Finnish war there was no family that hadn't lost a son, a husband, or a father—the entire burden of the Finnish war was borne by the Leningrad district, and now all the rest have died on the front, the university students were all sent to the front in the first dreadful months of the German attack ... I feel alien here in Uzbekistan, there's nothing to connect me with this country, but I have no home to go back to, none of the people who mattered to me from my generation is still alive."

We talked for a long time, and it felt as if we had always known each other. We parted late that night on the narrow, dusty hotel balcony.

Next day I went back to general staff.

18. CHOPIN'S GRAND PIANO

BEFORE 1939 I had no idea how strongly the Polish masses could generally react to our poets and to Chopin, if sensitized by the blows raining down on them. When I speak of a general reaction, naturally I'm thinking of the poems that are recited most often, the most frequently overplayed ballads and mazurkas. At each painful stage of exile, at each turn in our history they came back to us, as if we were hearing them for the first time. On the whole this had little to do with the "pure" experience of art, the way esthetes and connoisseurs experience it, as art for art's sake.

This is how the Jews hear their prophets.

Poems by Mickiewicz that had gone stale in school, such as "Ordon's Redoubt" or "To a Polish Mother," recited a hundred times at official celebrations, were coated in a veneer of boredom, and for some had simply ceased to exist. But at the Starobilsk camp on November 11, 1939, the first anniversary of National Independence Day, which once again we weren't allowed to commemorate, we listened to them dumbstruck, with lumps in our throats.

I can still see the set expressions on those boys' pale faces, and the childlike tears running down the gray beards of men who'd grown old in a single month. There, in the former Orthodox church, in front of five levels of bunks so low they looked like boxes set on top of each other, into which their occupants had to crawl like dogs, standing under a long black cross made of two boards nailed together, one of our company recited:

Our Redeemer as a child in Nazareth
Toyed with the cross on which he saved the world.
O Polish mother, I would have your child
Play with his future toys.

While he is small, bind his arms in chains,
Bid him be harnessed to a barrow,
So he won't pale before the headsman's ax,
Or flush at the sight of the gallows.

At that moment these poems were sanctified anew.

Lieutenant Kwolek, a tall, thin young man with a dark beard and a kind expression behind his spectacles, was in charge of this "hall," the largest and most populated at Starobilsk. He had organized this commemoration and had hung up the black cross among the bunks. Straight after this event he was taken away from us and deported to a remote mine beyond the Arctic Circle, where he died in 1941, "harnessed to a barrow."

At the same camp in Starobilsk, as we were wading through the snow with buckets of soup for our comrades, or carrying wooden beams, we would suddenly be hit full on by a radio wheezing out scraps of Chopin's *Revolutionary* Étude or the Polonaise in A flat major, and we felt as if this music were being played for us alone, being heard in secret by us alone, as if it had been written just to help us, as if we had rediscovered ourselves through this single rhythm, this single beat that united us all.

In Uzbekistan I heard a small boy, exiled for almost two years with his mother to a starving collective farm, declaiming in a shrill voice: "... and when they must, one by one they go to their death" (a quote from "My Testament" by Juliusz Słowacki). His mother was gazing proudly at her son, who had learned this poem in Asia; I don't think she realized how much danger lay hidden in that poem or sensed that one day it would sound like a command to him, just as it had spoken to thousands of young men who had had little to do with poetry apart from the few verses they'd been made to learn by heart in childhood.

It wasn't just those famous poems by Mickiewicz, or even Słowacki, which every Polish child knows, but even the work of the "obscure" Norwid, whom Krasiński criticized for being unintelligible, suddenly revealed itself in those years of war and exile to people who barely knew his name.

When we produced an issue of *The Eagle* devoted to Warsaw, I could find no better motto than Norwid's lines:

> from your cobbles I'd be glad to have a stone
> that does not shine with blood and tears.

Newly released from the camps, crowded into a cold hall at general staff in Buzuluk we listened to a slender young woman with fair hair named Domańska. Later to establish our theatre in Iraq, in a low, resonant voice with an unforgettable accent she recited "Chopin's Grand Piano":

> The building was ablaze, the flames died down,
> Then flared again—and there—below the wall
> I saw the brows of mourning widows
> Shoved aside by rifle butts—
> And then, though blinded by the smoke, I saw
> Before the porch's columns,
> An object like a coffin
> Hoisted out . . . it fell . . . it fell—Your piano!

On the day of my return from Tashkent to general staff a young man came to see me at my hotel. He had large, very pale eyes set in a narrow white face covered in freckles, so pale, so white that he was almost as transparent as a communion wafer. A pair of thin, delicate hands with very long fingers protruded from the too-short sleeves of his worn-out jacket. He cut such a frail figure that it looked hard for him to remain upright.

He came to see me, citing the Młynarski family as a mutual connection. His name was Jan Holcman, and he had heard that the son of Emil Młynarski, founder and the conductor of the Warsaw Philharmonic Orchestra, was with us in the army. Jan was a virtuoso musician, from a family that was well known in Warsaw's musical circles. His father was a pianist, a pupil of Professor Michałowski, and for many years his uncle had played first violin for the Philharmonic Orchestra; the boy's homeland was the Warsaw musical world, the Philharmonic.

To save him from the Germans, his parents had sent him to Lwów, while they remained in Warsaw. He had been unharmed in occupied Lwów, where the Russians had taken an interest in his great talent and had sent him on a scholarship to the conservatory in Moscow. During the Soviet-German war the conservatory had been evacuated to Tashkent, where this institution was vegetating in naturally very tough conditions. Holcman had headed after the conservatory too, but only loosely attached to it on foreign ground, he was dying of hunger. He had no idea what had happened to his family, who were shut in the Warsaw ghetto;* all he knew was that the Philharmonic had burned down. He only lived for music. He never complained about the Soviets but stressed that he had studied with superb teachers in Moscow and owed them a lot. But he was starving to death, and dreamed of continuing his education, of Paris, America, and Palestine, where he had distant relatives and numerous acquaintances. But how could he get away, how could we help him? Whatever he was, he was unsuitable for the army. He couldn't have lifted the lightest rifle, and in any case there were Soviet decrees acting against him. A decree of December 22, 1941, established that anyone living was in the eastern territory of Poland before November 29, 1939, when it was occupied by the Soviets, was by that token a Soviet citizen, and only had the right to report to the Polish Army if of Polish nationality. Ukrainians, Belarusians, and Jews were denied this right. On the basis of this decree, in June 1942 General Panfilov, the representative of the Soviet authorities attached to the Polish Army, had insisted

---

*His father died in the ghetto of TB, and his uncle was killed by the Germans along with the entire orchestra.

that our commanders must expel a large number of soldiers of these ethnicities from the army. It was of no significance that these people might consider themselves, or actually be, the greatest citizens and patriots of the Polish Republic. Of course, none of these soldiers was handed over to the Soviets, but every time a Polish citizen with a non-Polish surname was enlisted, the Soviets imposed major difficulties, which naturally were always having to be evaded or overcome in one way or another. Unfortunately, our own native anti-Semitism, with its innate mindlessness, sometimes accommodated Soviet orders. Holcman, who had been living in territory occupied by Russia before November 1939, and who had spent two years at the Moscow conservatory, could not, in Soviet terms, be "legally" recruited into the Polish Army. Although in this case the word "legally" made no sense at all, because the Soviet decree had been adopted unilaterally by the Bolsheviks, without the agreement of the Polish authorities. I took the boy to Yungiyul with me. With the commander's consent we immediately put him in British battledress and a pair of heavy British army boots. He was at once assigned to our military orchestra, tasked with copying out the notes. He spent a lot of time in our propaganda department, where on an old rinky-dink piano he played whatever we wanted to hear by Bach, Chopin, Beethoven, Schumann, Szymanowski, or Scriabin. We were hungry for music after such a long time listening to nothing but the camp radio, and we were delighted by Holcman's high-class playing.

We very soon took advantage of his presence. We set up a grand piano, an old wreck, on a garden stage among the apple trees, under a poor, leaking little roof the shape of a large shell. Underneath it, at the back of the little stage, we hung up a gouache head of Chopin. It looked like the head of the shattered Chopin monument in Warsaw, and also like Delacroix's famous portrait of him, with his face slightly raised in three-quarters profile. On either side of it we placed two small bouquets of bright yellow buttercups, the most common village flowers, in Uzbekistan as well as in Poland. That was the entire setting for the old piano, which stood with its lid raised, "resembling a coffin."

We dragged every last one of general staff's tables and chairs outside, but so many people assembled, soldiers and officers, that a large number had to stand.

The concert was held in the evening. Holcman played nothing but Chopin: études, preludes, mazurkas, and nocturnes, the Scherzo in B minor, the Polonaise in A flat major, and the ballads. He played superbly and bountifully. This frail boy had resolution, clarity, strength, and that impulse—nervous and passionate, but also precise, rhythmic, and confident—which has always seemed to me to be the essential qualification for a performer of Chopin. The purity of his touch was palpable, for the loud or the softest phrasing, and for the rising crescendo, even though the piano was out of tune and some of the keys gave a hollow or trembling tone.

The entire audience sat as if spellbound by the music, and many had tears in their eyes. Suddenly, during the *Raindrop* Prelude it began to drizzle, then the rain started to fall harder and harder. It even started leaking through the shabby tin roof and dripping onto the keyboard. Although his fingers were slipping on the keys, our virtuoso went on playing. Ten minutes later the rain stopped.

I was watching the audience. Nobody went to fetch their coat, even though the staff cloakroom was only a few steps away, nobody tried to shelter from the rain—so strong was the spirit of the music, its charm and power over the packed crowd of Poles.

Was it just the memories it evoked?

Memories of nocturnes, mazurkas, and ballads, played awkwardly, urgently and loudly through hundreds of open windows in springtime Warsaw, of the long auditorium at the Philharmonic (where Hofmann and Rubinstein performed), of the shattered monument on Ujazdowskie Avenue, the head of Chopin now a martyred piece of rubble amid the ruins of the capital, just as we had seen it on a photograph sent from London. No—for these people the music was not just a heartrending reminder. For these immobile people its uneven rhythm, suddenly rising with passion, then falling to the softest pianissimo, then erupting again with unrestrained, profligate power, this feverish breathing, was not just a memory, it was:

... Poland—from the zenith
of history's perfection
captured by a rainbow of delight.

Perhaps for the first time we had a reason to be grateful to the Soviets—grateful that here we could freely listen to the music of Chopin, now banned by the police in Warsaw.

19. THE DEATH CELL

JÓZEF Z.,* my closest colleague in the department, was calmly and unhurriedly shaving in his quarters, while I sat there, waiting for him, growing impatient as usual, accusing him of dawdling and saying we'd be late. We were going to celebrate the *White Eagle*'s first "jubilee." It was the twenty-fifth issue of our weekly, including a replication of the May 3 parade at Yungiyul, Bishop Gawlina's sermon, and a major article by Racięski on the successes of the British air force and, as ever, some current, highly popular caricatures by Włodzimierz Kowańko.

Our printers worked in extremely unhealthy conditions—it was terribly stuffy in the print shop, and it took many weeks of effort, and that with the support of our highest authorities, to get the milk rations due to them. In every matter of this kind we had to surmount the Soviet bureaucracy, which is hard to imagine without having had to deal with them in person. Only the highest ranks, in this period even Polish ones, had the magical power to remove these difficulties. As a result, every one of these trivial things depended on our quartermaster, later chief of staff, General Wiśniowski, or our head of purchasing, Colonel Indyk-Czajkowski, who supported our requests with their full authority whenever there was a need. The print shop was our pride and joy, because every single issue of *The Eagle* demanded a new fight to overcome new difficulties; the mistakes were noted and ardently criticized by our colleagues, but every article in *The Eagle* also had a response it would probably never have again, although later on the texts were often better, and the range infinitely wider.

*Antoni Józef Zielicki.

Józef, a mathematician by profession, had been a scout leader in the Lwów area. He had led Lwów's only prewar scout group for craftsmen, and just before the war he had been deputy commander of the Górki scouts in Silesia. During the war he went back to Lwów and immediately got involved with the resistance. As one of the five-member staff of the Union of Armed Struggle (ZWZ) he was arrested in June 1940. After a year's inquiry in Moscow he had been sentenced to death, and in June 1941 was taken to a death cell at Butyrki prison, where he remained for thirty-nine days.

He was the first of my friends condemned by a Soviet tribunal to escape execution thanks to the signing of the Sikorski-Maisky agreement.

Both overloaded with work, we hadn't yet found a moment in all these weeks to talk about our recent past. Everyone, literally everyone encountered in Russia in those days had a full and burdened past behind him, but we only found out about each other's experiences by accident, all of a sudden, often at times when we felt as far as we could possibly be from confessions. But that was the day when I heard Józef explain how executions were performed at the Lubyanka.

So there I sat, gazing at this thin, frail figure, leaning over a little Soviet mirror, at a face with small, boyish features, very blue eyes, and the faintly livid lips typical of people with heart disease.

"How do you know exactly how they do away with condemned prisoners?" I asked.

"There was a man called Lutz in the death cell with me," he replied, continuing to shave. "He was the manager of a railroad junction, at Kalinino apparently. He had been locked up as a saboteur for an incident that occurred two years after he had retired. He was an entirely trustworthy man, very well read in historical works, self-educated. He was suspected of running a gang of saboteurs. He had already been in prison for two or three years and had spent several months locked up with NKVD men of the kind who had carried out those sentences for years on end, before they themselves came under suspicion. They told him in detail how it was done.

"There was another well-informed man in our cell, an Armenian called Drastomat Hadjiturovich Sadjumian, who as chairman of the supreme court of the Azerbaijan Republic had very often passed the death sentence himself.

"These people told me that the condemned man is taken to the Lubyanka, because they don't do the shooting at Butyrki, where our death cell was located. They're taken down to a row of cubicles lining a corridor in the basement at Butyrki jail. There all their *kvitantsye* are collected, meaning receipts for the deposit of their belongings, then they're called out of the cubicles one by one. If they call you out of the cubicle with your things, that's a good sign, because then you're taken away for a search, and from there to the prosecutor, who announces a reprieve, and instead of the death sentence you get fifteen or even twenty-five years in the camps. But if they tell you to leave your things in the cubicle, you're sure to die. It means you'll be taken by car to the Lubyanka, where once again they'll read out the confirmed sentence, then take you down a long corridor in the basement of the Lubyanka, accompanied by the prosecutor, a doctor, and the prison head. Two NKVD men hold the condemned man by the arms, while a third puts a gun to the back of his skull and fires."

Józef was reluctant to talk about these things and had to overcome his own inner resistance. In any case, he was finding it hard to get going that day; wishing to take advantage of the conversation we had started, I reconciled myself to the fact that we'd be late for the printer's. Once he got started, he spoke precisely without omitting any details, and his storytelling was more like a dry, commercial report than "literature" in the negative sense of the word, where it is so easy to take liberties and twist the facts.

"I came closest to death eighteen days after my sentence," he continued. "On July 12 I was summoned with a Latvian minister called Marġers Skujenieks, an old man,* very pleasant and civilized, who had also been sentenced to death. They led us down a corridor in the basement to neighboring cubicles. These cubicles were strung the

---

*Born in 1886, Marġers Skujenieks, was fifty-five at the time of his death. —*Trans.*

length of both sides of the corridor: tiny little cubbyholes, where you could only just sit down with your things on your knees. Each one had a peephole. Skujenieks was put in the cubicle to the right of mine, number thirteen. I had only met him in the death cell, but I had grown very fond of him. He was adviser to the president of Latvia, a government minister, and a sincere friend of Poland. As far as I remember, for some time he had been chairman of the Polish-Latvian Society. He used to have his own yacht and spent part of the summer sailing. He had often been to Sweden and Denmark, and had always stressed Latvia's affiliation with that cultural environment. When the Soviet troops invaded Latvia he had received an offer to leave at once for Sweden but had refused. He was arrested soon after, naturally as an 'enemy of the people,' and deported to Moscow.

"When we were taken off to the cubicles together, I needed something to tie up my bag of rusks, but I had no string or rag. After a brief hesitation, visibly struggling with himself, Skujenieks took his handkerchief from his pocket and tore it in half. That handkerchief must have been his most valuable keepsake. He kept the half embroidered with the letter A, which was his wife's initial, sewn on by her or maybe by one of their children, in plain cross-stitch. Then he gave me the other half of the handkerchief to tie my bag, and I still have it in my keeping—maybe one day I'll be able to give it back to someone in his family.

"We sat in the cubicles for about an hour, while the prison head and warders went from one to the next, checking the names three times. After an hour there was some activity, and we were taken out of the cubicles one by one. About a minute went by after each man was taken out, presumably enough time to escort the prisoner to the car. Sitting in my cubicle, I could hear them getting closer and closer, as each man was led out and asked in turn: *Vasha familiya?* ('Your surname?') And then: *Veshchi ostavtye, pozhaluysta.* ('Please leave your things.')

"One of them was also told: *Ostavtye pidzhak* ('Leave your jacket')—clearly one of the warders liked the look of it.

"So you had to leave your things in the cubicle—meaning certain death, according to my informants. And so, cubicle after cubicle, they reached my neighbor Skujenieks; they took him away too, telling him to leave his things as well.

"After Skujenieks it was my turn. Apart from me there were only a few prisoners left in the cubicles on the other side. Silence fell, broken only by the steps of the man walking up and down the corridor to keep an eye on us, and by murmurs from a few of the occupied cubicles.

"I was sure the delay was because the car was full, and once the prisoners who had already gone had been delivered, they would come back for us too, but that it would take at least an hour. I had been to the Lubyanka from Butyrki for interrogation, so I knew it took about an hour for a car to drive there and back.

"One's thoughts are very strange at a time like that..."

He stopped shaving, and with half his face covered in lather, holding his brush and shaving soap in his undersized, sallow hands, he stood up straight and cast his blue eyes about the room, as if looking for something.

"Were you afraid?"

"No, not in the least. At one time I had been, when the sound of footsteps had woken me in the night and the warders had escorted the condemned men out of the neighboring cell, but there in the cubicle I wasn't afraid. What grieved me the most was that I would never have the chance to speak a word of Polish to anyone ever again (apart from a couple of encounters lasting a few minutes at interrogation nobody had spoken to me in Polish for a whole year), and that none of my loved ones would ever know how I had died, I could neither tell them nor write to them. And also that they would shoot from behind... It was treacherous, I'd have preferred them to shoot me openly in the chest."

He carefully wiped the soap from his chin, his pale, greenish cheeks, and his upper lip. As he talked, he showed uneven, slightly protruding teeth.

"An hour later the warders came back. They opened my cubicle door, and then something strange happened. The head of the prison handed me my receipt, and instead of taking me to the car, I was led away with my things, back to the death cell. The other prisoners were taken out of a few other cubicles and escorted back to the death cell too. I assume they were all Poles, whose death sentences had been suspended at the last moment in connection with the negotiations going on in London. But at the time all I knew was that Germany and the Soviet Union were at war, because one time a bomb had ripped into the building, all the electricity had gone off, and then I had heard them shifting bricks and running about the place. But I knew nothing about the Polish-Soviet talks."

He broke off his account; by now we were very late for the jubilee. At the print shop there was a cordial atmosphere, faces glowing with benevolence and sweat—it was extremely hot. Naturally there was vodka and speeches. Our amiable printer, a longstanding employee of *Robotnik* (The Worker), and chairman or deputy chairman of the Polish printers' union, who traveled with *The White Eagle* through every stage of our adventures, made a speech worthy of a trade union conference, and our best typesetter, nicknamed Piecyk ("Little Oven"), peeping into his glass again and again, promised us most solemnly that he would never let vodka pass his lips again.

We left the print shop quite soon and went up the hill, above the river, to the top of the garden. The thick grass had already started to go yellow and dry up. The brown water of the Kurkuldyuk River was crowded with soldiers bathing, and we could hear their shouts and laughter. As we lay on the grass, there was already a touch of freshness in the air; we gazed at the sapphire-blue sky, darkening toward evening, filled with heavy, motionless white clouds like snowy peaks.

"When I got back to the cell," Józef began again, as if he hadn't interrupted his story at all, "I was received as if I'd returned from the dead. The old professional executioners claimed it was the first time they had ever witnessed anything of the kind. I was kept there until July 31, thirty-nine days in all.

"In this cell, where I had only ended up after sentencing, and thus just after the outbreak of the Soviet-German war, there were always from three to seven of us. The main part of Butyrki is an old building with towers. In the old part there is a courtroom and investigation rooms, and in the center of the courtyard there is a church that has also been converted into part of the prison. Divided horizontally into several floors, that is where those already sentenced and destined for the labor camps sit it out in enormous rooms. Besides that there is also a new building, a large square block dating from the late nineteenth century with an inner stairwell, where all the cells are for prisoners under investigation.

"On the ground floor of this building there was originally just one special cell for those sentenced to death, but during my time there the number of death cells was increased to cover almost the entire ground floor and part of the floor above.

"Our cell was well lit, because it had a long, low, as if inverted window with frosted glass behind a metal grid. One part of the window opened like a vent. The bright light distinguished it from the cells in the Lubyanka, where the windows were ordinary, but each one had a metal screen in front of it; as a result, only a little daylight could get in from above, so it was always semidark in there.

"As soon as the war with Germany broke out, all the prisoners at Butyrki were evacuated, except for those sentenced to death.

"Apart from Skujenieks, who was taken out of the cell along with me that time and never returned, there was another Latvian, W. He lived in Riga, where he had left a fiancée. He belonged to the entourage of the commander in chief of the Latvian army and had been with him in Moscow three days before the Soviet troops invaded Latvia. He told me in detail about the commander in chief's visit to Stalin. During that final audience his commander asked Stalin whether he was satisfied with Soviet-Latvian relations.

"Stalin replied that he was extremely satisfied with them, that the Latvians were keeping to the letter of the treaty, and that Latvia and the Soviets had never enjoyed such good neighborly relations before. That same day the commander in chief was due to go straight back to Riga. Only later did it transpire that the railroad linking Moscow and Riga was already packed with trains full of Soviet troops, on their way to occupy Latvia.

"Apart from the Latvians, there was the Armenian, whom I have already mentioned, named Sadjumian. As a child he had been a shepherd, but the revolution had elevated him and he owed it everything. He was the only man in our cell who was still an enthusiastic devotee of Stalin. He took pride in his origins and sang Armenian songs, but he admitted that his children no longer spoke Armenian, only Russian. This thirty-something-year-old man with a round face and a cunning, not very likeable expression was, as I have told you, chairman of the supreme court in the Azerbaijan Republic. He had been condemned to death for having issued too many death sentences, as if doing it deliberately to set Azerbaijan against Stalin. He bore his sentence the worst of all of us, stubbornly insisting that he was innocent and ever loyal to Stalin. He was extremely quarrelsome and constantly taunted me with critical remarks about Poland, mainly aimed at Piłsudski. He had demanded a new inquiry, but once sentenced he was never summoned by any of the investigating magistrates. He didn't know how to draw attention to himself. One day he grabbed all our mugs and toothbrushes (the mugs were made of aluminum, and the brushes were of bone), tore the handles off the mugs and swallowed them. He also swallowed all our bone brushes. As a punishment, they refused to give us any more mugs or brushes from then on. Though he appeared to be suffering no ill effects, they took him away for a day to pump out his stomach.

"The prisoner who bore his sentence the most painfully, but more quietly and without trying to draw attention to himself, was a young Rusyn, Yanush Yanushevich Polonchak, from a village in Trans-Carpathia; he was seventeen or eighteen, with a fair, downy growth of beard and the thin, chiseled face of a highlander. With a very poor grasp of Russian, he found it much easier to communicate with a Pole, so he talked almost only to me. He told me the story of his fate, always in the same simple words; he had no idea what it all meant or why on earth he had been condemned to death. His father had owned a couple of dozen acres of land in Trans-Carpathia and a profitable store. In 1940 some Soviet agitators had turned up there, saying that America was nothing compared with Russia, and that Russia was an extremely prosperous place, a real El Dorado. So the young man and a couple of his friends had headed off to this new America. As soon as they crossed the Soviet border, they went straight to the guard post—at last they were in the paradise where they wanted to live and work.

"Of course they were locked up right away, and so badly beaten that the boy confessed to everything they tried to pin on him, and thus that he was a spy, an enemy of the Soviet Union, and so on. He told me they beat him up so badly that he would have signed anything or confessed to any crime at all.

"Condemned to death, the boy was in total despair at the thought that he would never return to his family. He wished he could let his parents know what had happened to him, and as he waited for his execution, he wept copiously, endlessly trying to understand why on earth they wanted to kill him."

20. THE GOLD COIN

"THERE was only one man in the cell whom we regarded as having a chance of coming out alive. This young man had been sentenced for armed robbery and was the only nonpolitical prisoner in there. He swore he had never had a murder on his conscience, but he earned his living waylaying cashiers, and had been accused of organizing an entire gang of robbers. He had a broad face with high cheekbones and large black eyes inherited from his Mongolian mother. He was highly intelligent, incredibly quick-witted, his name was Vasily Yakovlevich Radionov, and he had been sentenced twice before for the same thing—this was his third indictment.

"Every day in Moscow the cashiers go around the state stores collecting the money. Vasily was an electrician by profession. The first time he was caught robbing a cashier, 25 percent of his salary had been deducted as a penalty. The second time he was sentenced to a year in a labor camp; he had served the sentence and gone back to the same practice again. He told us he had only ever had the determination to commit these acts when drunk, never while sober. Both his parents worked at a meat-processing plant and lived in virtual poverty. The boy talked about his mother with great emotion, saying she had always been good to him and that she would cry her eyes out for him; as it was, she was going blind and had to earn a living by sewing. The young man had been sentenced by a municipal court and then, once he was already in our cell, a confirmation had come from the district court. Now he was waiting for the reply to an appeal to Kalinin.

"In our cell we held a series of talks—I spoke about Einstein's theory, Skujenieks about economic issues, and Lutz, the stationmaster from Kalinino, gave us a history lesson, and was even quite objectively knowledgeable about Polish history. Radionov drank up our words. He had an extremely good memory. He admitted to us that it was the first time he had ever been among people who spoke entire sentences in succession without a single swearword. Once he even told us that if he got out of prison, he wanted to change his life for the better, by running away to Poland.

"This Vasily Radionov comes into a story that is quite funny, but at the same time it is very sad and matters to me. It's the story of the coin I managed to smuggle through every prison search.

"My old aunts in Lwów had once given me two Austrian ten-crown coins. 'Maybe you'll need them one day,' they'd said. I always carried them on my person in a large leather wallet. When the Bolsheviks arrested me, I had them with me too, along with some kopecks and some Polish groshy, which by then were no longer in circulation.

"At the time of my arrest in June 1940 they didn't touch my money, but the next day, when I was taken to the prison in Zamarstynów, they spilled my rubles and kopecks onto a table and issued me with a receipt for them. My other Polish coins were put aside in a small pile as currency that was out of circulation.

"At this point I decided to steal my own money. The NKVD official hadn't noticed the two gold ducats among the groshy coins. When I was told to sign the receipt, accidentally on purpose I covered one of the ducats with my hand, and when I withdrew my hand, I took the gold coin with it.

"At Zamarstynów I was put in cell number forty, where I was given a place on the bunk with one of Lwów's typical petty crooks, already highly experienced in the field of imprisonment on one side of me, and on the other a young student who had been arrested for being in possession of a gun. Two days later I confided in them that I had the ducat. At this point my experienced neighbor explained to me that every two days here they conducted a search, which in prison they call a *khatranka*. On each occasion they take everyone out of the cell, strip them naked, search every fold of their clothing and every cranny of their body; meanwhile another party of warders searches the cell, taps on the walls, and sometimes even tears up the floorboards.

"My neighbor offered to sew the coin into a seam on my shoulder. He did it with great skill and care (despite numerous searches he had a needle and thread on him). Thanks to this I managed to keep the ducat through the next few *khatranki*.

"Then I was sent to a prison in Kiev. It was the only one where my cell had a window overlooking a square, through which I could see the roofs of moving cars beyond the prison wall. I could also look at a large building opposite, where people were living at liberty. It was August, and extremely hot. In the evenings the rooms in that house would fill up, the people would bustle about, and come out onto the balcony... I could watch them all.

"In that prison the searches were a daily event. All my seams were felt. After getting away with yet another search, I unpicked the seam and spent a long time wondering where to hide the coin; at first I wanted to put it in a little bag of sugar that I had with me, but finally I decided to bury it in a chunk of bread.

"A few days later I was sent to the Lubyanka in Moscow, and from there to Butyrki. Only when I arrived at the Lubyanka did I find out what was really meant by a search—all those previous searches were a joke. In the Lubyanka they unpicked all my linings, rummaged in the padding of my jacket from the inside, and especially in the shoulder seams, from where a few days earlier I had removed the ducat; all my sugar was spilled out of the bag, my soap was cut in half, and then they got around to my bread and started to cut it into thin slices.

"At that point I thought that if I got away with it this time, I'd survive prison in one piece. My NKVD man took the chunk of bread in which the ducat was hidden, cut it in half very, very close to the coin—it was even shining through the cut... and put the bread aside. Then I took courage and started to complain that they'd ripped my clothing and ruined my food, but from then on the ducat was like a talisman for me. I continued to keep it in the bread, but that wasn't easy either.

"At first in Butyrki they put me in one of the towers, known as Pugachev's tower because apparently Pugachev had spent the night there before being quartered. I don't know if that was actually true.

"We were shut in that tower in pairs. One of my companions was a worker at a Moscow factory that smelted gold imported from Kolyma, and he had been caught trying to steal gold. He was from Ivanovsk province and had escaped to Moscow with his wife and small children from a collective farm—they lived in such a cramped basement that when they all lay down on the ground to sleep there wasn't any floor space left at all. He worked sixteen hours a day, two shifts in a row, because otherwise he couldn't feed the children.

"When he was taken away from me, in his place came another worker, Dmitri Smirnov. He was in prison for the second time for *boltovnyu*, as he put it, meaning for idle talk.* After four years in a camp on the Solovetsky Islands and another year in prison, he had been released, had got his job at the factory, married, and started a new life. But a report by one of his former fellow prisoners reached his factory, accusing him of more careless talk in prison, and he was rearrested. He had already spent several months under investigation, and was deluding himself that they would release him because it was all a misunderstanding. He had started life afresh, his wife was pregnant, and he was determined to build a happy family, but most importantly, he was a genuine supporter of Soviet Russia. When I told him that in Poland there was national insurance, and that our railroads were among the best in Europe, infinitely better than the Soviet ones, he refused to believe me and stubbornly kept repeating: 'I don't believe a word you say, I don't believe anyone, whatever the proof—I only believe what I read in *Pravda* and *Izvestiya*.'

"Our tower was a damp place, and I realized to my horror that my chunk of bread was going moldy. Whenever they searched our cell,

---

* Wondering why most of the men had been deported from a village in the Mordvin province, an exiled Polish woman asked the wives and children the reason for their deportation. The only answer they gave her was "for words," and that was all she could discover.

usually in our absence, they threw the moldy bread into the slop bucket, so I kept picking the mold off the bread, trimming off tiny pieces where the mold was visible, or else I shoved the coin into a fresh chunk.

"In January I was sent the money they'd taken from me the day after my arrest in Lwów, and in exchange for those rubles I was allowed to buy some white bread. I used it to make a bag of rusks and hid the coin inside them, but the rusks dried out so much that they cracked at the point where it was hidden. I had a lot of bother with it, but I managed to get through every single search, all the way to the death cell, with my rusks and my ducat.

"By the time I was called out of that cell and was sitting in the cubicle, waiting for death (which I thought certain), as the guards came closer and closer, taking the prisoners from the cubicles one by one without their things, I felt ashamed that I had brought the bag of rusks and the ducat with me. Now it would be of no use to anyone. I reproached myself for the fact that at such a moment, when I was almost certain my sentence would be carried out, I had been so selfish and so attached to material things that instead of leaving the rusks and the ducat for Radionov, the one prisoner who had a chance of getting out alive, I had taken them with me when I left the cell. Later on I heard about people on their way to their death who even threw off their shoes, gave them to their comrades, and went barefoot.

"After being escorted back to the cell, I remained there until the night of August 1. That was a dreadful night. The prison was bombarded. The adjutant to the Latvian commander in chief, whom I told you about, was seriously ill with sudden stomach pains and vomiting. He thought he was dying and commissioned me, in the event of my release, to inform his fiancée; the supervisor kept stopping by our cell to shout at me for sitting beside the sick man. Suddenly at two in the morning I was told to pack my things.

"I deliberately dawdled over the packing, said goodbye to everyone, and then handed the ducat to Radionov. Tears streamed down his face, though he said he never cried. I told him the money might come in handy and made just one request of him, which was not to spend it on vodka. But he swore to me that he wouldn't part with it for anything and that one day he would give it back to me...in Lwów.

"I wasn't set free until the end of August. I decided to go and see the boy's parents. At the time none of us was being watched, so we could go where we liked. I had a hard time reaching the house where the parents lived: in a remote suburb of Moscow, it was a huge, shabby barrack, with long, dirty narrow corridors. At the end of each corridor there was a small communal kitchen, with tiny rooms on either side, where the workers lived with their families. I found the parents' room, where they were living in extreme indigence, with old Radionov's sister. Both were very friendly, and what struck me most was the mother's face, of a light, already very mixed Mongolian type and an engaging expression of quiet goodness.

"At first they were very wary, but when I told them details about their son, they believed me, and both began to cry. As he wept, the father said his Vasily hadn't been such a bad boy, it was just the circumstances, the company he'd kept...

"'Hadn't been?' I asked.

"Only then did the father tell me that Vasily had been summoned before the prosecutor a few days earlier and told that Kalinin had refused to show clemency. So he hadn't been pardoned. The prosecutor had informed the father that the sentence had been carried out on August 27."

21. "RUKI ZAGREBUSHCHIYE"

THE SUN had gone down, but we were still lying on the grass. The green of the poplars and the maize stood out even more sharply, even more brilliantly in the last rays of the sun. In the east the sky had changed from sapphire-blue to lilac, and the white clouds had become slightly, then more and more intensely pink, until they shone as red as geraniums, almost the artificial color of Bengal fire.

"Did they beat you?" I suddenly asked my friend.

"In Lwów I knew a very large number of people who were beaten by the NKVD—compared to them I was treated far less cruelly and beaten less. My first interrogation took place in the former luxury building of the Lwów power station. I was interrogated for forty-eight hours without a break, by several men taking turns. I was hit with a rubber truncheon on the back and thighs, and very painfully on the head. Not in the face, but very hard on the neck with the side of the hand. A blow like that, inflicted by a trained hand, makes the neck swell, and it's very hard to move your jaw. The first beating seemed to me less painful—you try to defend yourself, to fight back, and the first shock of rage kicks in. I found the second beating much more agonizing, but by then I was aware that there was no hope of rescue or defense.

"After the first beating I was immediately treated to a superb dinner, in the very same place, at the magistrate's elegant desk. There was even beer, and the magistrate praised our Lwów brand: 'There's nothing like it, not even in Soviet Russia.' He tried to pour me a second glass when I'd drunk the first. Although I was extremely thirsty, I refused, because I knew from the others that the NKVD were in the habit of hitting prisoners on the neck and head with empty bottles, which was particularly painful. I was counting on the fact that if I didn't finish the beer, the magistrate wouldn't want to pour the rest of it away, and maybe I was right—I wasn't hit with a bottle.

"In Moscow nobody touched me, but I did learn a great deal about Soviet torture methods from my cell mates. There was a former secretary of the Soviet embassy in London at the Lubyanka with me, charged with Trotskyism, and he was cruelly beaten, but for this torture he was taken away to Lefortovo prison just outside Moscow. When he returned to the cell after the first beating, his back was a single wound. At the Lubyanka he was carefully nursed, and once his back had started to heal, he was taken back to Lefortovo for more 'questioning.'

"One of our colleagues, later deputy regiment commander N., was tortured for several nights in a row in Lefortovo. On one of these nights, as he was waiting to be summoned, at about two in the morning he dozed off. Suddenly the door opened wide, and a tall old man with white hair was flung into the cell. The door was immediately bolted again, and the man crashed to the floor right beside his couch. He was bleeding profusely, his pants had been torn to shreds, and his legs were badly bitten. Our colleague jumped up, tore strips off his shirt, and tried to bandage the man's wounds. The old man explained that during his interrogation a large wolf had been set on him. Soon after, our colleague was summoned to the examining magistrate. And there beside the magistrate sat a wolf, with its ears pricked up.

"The entire scene in which the old man was flung into the Polish officer's cell covered in bite marks was in fact staged as a way of creating a psychological mood designed to extract confessions from the Pole, who had already been questioned and beaten for several nights on end. Sometimes our men were also beaten on the heels. Straight after the signing of the Sikorski-Maisky agreement, one of the commanders who had organized our resistance against the Soviets in Wilno was released from Butyrki and dispatched with all honors and an entourage of NKVD officers to a large camp full of Polish soldiers.

As a representative of high command, he was there to encourage them to join the Polish Army in the Soviet Union at once. Leaning on two sticks, he could hardly drag his swollen legs along the lineup of several thousand prisoners of war, so badly crippled and injured were they from hundreds of blows to his heels."

Dusk was falling, and Józef stopped talking; we had to go back but I urged him to finish his own prison story.

"As I said, on the night of August 1, I was removed from the death cell, but instead of going to the cubicles in the basement as before, I was taken to a large cell, where there were about forty people, including twenty Poles, a dozen Russians, and one Lithuanian.

"The first Pole I met was Father Cieński, a priest from Lwów. He went around hearing our confessions and giving us absolution. Not only had he been tortured in Lwów, but in his presence they had tortured a young woman whom he didn't know, as a way of forcing him to spill the beans about the Polish resistance.

"An hour later the door opened, and they began to take us Poles out one by one to another cell. There at a table sat some NKVD officers, bedecked in medals, who made the same announcement to each of us Poles: 'The Soviet Union, Britain, and Poland are fighting a common enemy. We're not going to kill you. Don't be afraid, just wait patiently.'

"Back in our shared cell, we Poles got together. After a whole year, I was with Poles again, at last I could talk in Polish, and finally I understood why my sentence hadn't been carried out. All of my Polish fellow prisoners had been condemned to death as well, and just like me their sentences had suddenly been revoked because of the ongoing Sikorski-Maisky negotiations in London. In the same period the death sentence was commuted to exile for some Russians and Lithuanians,* who were now brought to the same shared cell.

"As most of them were highly talented people, maybe it was significant that their professional knowledge could still come in useful

---

* They included General Antanas Gustaitis, a construction engineer who was head of the Lithuanian air force; however, he was shot on October 16, 1941.

for the lethally endangered Soviet Union? That at least was the view of the two most eminent Russians I met there, who both spent those few weeks with us, my last ones, in Butyrki.

"Both were Europeans to the core, and perhaps the only genuine friends of Poland among my Russian fellow prisoners. They hadn't a shadow of the enmity, prejudice, or suspicion that I had come up against so often. When it came to Poland, even the convicts who hated the Soviet authorities, simple peasants and simple workers, would make tendentious, almost always hostile remarks about Poland and the Poles.

"The first of the two friends of Poland was Alexander Ivanovich Ogilvy, a balneologist and university professor. He had produced a vast work on the geological properties of the Caucasus and was conducting research on the radioactivity of springs in that part of the world. Even in the death cell he had been allowed out every day to sit in the examining magistrate's office, where he could carry on with his research; an old man, he was still sustained by his work, and the thought of those hours had kept him alive. He told us the reason for his sentence. On the basis of his instructions and calculations, a hill had been excavated in the Caucasus, where he was counting on finding a spring with valuable properties. The spring had not been found, and as a result Ogilvy had been sentenced to death for sabotage.

"Our other friend, who had been in prison for a year by then, condemned to death for alleged espionage on behalf of Britain, was a world-famous geneticist and cultivator of domesticated plants, Academician Nikolai Ivanovich Vavilov.* For some years this scholar had been the pride of Soviet science. He told me he had traveled all over the world, except for Australia. Right across Russia, from the Arctic Circle to the Chinese border, he had hundreds of experimental fields, and there were two thousand assistants working under his management. He had been to Abyssinia, where he had discovered wheat growing wild. By crossing Soviet wheat with the wild variety, he aimed to make it resistant to a range of diseases. In Bolivia he had

*Brother of physicist and fellow Academician Sergei Vavilov.

concluded that potatoes growing wild on plateaus at thirteen thousand feet above sea level can reach over two pounds in weight. Then he had confirmed that the climate in those subtropical mountains is the same as the climate in Leningrad in summer, except that the days are as long as the nights. He set up a number of experimental fields just outside Leningrad, where he shielded potato plants from the light of the white nights from six in the morning. He swore to me that in this simple way he had managed to increase the size and weight of the potatoes. It was fascinating to hear Vavilov talking about plants, various methods of cultivation, and discoveries about nature.

"Vavilov had been condemned to death on the basis of a denunciation by another scientist, his deputy Lysenko, who had accused him of defending 'bourgeois-clerical' science. In 1940, just after Bessarabia was occupied, he had gone to Chernovtsy to set up some experimental fields there and to research the cultivation of various plants. It was there that he had been arrested for 'espionage' and given the death sentence. When he was moved from the death cell to our shared cell, he was expecting to be exiled for fifteen or twenty-five years, but in conditions where, though behind bars, he would be able to continue his research.[*]

"Shortly before his arrest, Vavilov had also been to Małopolska [the area centering on Kraków], where he had spent time just after the occupation. He told me about a man called Sienkiewicz, whom he had visited near Lwów: he had a small farm where he did biological experiments. Vavilov was delighted to find that on only a few acres Sienkiewicz had achieved some astonishing results. In Lwów he had

---

[*]He featured in a book by David J. Dallin and Boris I. Nicolaevsky, *Forced Labor in Soviet Russia* (Hollis & Carter, 1948), in a carefully researched chapter about the labor camps in Kolyma, as follows (p. 145): "Even such achievements as the acclimatization of oats and cabbages ... have been bought at the cost of the lives of the brilliant men who made them possible—men such as N. I. Vavilov, a scientist known the world over, and member of the Soviet Academy of Science, whose ideas on the mutation of plants failed to agree with the official Soviet interpretation of dialectic materialism, and who died in exile in Magadan from the effects of vicious climate."

become familiar with an atlas produced by Polish geographer Euge-niusz Romer, who was a local professor. Though familiar with various substantial atlases, Vavilov had never found a better one, in terms of graphic design, accuracy, and clarity of presentation. He also expressed his great admiration for the Dzieduszycki Museum in Lwów. He often repeated the conviction that very few Russians are aware that it was the Poles who taught the Russians agriculture and how to cultivate plants. This man was able to respect and celebrate everything of value that he had seen in Poland and every other foreign country.

"Apart from these two scholars, of whom I have retained warm and grateful memories, there was a Marxist professor called Alexan-der Lupol; having often been to Germany for philosophy conferences, he had been condemned for espionage. There was also an émigré writer called Andreyev, who had returned in response to a summons issued to the émigrés by the Soviet writers but had immediately been imprisoned; this was his second or third year in jail. There was also a man called Hirschfeld, a former secretary at the Soviet embassy in Paris, arrested in the years when almost the entire staff had been replaced, brought home, and shut behind bars.

"These people were all convinced that any Soviet citizen who went abroad would sooner or later be imprisoned for espionage or for col-luding with the enemy.

"In the same cell I was given a 'hot-off-the-press' account of a scene that I'd like to describe to you:

"Another of the prisoners in Butyrki was an Estonian government minister, one of the main organizers of the Estonian cooperative movement. As you know, the Estonian, Lithuanian, and Latvian cooperatives were among the best in Europe. In 1940, in the honey-moon period of Soviet-Baltic relations, when the Baltic countries were forced to agree to Soviet bases, and the Soviet government was still doing everything to convince them that the USSR wasn't going to infringe upon their independence, a group of Estonian ministers and eminent social activists were invited to Moscow. Stalin gave a dinner reception at the Kremlin, at which he questioned the minis-ter about the Estonian cooperative movement. For about an hour the minister told him about the development of cooperatives in the Baltic states. Stalin listened very carefully, said: '*Khorosho, khorosho, vy eto sdelali*—You've done very well,' and then took the Estonian minister by the arm and walked about the room with him. They passed Zhdanov and Molotov, who were sitting next to each other, engaged in lively conversation.

"Stalin pointed at them and said with a smile: 'This is what they'd like to do to the lot of you...' and he made a hand movement, as if scooping something up, 'because they are from Great Russia, and they have *ruki zagrebushchiye*, but I won't let them.'

"Only three months had gone by since this conversation, Estonia had been annexed, and the organizer of the Estonian cooperative movement, so hospitably received at the Kremlin, came to Moscow again, but this time in a prison car on his way to Butyrki.

"*Ruki zagrebushchiye* is hard to translate, and I don't think those words feature in the Russian dictionary either, but naturally what he meant was hands that are like rakes.

"On August 25, I went from Butyrki to the Lubyanka, where I finally learned about the signing of the Sikorski-Maisky agreement and the so-called amnesty. I was summoned there a couple more times to the examining magistrate—I remember that his name was Khorbatenko, and he treated me politely, in total contrast to all the previous magistrates, but strongly urged me to sign a document agreeing to cooperate with the NKVD, stressing that if I didn't, I might never be released. By then I knew from a fellow prisoner at the Lubyanka, a Polish staff officer, that our army was being formed in Russia, that General Anders had been appointed its commander, and that he had already been released. Naturally I feigned ignorance and wriggled my way out of it as best I could, explaining that I was ready to sign anything on one condition, which was that someone would come to the Lubyanka from our embassy and order me to sign it, because that was the authority to whom I answered.

"I was released on September 3, thanks to pressure from two of my colleagues from Lwów who had been released before me.

"I was transferred to a smart Moscow hotel, and my examining magistrate Khorbatenko was tasked to look after me and provide me with all the pointers and help I needed."

By the time Józef finished his account, it was almost dark. We got up from the grass and hurried to the mess. In the doorway we ran into a couple of equally belated colleagues.

"Where have you been?" asked one of them, brushing the grass and straw off the back and shoulders of my battledress. "Come on, admit it, where did you sneak off to?"

Józef said nothing but just gave him a crooked smile. We sat down to eat.

"Why didn't you tell him where we went?" I asked. "Why are you so fond of secrets and mystery?"

"Look at it my way," he replied after a long pause for thought. "I've been through twelve months of interrogation, and it leaves its mark—whenever I'm asked a question, even the most trivial kind, rather than answering, my instinct is to keep silent."

22. THE BRANCH OF LIFE

AFTER returning from Tashkent, I dropped in a few times to see the friend with whom I had originally shared accommodation at the home of the kind Ukrainian ladies. One day these two women, a mother and daughter, were feverishly dashing from cottage to cottage, preparing some sort of parcels. At dawn the next day they set off, carrying lots of bags, and one of them had a jar of buttermilk too. We didn't find out where they had gone until they came back that evening. Their faces were wet with tears. What was wrong?

Two years before, in 1940, Stalin had issued a decree mobilizing Soviet children aged from ten or twelve to sixteen years old (a fixed number from each village) to go to factory schools. The boys had to undergo technical training for qualified workers, so that, "in case of need," they could replace the older ones. At this point our younger landlady's only child had been mobilized, a boy in his teens called Seryozha. He had been sent to Moscow, where he was put up in an *obshchezhitiye*, a student dorm. The boy was fun-loving and liked to play pranks.

One day, a few weeks after arriving at the Moscow dorm, for a joke he tied a sleeping colleague's foot to his bed. In the morning, when the alarm rang and the boys awoke, without noticing what had happened, the boy whose foot was tied to his bed got up with the others, and fell on his face, knocking out two teeth. The Ukrainian boy, who had unintentionally caused this accident, was so terrified— he was guilty of actual bodily harm, which carries a severe penalty in Russia, regardless of the culprit's age—that he ran away from Moscow;

pretending to be a *bezprizorny* (a homeless child), along with some other boys he had fare-dodged all the way back to his mother in Uzbekistan. Naturally, he had been caught a few days later by the NKVD and immediately deported. For over a year the mother and grandmother had received no news of him and had no idea whether he was alive or dead, or what had been done to him. Suddenly a card had arrived from a prison twenty-five miles away from Yungiyul, saying that the boy had been in prison there for the past year, that he was sick with consumption, and that the mother was allowed to send him some extra food. So the women had set off, taking some bread, eggs, and buttermilk with them.

I don't know if they were allowed to see the boy; they just came back the same day in tears. No one had concealed that he had consumption and was in the prison hospital. They had left their bundles and the jar of buttermilk there. But nobody had told them how long his sentence was or whether his serious illness might lead to a reduction in his punishment for the "crime."

Every morning on the streets of Yungiyul I was struck by the look of sorrow on the people's faces, their mechanical way of moving, their sallow complexions and total exhaustion. At that time, the whole town would be on their way to work at the factories; some dragged along on their own, as if lacking strength, sticking close to the walls of the houses (something to lean against if they suddenly felt weak), while others came down the middle of the street in groups. Against the background of glaring heroic posters and bright slogans inscribed on the walls, they almost always walked in silence, with their heads bowed, all wearing the same miserable, colorless rags. In this general atmosphere, where the Soviet world around us seemed more and more synonymous with dull apathy or barely disguised despair, if I heard a sudden burst of youthful laughter from a courtyard or saw a look of joy on a couple of young faces I met in the street, it was a happy surprise that moved and pleased me.

In the town, across the Kurkuldyuk River, on a poorly paved, dusty street, behind a low wall made of compacted clay, stood a cottage with a small garden, where one of my colleagues was billeted. There was an *aryk* running down the side of the garden, which was entirely overgrown with young poplars and occupied by a flock of hens. My colleague was on very good terms with the Russian family who occupied this house: the father was a communist, a qualified worker, who went off to work all day beyond Yungiyul; the weary-looking mother was also employed all day at a nearby canning plant and came home in the evenings pale and exhausted, at an unsteady pace. Their fourteen-year-old son not only went to school but in particularly busy seasons was sent with his school friends to help with the cotton harvest. There was also a Ukrainian girl called Shura living with this family, who was treated like an older daughter. She also worked all day in a canning factory, then came home and summoned up the energy to do more work, helping the mother, cooking, doing the laundry, sewing for the boy, and helping to run the house.

Fragile, with a very fine complexion and fair hair, this girl of at most twenty-two or three was on the move all day. She was not so much pretty as charming. Her attraction relied above all on her unfailing cheerfulness and instinctive goodness; always joyful, she bestowed this positive benevolence on everyone around her without distinction. We chatted on a number of occasions. She spoke animatedly about the new tasks her bosses had given her to perform at the factory or in the village and repeated the latest Moscow slogans without a shadow of skepticism; she always seemed uncritically loyal and dedicated to the Soviet regime. Looking at her, I thought: So the Soviet Union is capable of raising good, happy, devoted citizens. Her winning smile was slightly marred by a scar on her upper lip, the result of a childhood accident. Whenever she laughed or blushed, and she blushed extremely easily, the scar showed as a white mark. It cut across a corner of her mouth, giving her smile a strange quality, an almost painful contraction but one you forgot as soon as you looked at her pale eyes with their long lashes.

Sometimes towards evening I would drop in at Shura's house. One time, tired after working all day in the heat, I went to see her. The air was still close, and on the compacted earth in the courtyard Shura was feeding the hens. The boy was sitting on a bench, cutting himself poplar sticks. From a distance I could hear the girl's soft alto laughter.

Soon we were sitting on the grass in front of the irrigation channel. I had been longing to ask her why she, a Ukrainian, was here in Turkestan, living with an unrelated Russian family, but I hadn't dared. That evening I didn't hold back but asked her about her childhood; her little face suddenly grew serious, and she unhesitatingly began to tell me the story of her past, as if she had been expecting the question for a long time. Chewing a piece of grass and without looking at me, she told it in a single go, as if in a hurry to get it all out of her.

"My childhood was terrible."

Blown by the wind, the poplar leaves now cast shade, now suddenly lit up her face, her hair like golden down, and her dark skin, extremely smooth and fine, almost like a child's.

"My father was a smallholder in the Kharkov province. He had a cottage, a few horses, and some cows. So naturally he was a kulak," she added more quietly, lowering her head.

"As soon as they began to introduce the collective farms, my father was exiled to the far north. That same year my mother died of starvation. Three years later my father was released from the north, but by then I was no longer living in our village outside Kharkov—after my mother's death I was sent to a collective farm in the Crimea, where I was working. He came to see me there." And at this point, although her face had been calm as she spoke about her father's exile and her mother's death, she began to tremble and said with difficulty, as if forcing herself: "I had to call him *dyadya*—uncle, I couldn't admit he was my father, and that I was his daughter, or they'd have expelled me from the collective farm."

Clucking insistently, a black hen had toddled up to Shura and was pecking at something in the grass. She shooed it away with a nervous gesture that was most unlike her and continued: "My father returned to our home village and was given permission to work there, but he only stayed for a few days. The man who had been the cause of his exile to the north, and who three years on was playing a major role in the village, invited him for a drink. My father refused, saying he knew who had been responsible for his deportation.

"My father was immediately denounced again, and exiled to the north again, but for five years this time. This happened almost five years before the war, and since then I have had no news from him or about him. I don't know if he is dead or alive."

That was all she told me about her past. I met her at least a dozen times more, ever the same kind, busy, jovial girl, always looking for ways to help others.

Some of my colleagues did not live in the town but in a purely Uzbek village, about a mile in the opposite direction from general staff. A wide, rutted road ran through the village, partly overgrown with grass and full of deep, muddy potholes. Amid a network of irrigation channels, the whole village was drowning in the greenery of vines, maize, poplars, and flowering lilacs. There were dogs barking, people herding a special breed of *kurdyuk* sheep, with huge tails filled with fat. Some of the sheep had such enormous fat tails that the Uzbeks tied wooden slats to them to make it easier for them to carry the weight. The Uzbek children herded mooing cows with long switches. I don't know to what extent this village had been collectivized, but I was told collectivization had been carried out in this area with great delay, or rather caution, for fear of rebellion or violent resistance by the local population. I never saw a single propaganda poster there or even a newspaper. The people's faces were suntanned, and if tired, it was with a different, rural tiredness. Maybe it was a mistaken, superficial impression, but I thought this village world seemed happy, because it was far away from politics, immersed in hard work on scraps of land, very like our Polish villages, or any village on earth.

After a Sunday spent there with friends, the only real Sunday that I remember enjoying at leisure in Yungiyul, on my way back along the narrow village paths I came upon a cottage inhabited by a young Polish couple, Mr. and Mrs. K. He ran physical training and gymnastics in the army, and in Poland he had been a top trainer at the

State Institute of Physical Education in Warsaw. They had both spent a year in exile at a collective farm, and only a week earlier their son had been born. I found Mr. K. in the yard of their Uzbek cottage, mending a large black baby carriage on low wheels. He had gotten this pram, a real treasure, from someone here—it had come all the way from Warsaw. His wife was very pale, exhausted by the heat, which was especially acute that day, and was lying in a deck chair. The baby was asleep beside her, under a mosquito net acquired from goodness knows where.

I was moved by the sight of these brave people, the father working away, the frail woman with large black eyes, and their child. I told them I admired the touching madness of having a child here in these conditions, with such an uncertain future ahead of them, and said that evidently they accepted and loved life, and believed in it. Mr. K. broke off his task to answer me (he was banging large nails into the bottom of the overturned pram). He wiped the streams of sweat from his face with a sleeve and sat on the grass. An athletically built sportsman, he gazed lovingly at the petite figure of his wife and their child.

"What do you mean?" he said after a pause. "Do you think we're the only ones? Lots of Polish children were born at the collective farms. I know a little boy who was born at our farm, in quite appalling conditions, more than two months premature, and now he's the picture of health!

"Go to Yungiyul station and see how many of our women are down there with children. They're emaciated, they've got lice and no roof over their heads, and their men have gone to join the army, but even there there's laughter and joking. They keep their straw mattresses outside, and when it rains they put them away in the Uzbek houses, though the Uzbeks, with whom they cannot communicate of course, throw them back outside. But it doesn't matter. The women laugh and gossip, while the children play.

"'Why should I worry?' I heard one of them say. 'Poland is right here—let general staff do the worrying for me.'"

I went home thinking that the "golden branch of life" really is "eternally green."

23. WITHOUT A FLOURISH

MAY AND June have stayed in my memory as a time of gradual development, while the organizational work in all sections of our department struggled to come together; I also remember this period as a time of increasing weariness in ever more tropical heat, and above all exasperation because of constant obstacles, interruptions caused by serious illness, fears for the lives of our closest colleagues, and the disaster of one epidemic after another.

At the end of May we organized a conference for the education officers at general staff. Such an apparently simple task! But in those conditions just bringing in, accommodating, and feeding several dozen extra people at general staff meant a whole world of difficulties. My main reason for organizing this assembly was to have personal contact with the workers in the field, to gain direct understanding of the needs, shortages, and also the grievances of the education officers, with whom contact was so difficult and always too rare. I managed to get the chief of staff's signature for this conference, under a directive defining our rights, duties, and range of competence. This directive, devised by us "in agonies" was accepted in its basic shape by army command, but only after lengthy discussion and a series of amendments that limited our far-reaching ambitions.

My aim was to establish a common course of action, a common strategy. Our propaganda tasks in the field were in general outline indisputable: to maintain the will to fight for Poland in every circumstance, regardless of political party or racial differences, to have the closest possible contact with the soldiers, to help them in every respect, and to keep them informed of the situation. It was up to our department to obtain as much information as possible about Poland, about resistance and fighting there, and about the fighting on all fronts. The education officer in the field was responsible for organizing efficient distribution of our publications, information, and bulletins, and also of the material reaching us in an irregular stream from Britain. After all that time in the camps hunger for information was acute and universal. Apart from the journals and bulletins that came from general staff, each of the larger units also issued its own bulletin, based on radio broadcasts and materials that we provided. Even the smallest units issued their own wall newspapers. The education officers started up clubs, small libraries, and the first training centers for the youth. The lion's share of the effort went into overcoming basic difficulties—few armies can have had quite so many of them, hence too our battle to be assigned the most dynamic, energetic officers, and hence our constant complaints when we were fobbed off with idlers as education officers, because at the time our entire operation was regarded as a harmful sham.

The above-mentioned basic difficulties included in the first place a lack of paper. Many schools and hospitals had to use the cut-off edges of newspapers, gray cardboard from packaging, wooden slats, or even birch bark. Any sheet of paper that HQ and the education officers managed to obtain in whatever way they could was worth its weight in gold.

There was a lot for us to learn from Soviet propaganda, as far as organization and operational techniques were concerned, though naturally not with regard to their repeated political contortions, as we had been at war with Hitler since 1939, not 1941.

The Soviet propaganda apparatus taught us how to reach the highest and lowest levels of the army via active groups, propaganda journals, leaflets, and daily *politchasy*.* We constantly had to combat the automatic suspicion and aversion of many a unit commander

---

Politchas—an hour spent reading the newspapers together with a *politruk* explaining or commenting on events.

toward this "weapon," which among the Soviets and the Nazis possessed such fantastical methods and prerogatives.

But thanks to the support of our senior command, we had the opportunity to build up our apparatus considerably and broaden its sphere of activity, and through the more energetic education officers to have an influence on the relationship between officers and private soldiers, leading in a few instances to the removal from their post of officers whose attitude to the men was unfair or thoughtless.

In our attitudes to the Soviet authorities, we placed emphasis on defending our rights, but also on loyalty in fulfilling our obligations and on nonaggravation of a relationship that was in any case increasingly difficult.

For the conference I prepared a report comparing the propaganda methods used in Russia, Germany, and the democratic countries. I received the richest and most interesting material from our "guardian angel," Captain Sokolovsky.

A few days before the conference three of my closest coworkers were taken off to the hospital. Each of them had been due to prepare a report, and they included my deputy, who was responsible for the entire organization of the conference.

Creating positions on paper meant nothing when the lack of personnel to perform the increasing number of tasks was making itself more and more acutely felt. My most active, responsible staff members were out of the picture. In a job where we constantly had to improvise, where direct dealings with general staff, with the heads of various units, and with the commanders often meant everything, because everything had to be done at once, verbally, in person, or else it would be too late—the constant changes of personnel put us in a situation which frequently appeared inescapable. Over half my team were in the hospital and new people kept appearing instead of those who already knew the ropes.

But our department was no different from any other—all our formations in Turkestan were suffering from the same difficulties, and in a number of places their state of health was truly tragic.

*

The spread of illness and epidemics was so serious throughout the army that the possibility of creating any combat units within the USSR was in serious doubt.

Almost half the army (44 percent) passed through the isolation wards in our hospitals. Most soldiers fell victim to typhus, typhoid, dysentery, malaria, and so on. In Turkestan alone more than two thousand soldiers died of contagious diseases (not counting the people who died on the threshold of our army, the men, women, and children who, already infected, died on the way, at the stations, in the mud, in the snow, and in Uzbek tents).

Perhaps most tragic of all was the fate of the Seventh Infantry Division; on average more than half the division was in the hospital, and at the worst stage 73 percent of them were sick. In February and March of that year, in this one division 2,261 men came down with typhus alone. Nowadays we only have to study a lucid little book full of figures and graphs, shocking in its laconic eloquence, by Dr. S. Ehrlich, *At the Foundation of the Polish Army in the USSR,** to understand what tasks the doctors, nurses, and orderlies were facing. Their job, essentially, was to ensure that the entire army being formed in Russia did not die of contagious diseases.

Soldiers wounded at the front, being visited by their commanders, hospitals at the front lines—how eagerly every form of propaganda seized upon this noble theme; this was the suffering of heroes. But thousands of men dying in hospitals barely equipped with medicines, in hospital blocks unheated in winter, on the steppes bordering the Volga, or on the compacted clay of Uzbek tents in tropical heat—these were shameful facts; our Soviet guardians forbade us to talk or write about them, let alone photograph these conditions. We managed to export from this "paradise" a handful of horrific documentary photographs of children and soldiers dying in our hospitals, taken on the sly.

**U podstaw Armii Polskiej w ZSRR*, Biblioteka Towarzystwa Wiedzy Wojskowej 2 Korpusu, vol II.

The doctors and nurses fought the epidemics to the last limits of their strength, and it was a fight without a flourish, without the accompaniment of any kind of propaganda. Equally without a flourish, without having held a rifle, hundreds of soldiers quietly died.

At the army organizational center the average number of people sick was more than 69 percent. They were stationed at Guzar in Uzbekistan, which had been depopulated by deportations and executions following the last uprising in 1936. Our people lived in Uzbek and Tatar tents and shelters dug in the sandy fields. Of course, the rallying point was the main focus of epidemic. Louse-infested and already infected, large numbers came pouring in there to join the army. There was no underwear. The rallying point had a total of fifty tents for a population of 3,800. With thirty living in each tent, it was hardly possible to sit down. Some two thousand people lived under the open sky when at night there were still frosts and snow, and during the day it thawed and rained. Many dug themselves pits in the ground, where they sat in their rags, soaked and frozen. Others escaped to the neighboring villages and towns to spend the night under cover, walking miles each day to return at mealtimes, and bringing new lice and new infections back to the camp with them. It was easy to slip past the sentries, who didn't even have guns. Carts carrying the sick were pulled to the hospital by hand for lack of horses. Water was carried nonstop in buckets to a single cauldron over four hundred yards uphill. For lack of paper, there was no question of keeping any records or noting the course of an illness. The highest mortality rate in Guzar was among the staff at the hospital for contagious diseases, where 14 percent of the orderlies and 38 percent of the doctors died.

In the same area, there was a Junaki orphanage at a place called Karkin-Batash; the local well only provided ten buckets of water per day, while the irrigation system was constantly closed for several days at a time. The children were so worn out that they couldn't eat up their meager rations, and mortality among them reached 12 percent.

At other military centers the state of health was no less appalling; not until April did a slight improvement occur. The line units set up their own disinfection facilities, bathhouses, and laundries, gaining the opportunity to resist and defend themselves against contagion.

In Uzbekistan alone 49,411 patients suffering from contagious diseases went through our hospitals. According to Ehrlich, who worked as a Polish Army doctor from the very start, "at the beginning of the organization of the Polish Army one in three of the soldiers was suffering from an infectious disease, and in the period when the pace was particularly high, the number increased to almost one in two."

That was the situation.

One should remember that we had ended up in territory inhabited by a population that was also stretched to the limits, living in the most primitive sanitary conditions, where every inhabited place was an endless hotbed of typhus, typhoid, and dysentery.

In the early months of organizing the army it was typhus in particular that decimated the soldiers, followed in May and June 1942 by dysentery, with malaria coming in its wake.

After two years in prisons and labor camps, where none of the inmates had seen a single vegetable or a single fruit, people's hunger for raw food was so acute that it was impossible to restrain, and no prohibitions worked. As a result, from May dysentery raged in the army in an extremely virulent form.

In May too, once the mosquitoes had hatched, malaria began to spread at an alarming rate, reaching its greatest intensity in the Sixth Infantry Division, where at one point 96 percent of the men were sick. This division was mainly stationed at clay-based, treeless settlements in the vicinity of Shakhrisabz (Uzbekistan), where for some years the Soviet authorities had banned the cultivation of rice, for fear of malaria. But in 1942 the ban was lifted; our camps were pitched along the waterlogged paddy fields. The mosquitoes infected the entire army and the entire local population.

In Sixth Division alone, naturally the six-hundred-bed hospital wasn't large enough, and every ward was packed to bursting with patients lying side by side. There was never enough medicine, as in these circumstances even quite large stocks ran out at lightning speed. Naturally, mosquito nets were out of the question.

At the end of May General Anders came back from his first trip to Britain. The news he brought was bad—the British saw no possibility of arming our troops while they were on Soviet terrain. By now nobody was still under the illusion that the Soviet government would give us the promised weapons. The British tried to arm our troops by including equipment for the Poles in a general contingent allocated to the Red Army, but the Soviet authorities refused to agree to this solution.

At the same time, there were ever more persistent rumors that the Soviets were creating a new Polish army but a Red one of their own. In March I had met a swarthy soldier boy who spoke Polish badly and claimed he was off to join the Polish Army, but in Siberia. I regarded it as a misunderstanding, but one of our colleagues had apparently met some Polish officers recruiting for this new army. By now everyone, from Anders to the very last soldier in Turkestan, could tell that the honeymoon period of Polish-Soviet friendship was over. The Russians were increasingly often questioning the right of citizens of the Polish Republic of non-Polish ethnicity, who came from territory occupied by Russia, to join the army. The Soviet authorities were fanning the flames of local disputes, and our commanders were being showered in protests from the Soviet officers assigned to us because of the emblems of Lwów or Wilno that our soldiers stubbornly continued to form out of white pebbles in front of their tents on the desiccated Uzbek soil. (How many of those emblems I later saw on the desert sands of Iraq!)

At the same time soldiers and officers started to vanish from the Polish units, suddenly kidnapped by the NKVD. Just as Ehrlich and Alter had been taken from the embassy a few months earlier, in the same way one of our officers was kidnapped from the staff courtyard, pushed into an NKVD car at lightning speed and driven off. Our protests were of no use—the man had vanished into thin air.

The NKVD men at general staff were still exceedingly polite. At a reception of theirs, where as ever there was plenty of alcohol, and where for the umpteenth time one of our senior officers questioned an NKVD man about the missing prisoners from Kozelsk, Ostashkov, and Starobilsk, he was told, in the strictest confidence, not to talk about the matter because he might spoil it all by being too eager: "July and August are the only navigation periods in the Arctic Ocean, on the route furthest north to Franz Josef Land..."

We clung to this shadow of hope, and this final Soviet ruse still worked.

Or maybe a year ago, we thought, during the high-speed advance of the German army the Bolsheviks simply couldn't get our comrades out of there, but now that the situation was changing for the better, maybe they'd manage to bring them? The Soviet aim at the time was always that we shouldn't speak to the outside, and that we ourselves shouldn't entirely believe that defenseless prisoners of war, Polish officers and soldiers, could have been massacred.

In the second half of June the Soviet government suddenly got rid of all the Polish diplomatic posts, a total of nineteen on their terrain, with the exception of the embassy in Kuybyshev and a certain number of intermediaries. These posts performed the role of unofficial consulates, providing for the mass of Polish exiles. The role of these local posts, the range of their competence and capacity to take action depended on the personal character of the Soviet representatives on the spot and the skills and initiative of the diplomats.

These diplomatic posts made it easier for many people to reach the army, provided information on the new Polish Army—months after its establishment very imprecise reports were still in circulation—and also contributed to the release of prisoners who were still being detained in defiance of the "amnesty."

At the same time the military posts were closed down which our army command had sent into the field to steer the liberated Polish citizens toward the army, expedite the journey for the convoys, and obtain rations of bread for the weeks they would spend traveling. Through the diplomatic posts the embassy distributed welfare for the Polish population, including food from Britain and the United States, and clothes donated by Polish Americans.

This aid was limited compared with the need, but it was there, and that annoyed the Soviet authorities. At the time, one of the high-ranking NKVD officials said to our chief of staff, General Szyszko-Bohusz: "You'll be on your way soon, but it'll take us over twenty years to digest the buckwheat you'll have cooked up by being here."

Despite the many things that these posts lacked (they must have been improvised at high speed and were not always properly staffed), every Soviet citizen must been have struck by the democratic nature of the diplomats from "reactionary" Poland compared with the Soviet officials, the lack of the distance that between the Soviet authorities and their population was created by fear, and how easy it was to criticize the Polish authorities (which no Pole failed to do). As well as this, the free distribution of canned foods unheard of in the Soviet Union (the greatest avidity was prompted by corned beef, for which one could exchange items that were unobtainable in the USSR, such as reels of film, cameras, and car tires). The used shoes and old clothes from the United States were real treasures, and all this came pouring in from the capitalist world, supposedly "steeped in poverty." For the hungry, impoverished Soviet population cut off from the outside world all this constituted dangerous propaganda.

In June, once all their offices and storerooms had been sealed, one hundred diplomats and diplomatic post staff were arrested, and so were our "intermediaries." Among those arrested was my cousin Henryk Żółtowski. We had been childhood friends, but I had lost sight of him for many years. I retained a memory of him as an extremely able man, open-minded, very kind and attentive. Originally from the Poznań region, he and his wife and three children had taken refuge in Wilno in September 1939 but were then deported into the depths of the USSR. Liberated following the "amnesty," he was appointed by our embassy as the diplomatic representative at Barnaul (in Altai Krai). The people arriving from there were full of respect and gratitude for his work. "He was our best diplomat," his boss told me. In May I received a letter from him. He wanted to leave his post to come and join the army with his wife and children. He asked me for advice and information. I could see what was happening all around me; I considered the wave of people leaving difficult but already "domesticated" places of exile or deportation, I saw them starving here on Uzbek terrain, clinging to the underfed army that was being ravaged by epidemic, trying hard to survive with this army through thick and thin. Further disasters were imminent. The evacuation of the army to Iran was still very problematic, and evacuating the civilian population along with it seemed at the time fanciful in the extreme. I wrote back advising him against leaving, urging him not to abandon such important work, of which I had heard so many good things. I don't know if my letter had any influence on his decision not to leave Barnaul.

Only a few weeks later Henryk Żółtowski was arrested and died in prison. The food parcels his wife and children brought for him, by selling off everything they had, were still being eagerly accepted two months after his death.

Any piece of guidance given at the time, like the advice I sent to Barnaul, could bring salvation, doom, or death. Today each of us is examining his conscience, wondering how many times he was to blame for a death because he gave one or another piece of advice, or because he dared not give any. At general staff we were being showered in requests for guidance. Quite reasonably everybody thought that at general staff we had a better idea of how Poland's fortunes would develop, and few people can have realized to what extent the future of the army being formed was still in doubt.

After the arrest of all the diplomats, the Polish population scattered across the whole Soviet Union was again utterly at the mercy, or lack of mercy, of the Soviet authorities. The "illegal" influx of Polish families to the army, strictly prohibited by the NKVD, only increased.

As soon as he came back from London, General Anders began efforts toward a new audience with Stalin, with the aim of elaborating further recruitment, which on March 19 he had already discussed with Stalin before leaving for Britain. The aim was to be able to send those recruits to our units located in Iran for training. General Anders was also determined to secure the evacuation to Iran of the forty thousand soldiers and their families still in Russia. The turn of events in Uzbekistan and the neighboring republics, and the conditions prevailing there, proved the need for evacuation a thousand times over.

By then we all understood that the extremely difficult task of forming a modern Polish army out of the mass of physically exhausted or ailing Poles was only a realistic endeavor outside the borders of Soviet Russia.

In Turkestan the epidemics did not let up. Apart from outdated training weapons for a single division, the Soviet government could not or would not provide any guns. Meanwhile the Soviet officers attached to our army were starting to drop hints again about the eventual limitation of rations for the Polish Army, suggesting that soldiers who couldn't be fed were to be sent off to forestry sites, factories, and collective farms—forced labor camps, whatever they were called.

General Anders was not invited to Moscow; evidently Stalin had ultimately realized that he would never be able to make him into a blind tool for his policies.

In July a telegram came from Stalin agreeing to the evacuation of the rest of the Polish Army along with their families to Iran but refusing to allow further recruitment on the territory of Soviet Russia.

I cannot say much about this final period in the USSR or about the evacuation from my own personal memories.

Early in July, the day after being inoculated with some wonderful anti-typhus vaccine sent from India, I came down with a fever. Typhus? Malaria? A few days later it was confirmed that I had both of them at once. In a not entirely conscious state I was taken to the hospital in Ak-Altyn. Discharged at the end of August, by which time the basic evacuation was already over, I was transferred with the rest of the stragglers, sick people, and children via Ashgabat to Iran.

24. AK-ALTYN

AN ESCAPE—I don't know what else to call it, how else to define my illness in Ak-Altyn.

I remember the first half of July at general staff as a period that was hard for anyone to endure. I was no exception.

"I'm just longing to fall sick," as the member of our team who was toughest on himself and the most experienced of all had said to me at the time—it was Professor Aleksandrowicz, who in the schooling section was endlessly battling against insurmountable obstacles. "That's my one desire—other people carry out inspections and are lucky enough to be able to forget, but I remember everything, and it won't give me a moment's rest. There's so little I can do to help, if anything at all."

A few days later, it was not the professor who fell sick but his right-hand woman, Janina Pilatowa, small and frail, but dynamic and determined. She too was taken off to Ak-Altyn, suffering from typhus.

We all knew this Soviet hospital for Polish soldiers. For weeks we had been taking advantage of the hot siesta hours or evenings after work to dash over to this place, where so many of our people were battling with death. We would drive there with a jar of stewed fruit, which would spill on the way, a bottle of wine or rusks—first through the streets of the town, passing long strings of pensive camels led by a small donkey, then past huge depots, entire "ricks" of cotton, and down a dry, potholed road along the vast cotton fields (that was why this place was called Ak-Altyn, meaning "White Gold"). Then we would pass through the narrow streets of Ak-Altyn lined with clay cottages and drive up to two small whitewashed blocks, separated by a bed of multicolored flowers and some paths. On one side of the white buildings there was a fence dividing it from the street, and on the other there were some small mulberry trees, with a few little benches underneath them. A carefully tilled cotton field came right up to the hospital.

When we first saw the hospital, although it was poor and cramped, we all shared the same pleasant impression of a place that was well looked after. The people who worked there were utterly dedicated to their profession, and all the patients knew that here they would be treated by experienced, sensible doctors, and that the nurses would attend to them with maternal care.

The first of our staff whom we visited there was Wiktor Ostrowski, suffering from typhus. We couldn't enter the isolation ward, so we talked through the window. I had first met Wiktor in Gryazovets; he was very thin with a shaved head, no beard, regular, gaunt features, and an intent, glassy expression in his eyes—at the time he reminded me of a medieval monk in a padded jacket. Interned in Lithuania, after the Soviets occupied it, in 1940 he had ended up in Kozelsk, from where the NKVD took more than 4,000 of our officers to Katyn and murdered them. Ostrowski and 1,500 others had been transferred to Gryazovets once the German-Soviet war had begun, and thus in the summer of 1942. There he had caused a sensation with his talks, which the entire camp enjoyed, about his mountaineering expeditions and the peaks he had climbed in the Cordillera, the Caucasus, and the Alps. His book about the Caucasus, which he had managed to bring with him, clearly and popularly written, taught us not only how to climb peaks nobody had conquered but also how to love a tough life full of dangers. By profession an engineer and a good organizer, he had joined Propaganda from day one; despite suffering from wounds caused by scurvy, he had set up our film and photography department. In Ak-Altyn he was being nursed by a very young Ukrainian called Gala. He owed his recovery largely to this girl's constant care. He was the first to tell me how devotedly our nurses worked at the hospital. There was no service, no effort these women shied away from. Gala was no exception. Ostrowski saw her spend four nights in a row by the side of a dying man in the same ward, while also giving her own blood for a transfusion. I choose to mention this because of course, throughout the war many nurses worked selflessly all over the world, but amid such brutal living conditions in the Soviet Union, amid our memories of the camps, where people were treated worse than cattle, this warm and merciful attitude was extremely moving, like rediscovering the world of our childhood, like rediscovering our homeland.

Ostrowski had not yet returned from the hospital before my deputy Józef Zielicki was taken there. For a whole week he had a pulse rate of 117, a raised temperature, and an ashen face. There were dozens of urgent jobs to be done, and the education officers' conference was due to take place in a few days' time. Józef worked superbly, ardently, almost tirelessly, with no nonsense or what the Silesians call "making wind" (not that he suppressed it, he simply had no such tendency). Whenever he wiped his small hands, with short, slightly curled fingers, whenever he smiled with that strange look that was always on his gaunt face, his burning eyes, so pale they looked white—it was for quite specific, service-related reasons: either he had managed to establish a youth department, hold an education officers' briefing, secure a new job for a valued employee, or obtain provisions for one of the centers. All the while he did his job so discreetly, so quietly that few people knew to whom they owed the help they had received. He always took on the tricky conversations and sorted out all sorts of complicated matters. He said what he thought without pulling any punches and, though not always tactful, he always stuck to his guns, which meant that he did have enemies. But behind a prickly, sulky exterior he had a heart of gold and performed the lion's share of the real and most essential work in our department.

At the hospital he was initially diagnosed with typhus, and was duly treated for it. It was a few weeks before they realized that he had sepsis, a general infection of the blood and the pericardium. He was given a series of different treatments for each presumed infection, and ultimately intravenous doses of Rivanol, which finally began to have an effect.

He lay in the hospital in tropical heat, white as the sheet he was

under, pouring with streams of sweat, because each day his temperature fluctuated, rising to about 104°F, and then falling below 97. I
usually visited him when his temperature had gone down. The doctors
were feeling helpless, and for some weeks they couldn't even define
what infection he had. He remained very calm. During my short
visits we talked about many specific details of our educational work.
But despite his great self-control he was obviously growing weaker.
Not long ago he had told me how he had escaped death by a whisker
in Butyrki; he was still physically debilitated after all those months
in prison, undergoing tough interrogations. Nor could I forget that
his father had died very young of heart disease. How long would his
heart hold out against the daily swing in temperature?

"If he comes down with any other infection, he'll be done for,"
the matchless Dr. Duczymińska told me—she was always on the go
between general staff and the hospital, caring for our patients nonstop.

So would I have to come to terms with his death too?

He wrote me little notes, always passing businesslike comment on
the stewed fruit I sent, which was the only thing that gave him any
relief, saying that it was overcooked, undercooked, or had come too
late. In the same spiky, Gothic script he wrote asking me to bring
him a few small things he needed, including his ring with an eagle—
this last request was underlined. It was a black ring with a small white
eagle carved on a red background by a sergeant from general staff,
using part of a red toothbrush. Only once did Józef write: "I only
have enough strength for another ten to fifteen days. I'm losing the
will to live, and all my joy at life." I had always admired his will to
live, his ability to enjoy life despite having a very sad look on his face,
while also dedicating himself to our work, from which I had lately
derived so much stress and resentment toward myself and others. He
told me that while he was in prison he hadn't killed a single living
thing, not even a bedbug, because he loved life so much. How far I
was from loving life at the time! How greatly I admired and envied
him. A phrase of Dostoevsky's came to mind: "One must love life
more than its meaning." How does one achieve this attitude to life
if one does not possess it by nature?

As I was returning from the hospital at dusk, I thought about all the close friends I had lost. So was this to be my lot—the death of my friends? Was Józef Zielicki going to die too? Each death intensified the feeling of having no more strength to form new attachments and start life over again. The sudden disruption of our camp friendships and the increasingly niggling belief that my closest friends from Starobilsk were already dead had severely undermined my will to live. Now work and friendship had brought me close to a few people once again, and maybe this attachment felt so vital because it was having to replace everything that had been torn away from us, our country and the loved ones we had left there, and those whom we had only just lost; once again death was going to snap those threads. I thought with bitter envy of people who were capable of "cocooning" themselves in old age, guaranteeing themselves a sort of restricted happiness by caring for nothing but their own health and a peaceful decline. The charming X., friendly and obliging, whom I had known in Paris, could not resist telling anecdotes at the funeral of his son-in-law, in whose home he lived and to whom he was very attached; when his own wife had been buried (after several decades together in perfect harmony), he had come out of the house, in front of which stood the funeral cortège, and automatically said with a smile: "*Quel beau soleil!*" Only on noticing the hearse had he dropped his gaze and added: "*Mais quelle triste journée!*" One can teach oneself self-protective egoism by being standoffish for years on end, and if not egoism, then perhaps to be more detached toward fragile personal affections, more abstract. But what use is that, if I have never been able to see things other than through people? Even Poland has always been embodied for me by a few faces of the living and the dead.

Throughout this period the work had to continue in every section. To cap it all, the heat never let up but intensified; it was even hard to breathe at night. I found it much harder to bear than later on in the Iraqi desert, maybe because the wind was not as dry, or I was still, like everyone, malnourished. In the morning the work was solid and intensive, but later on it became increasingly foggy, the brain slowed down, the number of papers on the desk increased, the number of people with whom or for whom one had to do something also rose, and I found myself losing control over things and people. The only consolation was that I was aware of it—I could see that I wasn't in control of the system, that it was coming apart in my hands. I have found the following extract from the diary I kept in Yungiyul in this period: "What's the point of life? An electric button by the bed that you can press for instant death—that is my cowardly, passive dream." There was nothing metaphysical about my state of mind. It was as far as possible from the Christian attitude to death, the self-sacrificing, courageous approach, where there is both love of life and sacrifice of life; all I could feel was a longing for nonexistence and sleep. In this defeatist mood I was gripped by fever, aching bones, and a violent headache. I was immediately dispatched to the crowded infirmary at general staff. And here again I endured the frequently experienced, unreal, and "ultimate" attitude to illness. Maybe death was coming now; I felt no fear, just clear awareness that death is only terrible when other people die.

Lying in the stuffy infirmary, from far, far away on the Kurkuldyuk I could hear the sounds of our orchestra playing dance music, someone calling "Hello, General!" and singing. I admired these people who still wanted to live after all they had been through.

As I was in a high fever, I do not remember much of my first few weeks in the typhus ward, apart from the broad, kind face of Nina Fyodorovna, the senior ward sister, leaning over my bed with the light behind her. Many of the patients and nurses called her "mama." She was the daughter of a peasant from somewhere on the Volga. Without raising her voice, but with unwavering authority she ran the hospital's isolation ward. One of the white hospital buildings and part of the other one were under her command. I had the meek and happy feeling that others were thinking for me, that I could be totally passive, and that nothing was being asked of me beyond swallowing some pills and having my temperature taken.

As soon as my temperature began to drop a little, I had time to think in the stifling heat of the day, and at night too I could ponder in solitude the last few weeks of work and do some bitter soul-searching, identifying all the deficiencies and all our mistakes. My friends and colleagues, though not allowed inside to see me, did visit by looking in at the windows. The care and warmth bestowed on me from the very start by my friends and the nurses were the starting point for my long and beneficial psychological recovery. I slowly started to regain an attitude to life, to people, and to myself that was not strained, hostile, and nerve-racking. Ak-Altyn gave me the chance to catch my breath.

"We only paint a fraction of contemplation," writes Norwid, but we only live a fraction of contemplation too—when that moment of respite, of solitary gazing, of disinterested communion dies, not just indifference but a loathing for life sets in. It is hardest during war, when every gesture must hit its target at the shortest range, must support this world of thoughts and contemplation. But as far as my work was concerned, it could never be finished—it demanded nonstop communication, supervision, and endless hammering away at the important issues, as well as at the seemingly trivial but no less necessary ones. All this demanded smiles, compromises, pressure, even vodka drinking, and the tide kept on rising above our heads, overwhelming us. As well as maintaining a sense of duty and an ability to impose my will, I had to be capable of keeping it in check.

I'm trying to decide what contributed to my salvation in Ak-Altyn, apart from human friendship. I spent hours gazing out of the window, looking at the cream-white window frame against a pure blue, almost always cloudless sky, very bright in the mornings, then gradually darker, then brightening again, taking on a greenish hue. I thought about how a painter could pick out the "sound" of that perfect blue, the "shout" of the white window frame against the azure sky; I could only summon up the memory of a few pictures that gave me the right evocation of a pure blue sky with objects set against it (although I had seen thousands of paintings of the sky).

I thought about Matisse and his southern Moroccan canvases (featuring windows, sky, and white curtains), where the shout of colors was rendered with incomparable, singular force, and at the same time almost childlike simplicity (or so it seemed, for in fact it was highly conscious); I remembered Guardi's *Piazza San Marco*, a painting I had seen in Paris in 1935 at an exhibition of masterpieces from the museum in Grenoble, and which Pankiewicz had pointed out to me. This picture also featured the same brightness of a smooth sky, and also the logical waxing and waning of this brightness, from the illuminated houses on one side to the shaded ones on the other. Later, when I was taken outside the hospital to sit in a deck chair, I gazed at the flower beds, filled with dark-red velvety-looking sprays of dahlias and asters, yellow chrysanthemums on big, luxuriant bushes, masses of familiar flowers of every color mixed with ones I didn't recognize (including some pink flowers growing thickly on tall stems with green leaves turning yellow); and remembered that a bed of this kind, overgrown with all sorts of flowers, had once interested me enough to provide my mind and memory with endless material to work on for several days. This lost world seems to me totally unattainable now. Yet even the memory of it gave me support and spiritual nourishment.

After a few weeks I was transferred to the other wing, where Ostrowski had been lying earlier. There I ended up in the merciful hands of Gala, the Ukrainian nurse. The small ward housed ten of us, all typhus patients, lying very close together. It was still stuffy, and there was always someone having an enema or "sitting on the throne," so there was a constant sickly-sweet smell in the room. I spent the first night beside patient S., who was unconscious and in such a hopeless state that he couldn't control his bladder. Every time he had an accident, Gala would call in a colleague from the next ward and, as gentle as an angel, would change his entire bedding. Two days later the poor man died. Right to the end, Gala hardly left his side. Once I had recovered, I reminded her of my neighbor who had died.

"You're talking about Janek, oh yes . . . he once showed me a photograph he always had on him, of his young wife and two lovely little sons, and I felt so sorry for him, so sorry . . ." and she fell silent.

In this ward there was also a pleasant sergeant from Vrevsk. He had a son in the Junaki, who had spent a few months in the hospital too, and had only just survived. The father was calm and solemn, with white eyebrows above large sad eyes, and a white beard grown in the past few weeks. He had severe complications. The nurses were not entirely certain he would recover. He bore his severe condition with total resignation. "I've already told myself that if God so wishes, that will be my fate." Beside him lay another man, who had gone almost totally deaf from typhus, with a yellow complexion and hard stubble on his chin. He never said a word, except for the occasional torrent of invective, either against the propaganda department, which was useless, because it had been late issuing an announcement, or against our best doctor, because she spent too little time talking to each patient and was evidently "proud," or against the meager dinner.

By now I was feeling better. My temperature had dropped, and my colleagues were coming to see me through the window, even Mrs. N., who wasn't tall and had to jump up to show me the tip of her powdered nose. On the final Sunday before the army left Yungiyul (the evacuation was now in full swing), the guards' orchestra came to say goodbye, with all the officers. Through the open windows a very young woman sang us a song about Warsaw, popularized by Zosia Terné, and then a song about going home. The patients began to sob, and at this point Nina Fyodorovna immediately put an end to the concert. One of the patients in the neighboring ward was still in a serious condition and had been seized by such a fit of weeping that she couldn't be exposed to such emotion any longer.

There is a strange slackening of the nerves after an illness, and perhaps of the tear ducts too. I noticed it in others, and felt it very strongly for myself, although in normal life, even in misfortune I have hardly ever known what tears are. After the cold and bitter mood I had felt before the illness, now I wept at every opportunity, or without an opportunity, inventing reasons for it, but they were good tears, of affection, marking a return to life. I remembered the passage in *The Brothers Karamazov* describing a murderer who confessed his crime many years after the fact. Father Zossima said that not only did he experience total relief, not only was he happy, but God had even granted him "the gift of tears." And in fact most of the convalescents in Ak-Altyn had this gift of tears. I remember crying about two things on one of the first evenings after my temperature came down. The first was a Chopin concert in Warsaw. I imagined the first concert that would be staged after the Germans had been driven out; when I heard that they had banned Polish music in Warsaw, and Chopin in particular, it prompted me to imagine the Philharmonic being rebuilt at high speed, a crowd too large to fit in the concert hall filling the surrounding streets, loudspeakers, all Warsaw and us, come home from afar—and I wept tears of joy. At the time I believed it would happen. The other reason was Eustachy Sapieha's last visit. He was finally leaving for Tehran and had come to say goodbye. I wept out of affection for him, remembering how this old man with a face straight from a painting by El Greco, very white teeth, splendidly thoroughbred features, burning dark eyes, and a slight limp caused by gout or rheumatism, had been assigned to Propaganda.

Released just after the "amnesty" following two years in prison and a death sentence for having been Poland's foreign minister and for having signed the Riga peace treaty, he had ended up at the embassy, where he was assigned to the filing. The former minister, highly rated by Piłsudski in 1920, then ambassador in London for many years, was in addition a prince, and a pillar of the Nonpartisan Bloc for Cooperation with the Government—undoubtedly a disastrous set of references at Kot's embassy. He had been left on the sidelines, and when I arrived at the embassy, the impression I had was of a man who clearly deserved respect but was probably no longer capable of work demanding energy and initiative. He was among twenty people earmarked to be sent from the embassy to a diplomatic post outside the Soviet Union. One day all these people arrived in Yungiyul, which was near Tashkent, from where they were supposed to be traveling onwards. At the last moment the Soviets stopped two of them and ruthlessly prohibited them from crossing the border. They were the communist poet Broniewski and the former minister, Prince Sapieha. A decision was made to take them into the army, so that they could leave Russia with the troops as Polish Army officers, at which point

Anders assigned Sapieha to Propaganda. Most of us had doubts about this, seeing it as a totally fictional "courtesy" appointment. There was tons of work to be done, and not enough people to do it. "He's just going to take up a staff post."

Only one of our colleagues persisted in loudly calling him "Mr. Minister" and "Prince" every other word; meanwhile, with his consistent but rather childish sense of democracy Józef would have died rather than address him as "Prince," and apparently once told him off like a twenty-year-old cadet. Sapieha took it calmly, as the simplest thing in the world. His task was to run the garrison lecture department.

It was amazing to see how this man got down to work, running three or four miles a day in the hot sun, never complaining, arguing with the unit commanders about times, finding lecturers, and going to hear and supervise each talk—he was so morally upright that he even supported and praised lecturers to whom at first he had violently objected, once he discovered that his judgment had been incorrect. So it was with the famous writer Mrs. Nagler, who worked in our publishing and library department, when she insisted on giving a talk about Polish poetry, including Słowacki, to a company of drivers. Sapieha was on the defensive: "Can this really be of any interest to the drivers?" But the talk went ahead, and was a big success. Sapieha was very pleased about it, and from then on he supported Mrs. Nagler wholeheartedly.

In this same period Czuchnowski, the communist poet, joined our department too. He was going to give a series of anti-Nazi talks, so as a lecturer he was answerable to Sapieha. The same colleague who so loudly greeted "Prince" and "Minister" Sapieha could not come to terms with the presence of Czuchnowski among us, whose extreme radicalism was notorious in Poland. "That Bolshevik!" he boomed indignantly.

I can still see Sapieha and Czuchnowski sitting together, discussing the text of a future talk at the long table in our propaganda department, those two faces, the calm, bony face of the old prince, like the profile on a medal, and the thin, nervous, birdlike face of the peasant poet. Old Sapieha took him to the lectures, conferred with him, and praised him.

"He's good, he speaks well, you just have to rein him in a bit, because he's very passionate and tends to overshoot the mark," he told me after one of Czuchnowski's talks.

After only a few days with us, Sapieha had nothing but friends. He spent all his spare time at the department, at the same long, narrow table. He brought interesting books for the library about Uzbekistan's past, about Tamerlane and Genghis Khan, and read up on them.

One time a fat man called Bau came to see me, the driving force behind our *Eagle*. He was a born journalist, with a tabloid past, who loved sensational stories and was very good at observing people, then making witty but never really spiteful comments.

"I never imagined I'd have such extraordinary conversations here!" he said to me one day, waving his hands about. "What sensational memoirs they'll make. A few days ago, here in Propaganda, L.* told me that before the war he met Ribbentrop at a bathhouse in Venice, and that Ribbentrop told him about the annexation of the Ruhr, admitting that it had been Hitler's bluff, but the only one, because all his other moves had been supported by a commensurate military force. How many dollars I could get for this information in New York! And now, yesterday I was sitting in the orchard with Prince Sapieha, wetting our feet in an *aryk*. He told me the entire story of the 1919 coup d'état, and at one point I asked him what he believed was the most important act he had ever signed into law. He thought for a long time and then replied: 'I think it was the Franco-Polish alliance.' Recently he told me about the days when the Bolsheviks advanced right up to Warsaw. He was foreign minister at the time. I asked him where he was at the moment when the news came through that the Bolsheviks had been repelled. It seems he was in the street—he had immediately raced off to the ministry on Miodowa Street, but that's not the point: as he was telling me, he had big fat tears in his eyes."

*Eugeniusz Lubomirski.

I hope to read Bau's memoirs one day—he really should write them. They'd be interesting, often moving, and certainly funny too. Once he told me in a whisper, very seriously: "What do you think, Captain, the entire scandal involving 'Rudy' Radziwiłł and Mrs. Suchestow was my doing! The editor demanded a scandal without fail within the next two weeks, because the readership was falling—so I came up with Radziwiłł!" As he said this, he had the look on his face of a commander describing a great victory he had won.

After a few weeks working with us Sapieha fell sick with a particular form of malaria. He was taken to the same hospital in Ak-Altyn. He was in a large ward, where I remember seeing him one hot afternoon: the sun was blazing through the window, and he was lying naked, barely covered by a sheet. With those dark, burning eyes, sparse, ruffled snow-white hair, emaciated ribcage the color of ivory rising above the pushed-back sheet, and those thin arms, he no longer looked like a painting by El Greco, but like Saint Jerome the hermit in a small canvas, by Titian perhaps, which I vaguely remembered from the Louvre. His eyes hurled thunderbolts, and now and then he erupted, complaining that they were poisoning him with medicine (he threw it all away), forcing him to eat out of spite, when he insisted on fasting, *parce qu'il faut faire jeûner la fièvre.** Ultimately the cause of all this was an obsession with the idea that once again he had been "put away," and that they would never let him out of there—the trauma of a man who had spent almost two years in prison and several weeks in the death cell.

After much difficulty we persuaded the kind doctors to let Sapieha leave, because they weren't helping him anyway, if he was throwing away the medicine and starving himself. He returned to general staff, and there, in conditions that were a hundred times worse, he very quickly recovered.

As I lay in the typhus ward, I found out that Sapieha was now definitely leaving for Tehran with some of the troops. Throughout his work at the office I had hardly crossed paths with him, and he

* "You have to starve a fever."

even resented that I took so little interest in the needs and difficulties of his section, but now in a state of illness I was overcome with affection for this man, his age, his past, his modesty, style, and noble character.

For my final week in the hospital I was back with Nina Fyodorovna, in a section for typhus patients within the large ward for those suffering from dysentery (there were more than forty of them). The patients in my section included platoon sergeant Orzechowski, whose parents had died in Arkhangelsk oblast and whose two brothers had been killed defending Grodno from the Soviets. A third brother from the guards division came to see him, bringing chocolate and money. "There's just us two left, we met up in prison, and we're still together," he said. "You're not going to die, are you? You are going to live? Because"—at this point he turned to me—"if a man's number's up, he'll die, but if it's not, he won't." He said it right in front of his brother, who had a temperature of 104°F and showed no reaction to his questions and adages at all. I lay beside him in the same room for several days, and I don't think he said a word in all that time.

I hardly had any contact with the dysentery patients. I was not allowed to go near them. During my time there one of them died, wheezing and groaning terribly in the process. On the other side of a latticed partition lay a small boy, strangely quiet. Nina Fyodorovna didn't believe he was curable, and they were giving him whatever he wanted, chocolate and beetroot soup, and persuading him to let them carry him out into the sunshine. He didn't want to move from the spot and lay like a mouse, silent and sad, not weeping, but never smiling either.

There was one other patient whom I wish to mention: a large man with rather a brutal face, a powerful jaw and a permanently unshaven chin. Emaciated, suffering from dysentery, he dragged himself unsteadily about the ward. His name was Grad, and he came from Małopolska. He was a settler, originally from near Grodno. His parents had been deported to Arkhangelsk oblast and forced to work there. His father was seventy-three and his mother seventy-eight—they had both died after being moved to the Vologda area. His wife had died in Tashkent. He said that fifty-two members of his family (which included sons-in-law, brothers-in-law, and their families) had been deported.

"Now there are only five of us left alive—all the others are dead, the truth is they starved to death. And now I know that from my village, out of a total of thirty houses they took everyone from sixteen. I'd like to go home before I die, just for half a year!"

"Why for such a short time?" I asked.

"To meet up with my Ukrainian pals—they were the ones who informed on me, they tortured me. I lay under a board—do you know what that's like? They make a man lie under a board, and then they whack it with an ax—people die like that, it damages your kidneys and rips out your innards. I survived it, I lay there for six weeks and got out." When he spoke of the Ukrainians, his cold, fierce hatred was evident.

For almost two years the Soviets had occupied that territory, inhabited for centuries by Ukrainians and Poles, where there was no village without mixed marriages, where people with Ukrainian surnames were so often Polish patriots and people with Polish surnames ardently supported the Ukrainian cause; three years ago the Bolsheviks had deported both Poles and Ukrainians alike in cattle trucks to the east, and deadly mutual resentments were still in play for deadly mutual crimes.

During my last week in the hospital I was allowed to go and sit outside on a deck chair, which was an immense joy for me. After the ward full of patients and its sickly smell, and the unchanging "landscape" of beds and nightstands, I could enjoy the pure, clean air, the beds of multicolored flowers, and the distant view of the cotton fields, white with blossom, like modest little wild roses. From afar, the Uzbek houses made of baked clay and the fields during the sunset, and then under the stars were a feast for the eyes. In the last few days I was allowed to spend almost all my time in the dense shade of the small mulberry trees. This place where there was so much famine and poverty now seemed to me not only beautiful but wonderfully fertile, like the Promised Land. Next to the cotton farm was a silk farm, and then the paddy fields, cultivated by Koreans, deported from Manchuria or Korea. While I was convalescing I was brought fabulous fruit from the neighboring orchards, including grapes, and peaches with dark flesh, like apricots, of a size I'd never seen before.

I was told that this area had only been changed into collective farms four or five years earlier, and that the government had proceeded with "extraordinary restraint" to avoid further unrest in this region. On the other hand I heard that only a few years before then, none of the Bolshevik agitators sent to these parts had ever returned, because the Uzbeks had murdered them. So a few years ago they had simply deported all the richer Uzbek property owners to a place about fifty miles away. "They and their families left everything behind," a Bolshevik nurse told me. "Everything?" I asked in surprise. "Yes, everything, because they had to leave their houses and what was in them; naturally all their land was taken from them for the collective farms. Now, several years on, they've been allowing more and more of those Uzbeks to come back, but as members of the collective farm."

A few wards away from me, in the other building Janina Piłatowa was also suffering from typhus. We had only just met before falling ill. Here I was in very close daily contact with her, purely by letter. She was a unique person, enterprising, intelligent, and forceful in her reactions. A philologist by profession, author of a series of school textbooks, she was from Lwów and had been a student of Professor Lehr-Spławiński; with rare efficiency she had set up Polish schools in Kyrgyzstan. Then in Yungiyul she worked in our education department. After we left Russia, in Palestine we owed her among other things the three-volume *Polski szlak* (The Polish Way). It took a miraculous degree of persistence, energy, and inventiveness to select such a wealth of first-rate pieces of Polish prose and classical poetry, photographs from all over Poland, and up-to-date texts from the course of the Polish fighting since 1939. I remember my first impression of her: petite, with glittering eyes and stiff, cropped hair. Suddenly we began to correspond, writing each other long letters, and fighting over seemingly trivial but actually vital matters, wounding each other mortally, and then making it up again. The good-natured nurses thought we were crazy. Once we began to improve and were put outside on deck chairs, we spent long hours together in the shade of the trees. I was dazzled by the rare degree of her precise intelligence, that of a scholar with a permanently live stream of painful Polish susceptibility, a stream that went back to Słowacki and Żeromski. Our conversations in deck chairs only went on for a few days before her temperature started to rise again, just a couple of degrees, but soon after she was forbidden to lie outside. Nonetheless she kept walking, dragging the heavy deck chair by herself—she was defiant by nature, so she tried to hide her fever but overdid it. When I left the hospital she had a high temperature again, and her wide, feverish eyes twinkled in her small face; at that point it wasn't at all certain if she would recover, or if she would be well enough to travel abroad.

The closer my departure, the more time I spent out of doors. Nina Fyodorovna was on her feet all day. In the evening there was a *politchas*, when she sat on the wall surrounding the hospital, with the nurses gathered about her, and explained the latest news from the front to them. Once darkness had fallen, she often sat at my bedside. Nina Fyodorovna was a widow with an adult daughter, a medical student called Vera. Vera was young and pretty, with a complexion that radiated health, very black, lively eyes, and black hair that was always willfully escaping from under her white headscarf. She worked in the same unit as her mother, under her management.

One day I was lying on my deck chair as usual. It was almost night, the air was fresh, and in a still greenish, not entirely dark sky the Great Bear began to twinkle above the cotton field. Her day's work done, Nina Fyodorovna sat beside me on a stool and turned her tired gaze on the field. I told her how much I liked her daughter, and how well she looked.

"If you knew what she's been through, and how she looked in March! She arrived here barely alive. She's a medical student at Leningrad University, and she only has one more year to become a doctor. She was in Leningrad during the siege, the worst of the cold weather and the heaviest fighting. She was told to evacuate an old, reliable worker who was a patient there. She must already have been sicker than he was at the time—all winter she had lived on a daily bread ration of four and a half ounces, and she was terribly famished. She took him to Vologda and left him in the hospital there, then traveled on to join me. If not for one of your people who helped her on the way, I might never have seen her again."

A couple of days later, in the same spot Vera told me what had happened.

"I traveled by train from Vologda with a woman and her children. At one of the Siberian stations we were told that the Tashkent train, in which we were traveling, was stopping there for three days, so we should go and get provisions. I got out to find some provisions for the family I was traveling with and myself, but meanwhile the train went off with all my things, including my travel documents. I had to catch it up. It was night. After waiting for several hours I was told there was a train going in the right direction standing at track nine. I didn't know what was wrong with me, but I already had a high temperature. I felt so weak. It was dark. I hardly had the strength to walk around or under the very long trains that were standing at the station. Finally I found track nine—where there was no sign of a train—and in the distance there was a man standing in the snow under a lamppost. Making a final effort, I forced myself to walk up and ask him what I should do—maybe he worked for the railroad. But he was a Pole, and like me he was looking for the train to Tashkent. He was going to join the army. To catch up with my original train, I would have to buy a new ticket; I only had forty rubles and there were two terribly long lines for tickets at the station. The Pole whom I had met by chance expressed himself in a very refined way, despite looking gaunt and being dressed in rags. He had graduated from an institute, but I can't remember which. He could see I had a fever and was fainting with tiredness, so he gave me his letter of referral to Tashkent, assuming that as he was going to join the army he'd get there anyway. He found me a place in the packed waiting room, took off his jacket, laid it on the floor, and told me to lie down on it.

He went foraging for me, and stood in line for me. Suddenly, late at night we were told there was a train leaving for Tashkent, so without tickets we fought our way onto the closed platform and got into a dark freight car full of people. There the Pole found me a place again, laid me on the ground, and I passed out. Only at dawn did I come around and wonder where my guardian was. My traveling companions told me that he had jumped out at one of the stops to fetch me some tea, but the train had departed, leaving him behind.

"And I never saw him again. Every time they bring in a patient I wonder if it's him. I don't even know his name, but it's thanks to him that I'm here at all. I was in such a bad way that if not for him, I would never have moved from that station. I reached my mother in Ak-Altyn, and once I was here it was confirmed that I had typhus."

For Vera and her mother I translated a series of poems by Baliński and Słonimski, the same ones I had read at Tolstoy's house, and at Vera's special request I dictated a selection of them to her. The one she found most moving, and wrote down first, was Baliński's poem "The Other Name of Solitude:"

> …But there is another solitude, without any tears or
>   feelings,
> Solitude that knows no audience and no sympathy
> And that discovers the world like an aimless abyss,
> Were you to look into it like a mirror. Genuine solitude.

The next day she came along looking very embarrassed, and shyly asked me to dictate my translations of the poems to her again. She'd read them to her friends, who'd liked them so much that somebody had pinched them from her bedside table.

At the end of August I left the hospital. All my colleagues had already left the Soviet Union. General Anders was now in Iran as well, and only the closing staff were left, headed by General Szyszko-Bohusz.

Although I wanted to go, I was sorry to leave the hospital, the people to whom I owed so much and whom I had come to love. At the same time I gazed sadly at one of my neighbors in the ward, knowing that he was not leaving—among the dysentery patients there were plenty of hopeless cases whose days were numbered, and who were only kept alive by the hope of evacuation.

Just before I left there was a very unpleasant incident. Our departing units had left quite a lot of things behind: canned food, medicines, and kit sent to us from Britain, which we passed on to the Soviet troops. As we owed the hospital a great debt of gratitude, we tried to give it as many of these items as possible. Among other things, we provided twenty-seven pairs of shoes for the staff. Nobody who wasn't there can imagine what great excitement an ordinary pair of English shoes could prompt in Russia at the time. I noticed that not a single pair had reached the isolation ward, where most of us Poles had been treated. I immediately wrote to the quartermaster with a request to send me a few more pairs of shoes, so that I could distribute them to our caregivers. The next day I received the shoes and handed them out to the nurses, who were very pleased and grateful.

On the day of my departure I found out that this fact had been reported in a neatly typed-out denunciation aimed against the nursing staff in the isolation ward. I saw this denunciation on the desk of the hospital *politruk*, who summoned me and subjected me to a long diatribe. The only nasty person in the entire hospital, he was accusing these women of acting "against the collective" and of evidently having complained to me about the injustice of the way things had been shared out, etc. I had to defend them and myself, by explaining some basic things, including that I had not needed any complaints because it only took one glance to see what worn-out clogs they were going about in, and that I simply wanted to help the hospital.

This conversation reminded me again that I was in a Soviet hospital—the barely disguised suspicion of the NKVD representative, his nastiness, his carping at a deed I had no reason to be ashamed of, and the impossibility of explaining to him the obvious fact that after a few weeks of being cared for in this hospital I had every right to ask the quartermaster for a few pairs of extra shoes for the best and most caring nurses, and that it had absolutely nothing to do with revolution, capitalist encroachment, or "lordly" Poland, but was just my way of saying thank you to these women.

I left, worried that the gesture I had made without consulting them may ultimately have been to their detriment.

25. KARAKUM

By now the army was in Iran. I spent a few days in Yungiyul, which was almost deserted apart from my last few colleagues at general staff.

With no strength, and with my heart acting up, I trudged about chatting till late at night, worrying about a hundred matters and people with exaggerated emotion. By then I was recovering from a second bout of typhus, and once again I had a strong reaction, a physical feeling of total transformation combined with an irrational sense of bliss.

The close-down staff left on a specially reserved train, while the recovering patients traveled separately. They wanted to put me in charge of the latter convoy, but I took advantage of a convalescent's privilege and not only wriggled out of this duty but also, thanks to an obliging colleague, obtained an individual travel document.

I stood and waited at the station, alongside more than sixty malingerers, soldiers and officers, including forty convalescents, some of whom could hardly stay upright. They had been promised their own railcar, and they had a group travel document, with the number 9 on it, denoting the coach assigned to them.

The train pulled in, only stopping at our station for two minutes. Clutching my individual ticket I scrambled into railcar number 8, as directed, and found it to be packed solid, but I squeezed in anyway. Amid crying children, women, and soldiers, in the cramped, stuffy atmosphere of the "hard" class, with the benches raised, people and baskets crammed in alike. Unable to move an inch, I thought with envy of railcar number 9, assigned to my colleagues, who would all be traveling together, not in a crush, with the whole car to themselves.

But a number of stops later on I found out that their specially reserved railcar had arrived at the station full to bursting, and none of our people had boarded the train, because they had a group ticket. So in fact I had got off lightly!

My first acquaintances were two young Jews from Kishinev. They were going to an island in the Aral Sea where, so they told me, it was terribly hot, with no trees at all, to work as doctors at the island's medical unit. They were both visibly nervous about it, but I could also sense youthful hope in them; one had only finished his medical studies a year earlier in Lwów, and both were missing Lwów in 1940, when it was still the epitome of culture and comfort, though by now it had been plundered and abandoned.

We got on well from the start, and they confided in me that the only reason why they hadn't been sent to the front, or anywhere near it, was that they were from Kishinev, and thus in Soviet eyes not above suspicion. They spoke French quite fluently, and showed me a French book published in about 1900, the only one they had managed to obtain in Tashkent from a bookstall. It turned out to be a pornographic novel printed on coated paper, with inset illustrations depicting "elegant" ladies with ample bosoms and wasp waists, in little straw boaters or elaborate coiffures in front of the sea, flowers, smart villas in Monte Carlo and San Remo, yachts, carriages, and "stylish" salons. The young men were traveling first by rail, then along the Amu-Darya River to Nukus, and finally by sea to the island. I did not dare tell them what I knew about this land of indigence. Following the "amnesty," some of our people had been sent down the same river on barges to collective farms in the Nukus area. These people, already "free" by then, were given provisions for two days, but the voyage lasted for two weeks; every day they were obliged to throw a number of corpses overboard as people died of hunger. That had only happened a few months earlier. Those Poles had then been housed at the miserable collective farms around Nukus, where they continued to die like flies. These tales were still fresh in my ears.

The young doctors proudly pointed at the book, saying they would use it to "hone their French-language skills," or at least not to forget

XXV

Wojsko juz w Iranie. Spedzam pare dni w prawie opustoszonym Jungi Julu; ostatni rzut sztabu, paru kolegow.

Ledwo sie jeszcze trzymam na nogach, z nawalajacym sercem laze i gadam do poznej nocy, przejmujac sie stu sprawami i ludzmi z ustokrotnionym uczuciem. Juz drugi tyfus mam poza soba i drugi raz przezywam z rowna sila ten potyfusowy powrot do zycia, fizyczne uczucie zupelnej przemiany zwiazana z tym irracjonalnym poczuciem blogosci i radosci zycia.

Sztab likwidacyjny wyrusza pociagiem zarezerwowanym, ozdrowiency jada osobno. Chciano zrobic mnie komendantem tego ostatniego transportu, ale wykorzystuje przywilej rekonwalescenta i z funkcji tej nie tylko sie wykrecam, ale jeszcze zdobywam, dzieki uprzejmosci kolegi indywidualny dokument podrozy.

Czekam na stacji z moim biletem, razem ze mna czeka szescdziesieciu kilku maruderow zolnierzy, miedzy nich oficerow wsrod ktorych 40 ozdrowiencow.Sa tacy, ktorzy sie jeszcze ledwo trzymaja

Manuscript of the first page of the chapter headed "Karakum" (here still with its original title, "The Border") and a watercolor depicting the Iranian landscape.

what they already knew. This book was a symbol connecting them with the West, a piece of treasure they were taking with them on their journey into the unknown.

I left the two young doctors with a large can of English tea. They thanked me effusively. The Roman name for a coin that was placed in the mouths of the dead so they would have something to pay Charon to ferry them across the River Styx was a viaticum; maybe this can of English tea (rather than the French pornographic novel) would serve them as a viaticum on the Amu-Darya.

I had some provisions with me, including chocolate and jam. I treated the children to chocolate, which caused a sensation. I gave the lady conductor a large handful of tea, with a request to make some, and when she brought me a large pot of it, half the railcar held out their mugs and chipped containers.

The stuffy, crowded atmosphere obliged me to reconnoiter, and by complaining of my convalescent state, and better yet by offering the tempting promise of tea or sugar, I managed to win over the conductress in the "soft" railcar, and a few hours later I was in this coach for the privileged few, at first in the corridor, but later in a compartment.

I made new acquaintances. Now I was with the aristocracy: an intelligent gentleman with gray hair and a Jewish surname, married to a very young ballet dancer, with whom he was hopelessly in love, constantly steering the conversation onto her, showing me her photograph, and claiming to be thirty-nine years old himself (I'd have sworn he was fifty). He told me a lot about Moscow, about his elegant apartment there, and how before the war he had organized all the talks at the Writers' Union, and receptions for foreign writers too; he was thrilled by the wide variety of luxury food products that were available in Moscow before the war—to writers who were loyal to the regime). It reminded me of the distaste with which, in *Retour de l'URSS*, Gide described the gastronomic orgies enjoyed by the Soviet Writers' Union. Eventually I found out that my interlocutor was "for the time being" deputy director of the circus in Ashgabat.

Towards evening, before we reached Samarkand, I had my first sense of thrill on this journey: a landscape with such pure, resonant colors, and such soft shadows that it looked transparent. Flowing, gently sloping stretches covered with lemon-yellow stubble fields, now completely empty, except for occasional small stacks of wheat or maybe barley, they ran dozens of miles into the distance, toward jagged mountain chains, which in the evening light were a delicate sapphire-blue or purple as amethysts. The land seemed deserted; now and then there was a small clay hut, sometimes whitewashed, or someone riding a small donkey, like a moving pinhead in that broad yellow-and-purple landscape, under the greenish-gold evening sky.

I was given bedding for the night: a pillow, clean sheets, a quilt, and a place in a compartment, where I found an elderly Georgian getting ready for bed. As he scratched his thin hairy chest and took off his socks, he told me at length and in detail about Tiflis, about its streets, fruits, and trees; he complained that for years as a railroad clerk he had had to work on nothing but northern routes in the Arkhangelsk oblast, and that he hadn't seen his hometown for five years now. On the upper bunk lay a large, redheaded peasant in snow-white pajamas. The Georgian explained to me that apparently he was the vice-chancellor of Moscow University, or the dean of the medical faculty in Moscow. He had a heavy, crafty face, square with a red beard, and shoulders like an ox—that must have been how Count de Vogüé imagined *un moujik russe*. An intelligent, excellent chess player, he played chess all day from dawn to dusk, beating everyone. I tried to draw him into conversation, by commenting on politics. I failed— chatting to a stranger in a railcar, and a Pole at that—he wasn't dumb. I got nothing out of him except for a few very scathing remarks about the British.

Early the next morning (during the night we had gone through Samarkand and Bokhara) we entered the hopeless terrain of the Karakum Desert. There wasn't a single person for hundreds of miles, just a gently undulating sandy expanse. The only plants to be seen were very occasional dried-up bushes resembling our juniper. At vast intervals there were small settlements, little towns, a bit of gray vegetation or some clay houses with no trees, exposed to the scorching heat of the sun; I only saw one settlement built in a more methodical, modern way, with identical small white cottages and large reservoirs of crude oil.

Across this hopeless plain flowed the Amu-Darya, at least a mile wide, and so very shallow that the bottom was often visible, or small sandy little islands. We stopped for about an hour before crossing an immensely long bridge, and when asked why I was told that they had to get everyone off the roof. We meanwhile were ordered to close all the windows.

Damage to this bridge would have blocked the only line from the Caucasus to Krasnovodsk and Tashkent, which because of the German attack and the threat to the Volga was the only railroad behind the front connecting the Caucasian oil basin with Russia.

After hours of desert, this large blue sheet of water was refreshing and comforting. Once again there were a few trees in sight and a few houses, and then the whole day went by without a change in the desert landscape, the heat of the sun, and the sand getting into every crevice.

In the corridors of the railcar I encountered some *bezprizorniye*. God knows where they were going, thin adolescents in rags. By the door into the restaurant car, the first in Russia where I could possibly eat the food—a little chopped meat and noodles—stood a teenage boy in a torn jacket, with a broad, open face, and hair that hadn't been cut for a long time; he was stubbornly silent, asking for nothing. One of the serving men came out of the restaurant car and thrust some scraps at him in newspaper. *Idi, idi*, he said without malice—"Off you go." Without a word the boy went off with the scraps to another corridor in another railcar. I saw five boys like that one.

Despite being very strict towards people who illicitly pushed their way into the railcar, the conductress did not throw these children out, and the passengers closed their eyes to them too; some gave them pieces of bread or leftover food.

On the third day of the journey, I woke up before Ashgabat, and saw the same endless expanse of sand, and the same withered bushes of Karakum juniper.

Ashgabat—capital of the Turkmen Republic and a border city. At dawn I left the station and walked along new avenues, past huge statues of Stalin and Lenin, past monumental new buildings, immense posters about the war and slogans on red faded calico.

I dragged myself and my luggage to the House of Soviets, which is a hotel; just behind the building I suddenly discovered a whole new world: out of the flat, infertile plain stretching a dozen miles into the distance some lofty, silent mountains suddenly rose to a height of over 6,560 feet above sea level, pink, and totally bare, with soft, undulating contours. Along these peaks ran the border—on the far side of this pink-and-gold wall, under a turquoise sky, lay Iran.

26. THE BORDER

I SPENT twenty-four hours in Ashgabat. Apart from people officially sent to Ashgabat for transfer there was also a "wild" influx of Poles at the time.

One of the residents of the House of Soviets was Colonel Perkowicz, who with a few dedicated assistants and a handful of drivers was managing the evacuation of the Poles to Iran. He took advantage of every opportunity to add to the set number of evacuees agreed with the authorities and to squeeze in a few more of the Polish women and children who sat waiting in a camp, frantically longing to get out of the Soviet Union.

In the third volume of Melchior Wańkowicz's *Monte Cassino*, this same Colonel Perkowicz, who managed the evacuation in Ashgabat in 1942 and took part in the battle of Monte Cassino in 1944, tells the author how the Narkom (Council of People's Commissars) of the Turkmen Republic suddenly ordered Perkowicz and his team to stop the second evacuation, because the number of evacuees had reached seventy-nine thousand, exceeding the agreed seventy thousand. He describes how he spent three hours walking about, trying to force himself to go to the Polish assembly point, while wondering what to say to these people; he couldn't think of anything, so finally he told them straight out. They were devastated and sat there all night weeping; Perkowicz wept with them, feeling helpless.

On that occasion he had managed to squeeze through another 110 persons. That was all, and the rest of the Poles gathered at the Ashgabat evacuation camp were forced to go back to their old life of hunger and homelessness.

When I arrived in Ashgabat, American Dodges were still driving Poles across the pink mountain range each day without hindrance.

During my day in Ashgabat, I was too physically weak to tour the city, and have not retained much in my memory: the statues of the leaders, the Corinthian columns on bombastic, over-ornate new office buildings, Russian and Turkmen inscriptions and slogans everywhere extolling work and heroism, and on the baking hot streets Russians in faded clothes, moving about in a crowd like sleepy flies, or rare Turkmens in huge sheepskin hats silently riding by on donkeys, and slender Turkmen women with dark skin and very black hair, in long colorful robes and strange red headdresses, like top hats without brims, narrower at the bottom, wider at the top, studded with coins and beads. I only saw a few of these women, lost among the crowd of Russians. Far beyond the European city, against the pink mountains were the delicate outlines of small mud houses, built one on top of another, the city of the Turkmens and the women in red headdresses.

My departure from Ashgabat was at seven in the morning. That day Colonel Perkowicz was sending sixty children, mainly orphans with female caregivers and a few mothers. He let me travel with them. Three huge vehicles were transporting them to Mashhad in Iran. From there the children would travel on to Bombay, though for the time being they would have to be accommodated in Iran. Which meant sixty children and several women, out of a total count of hundreds of thousands murdered or gone missing; these thoughts, bitter and indifferent, were wandering about my mind as I gazed at the children. Most of their little faces were emaciated but full of curiosity and joy, as the mothers and caregivers nervously loaded them and their meager luggage onto the trucks.

We set off toward the mountains along an asphalt highway, crossing a seven-mile plain as flat as a table, under a dazzlingly bright, cheerful sky. At once yesterday's sense of enchantment came back to me, though at first I found it hard to look at this severe, haughty landscape with a painter's eye. My view of the mountains was encumbered by my memories of terrible oriental daubs, or biblical scenes painted by various dabblers, such as a Palestinian panorama with equally pink mountains—naturalistic, impotent attempts to make the mountains look "just as they really are." But these memories quickly died away, and my delight remained. Since Yungiyul I had been trying to work out what made the local sky look so distinct. This shade of blue had an extremely intense turquoise tinge to it, for which I couldn't find the right Polish term—the only word to describe it was the English "strident." Old turquoises do in fact acquire these rich, greenish-blue shades, but the sky also had a unique brilliance and freshness. It was the same sky that I had admired through the branches of the Yungiyul apple trees, but today beneath it stood a rampart of mighty pink mountains, which our three huge vehicles would soon start to climb. Cleaned and polished, these covered Dodge trucks shone like black mirrors. I sat next to the driver, platoon sergeant Józwa in a pith helmet. Those first cork pith helmets that I saw on Polish soldiers looked enormous—I found them both comical and pleasing. While I was having dinner at our post the day before, some of our drivers had come in, strapping fellows, and the pith helmets had made them look like British army commanders in India or Arabia (as seen in movies and illustrated magazines). I was happy to see Józwa's broad, suntanned face under the first helmet, and his very blue, very Polish eyes. A cavalryman from Fourth Regiment of Mounted Rifles, he drove the truck leading the convoy, at a steady pace, with nerves of steel, confidently tackling a long series of difficult bends. Józwa had driven this route several dozen times before and knew every twist and turn. Calmly keeping his huge, bronzed hands on the black steering wheel, he tossed me the occasional piece of information. First we drove down into a gorge, then along an excellent highway, climbing higher and higher up switchbacks, until suddenly the entire Soviet side lay beneath us in the light of the morning sun, the vast plain of the Karakum Desert and the white city of Ashgabat at our feet; at the edge of the sky blue shadows merged with the ground, looking deceptively like the sea, and at closer range, the undulating slopes of the bare mountains had the exact shapes, to scale, of a crumpled gray blanket thrown aside, the same rounded folds and hollows, in some places the same shade of gray, even the same "fabric."

The wild emptiness of the mountains, withered thistles on the scree, and a few wretched clay settlements in ruins—that was all. High up in the moonlit landscape Józwa pointed out a few tiny yellow cottages and a manège, where some soldiers were exercising on a dozen or so horses; in another little square a small unit was doing rifle drill. From a distance they looked like little lead soldiers. There wasn't a single tree (everything was brought in there, including water). I thought of Pechorin, in Lermontov's *A Hero of Our Time*, looking for the most dangerous adventures he could find in the wild mountains of the Caucasus to kill the boredom that was gnawing away at him, and of his kindhearted friend Maxim Maximych. I wondered if there were people like that nowadays at these border posts. Lermontov's novel is set in the wild Caucasus Mountains, which are rich in plant life; here there were just the arid peaks of the Persian border, but still the same small forts, lost on the outer edges of a huge state, and people living a similar life there, cut off from the world for months, maybe years. Centuries go by, regimes change, but people remain, just the same, despite the spread of education and propaganda.

We were almost at the top of the range, which forms the Persian-Soviet border. Gaudan is less than twenty miles from Ashgabat, 6,560 feet above sea level. On the bare slopes there were a few one-story cottages with arcades, and a dozen sleepy soldiers sitting in the shade of the houses. I asked one of them what these slopes looked like in the spring.

"They're all green," he replied, "with lots of flowers, red and yellow tulips."

Today all I could spot on the nearest hills were very occasional dark clumps of bushes, and tall, withered, greenish-gold thistles along the highway.

The customs officers were sending off some gas tankers and weren't in a hurry. We waited. Thanks to the altitude, the "underside" of the air was fresh, but the sun was shining fiercely. The climate in the room where the customs inspection took place was more bearable. I was one of the first to be inspected. I asked the customs officials if I could stay in there until my traveling companions' inspection was over. I hardly knew them yet, and here amid feverish unpacking and repacking of bags, boxes, and parcels I became acquainted with the children and ladies in our group. I looked at the thin little bones of Jaś Pajączek, at his lively hazel eyes and small, slightly upturned nose. I met the Starczewski brothers, the Grzeszczuk brothers, the Dąbrowski family, and many others whose names I no longer recall. Miss Dąbrowska was six years old, with a tiny nose in a freckly, flushed little face. She was wearing a dark cherry-red dress and a little straw hat, pushed back on her thick, dark-red shock of hair; there was a small bunch of red and blue flowers pinned to its stiff brim. After much persuasion she recited "Kizia Mizia"* for me, extremely fast and quite incomprehensibly. Then she was going to do some singing and dancing. But suddenly she imposed a condition on her mother that she had to have a thimbleful, and right away. For educational reasons the mother could not agree to this particular ultimatum. The situation was saved by her eight-year-old brother Januszek, who immediately agreed to recite something, and concentrating hard, declaimed:

> "And now you are dead, Marshal Piłsudski,
> Our leader will never come back.
> The black flags are flying, the funeral banners,
> The faces are veiled in black."

"How do you know that poem?" I asked.

"Grandpa sent some old copies of the children's magazines *Płomyki* [Little Flames] to Turkestan."

One after another I came to know these children's faces, each of them unique and irreplaceable, and realized how valuable this little group was. Taking these indigent Polish kids away to better conditions, overcoming thousands of difficulties for this purpose, seemed to me a task of the most vital importance. "Do not despise the feeble child—it might be the child of a lion," says an Arab proverb. By some

---

*A children's rhyme roughly equivalent to "Pussycat, pussycat, where have you been?" —*Trans.*

miraculous effort of constant care and a lucky chance amid unlucky circumstances these children were still alive, and not, like tens of thousands of others, lying in shallow mass graves in Russia, Siberia, and Turkestan. I remembered the winter in Buzuluk when an epidemic had killed several dozen of our children, purely because there was no medicine. Mr. and Mrs. Z.'s little daughter had died then—the father had managed to obtain a single injection in exchange for a gold watch. He brought it in as his daughter lay dying. He also brought her a piece of treasure—a small bar of chocolate from the welfare service. Though on her deathbed, the girl was fully conscious and said: "I don't need it any more, give it to Zosia, Mommy." (Zosia was another little girl.)

The customs inspectors at Gaudan were extremely thorough, but polite. Each written document was examined by a special clerk who could read Polish. I got through without any trouble, saved partly by my handwriting, which I myself find difficult to read. I had very few things, but I did have the notebooks I had filled with stories from the prisons, and some diaries. The customs official examined my ID and some of my letters, and passed on to other work.

Now came the turn of the bags and trunks being carried through by the women and children. The contents of their luggage were the perfect illustration of all the misery of their lives in exile, the mothers' relentless efforts to provide for their children, and the whole struggle for existence. One of the ladies pulled out a bag of ancient rusks made of some awful flour, which looked like brown stones and grit, but after spilling the entire contents onto the dirty table, where the official prodded the bigger pieces with a special tool, Mrs. X. carefully gathered it all up again, all those crumbs reduced to sand along with the dust from the table. Iran? Bombay? How could she know what it would be like there? They might be starving again. The tribulations of the past three years had taught her mistrust. Then out of the trunks came dozens of small rags, old buttons, and bits of string, terrible old junk that not even a ragpicker would have glanced at. With unruffled calm the customs official unrolled every last rag and stuck a metal stick into every can of food for the journey and every jar of melted butter or honey. And there were a number of these;

Mrs. D., the mother of two of the children, had rather unusual luggage. She had evidently come from a more prosperous collective farm, because she had gingerbread and three large bottles of honey, melted butter in one jar and fresh butter in another. I was amazed by the amount of honey.

"At the collective farm I was paid in honey," she explained.

Then came other families with more trunks, filled with every sort of drapery to furnish a modest urban apartment, and thus curtains, colorful rugs with shapeless storks sewn on them in white yarn, or garlands of poppies in red yarn or silk on black velvet, fat embroidered pillows with tassels and crocheted curtains, all carefully laundered and folded. These objects were a treasure and a lifesaver. These women had had great success selling them in the depths of Russia and had managed to feed their children. Those who had been lucky enough were now taking some of these remaining souvenirs of the family home into the world with them. After the inspection all these items were rapidly but carefully repacked into the battered trunks, and into bags quickly tied with string by the older children. Some of them, mainly the older boys, did it with speed and proficiency—it clearly wasn't the first time they'd had to pack. How many bitter tears those objects must have seen, those embroidered rugs, to a point where one ceased to notice how hideous they were. For at least these children traveling with their mothers were cleanly dressed, and some of them even looked quite well.

"Please sir, there's nothing more awful than when a child is hungry and there's nothing to give him to eat," said a middle-aged woman with gray hair and dark rings around her eyes, who was sitting on a trunk, leaning her tired head on her hand.

I talked to many of the orphans. Each one instantly told me about himself with complete trust.

"Where's your father?"

"I don't know."

"Where's your mom?"

"Dead," or "She stayed at the collective farm," or "They didn't let her out"—that was the most frequent answer. "Mom was left behind at the station—she got out to get us some food and didn't come back"—I heard that over and over again.

There was a small, very pale girl in our group, with a full forehead and two little braids like mouse tails. I was told her story. She had arrived at the station in Ashgabat with her mother and brother, both of whom were seriously ill. They were to be hospitalized at once but were going to two different hospitals. As they parted in floods of tears at the station, the mother put a little box into the girl's hands and told her to guard it with her life, because "Mommy and Daddy's wedding rings are in there."

A few days later the mother died, the brother still lay seriously ill in another hospital, and the little girl, living in a tent, was robbed of the box with the rings.

Finally the inspection was over. While the trunks were being packed up again the children were wandering about the customs hall. There were lots of portraits on the walls, including Marx and Engels, Lenin, Molotov, Voroshilov, Budyonny, and of course Stalin. During a break while the customs official was absent, an eight-year-old boy called Michaś, so small I wouldn't have given him more than six, toured the room, carefully examining all the portraits in search of Stalin. When he finally found him, he raised a clenched fist toward the dictator's face. One of the older boys, of about twelve, told him off severely, saying it was a senseless thing to do, as one of the customs officials might see, but Michaś didn't seem at all perturbed or the least bit convinced.

I told one of the accompanying ladies about this gesture. She wasn't at all surprised.

"We always had this problem with the children at my collective farm too," lamented this nice old lady. "What did they ever have from Stalin except misery and starvation? Every child that went past his portrait stuck out his tongue, shook his fist, showed him the finger, or even spat at him, and it was quite impossible to train them out of it."

This child shaking his little fist at the omnipotent dictator was my last impression as I left the Soviet Union.

At about two we were off again. A few yards further on, the road narrowed. On the very crest of the mountains there were Soviet sentries, and within a barbed-wire fence fixed to trestles along the border there was a wire gate, which after a brief check they let us go through.

And we were in Iran. I automatically crossed myself and felt the driver's hand giving my arm a friendly squeeze as he said: "Well, Captain, paradise is behind you now." In a serious, brotherly way his blue eyes were smiling. "If it weren't for one man we'd all have died here," he added after a while.

We drove on through camps and passes, but downhill now. Against the sky I could see a huge black bird whose square wings had ragged tips. An eagle? A vulture? Under the radiantly turquoise sky the more distant mountains were still pink, but some of the scree was gray, though in this light it was a greenish gray. At closer range the hills were almost lemon yellow because of all the dried-up thistles. Some rats as big as rabbits ran across the road—the children thought they were hares—and some long-legged lizards of incredible size.

We reached Bajgiran, an eastern town of flat-roofed, baked-clay buildings. A few taller houses were assigned to the army: they also had flat roofs, but they were made of solid brick, with well-constructed arches, and their precise construction and size distinguished them from the rest. I found out that they had been built by the Germans during this war or just before it.

In Bajgiran there was a representative of Soviet power in charge, who checked our documents again. Bored, he was sitting in a stuffy little room overlooking the street, smoking a pipe; the bench he sat on was covered in thick fabric with a black, red, and dark-blue geometric pattern. The fabric was exactly the same as the upholstery on an old ottoman in my father's study. And suddenly I had a vivid memory of that couch, with the dents we inflicted by somersaulting on it, and all seven of us siblings squatting on it in turn. We used to sit on that couch under a large painting of the head of a black horse with a white blaze, listening to my father reading aloud. In turn he read us Sienkiewicz's *Trilogy*, *David Copperfield*, and lots of other books. How clearly I can see his face in the white light of the spirit lamp, his profile with the aquiline nose, dark bushy mustache, and carefully shaved chin moving as he read, above a stiff starched collar and his eternal black tie. I can see his head resting against the sloping back of a green leather armchair, and the tears he tried to hide, but which began to well up in the corner of his eyes as soon as there was a moving scene. I can still hear his embarrassed coughing whenever he came upon a passage that he thought unsuitable for children. (In the *Trilogy* all such passages were carefully outlined in pencil.) After all these years, in the burning heat on the Persian border, I could still feel the delight of that half-hour evening ritual, and our anxiety that it would soon be over, and we'd be told to go to bed.

From Bajgiran to Quchan was perhaps the toughest, as well as the most beautiful stretch of road. The bends were so sharp that the huge Dodge trucks were not able to go around them in a single sweep but had to drive slowly along a very low parapet of loosely laid stones above a precipice, occasionally backing up again before turning the corner. There had already been a series of accidents here since the spring, including one in which three Soviet vehicles had apparently rolled into the abyss. Soviet workmen were improving the road by widening it—at first it was mainly just Soviets whom we saw on this road. Then we drove into a narrow pass between bristling russet-pink rocks and then forded a stream. Wherever there was water, even the smallest brook, plant life had instantly sprung up, including slender young poplars and willows. We stopped, and the children happily cooled their feet in the water; generally they were extremely well behaved and not at all frightened by the precipice, as if our journey were a pleasant outing.

Now and then there was a village, consisting of a dozen or more small clay cottages, and one or two larger houses that were simply constructed but strangely beautiful in their simplicity. The outer wall would consist of thick pillars or wooden columns, with a recess behind them forming a narrow terrace. Behind that there was another wall, sometimes whitewashed, occasionally with a geometric decorative pattern, and arched doors. The poorest houses were simple and well proportioned, providing a beautiful architectural treat—they felt perfect just as they were, with nothing to add and nothing to remove. One settlement has stuck in my memory, at the first oasis we encountered on our journey across the wild mountains. In a mountain gorge between the rocks there were meadows with hundreds of sheep and stacks of golden corn. At the foot of a chessboard of small fields ran a stream, with huge maize plants growing along it, occasional sunflowers, and green plots of thick grass or clover. Below us we could see flat roofs, because the settlement was on a slope descending to the brook, and the highway passed through the middle of it. On each roof bunches of corn had been laid out, and further on just outside the village we saw dozens of sacks of carefully packed sheep's wool and camel hair. Here by the winding stream, after the burning summer, in August, the green of the meadows and the white-trunked poplars were still totally springlike.

My first impression of Iran was the incredible civility of the people—more than civility, cordiality. All the children and many of the older people waved to us. In Quchan, where we stopped for something to eat, two young men brought us grapes as a gift, knowing that as there was no opportunity on the border to exchange rubles for the Persian currency, the toman, we didn't have any local money. All our people had been passing through here for several weeks without any money, so these people's kind gestures were totally disinterested.

After Quchan the road was smooth; dusk fell, and then night. Most of the children were soon fast asleep in all sorts of positions. After traveling all day, I felt great weariness. My traveling companions kindly let me lie down on blankets inside the truck, and I fell asleep. When I awoke, we were driving along a smooth highway, in total darkness. From a corner of the vehicle I could hear one of the children whispering: "One of the girls at our place wanted to marry a Cossack"—he meant a Kazakh—"who promised her two carts of sweet melons, several sheep, and a camel"—this word came out distorted—"but on the day of the wedding he wasn't there, and the next day all the Poles left, and she did too. So we all laughed at her and asked if she wanted to stay behind with the Cossack, but she said no, she wanted to take him away with her to Poland."

I fell asleep again. At about one in the morning the reddish glare of electric lights and bumpy cobbles awoke us—we were in Mashhad.

27. FROM THE TORMENT OF EXILE...

MASHHAD at night; half-awake, the children and their escorts were taken off to the Polish children's center, from where they would be transferred to Bombay. Meanwhile, our hospitable representative assigned me accommodation in the "best" hotel, where he was based too.

I had a little room of my own, with two windows onto a small courtyard, which the sun hardly shone into, so it was relatively cool. Our representative informed me that I would probably have to stay put for ten days until there was a lift to Tehran. I was glad of the gift of ten days to myself before starting on a new stage in the organization of the Polish Army "somewhere in the East," whose troops were finally getting guns. I was also pleased that I'd be spending this time just outside Afghanistan, in Mashhad, a city where I knew nobody apart from the children with whom I had arrived.

To the Shiites, Mashhad is a sacred site of pilgrimage (properly Al-Mashhad, which means "the place of martyrdom"), the eternal resting place of the great imam Ali Al Reza, who was poisoned by black grapes served to him on a salver by his enemies and died in 818 AD, here in the province of Khorasan, while promoting the faith of Mohammed.

According to Shiite beliefs, Ali Al Reza, from the eighth generation of descendants of Mohammed, performed many miracles; at his intercession rain fell during a terrible drought, and the imam himself showed each cloud over which province it was to release its rain; he also made a garden go green in the middle of winter and caused grapes to ripen there. Ali Al Reza knew what was going on in people's hearts and the hour of their death. Believers ask him for protection on sea and land journeys, and also for salvation "from the torment of exile."

As I lay on the narrow bed in my little room in Mashhad, I took stock of the past few years.

Exactly three years ago—it was September 3—I had reported at the Rakowicki barracks outside Kraków, to the Eighth Regiment's reserve platoon. The line platoons were already in action at the time, and we were ordered to move that same night as a dismounted unit toward Dębica, where we were to receive horses. I had arrived in Kraków that day after a thirty-six-hour journey from Warsaw by train, on foot, by horse and cart, and by train again (some stations had already been bombed, and the line from Warsaw to Kraków via Częstochowa had been cut off).

I had already seen our wounded soldiers on the Częstochowa-to-Kielce line, and also German prisoners of war taken captive at Częstochowa, whom at a small halt our nurses were treating to... grapes.

That same day in Kraków, as I was circling the bombarded station, I had survived my first German bomb. It ripped into a convent a few houses away from me, leaving me with a memory of the defenseless, bewildered look on the face of the Mother Superior calling for help. The bomb didn't kill anyone, but it broke some water pipes, flooding the convent. Rather than terror, it prompted surprise and confusion.

A month later, attacked and surrounded by Soviet troops—at the time Hitler's allies—we were taken captive and made to walk in an endless column to Lwów, Tarnopol, and Volochysk, and from there by train to Starobilsk.

Then came a year in the camp, with lice, at first with no news of my loved ones, idiotic interrogations, the closure of that camp, and finally transfer to Gryazovets. (Why exactly was I one of seventy-eight still alive out of our four thousand Starobilsk comrades, when all the rest had gone missing without trace?)

A second year followed, in the camp at Gryazovets outside Vologda. I remember the subtle green of the birch trees in spring, burdock leaves growing before one's eyes to more than six feet in width in the

Lieutenant Józef Zielicki and Lieutenant Józef Czapski in Beirut. This picture probably dates from October 23, 1942, and was taken shortly before Czapski's departure for Damascus.

short but luxuriant, wonderful northern summer, winter temperatures of −50°F and deep snow in air as silent and pure as crystal, and the wall I was ordered to build out of enormous bricks which lay in heaps, the remains of a blown-up seventeenth-century church; we called it "the wailing wall."

In fact, there we had the right to communicate with Poland once a month, which was another exceptional privilege, when at the same time our four thousand fellow prisoners from Kozelsk No. 1 were already lying in pits in Katyn forest with bullets in their skulls.

This thin thread of contact with Poland was broken when the German-Soviet alliance ended, and news via London, Geneva, and Ankara was even rarer and more limited.

Then came the Soviet-German war, and our frenzy of enthusiasm and hope. Liberty, forming the army, the steppe, the journeys about Russia in search of our missing, massacred comrades, Turkestan, and evacuation.

Now the Germans had attacked Stalingrad, posing a threat to the Caucasus and the oil deposits, but despite their successes, there was a growing sense of certainty that the Germans would be defeated.

At that point, in Mashhad, why did I not think about what might lie ahead of us after the defeat of Germany? What stopped me from considering a new threat, of Soviet occupation this time? Faith in "historical justice"? A typically Polish "somehow it'll work out" attitude? That too, but above all the hope for change for the better after the war, all over the world, including Russia. Above all, overestimation of the moral strengths of the "great democracies." We chronically believed—how very few incisive, reticent pessimists there were among us—in all the promises, treaties, and Atlantic Charters. Words, words like Roosevelt's declaration that "Poland is the inspiration of nations," seemed to us a guarantee that once the war was won, we weren't going to be treated like just another card to swap in a game with the Soviets.

At that time, in Mashhad, where news of the war came from far away, as if muffled, I had no idea yet where the Polish Army would be formed—whether in Iran, Iraq, Palestine, or Egypt, or whether our road back to Poland would be across the Caucasus or the Balkans.

It never crossed my mind that this army's route would take it to Italy, to fight at Monte Cassino, Ancona, and Bologna, and that then we would have further exile ahead of us. But who among us could have seen the grim future at that time? No one, apart from Adolf Bocheński, politician and soldier, news of whose daringly courageous exploits in the African campaign had even reached us in Russia.

In my hotel room on that first day in distant Mashhad, all I knew was that a very important chapter in my life, the Soviet phase, was over. I felt that I wanted to emerge naked from this experience, devoid of all objects connecting me with it. All morning I searched for a new notebook, so that I wouldn't have to write in the same one as in the Soviet Union. What was the meaning of this strange need, almost physical, for a new skin? I knew I couldn't start life over again and that anyway what I'd been through in the past few years was too important for me to want to cast it off, even if I were able; in fact I wanted to process it all internally, look at it from the outside with detachment, and not forget the tiny details.

My new notebook had a gold inscription in Persian on its turquoise cover. As soon as I saw it I pounced on it like an alcoholic on vodka. At last I could write without fear of a search, or almost without fear, as there were two NKVD officers staying in the same hotel. I could write what I remembered, things that even with my illegible handwriting I hadn't dared to note down in Russia without using a code or being cryptic. Amid the golden minarets, the gold and turquoise cupolas of "the most beautiful mosque in the world," and the streets of this city, where a dense crowd of Persians, Arabs, and Indians moved along from dawn to dusk, each day I spent several hours immersed in memories of the Soviet years.

This crowd struck me as being far less mechanical and downcast than the Soviet crowd. The first impression was of a mood of satisfaction with life, and even the numerous beggars were absorbed into the lively bustle. But after a few days I saw some shockingly shameful scenes here too. Near a store packed with cakes a tall, withered man came by, carrying an infant that looked more like a corpse than a child. On the sidewalk outside my hotel lay a small boy with a high

temperature. Nobody showed any interest in him, and flies were settling in a black swarm around his eyes and his half-open mouth,
burning with fever. I saw a woman curled up in the middle of a side
street, obviously sick, probably dying of starvation.

Dozens of carpets were hanging in the numerous stores, or rather
deep recesses that opened onto the street, and amid garlands of shoes,
cobblers worked until late at night in the harsh light of spirit lamps
or large oil lamps without shades. Two-horse cabs ran jauntily over
the uneven cobbles, their drivers constantly pressing their scrap-metal
antediluvian car horns "made in Germany." The stores at the bazaars
sold turquoises by the handful, and leather suitcases, while on the
streets the most wonderful grapes were heaped in pyramids alongside
piles of peaches. All this was mixed with the ultimate in German
trash, no longer to be found anywhere in Europe: chunky mugs with
German mottoes in Gothic script: *Ein süsses Mädchen*, *Ein guter
Schuss*, and prints in gold frames. There was a colorful crowd of pilgrims everywhere, the white turbans of mullahs, and the black or
green turbans of Mohammed's descendants. I also saw Indians in
blue turbans, and women covered in black or white veils as big as
sheets, making them almost invisible. Many of the men had henna
stains on their hands, cheeks, and hair.

Still very weak after my illness, I lay in my room, writing up my
Soviet memoirs. Mentally I was on those frozen steppes, in the packed
railcars, or traveling from Gryazovets to Ashgabat. Every outing to
the Armenian restaurant next door, where the only decorations were
awful, grating American propaganda posters and portraits of Roosevelt, Churchill, and Stalin, or every drive to the mosque in a droshky
stirred violent emotions. It seemed to me that in this city, where as
well as the great imam Harun al-Rashid had died too, I really was in
the middle of the *Thousand and One Nights*.

The most fairy-tale building of all was the mosque, where I went
almost every day. Scraps of the history of this temple and of this city,
a history full of cruelties, invasions, and violence, reminded me at
every step how commonplace cruelty is in Asia, and how great the
indifference there to the fate and suffering of man. Massacres had

changed entire provinces into wastelands. In the fourteenth century Miran Shah, son of Timur, destroyed the neighboring city of Tus, putting the citizens to the sword. The only survivors were those who hid behind the stone walls of the "Bast," a holy site in Mashhad, in the shadow of Ali Reza's tomb. After that there were two bloody attacks on Mashhad by the Uzbeks in the sixteenth century, then Turkmen and Afghan invasions.

Born near Mashhad in the seventeenth century, Nadir Shah, the leader of a band of brigands famous for his cruelty, became the ruler of Persia, and it is to him above all that Mashhad owes the splendor of its temples. It was he who built the hundred-foot gilded minaret and the famous golden gate of Nadir Shah.

After attacking India and destroying Delhi, the Shah returned to Mashhad, scattering heaps of his enemies' skulls along the way, and bringing a vast amount of plundered gold, most of which was spent on the construction of the local temples.

In this same city, right beside the tomb of the imam—the great protector of exiles far from their homeland—the same Nadir Shah carried out an inspection of fifty-six thousand families, whom he ordered to be driven out or displaced from various provinces.

The one and a half million Polish citizens deported by Stalin into the depths of Russia, the corpses of children tossed out at the stations in Lwów and Tarnopol through the windows of cattle trucks packed with people being transported in the cruel winter of 1940, the starvation and impoverishment of entire provinces, the hundreds of thousands of women left to their fate on the bare steppe—from the perspective of Asia it all seemed terribly normal, only differing by the numbers recorded.

What is the value of a human life?

As I trailed about the streets of Mashhad, discovering bits of its history, I was struck not by the contrast, but by the similarity of our experiences, by the Asiatic nature of these horrors. So far from Genghis Khan, Timur, and Nadir Shah in time and space, full of nineteenth-century conceit and a faith in the "mechanism of evolution," we failed to admit the thought that such a fate could still come upon us.

Ya tozhe Azyat—"I am an Asian too," Stalin apparently said to the Japanese minister Matsuoka.

But to cap it all, Stalin the Asian had also eradicated and destroyed in the heart of every man subject to him the world of prayer. Here there was no similarity, but a contrast between the Soviet Union and Asia, which revealed itself to me in Mashhad, and caught the eye at every step.

After three years in a country where prayer was a source of ridicule and disqualification—I remembered the railroad worker who, passing a railcar full of deported Poles, heard them singing the morning prayer, scowled spitefully and snarled: "And they call themselves an intelligent nation!"—after three years in a country where prayer was hidden in the catacombs, I was stunned by the overtness and spontaneity of prayer here.

What a crowd, the human crowd reciting and wailing, women huddled up to the bars behind which, amid candelabras, chandeliers, and mirrors, stands the tomb of the imam Reza. Here there were large square courtyards, wonderful pools surrounded by flowers, turquoise convolvulus the color of the sky rambling up young eucalyptus and palm trees, between walls covered in ultramarine, cobalt, orange, and pink majolica. Some of the motifs were pure baroque, bird-people with human faces and wings amid stylized plants and animals (the Shiites are not as strict opponents of depicting people and animals in art as the Sunnis). Alongside eighteenth-century European motifs others looked as if they had been taken straight off Chinese vases. And against this colorful, fairy-tale background were pilgrims lost in prayer. The most sacred site is the tomb with two slabs superimposed, under a green velvet canopy. Every pilgrim—and there were a hundred thousand of them annually before the war—had to walk around the imam's tomb three times, cursing his enemies. The Islamic encyclopedia of 1933 still gives the names of the Christians who have succeeded, partly in disguise, to visit this place sacred to the Mohammedan Shiites.

I saw old men kissing the gray-and-green marble floor, hundreds of people squatting, fanatically praying before the doors forged out of silver, under stalactites of mirror glass and gold, under chandeliers of the most fabulous Venetian work, where on fragile white, pink, blue, and gold glass feathers and flower stems fat doves were calmly perched, the sacred birds of Mashhad.

There were people curled on the ground or standing with their palms turned upwards, singing plaintively, each for himself alone. I knew there was a vast gulf between Mohammedanism and Christianity, but watching these people kissing the bars surrounding the imam's tomb, and the women weeping bitterly at the foot of it, I thought of the dark chapel at Częstochowa, a place full of pilgrims, where the crowd kneels on the cobbles at the feet of Our Lady of the Gate of Dawn; I thought of those people who, amid the blows and misfortunes that they suffer, believe just as strongly in God Almighty, in His justice, and seek the mercy and protection of the "Queen, Mother of Mercy, sweetness of life, and our hope."

One day I took myself off to the mosque at dusk, where the chapels were in semidarkness. I entered the large mirrored hall with the biggest Venetian chandeliers, and an eleventh-century bronze candelabra in the shape of a tree, much taller than human height, in which votive candles are placed. Here in this huge space, in the very same spot where the day before a mullah in dark glasses had been squatting, another one was sitting, with a snowy beard, praying with the same fervor as his predecessor. About ten paces behind him stood a boy of about eighteen, of another race, with very brown skin, regular features, wonderful dark eyes, and a subtly chiseled nose and mouth. He was wearing a faded blue turban, and making strange gestures, occasionally putting his henna-marked hands to his lower lip, then bowing low, with his hands behind him; the look on his face was deeply pious, disconnected, and happy. "The world is a carcass; let he who craves particles of this world grow accustomed to living with dogs," said Caliph Ali, and also: "Happy are those who have renounced the world and only desire the life to come."

Suddenly the electricity came on. The high, mirrored ceilings were also illuminated by the pale evening light, and their bluish silver contrasted with the russet light of the electric lamps. In a gloomy side

A page from *Diary No.* 2: 3 IX 1942-23 V 1943. "From Mashhad"—a drawing by Czapski featuring minarets.

chapel, where the day before no one but women had been praying, once again I saw five or six women semisupine on the floor, wrapped from head to foot in gray penitential shawls, immersed in prayer. In the same room, many people were bowing their heads in prayer on the stone slabs, each with a sort of small block in front of him, positioned to let him beat his brow against it rather than against the floor. Among them stood a mullah in black, tall and gaunt, with a mouth strikingly similar to that of my friend from years ago, Father R., who had suddenly dropped his brilliant career as a world-class painter and entered a monastery. Father R. had beautiful eyes, which weren't like those of the praying mullah, but there was something strikingly familiar about this figure as a whole, in the way his head was tossed back slightly to pray, oblivious to the world. It was above all the large mouth, rather unattractive, and the nervous, impotent chin—their set and expression were exactly the same. A purely physical likeness? One a mullah, the other a monk, praying with equally ardent hearts, with the same pure and happy faith in God, the source of all grace and the aim of all desires.

"Happy are those who have renounced the world and only desire the life to come."

The day after arriving in Mashhad I visited the Polish children's home.

The man who had set up this transfer point for children traveling from Russia to Bombay was our deputy consul in Bombay, Tadeusz Lisiecki. This judicious, realistic, phenomenally dynamic man devoted himself body and soul to transferring children from Russia to Bombay. He had also brought the first convoy of aid for Polish refugees from India in twelve trucks, by an entirely new route via Delhi, Balochistan, Zahedan, and Mashhad. He brought gifts donated by the Relief Committee for the Victims of War, which was set up in India in 1939 under the banner of the Indian Red Cross. He had brought fats, medications, typewriters, and a dental surgery, and reached Ashgabat for New Year's Day 1942. I remember how that winter in Buzuluk fantastic news had reached us about a Red Cross convoy from India. The dental surgery in particular stuck in my memory, because I had a false tooth in my mouth that had been made in the prison camp out of a piece of cow's bone fished out of the soup and set in place on part of a broken needle. The convoy from India was an encouraging sign that contact was possible between the superbly equipped Red Cross in the world outside and the boundless indigence of the Polish exiles in Russia.

The center for Polish children (where there were 240 of them), excellently organized and equipped, was located in the wing of a home for 400 Iranian children. It was run by a robust and energetic blonde woman, Mrs. Jasiewicz. Part of the building and some of the beds had been given over to us, and whatever the need, the Persians—especially the manager of the home—hurried to our aid.

Several convoys had already gone to India. More and more were coming in from Russia, usually by night. The healthier children were sent on as soon as possible, the weaker ones, not fit for an arduous onward journey, stayed here, and any who were ill were put in the home's little hospital. Any child in an extremely serious condition was sent to the wonderful American hospital that had been operating in Mashhad for many years. I was at our home at dinnertime, and for the after-dinner siesta. The healthier children were lying on blankets on the floor, the weaker ones on little beds in other rooms. I also visited the sick ward. By the door lay two small children, a boy and a girl, skeletally thin.

Warsaw's best pediatrician, Professor Kopeć, who had ended up here via Kozelsk and Gryazovets, took me to see a small girl with a lovely little face, flushed with fever, with blue eyes and extremely regular features; turning back the quilt he showed me her arms and legs, like bones coated with skin. "These are by no means the weakest children," he said. "We send the very sick, very malnourished ones to the American hospital. There are about fifteen of them there." Then he added in a whisper: "One child died of starvation, here in the hospital. It was impossible to save him; his organs couldn't cope. The children are better off there; they start to eat, and that's the most important thing."

That same day I visited the American hospital as well.

The hospital had been run for twenty-five years by Dr. Joseph Cochran. It was beautiful, among trees and flowers. Stone corridors, big airy terraces, on which the patients lay outside. Above some flat-roofed houses stretched the "Seven Sisters" mountain range.

We looked in at the Polish children's ward. Almost all the patients were from the collective farms around Kermin, where the tropical heat in treeless, waterless settlements had been murderous for them. These starvelings included Basia Dymnicka, a child with terrifyingly thin arms and a sad, solemn little face; her mother was meant to be leaving for Iran with another convoy by another route, and for weeks on end the sick child had had no news of her.

A twelve-year-old girl with the same sad look was copying out—in nice handwriting but with some spelling mistakes—a song about a soldier from another child's handwritten text. I asked her where she was from and where her parents were.

"I was with Mommy and Daddy in Arkhangelsk oblast," she politely replied. "Daddy came south with us to the army, but he only served a week and then died of typhus. Mommy died at the collective farm."

The children were lying on snow-white little beds, with a colorful bunch of flowers in the background, lots of toys, and in the window a canary in a cage, apparently a gift for the children from Mrs. Cochran.

Three of the patients were being transferred today—how frail they still were!—from the hospital back to our home, because they were now out of danger. Lisiecki took note of each child's state of health, paying close attention to important and unimportant details, and so did the two ladies from our home who had come here with us. The children wanted to give each of them a farewell gift, little pictures and cutouts. As we were leaving, the youngest children burst into loud and passionate weeping.

On the day I visited this hospital, one other child had died of starvation; his liver had ceased to function, and weak lungs and whooping cough had also contributed. The head of the hospital, of whom the Poles spoke to me with the greatest gratitude, and our consul took me to the morgue, where a narrow little object lay wrapped in a clean sheet. The doctor folded back a corner of the sheet and I saw the agonized little face of Władek N., waxen and yellow, with dark-brown sunken eyelids, and a dark stain by his clenched lips. The funeral was to take place next day. We had to find a box, because there were no coffins, and bury him at the Armenian cemetery.

The next day I went to the cemetery with the consul for Władek's funeral. In the heat and dust, we drove a large truck, carrying the child's corpse in a little box made of thin planks knocked together. With Lisiecki at the wheel, we roamed potholed roads in the suburbs, until finally we reached the Armenian cemetery. The earth was scorched, and the surrounding wall was made of baked clay; only a few of the graves were cared for, with crosses and greenery, the rest of the place was strewn with uneven burial mounds, with not a single tree, no trace of grass or other plants.

Once again, Lisiecki had had to overcome a thousand obstacles. The little coffin was made of real planks, which in this treeless land were worth their weight in gold. He had also managed to provide a wooden cross and some gravediggers. Lisiecki himself had collected the body from the morgue and driven it here, then managed the improvised gravediggers, lowered the coffin into the grave himself and helped to fill it in with a shovel.

The priest who came to send the child off to his eternal rest was Father Cieński. He had been tortured in Lwów, then imprisoned at Butyrki and the Lubyanka, sentenced to death, and later, like all of us, "amnestied." He had walked hundreds of miles and driven thousands to visit all the most out-of-the-way collective farms in Turkestan, saying Mass and administering the sacraments to our exiles. In a faded Polish uniform and a white surplice, he said prayers over the grave of this child, who had died here of "the torment of exile."

We drove away, leaving behind the little coffin scattered with gravel and clay dried out to a state of dust.

"Do not let him fall into the hands of enemies and never forget him," says the prayer for the dead, "but bid Your angels receive him and escort him to heaven, his homeland."

28. FAREWELL

As a result of bronchitis and a high temperature, I too was taken to the American hospital and put in a separate room. There was a wide window looking out at vegetation and mountains, dark-blue drapes printed with brown and yellow flowers, a carpet covering the entire floor, a wonderful bed, and very fine bed linen. For supper I was brought a tray of food from the doctor's private kitchen. The tray was covered with a hand-embroidered napkin, and on it were silver flatware, a small silver mug of sweet juice, soup, vegetables, homemade cookies, and peaches already peeled, stoned, and sprinkled with sugar.

The next day I was given as much hot water as I wanted, and an egg, toast, and tea with milk for breakfast. I am not at all greedy by nature—my family even used to joke that if I were given pigswill I'd eat it without batting an eyelid. But after the tea on tin plates at the Soviet mess, after all the slovenly Soviet canteens, and the hostels in Kuybyshev, Chkalov, and Ashgabat, this accommodation and this food was like something out of a fairy tale.

I had my own room, unlike my recent experience in Ak-Altyn in the same ward as forty dysentery patients. I had warm, attentive care, and on top of that all sorts of "bourgeois" luxuries—it made me remember my most wonderful nurses in Ak-Altyn with gratitude. What a superhuman effort they made to create the same atmosphere of care in those conditions as here and to restore those people's strength and health. Here all the patients benefited from superb, meticulous medical care, the constant vigilance of the entire staff, a wealth of medicines, and extraordinary hygiene: numerous Persians, the Polish children from Russia, and now me as well. For me, it was my final week "in transit" between the Soviet Union and Iraq, which I spent writing up my notes about the Soviet Union in the most comfortable conditions imaginable, looking in on our starvelings, saying goodbye to them, and at the same time to three years of Soviet experiences.

Until nine o'clock the windows could be left open on the shady side of the building, but my window looked east and had to be closed from four in the morning. I only opened it toward evening, when the air was fresher, but as it was, from my bed I could see a lush green garden, all manner of fruit trees, and young ash trees with large dark leaves; beyond that were clay houses, yellow, russet, and gray, with flat roofs amid trees of various species and shapes, and many different shades of green, interwoven with slender poplars whose leaves were a fresher, almost springlike color. Behind the trees the ragged pink peaks of the Seven Sisters range rose higher and higher to the south, ending in the tallest, conical summit under a pure blue sky.

The Persian staff were cheerful and extremely courteous. We used sign language to communicate, and the two Persian nurses from Ashgabat spoke a little Russian.

I was given constant care. The nurses had a duty to report hourly to ask if I needed anything. The doctor's young daughters brought me everything they could find about Poland: Sopoćko's book in English about the exploits of our submarine, *Orzeł?*, and color prints showing views of Łazienki and Łowicz cut out of an American geographical magazine. The same little girls brought me tea, cookies, and grapes.

The entire hospital was very religious. Dr. Cochran's grandfather had been a pastor in Tabriz, and his father had been a doctor at this same hospital, so this was the third generation of the family to be living in Iran. During the day I could hear hymns being sung in the hospital. The Muslims and Protestants working there were always talking about God.

It was the middle of August, the first few days of Ramadan.

One of my nurses was an old man with a stubbly chin called Aga Ali. In broken Russian he explained the meaning of this strict fast to me: "If you yourself are hungry and thirsty, you know what it means for a poor man to be hungry and thirsty. That's why Mohammed established Ramadan."

He also told me that in the days when the Soviet and British armies occupied Iran, the Persians fought "like lions," and that if not for their ruler's orders, they'd have beaten the British and the Russkies—they'd already captured Tiflis but were ordered to retreat!

My other nurse was Ismail, who stressed that he was a Turk, not a Farsi, and came from Hamadan. He too was very religious, but was a Christian. Several times he talked to me about Christ and brought me meditations on the Gospels published in New York. He told me with delight about Hamadan, its beautiful fruits and lovely mountains, inhabited by Turks, Farsi, and Kurds. He told me the Kurds had killed the British consul and his aides and had massacred the Soviet airmen who came there. He was furious that the British and the Russians had occupied the country by deceit—apparently the Persian regiments had fought superbly, though there were too few of them. Growing more and more heated, he cried with fire in his eyes: "One Persian soldier is worth a hundred Russian or British!"

And the old man believed it; once again, as with Aga Ali, I felt aware of a nonexistent boundary between reality and fairy tale. The background to the legends I was hearing was a loathing of any invader.

Sister Ester Edger told me she was Assyrian, and that when Babylon destroyed Assyria, vast numbers of Assyrians had moved to the shores of Lake Urmia (in Persian Azerbaijan) and remained there. Her mother, a Catholic, was murdered by the Turks in 1919, during the massacre of two hundred thousand Christians. Ester Edger had been cared for by the Americans and sent to the American schools in Tehran and Beirut; now she was a Protestant and deputy to the head doctor, Joseph Cochran. Ester was very dark, with distinct, regular features, big black eyebrows, and a broad, heavy face. Was it her story that prompted me to think she had an Assyrian profile and could have been a daughter of Sargon?

And so I learned some geography and history in there, I discovered that the Assyrians still existed, and that Tabriz, Hamadan, and Urmia were more than just abstract concepts.

The courtesy and help afforded to so many Poles, as foreign exiles here, by the people of Iran was astonishing. At times this civility might have seemed almost servile to the Europeans, but isn't it quite simply an individual style, developed over many centuries, the traditional form of a country with an extremely ancient culture? "They're a cunning race, one should be wary of them," some people told me. What did they mean by "cunning"? The cunning of Aga Ali, who went out of his way to make life as pleasant as possible for me there? Or of the French-speaking Persian doctor, who when visiting his Persian patients would drop in on me as well to ask what he could do for me, and who told me rationally and without any fantasy about his country's difficult situation?

On one of the first days I was suddenly visited by my neighbor, an emaciated, jaundiced old man in a hospital gown, leaning on a crutch. He spoke a little Russian. He was pleased to be received with respect. The next day he brought along his brother, a fat merchant called Kadji Ali Visungi, who offered me his services, and even money. He gave me a long lecture on how Mohammed bade them be hospitable and that foreigners should be helped in every way, and finally he brought me some cookies, evidently meant for his brother. He was fasting, like all the practicing Muslims here, eating nothing from two in the morning to six at night for a month; he too explained to me that the point of this fast was to remind people to help the poor and the hungry. He was a follower of the Babi, or Baha'i faith, and claimed there were about one and a half million of them in Persia. He tried to explain the principles of this sect to me, that one should not fight one's enemy, or oppose evil with evil, one should not kill, one should love everyone including foreigners, and be kind to everyone, even though it is easier to love one's own family and one's coreligionists. He made it sound like a Persian version of Gandhism or the Tolstoyan movement, although this sect is much older—it features in the work of Gobineau, who describes the martyrdom of the founder of this religion.

As soon as my temperature began to drop, I too was invited into the doctor's garden, where I spent several days in a deck chair on the lawn.

The grass was thick and lush, sprinkled with tiny clover. The trees were mature, with tall, leafless trunks, spreading boughs, and leaves with silver undersides, shaped like maple leaves but much smaller and more jagged. There were asters, rosebushes, and tobacco-scented flowers. Every day two nice dogs came and fawned on us, both incredibly fat—a big setter and a very friendly little dog called Peggy, with thick hair covering her eyes.

In the shade of these trees, whose leaves were as lovely as large bouquets of flowers, a wide cherry-red rug was spread out, and our poorest children lay around it on deck chairs. They spent the sunny after-dinner hours there, and the healthier ones were brought out again after the siesta. Every day, four pretty little girls, the daughters of the doctor and the pastor, in blue dresses, as if straight out of an English eighteenth-century portrait, brought the Polish children presents: little color pictures with Bible scenes, tomato juice, thick milky cocoa, and inventive toys.

But the Polish children were all sad, as if prematurely old; they never smiled, but sulked, eating reluctantly or refusing to eat. Utterly emaciated, they only whispered to each other and swapped the "holy pictures." The youngest child was sitting in front of me, a small boy called Lopek who was suffering from whooping cough but had also had pneumonia; racked by a severe cough, he was in a solemn, sullen mood. Next to him sat another little boy, with skeletal legs, covered in red spots and with some sort of ointment on his head. These boys never once smiled in my presence, though they were the youngest in the group, about three or at most four years old. A little girl was put in a deck chair next to me—it was Basia Dymnicka, whom I had seen when I visited the hospital. The head doctor had less and less faith in her recovery; he sounded sadder every time he spoke of her, shaking his head and falling silent. She was slowly fading, refusing food, and constantly asking about her mother, and also her father, of whom there was no news either. At most ten years old, she had a very serious, thin little face, with no hint of a smile.

When I told her she must eat, gain strength, and recover her health, she only replied: "If only my mommy would come back ..." without finishing the sentence, but in the tone of her voice I could hear: "Then I'd be sure to get better."

I asked her some questions, and she started telling me her story, in a strangely matter-of-fact way, like an adult, with a sort of detachment.

"We're from Brzeszcz, outside Kraków. My father was the chief postmaster there. We had such pretty sunflowers, on all four sides of our garden, and on two we had raspberries as well—it was so pretty. There were two lovely forests, one damp, one dry, and I used to go mushroom picking there with Mommy. What lovely boletus and sulfur caps there were!

"When the war came, our parents took us to Lwów, from where we were deported to a village called Vasilevo in Arkhangelsk oblast. Daddy chopped timber for fifteen kopecks a yard—he didn't earn as much as a ruble a day. If not for Mommy, we wouldn't have survived, but she worked as a waitress, then as the head cook. When we found out the Polish Army was being formed, we all decided to go. And when they asked us to stay, they promised Mom she'd be manager of the crèche, and they also said: *Budetye pomnit, kak vashi dyeti z goloda budut umirat*—'You'll remember your children starving to death,'"— the girl said this in perfect Russian; she had clearly memorized this sentence—"but we said no. Everyone was going, how could we stay? We spent two weeks on a raft to Krasnoborsk, a whole sixty miles, then by ship to Kotlas, and from there by train to the town of Kasan in Bukhara oblast.

"Once we arrived at this town, near Bukhara, it wasn't too bad. Daddy worked, so did Mommy, and we had bread. Daddy went to dig canals, and then worked at a carpenter's, where he was meant to be the assistant but the carpenter was never there, and Mom worked at the hospital. That was where she fell sick with typhus, and she was ill for ages.

"The worst was after that, when we went to Kermine. There was no water, no trees, and a terrible heat wave. It wasn't so bad for me, because I was in a Polish shelter, but Mommy lived in a tent at the station, and she really suffered. And where has she gone now? Where is my mommy?"

One of the pastor's daughters, who had long, loose fair hair and was wearing a little blue dress, brought Basia a glass of tomato juice, and with the kindest smile encouraged her to drink it. Basia didn't even look up but refused by firmly shaking her head, totally indifferent. What a strangely subdued child. The soft grass, the trees and flowers—it was as if she couldn't see any of it, and only when she spoke about the damp and dry forests near Brzeszcz, about the sulfur caps and the sunflowers there, did her face come to life, and a hint of animation crossed it.

"What was it like traveling north by raft?"

"We went over sixty miles to the nearest city on that raft, with one other family, and it was hellishly cold. When there was a wind against us, we couldn't move, and we spent three days like that, stuck on the spot. Another time the raft hit a stump and had to be fixed, and we were stuck for three days again, though at night we went to some cabins. Daddy spent the night on the raft so it wouldn't be stolen. The other family was the Bogdanowiczes, who had six children. It was quite a business trying to stay the night in the villages, because sometimes we were let in, and sometimes we weren't. Generally people were kind, and took us in; they even gave us baked jacket potatoes and very tasty salted mushrooms—and there were some rich people, who had samovars, and when they'd eaten supper they gave us the samovar and some supper. There were some places where we sat for three days without having to pay a penny. One time it was so muddy and cold, but nobody wanted to take us in. It was a tiny village, and they were afraid. Then I began to cry, I felt so cold, and my sister began to cry too, so they let us in. But only Mommy and us two girls, not the Bogdanowiczes. They gave us supper and a place to sleep on the stove—it was wonderful, but the others went back to sleep on the raft, and one of the children died in the night. Then we found out that a second one had died soon after.

"While we were on the train from Kotlas my sister died, because she had the measles and pneumonia. I was sick too, I had a temperature of a hundred and four and I didn't know my sister had died. And now Mommy's not here . . ."

The pastor's daughters laid out some attractive toys in front of Lopek, including some colored building bricks and a painted cardboard box, but he wasn't at all interested in them.

The smallest of all the children sent to the hospital, a two-year-old orphan girl, was never brought outside with us. She was in a hopeless state, suffering from chronic dysentery, and her body was utterly exhausted. Each morning they carried her to Dr. Cochran's wife's room. The child wouldn't accept food from anyone except her and Sister Ester, the Assyrian nurse. As we lay out on the grass, we could hear the poor child crying nonstop in the doctor's villa. Not even crying—she was too weak for that by now, but whimpering, an endless low moan.

What was behind all the kindness we met with here, and why did we find it so moving? Not just the cocoa and tomato juice, or the Persian rug on which the deck chairs were set out, but this unassuming approach, the ever vigilant attention toward those who were suffering.

That day I saw the pastor's wife, a tall American woman, whose older daughter was very like her; slender, not a young woman anymore, but with very fine features, she entered the garden in a bright summer dress and a large straw hat, just as the nurses were carrying out some children with jaundiced complexions and cadaverous limbs to sit on the lawn. She stopped short, then stepped back a pace to let the nurses and children pass by. And again, it was the look in her eyes that showed brotherhood, a look of shyly hidden, intense sympathy, the look of a person who not only reacts to the suffering of which she or he is the helpless witness, not only sympathizes, but also feels ashamed for being well fed and relatively happy.

> "and so I hasten to give back my entrance ticket."
> —DOSTOEVSKY, *The Brothers Karamazov*

My temperature dropped and I was well again. Time to close this short chapter, I thought one quiet evening as I sat in a garden deck chair, smelling the scent of dried grass. Three years in the camps and the army, and suddenly here I was, at the end of the world, on an island of convalescence, amid flowers, trees, and kind people.

On the day I was due to leave the hospital, I was suddenly woken at six in the morning by the consul, Lisiecki. At four in the night he had brought in fifteen injured Junaki, girls aged fifteen to eighteen. Another vehicle was bringing three more girls who had been killed when the huge truck in which they were traveling had overturned on some jagged rocks. Two of the survivors were in a very serious state. The vehicle had skidded on the gravel turning a corner, though it had happened past the dangerous stretch before Quchan, where there were so many sharp bends and steep drops. The girls had fallen out, some into a river, some onto the rocks, and they had waited six hours for help to arrive.

By chance, an Englishman had driven by, who left them bandages and a first-aid kit, while he went to fetch help. A Soviet vehicle came along too, stopped briefly, and then drove on. Later in Quchan the Soviets officially informed our people that the girls were injured, but that they had everything they needed, because they had provided them with assistance.

I learned some facts about the girls who had died. Danuta Studnicka had a broken spine and a crushed skull. Her injured sister had been brought to the hospital; their mother had died in Poland, and their father had been deported and apparently killed. They were from Toruń. Seventeen-year-old Wacława Kaczmarska had died an hour after the accident; hemorrhaging from the nose and mouth, she had suffered badly. Her mother and sister had stayed behind in Aktyubinsk, sending Wacława to the army to join the auxiliary service. Aldona Trypuć had injuries to her head and her liver, which must have burst, because she had stains all over her body. She had spent three hours dying in agony. Her mother was a doctor.

That same morning, four of the girls who had arrived with Lisiecki and were not at all injured, just shaken, came to sit on the lawn along with the sick children. Radiant with life, their faces flushed with health, these teenagers exuded freshness and energy. In this foreign country, in a garden where they could speak neither English nor Persian, they could hardly communicate with anyone. After the terrible nocturnal accident and six hours among the rocks with their dead friends, these girls managed to remain modest and natural, even though they were all visibly in shock and completely exhausted.

The seriously injured girls were put in a ward right next to my room. Dear Aga Ali struggled to read out to me a long Russian sentence he had written down in Persian script, to say that he sympathized with the victims of the accident, but that they should trust in God and all would be well. He asked me to correct the text, so that he could read it to them.

The girl who prompted the greatest anxiety was Helena Bernacka. Lisiecki told me she had a fractured skull; brain tissue had been found in her hair, and she probably wouldn't survive after being left in such a dangerous condition for six hours without a dressing. But when the doctor examined her, it turned out that apart from severe bruising and concussion, she had no serious injuries. The brain tissue in her hair was from her friend, whose skull was crushed and who died beside her on the rocks.

Helena lay in a darkened room with the door set ajar. I was in the corridor at the moment when her sister arrived. She had been traveling to Tehran with a different convoy, had heard about the accident, and then taken every possible opportunity to turn back to Quchan, and from there she had reached Mashhad, not knowing if Helena was still alive. From the corridor I saw her lean over her sister's bed; I heard Helena's nervous sobs and her sister's tears as they hugged each other. Then I heard Helena describing the accident: "Then the truck slid off the embankment and we fell out ... it wasn't all that high ... but the rocks ... and the stones were very sharp, and I passed out. When I gained consciousness, both the girls who'd been next to me, Danuta and Wacława, were dead ... And I was sure I was just about to die ... I said a Hail Mary"—here her voice grew stronger, and without sniffling, but in a burst she added: "... and I thanked the Lord that I wasn't dying among the Soviets."

So this wounded child, lying among her dead friends, thought of death on the remote rocks of Persia as a happy death, because she was free, beyond the borders of the "Inhuman Land."

I went into the garden to say goodbye to them all, but neither Lopek, the child with whooping cough, nor Basia Dymnicka were on the lawn. The doctor had been keeping them indoors for a few days, because they were getting weaker.

I went back inside to the children's ward. There were abandoned toys lying on the empty, made-up beds, and the fat canary was chirping away in his cage. Only two beds were occupied—Lopek was asleep with his head on his little fist, breathing heavily, his face as serious as ever. Basia was also asleep, lying by the window. There was an exhausted look on her narrow little face, with fine blue veins on her transparent brow, and her long pale hands were laid on the quilt. Her fair hair was cut short like a recruit's. Above the bed a long rubber tube extended from a small white enamel container, in an attempt to drip nourishment into her waning body.

The child was moaning in her sleep. Afraid of waking her, I tiptoed out of the room.

One last time I looked into my room, where I had spent some relatively happy days among the kindhearted people who were so compassionately trying to restore life and joy to the children starved in the Soviet Union.

By now it was evening. The rich greenery of the garden, the clay walls and flat roofs were already cloaked in a thick veil of shade. The Seven Sisters range stood out, an intense shade of violet in air as pure as glass. Only the highest, conical peak, lit by the last rays of the sun, was purple, the color of blood.

PART TWO
The Fight

1. IRAQ

I STARTED to write this book in 1942 at the hospital in Mashhad, straight after leaving Soviet Russia. I wanted to preserve the memory of this multitude of recollections and to bear witness to what I had experienced, seen, and heard. Nothing more; but now, twenty years on, this book is to appear in German translation.

The German publisher suggested that I add an epilogue to bring the book up to date. "Please write about what has happened since that time between East and West," he said. I am not a historian or a politician, and I wouldn't have taken on this task, which was inevitably bound to outgrow the modest scope of these memoirs, changing the entire nature of the book, but I accept that after all these years it does need supplementing.

"Don't publish the book in German and don't write anything about Germany," said a friend from Poland. "Whatever you write, you'll be regarded as a neofascist."

These pieces of advice merely encourage me to publish this book in Germany, and to write an epilogue, without regard for politics, propaganda, pedagogy, or moral censorship. To bear witness to the past (all these things in the world, in us, belong not just to the *past* but potentially the *present*), not to blur or muffle anything, but by this means to bring oneself into the light, and maybe try to liberate others too from toxins, bitterness, and hatred.

In this epilogue I want to relate the further fortunes of the people whom I wrote about in the first part of this book, but how am I to do that without mentioning the news that came from Poland during those years, which at the time shaped all our thoughts and feelings?

The news that, while we were still in Russia, reached our camps via the Soviet radio, public announcements and journals, and later on, when we were at relative liberty, via the Polish and British journals that were sent to the newly forming Polish Army, along with photocopies of the underground Polish press and photographs of people who had been slaughtered or tortured, even including Chopin's head lying in the debris after the Germans had destroyed his statue.

We all had loved ones there who were in mortal danger, and that bonded us into a single family like never before. Hitler was lording it over Poland, heralding its destruction to fanfares of propaganda and enthusiastic, or at least passive acceptance of his aims by the overwhelming majority of the German nation.

The news from Poland was beyond our imagination: since the fall of 1939, to purge the land for German colonization, mass deportations had begun—thousands of peasants, and urban Jews and Poles from the towns and cities in the west of Poland adjoining Germany, had been expelled into the already overpopulated so-called General Government. Every day, trains full of refugees from the West came pouring in, "some of them filled with nothing but corpses," as Governor Frank himself stated in 1942.

Later, within the General Government, with the aim of settling Germans there too, entire territories were "purged," forcing famine and death on thousands more peasants.

All the academics at the Jagiellonian University (one of the oldest in central Europe) had already been arrested and deported to Sachsenhausen in November 1939, as part of an operation called "Sonderkommando Krakau." A number of the most eminent professors died in Sachsenhausen, after weeks of harassment and humiliation. These scholars, including sick old men, were forced to stand on parade for hours at a time, with their heads bare, dressed in rags, singing: "*Wir wollen singen und frölich sein.*"*

For what? For attempting to open the university—"a malicious act hostile to the German Reich."

---

*"We want to sing and be merry."

Because the Poles, decimated in their own land, had no right to exist, except as mute, entirely defenseless slaves, until the moment came when the sentence of physical extermination of the entire nation would be delivered.

For on June 6, 1940, in an interview for the *Völkische Beobachter*, Hans Frank, in charge of the General Government—the scrap of Poland into which more than one and a half million Poles and Jews expelled from territory annexed by the Reich had been crowded—said with reference to the posting in the Czech lands of news of the execution of seven Czech students: "If I were to give orders for news of this kind to be posted in Poland every time I have seven Poles shot, the Polish forests wouldn't be big enough to make the paper."

All these years on, must I go back to describing the nightmare of which everyone who ever wanted to know about it is already aware and would now like to wipe from memory? How am I to evade the memories of those years, which though superficially blurred by now, are still extremely vivid, even among those who were children at the time, still vivid for millions of people in Poland, not just thanks to the official propaganda that persists in being one-sidedly anti-German (because Katyn, a Soviet crime, is still a taboo subject in Poland), but often in spite of this propaganda. But the memories draw me ever closer toward the fundamental issue affecting all of us—our coexistence within Europe, the Pole's relationship *today* and in the future to the Germans, and the German's to the Poles.

I was one of the last members of Anders's army to leave the Soviet Union in the fall of 1942 across the Persian border. That year, seventy thousand Polish soldiers came out the same way, with fifty thousand women and children attached to the transport.

All the soldiers and adolescents capable of bearing arms or serving as auxiliaries in the army were redeployed to Iraq. In agreement with the Polish government, the British authorities had already sent the women with small children from Iran to India, Kenya, Lebanon, and even Mexico, where living conditions were provided for them that were the height of wise and cordial care compared with their wretched fate on the Soviet collective farms. In Iraq, soldiers from all the camps in Russia joined up with General Kopański's Carpathian Brigade. This formation had already been highly successful in combat against the Germans: Tobruk, the Gazala offensive, Libya, and further operations in Cyrenaica. Under the command of General Anders, who led us out of Russia, a new Polish army was formed, officially named "The Polish Armed Forces in the Middle East." Every soldier who had left Soviet Russia wanted above all to have a weapon, something the Soviets had not given him; he wanted to get to the front and fight the Germans as soon as possible. From October 1942, weapons had started coming in to the army but at a rate that the soldiers found too slow. At Khanaqin, our first camp outside Baghdad, a malaria epidemic broke out. In his memoirs, Anders describes visiting the sick, and adds: "The soldiers did not complain about their illness, or about the desert, or the heat. Their only complaint was that the guns and equipment were coming in too slowly for them to be able to train properly."

We finally received the eagerly awaited weapons and equipment—cannon, tanks, and thousands of jeeps. In chapter 7 of part one of this book I mentioned a Soviet expert on armored vehicles, General Panfilov, who was attached to the Polish Army in Russia; at the time he had claimed that training our soldiers to use the modern tanks was bound to take at least three years.

After several Soviet winters, where these soldiers, already exhausted, had endured temperatures that often went below 40°F, now they had to learn to use weapons that were new to them under the murderous Iraqi sun, in tanks that couldn't be touched with a bare hand without suffering severe burns. For these soldiers, most of whom were from the eastern part of Poland, a land of fields, soggy meadows, and dense forests, adapting to the climate, and to life in the tawny, dried-out desert, without a shadow of grass, was not easy. Each day we had several cases of severe sunstroke, and there were often cases of mental disorders. On a blazing hot afternoon, one of the soldiers on watch began shooting at the sun. The soldiers at the camp made "flower beds" on the dry, compacted earth. These were usually the emblems of their native cities, Lwów and Wilno, formed out of stones.

After only a year of intensive training, this army was a modern unit, motorized and ready to fight, and in January 1944 it went into action on the Italian front.

Those forests of tents at Khanaqin, Mosul, Kirkuk, and later in Palestine, Egypt, and Italy—was it an army in the classic, normal meaning of the word? It was a nation on its way to the Promised Land, to Poland. We did have soldiers in our army, but among them were old men whom no conscription board would have accepted, women serving as auxiliaries, and fourteen- to fifteen-year-old boys who had lied about their age in order to enlist. Within this "little Poland" in the desert we had to provide not just combat training for the soldiers but also save the broken or very thin thread of thought, culture, and science: four journals and three theaters were established (one of them performed plays by Fredro and Molière in the desert, and later in Italy). There were lectures, an imprint publishing books ranging from readers for the young people through to Mickiewicz's *Pan Tadeusz*, the national epic, which went all around the army in two editions of ten thousand copies each, and another imprint for pamphlets, essays, and poetry by the soldiers in the corps, works by young poets and writers. The point of all this was something far more important too. It was necessary to create conditions that would provide an education for the adolescent boys and girls who had been taken in by the army in Russia; many of them had forgotten how to read and write after three years there. For the young people of pre-conscription age, high schools and technical schools were organized, which stayed in the Middle East (Palestine, Egypt, and Lebanon) once the army had set off for the Italian front.

For the soldiers, the first general secondary school was set up in Palestine; later on, in Italy, each division had a general secondary school or a technical school, and at the Second Corps base there were as many as three.

A good many of the professional officers scowled at these ideas. Education? There'll be plenty of time for that sort of thing in Warsaw

—what these boys need now is to learn how to handle a machine gun. The rest doesn't matter!

An educational unit was organized under the management of an eminent academic, the former deputy minister of education Professor Aleksandrowicz. There was nothing bogus about it. The *matura* (or high-school graduation) exams, which these boys finally took once in Italy, had the normal demands of the Polish prewar tests. At the same time the young people were encouraged to go to university in Rome, Milan, or Turin, so toward the end of military operations some four thousand soldiers were studying at Italian high schools or universities.

Creating the entire system, finding the teaching staff—an element that was invaluable in the lines as well, so no commander wanted to let them go—was no minor achievement, and would have been inconceivable without the help of the senior command, who understood the importance of this matter. It was also necessary to reissue or make copies of a whole series of school textbooks. During the fighting in Italy, many of the young soldiers went on patrol with trigonometry or history textbooks in their backpacks; at the time, one of the lecturers, who had been a school inspector for fifteen years, told me that during his entire professional life in Poland he had never seen such diligence and that every night he had to go and switch off the lights in the young people's tents to make them stop studying and go to sleep.

During the Italian offensive, all the commanders kept putting in requests for these young students. In my Italian notebooks, on April 22, 1944, I recorded a ceremony held at Castel Pietroso to award *matura* certificates to several dozen of these young soldiers, who had already taken part in the fighting only three weeks earlier. The father of one of these boys, who was killed during the Italian campaign, said to me at the time that about 70 percent of his son's fellow students had already died in combat in Italy. They were the bravest, brightest element, the most willing to sacrifice their lives.

Nowadays I think of that first summer after leaving Russia, spent in Iraq, then Palestine, that year of military training and fervent organization, as a period in our lives that was full of hope, almost joyful. How can that be?

I remember the camps in the desert: the pure peacock blue of the sky, the subtle geometry of the white tents. As evening approached, in the dry air this bare landscape would be fully saturated with light the way Corot painted it; it had a captivating logic of transparent shadows, a logic that doesn't jump out at us in a rich, tree-filled, or built-up landscape. Tawny plains, now golden, now reddish, all the way to the horizon, as if drawn by a child, and sometimes, as outside Kirkuk, the subtle contours of rounded, pink, undulating hills, also as bare as a moonscape. No sign of a palm tree anywhere, now and then a dense clump of cactuses or thistles—of the same kind as the subtle twig the young Dürer is holding as a symbol of loyalty in his self-portrait for his fiancée—but here the thistles have grown to a tremendous size, into a bank of tangled bushes; fodder for camels, they are dry, yellow, and sharp as a sword. And then I remember these same white tents at night, the cupola of the sky without a single tiny cloud or a single tree to obscure it, all but shining with myriad stars.

As one of the proverbs of Solomon in the Bible says: "Where there is no vision, the people perish." We had a vision at the time; the whole patriotic, romantic tradition of the Poles, as if born again, prompted us to believe in "the justice of history." All the romantic poetry, which so many of the soldiers had studied at school and had often heard recited at official celebrations in independent Poland without really listening, suddenly came to life again, as if written for us alone.

Over a century earlier, Mickiewicz had prayed "For universal war for the liberty of peoples":

> For our arms and national eagles
> For a happy death in the field of battle.

(That was the time when the French historian Jules Michelet wept with emotion at the sight of the young Germans' standard.) Here we had our universal war; with good or bad faith, the entire Allied press was trumpeting that it was "for the liberty of peoples." We too thought that the "crimes of tyrants" had finally tipped the scale and awoken the world's conscience. For unbearably horrible news kept reaching us in more and more detail. In the first few months of 1943 we learned of new waves of deportations within the General Government. Fifty percent of the peasantry were deported from the Zamość area in late 1942, and in early 1943 another wave of deportations began. The Germans were planning to deport two hundred thousand people from several districts in the Lublin area, in order to resettle their own compatriots there from Croatia and Łódź. The deportees were being loaded onto railcars at the coldest temperatures. Those able to work were being sent to Germany for forced labor. The old people and mothers with infants were being dumped at overcrowded villages in neighboring districts. Later on, eyewitnesses gave me details of the heartbreaking scenes that had taken place at the time. Old people were abandoned on stretchers at the stations, in Siedlce forty frozen corpses were brought out of a railcar, and a little girl in a blue overcoat lay dead on the track. A witness to this scene heard some Germans laughing out loud and saying: *"Ein bödes Volk."**

The older children were sent to the Reich via Warsaw—to become Volksdeutsch. (In 1940 Governor Frank had already activated a plan to Germanize children with blue eyes and blond hair.) This news reached Warsaw at lightning speed and electrified the whole city, where the crowds at the stations risked their lives by trying to steal these children away; they managed to free several from the railcars and rescue them—from what? From the ultimate disgrace, for this city worse than death—the disgrace of becoming a German.

The partisan movement was growing by the month, dynamiting German transports carrying soldiers and equipment on their way to or from Russia and blowing up the tracks. Resistance attacks and open clashes were multiplying.

For us, 1943 was the year of the tragic death of head of state and Polish Armed Forces commander in chief General Sikorski in a helicopter crash off Gibraltar. That same year our army in the Middle

---

*"What crazy people."

East had already advanced to Palestine. There, before it set off for Italy, the final major maneuvers took place, with Sikorski's successor in the post of commander in chief, General Sosnkowski, in attendance.

The fall of 1943 was one of the bloodiest for Poland, a period of mass public executions. People were randomly arrested, even dragged off trams and put up against a wall—as hostages—and shot dead. Prisoners from Pawiak, Warsaw's central jail, were driven to execution sites in Warsaw's main squares barefoot and in paper shirts, after being given injections to stop them from struggling. To stop them from screaming, their mouths had been filled with plaster. After the executions the corpses were carted away. The pavement was scattered with sand to soak up the blood, and at once the square would fill again, as the citizens came running, throwing flowers and lighting candles that they placed on the ground; some people wetted their handkerchiefs with the sacred blood or gathered up the brains spattered on the walls as national holy relics. The Germans walked across the square with their heads lowered. "*Ein dreckiges, ein versauchtes Land*,"* said one of them angrily.

That year, Frank communicated that seventeen thousand Polish hostages had been shot dead without any sort of trial as follows: "There's no need to be concerned about the seventeen thousand executed Polish hostages, because they are victims of war."

The Nazi authorities had young people, not much more than children, sent from Germany to attend these executions in order to toughen them up by having them watch the agony of innocent people in Warsaw's squares with their eyes wide open. In that same year, a group of these youths, something like Nazi boy scouts, was sent on a trip to Mordy, a town near Siedlce. There they went to the cemetery, where they systematically smashed the old wooden crosses, knocked over the graves and monuments, and then marched off to my brother-in-law's garden. (Two years later he was deported by the Red Army and died in a Soviet camp.)

Outside the house there was a small plaster Madonna. On summer

_____
*"What a dirty, disgusting country."

evenings the children used to come and pray before this Madonna. The young German boys pierced her belly with bayonets and broke her arms. One of her little plaster hands lay on my sister's table for many years, evidence of this "petty" but highly symbolic gratuitous act by the German youths.

Except for the elementary schools, all Poland's schools and universities had been closed by the Germans throughout the country as soon as they occupied it. According to Heinrich Himmler's "Einige Gedanken über die Behandlung der Fremdvölkischen im Osten"* the Poles were members of the "*Untermenschvolk des Ostens*,"† who only needed to be taught to count up to five hundred at most, sign their names, and believe that "it is God's command to be obedient, reliable, hardworking, and honest to the Germans." Himmler did not consider it necessary to teach them how to read.

That year, the victims of mass shootings included young people who had been snatched from their schools, including many of the youngest generation of Polish poets.

Twenty-one-year-old Andrzej Trzebiński was publicly executed on November 21 in Nowy Świat, one of Warsaw's main streets. Like his predecessors, he was the third editor of the underground journal *Sztuka i Naród* (Art and the Nation) to be executed; the fourth, Tadeusz Gajcy, was killed at the age of twenty-three during the Warsaw Uprising, blown up with his entire insurgent unit.

> No ancient Greek hero entered into combat
> So deprived of hope, in their heads the image
> Of a white skull kicked by feet in passing...‡

their older comrade Czesław Miłosz would write years later.

In May of that year the twenty-two-year-old poet Wacław Bojar-

---

* "Memorandum on the Treatment of Racial Aliens in the East"
† "Subhuman eastern race."
‡ Czesław Miłosz, *A Treatise on Poetry*, trans. Czesław Miłosz and Robert Hass (New York: The Ecco Press, 2001).

ski had died of his wounds, hit in the stomach as he laid a wreath with a red-and-white ribbon at the foot of Copernicus's monument on the four-hundredth anniversary of his death.

> Copernicus: the statue of a German or a Pole?
> Leaving a spray of flowers, Bojarski perished:
> A sacrifice should be pure, unreasoned.
> Trzebiński, the new Polish Nietzsche,
> Had his mouth plastered shut before he died.
> He took with him the view of a wall, low clouds.
> His black eyes had just a moment to absorb.
> Baczyński's head fell against his rifle.
> The uprising scared up flocks of pigeons.
> Gajcy, Stroiński, were raised to the sky,
> A red sky, on the shield of an explosion.[*]

The year 1943 was also the year of the final extermination, first activated in 1942, of the Jewish population of hundreds of Polish towns and settlements, the total destruction of the Warsaw ghetto and of the Polish Jews and others rounded up in Germany and all the occupied countries. It was also the year of the Jewish ghetto uprising, the first mass rebellion on territory occupied by the Germans. It erupted on April 19, when Hitler was still at the height of his power, and it was hopeless, heroic, in the name of sheer human dignity and the Jewish race.

The liquidation of the ghetto, which the Germans assumed would be a three-day operation, continued for more than four weeks. A large number of Germans were killed in the process, and the Jews, defenseless, burned alive or gassed in their collapsing, blazing houses, in cellars or sewers, defended themselves to the last. On May 8 the leader of the uprising, Mordechai Anielewicz, and his entire staff were killed; not until May 16 did SS General Stroop report to his superiors that the "major operation" was over.

[*]Ibid.

At almost the same time news reached Poland, and also us in Iraq, that four thousand (at first there was talk of ten thousand) corpses of Polish officers, prisoners of war, had been discovered in Katyn forest—the officers for whom we had been searching, as I have described in this book.

The Katyn massacre, committed by the Soviets, a powerful ally of our allies in the fight against Hitler, filled all of Polish opinion, in Poland and abroad, with indescribable horror. How could we possibly ignore the political consequences of such a terrible fact?

Because I had come out of Russia and had searched for our missing comrades on behalf of the commander of the Polish Armed Forces, tormenting myself and others as I traveled to Kuybyshev, Chkalov, and Moscow, and then spent months and months on end working with an entire team of colleagues to draft, check, and supplement lists featuring the names of thousands of those men, the news about Katyn was confirmation, proof of the long-foreseen truth.

When General Sikorski presented the first news of it to Churchill, the latter phlegmatically replied: "If they are dead, nothing you can do will bring them back to life." "Be quiet, this isn't the time for mutual recriminations," said the British.

Whether Poles under occupation, Polish soldiers in Iraq or on any other front, or the Polish government in London, how could we engage in such "political" thinking? Under the pressure of Polish opinion from the world over, the Polish government approached the International Red Cross with a request to investigate the matter. The Soviet government, which naturally would not agree to this under any circumstances, took advantage of this proposal to sever diplomatic relations with the Polish government.

This rift had a decisive effect upon the further development of events on Polish territory, and merely facilitated Stalin's anti-Polish policy.

The news about Katyn made every Pole even more deeply aware that we were under lethal threat *from both sides*.

2. FROM THE ITALIAN LAND TO POLAND

FOR THE Allies, 1944 was the year of the Italian campaign, the Normandy landings, the capture of Rome and of Paris, the year when the Red Army crossed the Polish borders as they were in 1939; for the Poles it was the year of Monte Cassino and the Warsaw Uprising, and in Normandy, the Battle of the Falaise Pocket.

In January of that year the Polish Second Corps under the command of General Anders went into action after landing in Italy with a force of fifty thousand men, most of whom had come out of the USSR in 1942.

Italy is full of memories for us. The national anthem, which every child knows, "Poland has not yet perished, so long as we still live," was first sung in the Napoleonic legions led by General Dąbrowski. Hence the lines:

> March, march, Dąbrowski,
> From the Italian land to Poland.

If the magic of national history (which is usually rose-tinted) really does inspire one to fight with patriotic enthusiasm, it rarely elicits cold insight into the current political situation. In Italy our men, who had been through the disaster of 1939 and then Russia, were once again the proficient soldiers of an Allied army, armed with the most modern equipment. They believed they were going from the Italian land to Poland, and that they would restore their country's freedom—after all, that was the primary aim of this war, not just for them but, they had no doubt, for their powerful allies too. The desire to fight on the way back to Poland; an organic sense of optimism; faith in their own strength, and in that of the Allies, as well as uncritical trust in them; a desire to prove what they were, what a Pole could do in battle, right now, when following the truth about Katyn Soviet insinuations were starting to get through to the West that the Polish soldiers had left the USSR because they didn't want to fight—all these factors further intensified the will to fight unstintingly.

As soon as we landed in Italy the senior command was faced with a series of problems, all arising from the fact that the Second Corps was more than just a "classic," normal part of the Allied Eighth Army. It was not just an operational unit subordinate to British command, it was a symbol of the reborn Polish Armed Forces. General Wilson, commander in chief on Mediterranean operational territory, asked Anders at their first meeting how he was thinking of resolving the problem of supplementing the corps in case of losses in combat. After all, it had no reserves.

"Our reserves are not behind the army but ahead of it," replied Anders. The reinforcements would come from the front: Poles forcibly enlisted in the German army, Poles in hiding in France since the defeat of France in 1940, Poles from the Todt Organization,* right through, in the future, to soldiers released from the camps in Germany.

Wilson agreed to the creation of separate army camps for this new influx, even though he did not entirely believe that the corps would gain significant reinforcements in this way. Yet despite the skepticism of the Allies, as they moved forward, despite our losses, the numerical strength of our units did not diminish but grew. At the time of its dissolution in 1945, the Polish Second Corps numbered not 50,000 men, as on landing, but more than 110,000.

At his first conversation (to discuss organizational matters) with his direct superior, Eighth Army commander General Leese, General Anders also insisted on debating political matters concerning Polish-Soviet relations, including Soviet anti-Polish propaganda that was appearing in the Allied press, and thus had reached the Polish soldiers,

---

*A civil and military engineering group notorious for using forced labor. —*Trans.*

and the hostile attitude toward the Soviets of the men who had left Russia. General Leese demanded that Anders should not speak publicly on political matters, as it was not within the competence of the corps commander to do so. Never for an instant did Anders concede to this demand. The initial friction between them soon faded when Leese recognized not just the military merits of Polish Second Corps but also its unique political situation.

The senior German command had a perfect grasp of this situation from the start. A special Nazi radio station called "Wanda," which broadcast in the Polish language, appealed to the soldiers to return "home" by crossing the front lines. Leaflets in the same vein were dropped on our positions. One of these leaflets showed two dead black soldiers at the foot of Monte Cassino, with a Pole, "a white Negro," next to them, on the way to fight and let himself get killed too. "In the name of what?" said the caption underneath. In another one we read: "According to the wishes of the British, the Soviet flag is going to fly over your Fatherland." Or: "When the Red Army floods Poland, you will never see your family again." The leaflets included an explanation of how the Polish soldier was to cross to the German side, holding one of these leaflets in his hand. "Wanda" would give him a "sisterly hand."

The corps commander did not prevent anyone from listening to "Wanda." He was aware of feelings within the army, he knew that in spite of the hardships most of the soldiers had endured in the Soviet Union, despite Katyn, they would not fall for Nazi propaganda. Out of tens of thousands of Polish soldiers, only two Ukrainians, one Belarusian, and one Polish criminal were tempted.

In February of that year, in a speech to the House of Commons, Churchill offered 47 percent of the territory of the Polish Republic to the Soviets, as a guarantee of their security in the future. It is easy to imagine how this speech was received by the Polish soldiers, most of whom came from those parts of the country.

In the Allied press, and even in military newspapers such as *Eighth Army* and *Stars and Stripes*, there were more and more instances of news or comments inspired by undisguised anti-Polish Soviet

Briefing for Second Corps officers. Those in view include: General Władysław Anders (*in beret*) and Józef Czapski (*wearing glasses*), May 1944.

propaganda. I remember seeing in *Stars and Stripes*, less than a year after the Katyn graves were found, a caricature of a Polish officer with the caption: "One of the fifteen thousand *supposedly* murdered by the Soviet government." At the same time, in the name of Allied solidarity, the British censors prevented us not just from speaking openly about what we had experienced in Russia, but also from polemicizing with the theses being disseminated by the Soviets. Only after Monte Cassino did the British censorship loosen up a bit. Nonetheless, the cooling of the Allies' attitude with regard to the Polish question was ever more palpable as the wave of enthusiasm for Russian power grew. The entire press was fascinated by the wonderful successes of the Red Army offensive, which bathed Stalin in a halo of glory. On British and American cinema screens, Stalin prompted a storm of applause, and anyone who did not share this enthusiasm or, worse than that, took the liberty of criticizing him, was instantly suspected of being a Germanophile and even risked being arrested.

Soviet diplomacy took advantage of these anti-Polish attitudes at every opportunity: the Poles had "fled from Russia because they don't want to fight"; "the Poles are reactionary, the Poles are fascists and covert Germanophiles."

If all this failed to have a drastic, negative effect on the Polish soldiers' morale, it was largely because both the government in London and our senior command upheld faith in the Allies as much as possible.

"I did everything I could to reinforce the soldiers' faith in our allies," wrote Anders in his memoirs. "I believed that the entry of Soviet Russia into Polish terrain was temporary. I thought that, on winning the war, the United States and Great Britain would not allow a new partition of Poland to occur." This statement is typical of almost all the declarations and speeches made by our émigré politicians, government representatives, and senior commanders. At the time, despite the all-too-visible warning signs, the western Allies were our only hope. Could our commanders possibly be accused of "deceiving" the men?

As I reread our corps' press from that period today, I am struck by its extreme reliability, making use of every possible means and stratagem to give the soldiers true information, despite the obstacles posed by British censorship. The British and American attitude with regard to Poland, already ambiguous at the time, was presented without a shadow of rose-tinted propaganda. But in spite of all, our faith in the rightness of our cause, which was bound to triumph, engendered faith in the word of the Allies: none of us, or almost none, foresaw Yalta. Did those who looked to the future, despite the Allies' constant expression, to a point of bombast, of their appreciation for Poland and for the Polish soldier, see it in the darkest colors for Poland, even after victory over Hitler? Were they to stop fighting? What else could they do but fight and die, just as their brothers and sisters were fighting and dying in Poland? That was what Adolf Bocheński did, political writer and soldier, one of the brightest and most sober-minded thinkers I have ever met.

Bocheński was from a landowning family that lived in the eastern borderlands of Poland. His home terrain is now in Soviet Ukraine. He took a lively part in political life in Poland and wrote many excellent political articles and historical essays that appeared in *Bunt Młodych* (Youth Rebellion), and *Polityka* (Politics), a journal that was edited in those days by the current editor of the Paris-based *Kultura*, Jerzy Giedroyc. Bocheński was an active supporter of mutual understanding between Poles and Ukrainians, and in the days when the worst clashes between the two races occurred, his lectures in Lwów were attended by both Poles and Ukrainians. That was rare in those toxic days of mutual hostility. He was a consistent opponent of "blind nationalism and nationalist chauvinism." He dreamed of a Poland that was not ethnographic but federal, multinational, and truly liberal. A committed conservative, his cult of tradition was so extreme that it sometimes seemed anachronistic. But when they took a closer look at his conservatism, even the staunch "progressives" were surprised by the boldness of his notions and the vehemence of his attacks on historical falsification, and on what he called obscurantism, which he exposed and condemned, whether it was on the left or the right. What he sought was a return to the great traditions of Polish statehood; he spoke of Ossoliński with passion, as if he had known him personally, and dreamed of writing a multivolume work on him and the foreign policy he conducted in the seventeenth century.

If ever I knew a man who was capable of being an active patriot and at the same time a citizen of the world, it was Adolf Bocheński.

Author of a book called *Między Niemcami a Rosją* (Between Germany and Russia), he knew German history and literature extremely well, passed in Poland as a Germanophile, and strove for dialogue between the Poles and the Germans. In his view, it was not Germany but Russia that posed the greater threat to us. In their *Drang nach Osten*, the Germans, he claimed, would take away our land but awaken our national consciousness, while the Russians would simply *engulf* us. He believed that Hitler's rise to power destroyed all possibilities of agreement with the Germans in the short term, but he did not in the least abandon the idea for the distant future. Hitler's attack on Poland made this frail intellectual into a literally legendary soldier. Rejected by every draft, he succeeded in joining the army in September 1939, and fought his way through to France. He won his first Cross of Valor for Narvik and took part in the final phase of the French fighting; after leading his entire team from Brittany to Marseilles, right under the noses of the Gestapo, he took officers and regular soldiers across the Pyrenees to Spain, whence via Portugal they were able to reach Britain. He was an expert on the roads and mountain paths in the Pyrenees. Six months later, he traveled to Syria in the hold of a ship, and there he joined the Carpathian Brigade. At Tobruk, he set fire to a guard's tower at the rear of the enemy and went on a record number of patrols in the desert. He used to joke that he found it easier to go about on all fours than on two legs after all those patrols, where for miles he had moved on his hands and knees, picking the mines out of the sand. None of this stopped him from living the life of an intellectual—he always lugged books about in his backpack, wrote for journals and military newspapers, and made a lively contribution to the discussions organized by the brigade's young intellectuals. One of these discussions was devoted to the work of the German philosopher Keyserling. An outstanding officer, Bocheński had a unique style: when after intensive action in Libya the Carpathian Brigade returned for a rest just outside Alexandria, Bocheński was designated quartermaster, and at his own expense hired Arabs to erect the tents for his unit so that the men would not be overtired; on the first night he did not put anyone on watch but took a gun and performed this duty himself right through to morning. How many of these "antics" his comrades ascribed to him!

I only became better acquainted with him in Iraq. At the time, he was taking a navigation course in the desert; he knew the movements of the stars and talked about them as if they were old friends—nowhere do they shine so brightly and gather so numerously as in the desert. On our long nocturnal walks together among the tents he would recite by turns the pacifist poetry of Wittlin, the revolutionary verse of Broniewski, and page after page of *Faust* in German.

At Monte Cassino, during the battle for Passo Corno, he distinguished himself again by leading a patrol among the German bunkers. He got all the way to the summit of Monte Cairo. He received three light wounds, but there were nine holes in his battledress. He joked that at the hospital they would suspect him of having made those holes himself...with his pencil.

Many times we tried to save this brilliant mind, so crucial to Poland, by sending him as a correspondent to Algiers, but he always refused and said: "Right now my place is at the front—when the war's over, the moment will come when we have to start a new dialogue with the Germans, and then I can be useful." In his article about the battle for Passo Corno, which I am now rereading, I am struck by the combination of a purely professional report with a warm, human view, not just of his own soldiers, for whom he would have gone through hell at any moment, but also of the Germans, the ones who were firing at him and at whom he was firing, as well as the prisoners of war. The old tradition of the chivalrous warrior was still alive in him.

For the Italian campaign, Bocheński was awarded the Virtuti Militari Medal and a second Cross of Valor. At Ancona he was wounded in the groin, yet despite this injury he did not abandon his post for three hours. Wounded again in the right arm, he lost consciousness and was transferred to the shipment point. When his brother asked after his health, he impatiently replied that it was of no interest, because he was going to be blown up by a mine anyway. But he promised to spend a few weeks recovering, and to use the time to write. He took along a typewriter and thirteen volumes of Gregorovius's *History of the Popes*, intending to study it while convalescing. But on the third day, on the point of being transferred to a hospital far inland, he escaped and returned to the front. An expert at disarming mines, with his right arm in a sling, he now defused them with his left hand. Just when the Polish Army was being greeted with flowers as it entered the captured city of Ancona, Lieutenant Bocheński was killed disarming his twenty-third mine of the day.

Did Bocheński seek death? Did he desire it?

Si fractus illabitur orbis
*impavidum ferient ruinae.**

When still at high school, he and his brother had started to write a book titled *On the suicidal tendencies of the Polish nation*.

How greatly we miss Adolf Bocheński today!

---

*Horace, Book III, Ode iii, line 7, "If the world should break and fall on him, it would strike him fearless."

3. MONTE CASSINO

IF I REACH into my own memories of 1944, two dates, two events eclipse all others. The first, in May, is the battle of Monte Cassino, and the second, which had far more significant consequences, is the Warsaw Uprising, which broke out in August.

What do they mean today to the non-Pole, for whom the most memorable events in the war are the major German offensives in Africa and at Stalingrad, the Red Army's forceful counteroffensive, the Allied landings in France, all of which involved technical power on a previously unknown scale, as well as unimaginably large numbers of combatants and of fatalities? So what about Poland? How easy it is to forget its solitary fight in September 1939, the planned *Ausrottung** of the Polish nation from its own lands, the contribution of the Polish armed forces to the fighting on all fronts, and among these battles, the Polish attack on Monte Cassino, the obstacle blocking access to Rome. Why is Monte Cassino of such great significance for every Pole?

Monte Cassino was the first major battle for the Polish Second Corps, and its first clash with crack German units. For the Germans, the Polish soldier was from a country that seemed to have been crossed off the list long ago and had ceased to exist as an opponent worthy of their notice.

As for the Polish soldiers, their families were still in a country that was being subjected to inhuman oppression, which even SS brigade commander Dr. Schönrath described at a session of the General

---

*Extermination.

Government held at the Royal Castle in Kraków as follows: "No other nation on earth has ever endured the same degree of oppression as the Polish nation is now suffering." Thousands of these soldiers' comrades had been exterminated, murdered in German and Soviet camps and prisons, so they were longing for this sort of standoff with the Germans. At Monte Cassino, these soldiers were fighting for a country whose eastern borders had already been determined by their own powerful allies, to the advantage of Russia; Stalin had applied a brutal form of blackmail to "persuade" Roosevelt and Churchill that in case of victory over Germany, eastern Poland would be ceded to the Soviet Union.

Machiavelli advised against forming an alliance with a stronger partner, because in case of defeat, the stronger will always conclude peace at the cost of the weaker, and in case of victory, the weaker will find himself alone at the mercy of the victor. Such was the fate of Poland in those years.

The task assigned to Second Corps was to capture the monastery and the surrounding hills, from where the Germans had the entire Liri valley under their artillery fire, the only route to Rome. This stage of the fighting was fundamental to the offensive under preparation. Its aim was to break through the Gustav Line and the Hitler Line, the hinge of which was Piedimonte.

Monte Cassino was already famous, thanks to the fighting of the past few months, the wide offensive launched in January by the American Fifth Army and the French Corps, and then the second offensive led by the New Zealand Corps and the Indian division, with the narrower scope of capturing the fortified positions of Monte Cassino. This second phase of the fighting continued right through to March 24. Even though the Allied units had several times temporarily occupied the neighboring hills, and the monastery at the top of the mountain had been reduced to ruins by air bombardment, the Germans still held tight, determined to defend those positions to the last.

Also in March, the British Eighth Army replaced the American Fifth Army. General Leese proposed to General Anders that, within the new offensive under preparation, he should take on the section of the fighting at Monte Cassino, while at the same time stressing that he was not obliged to accept this task; if he chose not to, the corps would be moved to a different place, where the fighting was not as fierce. General Anders accepted the task. As well as military factors, the political considerations were equally important here: the losses might be just as great on every section of the front, but General Anders was relying on a celebrated capture of this already infamous fortress to be resounding evidence of the military value of the Polish soldiers and a response to the Soviet propaganda. It would further reinforce the spirit of resistance within Poland, bringing it new hope, and would have an effect on the further course of Poland's fate. The Polish soldiers who had come here from Siberia via Iraq and the Libyan desert would take part in the fight at the point where it had the greatest significance and where it was at its toughest.

The order issued to the corps was as follows: "To capture Monte Cassino and push on to Piedimonte."

By April, the corps had occupied starting positions for the future assault on Monte Cassino, from which we were separated by three miles of the Rapido valley. This protruding German bastion running all the way to Monte Cairo (almost five thousand feet) dominated the entire battleground—every stretch of the Rapido and Liri valley was under close German observation. The experience they had gained from previous assaults had enabled the Germans to perfect their defense, founded, as General Anders writes, on a system of fire "superbly supplementing and flanking themselves, incredibly flexible, allowing for a great concentration of fire at any chosen point." The German troops, with whom the Polish soldiers were to contend, were an elite force: the First Parachute Division minus one regiment, and the Fifth Mountain Division plus Forty-Fourth Division minus one regiment, supported by mountain and alpine regiments. Despite losses, the First Parachute Division, consisting almost entirely of superbly trained volunteers, would remain one of the best German divisions to the very end of the war.

Each of our divisions had two brigades in an incomplete state, while the Allied Corps had full divisions, consisting of three or even four brigades. As I mentioned earlier, the Polish Corps had no reserves.

Bringing in supplies at night without lights was extremely difficult; our preparations had to be totally concealed from the enemy. At first the supplies traveled by truck, then they were transferred to light vehicles, and finally to mules for the steep mountain roads unsuitable for any vehicle, including tanks.

Coated in spring greenery and red poppies as it ran below the blue wall of the mountain with the massive ruin of the monastery on its summit, the Rapido valley was more and more filled with smoke. In this way the night was extended to conceal our preparations. This valley stood between us and the enemy. The signal corps worked feverishly to construct an entire network of communications there, digging miles of cables into the ground. Right to the last moment the enemy were unaware of an approaching assault from this side, but the secrecy of these preparations made forays and offensive patrols impossible, precluding any reconnaissance of the enemy defense.

On May 11 at 23:00 hours our artillery opened fire across the entire front, and two hours later our divisions moved into the attack, under enemy artillery and mortar fire right from the start. The German barrage, tested and upgraded on a monthly basis, was extremely effective. The Carpathian Rifle Brigade captured the bastion on Hill 593, advanced to Snakeshead Ridge, and fought for Hill 569, while the Wilno Infantry Brigade forced its way through to Phantom Ridge. The fighting took place in darkness at night, then in daylight on rocky terrain, covered in bushes and pitted with recesses, caves, shelters, and hidden machine-gun nests. Immediately a large number of soldiers were killed or wounded. The casualties included the commanders of battalions, companies, and platoons, so their deputies, and their deputies' deputies took command in turn. The enemy launched counterattacks from hidden bunkers and caves in the rock. It was impossible for the artillery to support the infantry because of the uneven terrain and because of losses among the artillery observers accompanying the infantry. The fighting continued into the afternoon but capturing those positions proved easier than holding on to them. On

May 12 General Anders gave orders for the units to return to their starting points. Trying to hold the captured positions was causing the number of fatalities to rise without stop, while the ground base for the attack was so narrow and the number of roads and paths so small that it was impossible to bring reinforcements into the field of combat. Fresh battalions of the Parachute Division had just arrived on the German side to provide relief, and as a result there were almost twice as many enemy soldiers as at the start of the action.

The advantage of this first assault, which like the previous ones ultimately collapsed, was that it fulfilled its task as required by the British Thirteenth Corps, which was attacking in the Liri valley. By diverting the enemy fire with our attack, we had made it possible for Thirteenth Corps to cross the river and to establish the necessary bridgeheads. The British advanced further down the Liri valley, while our Second Corps continued to harass the enemy with forays and patrols.

The next action started on May 16 in the evening. Ammunition supplies were brought up (so many porters of ammunition had been killed that the soldiers did not have enough). The same bloodied brigades advanced to attack right under the fire of their own artillery, but in a reorganized way, with three battalions formed into two, and a third composed of soldiers reassigned from antiaircraft artillery, drivers, mechanics, and even men who had been lightly wounded on May 11 and 12, sent back to their units from the hospital. The fate of the entire battle was at stake, and so was the fate of Second Corps.

On May 17, at 18:30 hours, the corps captured Phantom Ridge, and also San Angelo Hill, except for its northern part and Hill 593—Snakeshead Ridge. The point was to surprise the enemy as fast as possible, regardless of the losses, in order to overcome their artillery barrages. Once again, during the combat every last scrap of terrain passed back and forth several times. Once again, the losses were high, and the exhaustion increased on both sides. These were hours of the ultimate combat, the crisis point—which side would hold out the longest?

During the night from May 17 to 18, preparations continued to prolong the Corps' attack, but advance patrols confirmed that the enemy had retreated from the monastery mountain. The Third Division did not renew its assault, and a patrol from the Twelfth Lancers Regiment planted a red-and-white flag in the rubble of the monastery.

But on Fifth Division's stretch fierce fighting continued until evening.

On May 19, the Carpathian Lancers Regiment, and then the Fifteenth Poznań Lancers Regiment,* whose task until now had been to cover the right wing of the corps, now began an assault on Passo Corno, hill number 838. They had to cross the three miles and eight hundred yards from the starting point to the top of the hill under fierce enemy fire, clearing minefields, and capturing one position after another, one shelter after another, in terrain where every few dozen yards terraces rose at right angles to heights of up to sixteen feet. As no mule could have crossed that ground, the supplies were transported by men without any cover from enemy fire. Boxes of ammunition were hauled up on ropes; bringing down a single wounded man took eight others three hours.

Within the Carpathian Lancers Regiment, the Third Squadron distinguished itself. Some of its members were seventeen-year-olds from the cadet schools in Egypt, boys saved and brought out of Russia. During the advance, on starting to feel faint, they had poured water on each other from their canteens and scrambled onward. Only that evening did the enemy withdraw from the mountain massifs shielding the Monte Cassino positions to the north. The British Thirteenth Corps and the Canadian Corps reached the Hitler Line, but the British had to withhold their attack on the Liri valley because of flanking fire from Piedimonte, where the Gustav and Hitler Lines converged.

An armored brigade (reassigned from the Second Armored Brigade) made a bold attack on Piedimonte, on terrain where it was difficult for tanks to operate, and without adequate support from the infantry, which, after losing a lot of men, had at most 28 percent of its force on

*They were tank regiments reassigned to the infantry.

this stretch. The corps units forced their way through to Piedimonte, tying up the German First Parachute Division's only reserves and preventing them from acting against the British Thirteenth Corps.

The fighting still continued. On May 25, our troops finally took Piedimonte—our mission accomplished, the road to Rome was open.

The corps' losses totaled 923 fatalities and 2,931 wounded.

The British king conferred the Order of the Bath on the Second Corps commander, General Anders.

I did not take part in the combat; as the head of the Second Corps Press and Culture service I was responsible for publishing the bulletins and press, for dispatching them all the way to the front lines, for communicating with the journalists who came streaming in from all over the world, and for contact with the entire information apparatus inside and outside the corps. What do I remember of those days, apart from the nervous tension that I shared with the entire corps?

Perhaps my strongest memory is of the soldiers returning from battle through the cork oak woods, transformed into a thicket of lifeless stumps, or coming down the steep paths, amid fresh corpses, in a state of extreme exhaustion, their faces unshaven, white with dust, without a drop of blood, as if transparent. They had seen the death of their closest comrades, they themselves had fought, killed, and escaped death. When they met me, climbing up the hill after the battle was over, they greeted me like a brother from another world— there was such joy in them at coming back to life again, such a happy sense of brotherhood gained in battle that they even bestowed it on me. After all, I had welcomed these same men into the army on the steppes along the River Volga as wretched slaves, who had finally reached us after a hundred adventures, human shadows whom the NKVD had not yet managed to shoot by the ditches at Katyn or anywhere else, or grind down in the camps. This irrepressible joy at returning to life, or merely encountering death eye to eye, the experience of a close brush with death, produces an intense sense of willpower and love of life, a special glow.

I remember a narrow, zigzagging mule path above a precipice, known as "the sappers' road." This was the only path the tanks could take to reach Snakeshead and Phantom Ridges, where the fighting was going on. This zigzag route, this mule path, was so narrow that every tank that had to stop because of a breakdown had to be immediately pushed over the precipice, because it was blocking the road for others, at a time when there was fighting above and every second counted.

It was also the only road for the stretcher-bearers to bring severely wounded soldiers down to the dressing stations. During the fighting, there was one day when the wounded had to wait for more than eight hours until the "sappers' road" was free of tanks; only then could they be carried down to the hospital for first aid.

Among the wounded, a very pale young man was lying there in a pool of blood. There weren't any stretchers. When he was lifted to be bandaged on the spot, he was found to have a large wound in his back. He turned his head, looked at the pool of blood, and said quietly, as if to himself: "What a lot of blood Poland is costing us."

The victory at Monte Cassino was a short-lived military sensation in the world's press. Here too a silencer was put on the story—there was no need to annoy our Soviet allies with too much talk of those Poles.

4. WARSAW

The hand is worn out now
From stroking rough coffins
—TADEUSZ GAJCY

THE SECOND event I mentioned in the previous chapter, immeasurably more important, is the Warsaw Uprising, which broke out in August and ended after sixty-three days of fighting for every single house, for every turn in the wall; it ended in the death of the best combatants, the annihilation of an entire generation of young people whom the war and the occupation had torn from their schools, the massacre or exile of the capital's citizens, and its destruction.

A disaster.

Today there are innumerable books about this disaster, in which the people who took the decision for the uprising to go ahead and led the fighting are regarded by some as die-hard heroes, by others as irresponsible, and by yet others as no better than criminals. To this day I have rarely met a Pole incapable of evaluating this national tragedy dispassionately; twenty years on, I too find it impossible.

According to Napoleon, for every major defeat in war there is always a major culprit. Where is this culprit? Is it the commander in chief of the Polish Army, General Sosnkowski, whose attitude to the uprising in these conditions was consistently negative, but who could not or dared not impose his opinion? Or Prime Minister Mikołajczyk, who, brutally pressured by Churchill to yield to Stalin's demands, wanted to believe as he set off for Moscow that the uprising could carry weight in the negotiations as a decisive argument in defense of Poland's rights? Or General Bór-Komorowski and his staff, who took the decision to trigger the uprising, because he believed the Germans were on the point of collapse, and that the Soviet troops were going to capture Warsaw in a matter of days, if not hours?

Several incidents of major importance for the war occurred in the month of July preceding the uprising. There was fierce fighting for the Allies in Normandy, where at the end of the month General Maczek's Polish armored division landed, to participate in the decisive battle of Falaise, and the offensive in Italy continued toward Ancona, with General Anders's Polish Second Corps taking part in the fighting. July was also the month of the failed Stauffenberg plot to assassinate Hitler, and his cruel reprisals against the conspirators, the month when the German eastern front collapsed across a range of 685 miles, to be precise along the Heeresgruppe Mitte,* which surrounded Warsaw, with German losses of three hundred thousand men during the retreat. In this month too the Red Army advanced at lighting speed to the outskirts of Warsaw.

As a result of this offensive, between July 21 and 25 panic broke out among the Germans in Warsaw. The German administration ceased to function, they burned documents in the streets and courtyards, and all the women were sent back to the Reich. At the same time an uninterrupted flow of refugees from the east flooded the streets. How could this sight not have affected the citizens of the capital, and even the commanders of the Red Army, which in Warsaw alone had forty thousand men under its mandate, eager for open combat after five years in the underground?

I was in Italy with the Second Corps when the uprising erupted. What reached us at the time via the radio, London, and communiqués was news of a succession of incidents and their horror, but it did not and could not reflect the direct, human side of the fighting being

---

*The "Army Group Center" was the joint name of two German strategic army groups that fought on the eastern front. —*Trans.*

experienced physically, and visually, by even the humblest citizen of Warsaw.

In my hands I have the daily diary that was kept by my sister Maria Czapska, who had endured the first German siege of Warsaw in 1939, had not left the city, and survived the uprising there too—right in the city center. Her brief notes written from day to day at the time evoke more than anything I could say now, so many years later. I shall quote from them in this chapter.

"Evacuation activity throughout the city," she writes on July 15. "Slogans on the walls in coal, chalk, paint, and stencil: 'Poland will be victorious,' 'We'll be revenged for Pawiak' [the Gestapo prison], 'We won't give up the Eastern Borderlands,' 'Wawer, Palmiry' [the sites of mass executions], 'Oświęcim' [Auschwitz], 'Katyn,' 'Hitler kaput'... In the suburbs 'PPR,'* and in the center 'PPR = enemy.' No one will wipe those signs off anymore."

"Prisoners are being taken for interrogation, there's a passenger car preceding the paddy wagon, the Gestapo men are holding machine guns aimed at the passers-by... in the evening we exchange news. There was a bomb attack at such-and-such a café, a roundup in Żoliborz or Mokotów, X. was arrested, a new transport left Pawiak for Oświęcim... The shooting in the street never lets up, we've grown accustomed to it. People go into gateways to wait it out, each person hurries on his way. Today I was at the post office when someone was killed on Świętokrzyska Street. A wounded pedestrian was still lying in the street under the guard of a policeman. Nobody asks questions, nobody even looks around, everyone goes past the site of the attack to get away as soon as possible."

*PPR—the Polish Communist Party—was disbanded in 1938 by Moscow but re-formed in Poland during the war. By 1944 its hit squads were operating against the Germans; limited in numbers, but supported by Moscow, it was trying to take advantage of the uprising spirit and the city's eagerness to fight, while accusing the Home Army, to which it was not subordinate, of being passive, and further slandering it with posters on the walls of Warsaw claiming that Home Army command had fled the city. Units of the People's Army, which also fought the Germans in Warsaw during the uprising, were the PPR's military.

"July 23: All sorts of equipment is coming over Poniatowski Bridge and down Jerozolimskie Avenue, from gigantic armored vehicles on caterpillar tracks to tiny two-wheel barrows harnessed to shaggy ponies; rack wagons, Belarusian carts with bow yokes, upper-class britzkas, horses from the manor; on the vehicles some women and children in German army greatcoats, with cows and goats, horses and mules walking alongside. The debacle. At the crossroads there's a dense, silent crowd. The faces are inscrutable, the gazes hard ... The Home Army have been given orders to be on the alert. We're waiting."

"July 25: The administrative offices are being evacuated. The post office is closed, the telephones aren't working. In Chełm the 'government' has arrived, including Wasilewska, Rzymowski, and Żymierski, a 'government' appointed in Moscow."

"July 19: Can we really let them leave Warsaw with such impunity? Everywhere we can see them loading up, carrying away whatever they can, office furniture, typewriters, food—while we clench our fists. When will this finally be over?"

When will this finally be over?—the entire city was whispering. But the urge to evacuate and the mood of panic among the Germans only lasted a few days. The administrative offices went back to work. New troops arrived in the Warsaw area and in the city itself.

By July 22 (though Warsaw was unaware of the fact), for strategic and political reasons Hitler had decided to defend it at any price. Four armored divisions were brought in, and the renowned Hermann Goering Division was transferred from Italy by express transport.

This is the diary entry for July 30: "Sunday. A sunny morning. I was on my way home from Holy Cross church. On the corner of Traugutt Street and Nowy Świat there were three military cars. There were German soldiers asleep on the mudguards, the running boards, and the ground. Terminally exhausted, with torpidly slumped shoulders, drooping heads, furrowed faces beside others that were still childish, and soiled uniforms. They've had to come a long way to fall asleep 'safely' here—on a Warsaw street....

"Apparently the Germans are preparing a counterattack on the curve of the Vistula. For this purpose they have brought in large reserves. . . . '*Wir werden uns an diese Erde ankrallen**—it has cost us too much blood to be able to abandon it,' cried Governor Frank in a recent address."

Warsaw was thinking of the great Soviet offensive, extending across the entire front, *from the viewpoint of Warsaw*. The Home Army commanders were counting on the possibility that the Red Army would enter the city at any moment. Was it totally mistaken? Right up to July 30, the Ninth German Army and the Heeresgruppe Mitte, who were fighting against the Red Army, also figured that the Soviet offensive was heading *for Warsaw*. But historians Jerzy Kirchmayer in *Powstanie Warszawskie* (The Warsaw Uprising) and Hanns von Krannhals in *Der Warschauer Aufstand 1944* (The Warsaw Uprising, 1944) both state, on the basis of maps and documents, that the operational plan for the Belarusian troops, the Soviet army that had reached the outskirts of Warsaw, did not include the capture of Warsaw at all. However, directives issued by Soviet headquarters on July 27, gave orders for the *offensive to continue*.

Broadcasts by Radio Moscow encouraged the citizens of Warsaw to believe that the Russians would arrive at any moment. Here is my sister's diary entry for July 25:

"Radio Moscow is prompting us to rise against the common enemy, stressing the Soviets' positive intentions toward the countries being liberated. Helena G., who has access to a wireless of some kind, is thrilled by the Muscovite speaker's rousing speech . . . She's keen on the idea of the two governments uniting (meaning the government formed in Moscow and blindly obedient to it, and the Polish government in London) and explains the need for an understanding . . . The Home Army's *Information Bulletin* is calling for discipline and peace, and describes events in Wilno."

These pieces of news, written side by side in the diary of a citizen of Warsaw: the expectation that the Red Army would enter the city, and the dreams of some for the "two governments to unite," and *at the same time* the Home Army's communiqué about Wilno already

---

* "We shall hang on to this land."

show the contradictions of the political situation that was building up at the time. Nowadays the events in Wilno are not just well known but regarded as typical of the way the Soviet army behaved toward the Polish Home Army units. On the eve of the major Soviet offensive, in the night from July 6 to 7, the Home Army's Eighty-Fifth Regiment, a force of about 500 men, confronted the Germans in Wilno, while about 5,500 Home Army soldiers attacked the city from the outside. The German resistance was fierce. That evening the advance elements of the Soviet Army arrived. The fighting continued until July 14. The Russians took advantage of the Polish assistance and in several places even provided it with ammunition and antitank equipment. By July 15, in the recaptured city, the commander of the combined Home Army forces, Lieutenant-Colonel "Wilk" Krzyżanowski, was invited by the Soviet general Chernyakhovsky to join him for friendly negotiations to discuss the organization of a Polish infantry division, a cavalry brigade, and the provision of the Polish units with Soviet equipment. The negotiations were renewed the next day with "Wilk" Krzyżanowski's staff, while other Polish officers, from the rank of battalion commander upward, were invited to a briefing at a place called Bogusze.

In Wilno and in Bogusze they were all arrested. "Wilk" Krzyżanowski was deported to Moscow, where he was tortured by the NKVD and lost his hearing, then he was "freed" and returned to Warsaw but rearrested by the security police. He died in prison in 1951. The example of Wilno was repeated in various versions wherever there was a tactical attempt at joint combat: Lwów, Lublin, Kowel, and other less important places. Naturally, the inspiration for this sort of procedure came from above. Home Army command sent news of these facts to Britain but received no response on the part of its Western allies. Thus the Home Army, in combat against the retreating German army, was placed in an impossible situation.

As for the radio propaganda in the days preceding the uprising, it reached us very quickly in Italy too. I remember hearing the Soviet radio appeal on July 30 to the population of Warsaw, which I have now found in my sister's diary.

"People of Warsaw, to arms ... Strike at the Germans, foil their plans to blow up public buildings, help the Red Army to cross the Vistula. Send us information, show us the way. May the million residents of Warsaw become a million soldiers, who will drive out the German invaders and gain their freedom. The entire population of the city must join together to fight as a liberation army. Citizens of Warsaw, to arms! Attack the Germans, help the Soviet troops to cross the Vistula, a million citizens is an army of a million men, fighting for Polish liberty!"

On July 30 and 31 the German armored divisions went into action on the outskirts of Warsaw, in Wołomin and Radzymin. And it was there on August 1 and 2 that the Germans gained an important success. On July 31 a communiqué issued by the OKW (Wehrmacht high command) announced that the Russians had launched a general attack on Warsaw from the southeast, and a Soviet communiqué announced the capture of the commander of the German Seventy-Third Infantry Division, positioned at a bridgehead. Home Army command received news of Prime Minister Mikołajczyk's departure for Moscow. General Bór-Komorowski was expecting a Russian attack on the city from one hour to the next. A series of reports confirming this expectation reached his general staff but later turned out to be fake. Home Army command fixed the start of operation Burza (Storm) in Warsaw, meaning the uprising, for August 1 at 5:00 p.m.

What was the Home Army general staff's reasoning?

The Warsaw Uprising was bound to erupt, regardless of its chances of success, in view of the mental state of the resistance, who had been preparing for this open combat for four years; an order forbidding the uprising could have destroyed the morale of the best fighting forces in the resistance.

But what if the fighting resulted in defeat?

Even so, the uprising would have fulfilled its task—it would have dug an abyss between the Poles and the invaders for the next fifty years! The direct tactical argument was: "The Soviets are going to enter Warsaw at any moment and must find the city already liberated by us. We're in charge here." The same staff officers reckoned that the uprising would last for five or six days.

And London was informed accordingly. The disarming, deportation, and liquidation of Home Army units, as in Wilno or Lwów and all the other places where the Soviet army was cooperating with Polish units, could be repeated in Warsaw. General staff knew that was possible, but this time "the whole world will respond with a cry of indignation." There was not just hope but an undying faith in the Allies, in the overriding power of world opinion, the eyes of which were apparently turned on Warsaw.

If the will to fight for independence and the inviolability of Poland's eastern border, already determined by the Soviets and the Western allies (the British king has guaranteed our border, he has never betrayed a promise, said people in Warsaw) is regarded as an anti-Soviet act, then the Warsaw Uprising, anti-German in the military sense, was politically just as anti-Soviet, in the longer term militarily too; besides, that was more than understandable following recent experiences including Katyn, Wilno, and the liquidation of Home Army units as the Red Army advanced into Polish terrain. Naturally, Soviet command and Moscow were highly aware of this. So what aid was the Warsaw rebellion counting on? On the rapid, by now apparently inevitable advance of the Soviet army, and above all, immediate airborne assistance from the West.

On July 25, General Bór-Komorowski contacted General Sosnkowski by radio to request airborne and paratroop assistance. "We are ready to fight for Warsaw. The arrival of the Paratroop Brigade for this combat will have enormous political and tactical significance. Prepare to be able to bombard the airfields outside Warsaw on our demand." So was Warsaw counting on the Paratroop Brigade and significant airborne assistance? Under the terms of an agreement concluded by Sikorski with British general staff, the Paratroop Brigade was to remain at the sole disposal of the commander in chief and was set aside for operations within Poland. But at the end of 1943, Britain had requested consent to use the brigade for invasion operations, and after a few months of negotiation the British had given their demands the character of an ultimatum. After many conversations and efforts to reach a compromise, on May 6 Sosnkowski had placed the brigade at the disposal of the Allies. By the end of July it was destined for invasion operations, and the idea of it being assigned to Warsaw seemed entirely unreal. With a view to Russia, by then the British did not want to reinforce the Home Army too much by providing it with essential equipment; how could they have wanted to send an elite, very well-equipped combat unit to Poland, especially when it was so valuable for the invasion front? And the air force? In 1942 Sikorski already believed that no insurrection could start in Poland without the co-operation of the air force, and in 1943 Sosnkowski had informed the Home Army that the Polish air force could not provide independent support for an insurrection in Poland until mid-1945 at the earliest. Until then, the independent use of the Polish air force to fly to combat regions in Poland on the last of its fuel could only take place as an *act of desperation*. At the moment when the uprising erupted, 44 percent of our air force was involved in invasion operations in Normandy, and the rest, including a squadron stationed in Bari, was being used for other purposes, for instance to assist the partisans in the Balkans, and was not yet fully prepared for action in Poland. As for the Allied air force, its commanders put forward a series of not just reservations but direct objections. Air Marshal Slessor was strongly opposed to airborne action over Warsaw, which was located at the furthest limit of practical reach for planes from Britain. Capturing the south of Italy had somewhat shortened the distance for flights and reduced their danger; nonetheless the hub of airfields to the east of Lille, which could be regarded as a suitable takeoff point closest to the destination, was still almost two hundred miles from the Allied front. For Air Marshal Slessor, Warsaw was out of reach for effective airborne action; the flights could only have *demonstration* significance and could bring immense losses. The only possible solution would be to use air bases on terrain captured by the Soviet troops, where these planes could land after providing assistance to Warsaw.

The uprising broke out on August 1 at 5:00 p.m., even earlier at certain points. I return to my sister's diary:

"In our section the uprising had already started by 4:00 p.m. In Żoliborz it began at 3:00 p.m.—everyone wants to be first, the eagerness of our resistance forces for this battle is uncontrollable...It began with the capture of the Prudential (the tallest building in central Warsaw), which was mainly occupied by German offices... After the Prudential, the fighting was for the post office. Our lads attacked the back of it from Świętokrzyska Street. They had several revolvers and hand grenades. Some were armed with coal shovels—shovels against machine guns.

"August 2: Capture of the PKO bank on Świętokrzyska Street, and further arduous efforts to capture the post office. An attack on the police headquarters on Krakowskie Przedmieście and the Arbeitsamt (the labor exchange, located in the Agricultural Bank on Mazowiecka Street) are under preparation.

"All Warsaw has been cut up like a chessboard...the Polish flags on the Prudential and the PKO are stirring enthusiasm...Since this morning we've been hearing commands in Polish in our gateway. The radiant faces of young insurgents who have literally emerged from underground and surrounded us, spreading like flames. After five years of misery, keeping their heads down, hiding their emotions, glances, and words, they're ecstatic to be fighting in the open. Anyone who has a revolver cares for it like treasure. There's mutual benevolence, helpfulness, the entire nation is banding together in a sort of joyful brotherhood...Young girls, acting as liaison, deliver ammunition and orders, flitting like quails across streets under fire—several tanks have been burned out in the city center by the forces of children like these, with bottles of petrol."

Such is the experience of the uprising at the heart of Warsaw—a sense of intoxication, a belief in the usefulness and necessity of this combat.

"Missiles fired by six-shot grenade launchers land in the courtyard of 4 Mazowiecka Street, during roll call, several boys are killed on the spot, others are severely burned and taken to the hospital. The house is on fire, the firefighters are throwing boxes of books from the attic into the yard. Only just bound, not yet on sale, they are copies of the *Epistolary Essays* by Norwid—the émigré poet, unacknowledged for decades and venerated by only a few, Norwid, who in 1865 wrote:

'No good will come from a nation whose energy is worth one hundred but whose intelligence is worth three, for the former will always get ahead of the latter and jump out and betray any plan, and every twenty years or so there will be slaughter (*sic!*), the slaughter of the innocents, the slaughter of a generation... And there will be destruction and nothingness. And so it will be.'

"Under the trees, where the bound pages of unknown texts by Norwid are hanging like garlands or rosaries, the bodies of child insurgents are being burned, once again the 'slaughter of the innocents, the slaughter of a generation' is happening."

> And youthful arms
> carried away on the wind as anonymous ashes
> will be called the debris of history*

Further on, the diary describes horrific executions, and how men and women were tied to ladders that were then used as a shield for German tanks attacking the insurgents. The diary gives the names of people, friends and acquaintances, forced to run ahead of the tanks. These pieces of information about atrocities are not rumor but facts, events that actually took place. Now they are precisely known from evidence, including German statements, and not just Polish reports. Borkiewicz† cautiously mentions a figure of fifty thousand executed during the uprising. These figures seem incredible, but even in his book about the uprising the German historian von Krannhalls writes of fifteen thousand executions on August 5 alone, all along Wolska Street and the side streets leading into it. And the official German communiqués imply that ten thousand people were executed in the first two days of the uprising. Indeed, in the first half of August I find

---

*Lines from *Od Anioła do Szatana* ("From Angel to Devil"), a poem by Norwid, cited in the diary.

†Military historian Adam Borkiewicz was himself a colonel of infantry in the Polish Army and a member of Home Army chief command. His book, *Powstanie warszawskie. Zarys działań natury wojskowej* (The Warsaw Uprising: An Outline of Actions of a Military Nature) was the first book about the uprising. —*Trans.*

this sentence in the diary: "The joy is infectious, the eagerness, the ecstasy of combat. I don't think anymore, I don't reflect, I don't calculate, I'm being carried along on a wave of excitement at living through these days in Warsaw, and at the fact that after five years we are free." These words were written on August 12, when both the rapid entry of the Red Army and immediate, effective airborne assistance from the West had failed to materialize.

To this day it is hard to establish exactly when the first flights over Warsaw were made. Borkiewicz writes of some airdrops in the night of August 3–4, but according to the air force commander, Air Marshal Slessor, the first drops were made on the night of August 8–9. Polish pressure on the Foreign Office and on the Ministry of War was constant. But the British authorities put numerous obstacles in the way. More than that, we were met with the charge that the uprising was unrealistic and premature. Not just the Soviet press was silent about the uprising, but the British press was sparing in its reports too. In Washington, Secretary of State Edward Stettinius asked our ambassador whether the Home Army had acted too early.

Meanwhile in Poland, who was not waiting for help to come from the sky, for British aid to arrive as their salvation? In the diary on August 3 my sister wrote:

"This afternoon planes of an unknown type were circling low over the houses . . . Convinced they were Soviet, we raced onto the balcony, but they opened fire into the windows of the building. There was a deafening crash, flames, plaster came raining down, and we retreated in terror—they were German Stukas.

"August 4: High above the city a squadron of planes flew from west to east, people went crazy, crying with joy. Help from Britain— they're ours. People rushed to unfurl flags in the streets, everyone poured outside, stood in the windows or on balconies, chanting the Warszawianka, but the squadron turned out to be German, and that same day the bombardments began. We had showed them our districts ourselves. With a whistling sound the Stukas dived toward the roofs, aiming precisely. 'Small bombs,' people consoled themselves . . . Small perhaps, but they tore down four stories at a time.

"August 12: Hope persists that help is on the way. Nightly expectations of airdrops. But how are we to profit, when the city is divided into squares?"

On August 4 Churchill appealed to Stalin to provide help for Warsaw. Stalin replied that Polish reports of the uprising were exaggerated, and the Poles shouldn't be trusted. Churchill sent another appeal to Stalin on August 12. On August 16, Molotov categorically refused to allow any planes bringing aid to Warsaw to land on territory occupied by the Soviets. Air Marshal Slessor explains that this meant that "not only will it be impossible to fly shuttle flights," but also that "planes taking off from Italy will not be able to land in Russia, even if they are damaged and have wounded men on board."

On August 18 Churchill sent a telegram to Roosevelt emphasizing that Russia was refusing to provide any help for the Poles at all, although the Soviet troops were "not many yards" away from Warsaw. On August 20, Churchill and Roosevelt jointly appealed to Moscow to provide assistance for Poland. Stalin replied by telegram, insisting that the Warsaw uprising had been started by a group of criminals, and refused to provide any aid at all.

Through Churchill's telegrams and interventions in Moscow, the British continued to demand the right to land at Soviet airfields. In a letter to Roosevelt, Churchill insisted that action on a wide scale should be put in motion, to make landing on Soviet terrain a fait accompli. This was the only way to provide real help for the uprising. Not wishing to antagonize Stalin in any way, Roosevelt replied with a categorical refusal.

During the first month of the uprising, 159 planes were sent over Warsaw which, with a loss of twenty-seven machines, performed seventy-seven airdrops, forty-six of which were successful. These airdrops, achieved with great difficulty through the efforts and pleas of the Polish authorities, could not in any case tip the scale of victory, and had no real significance for the fate of Warsaw.

When new demands were made in September, Stalin was slow to respond. It was not until September 10 that an unexpected message arrived to say that Stalin was ready "in principle" to grant landing rights. This news did not reach the Polish authorities in London until September 12. At this point the Americans decided to make a major expedition to Warsaw, and the city was immediately informed of these plans. In the same period, after September 12, the Red Army carried out a few airdrops over Warsaw, on a very limited scale, but which were loudly publicized by the Soviet press. The sacks were dropped without parachutes and burst on hitting the ground, spilling pulverized hard biscuits, and the weapons, not the ones requested anyway, were also smashed.

Nevertheless the airdrops, and consent to use the airfields, seemed to indicate a change of Soviet tactic, again prompting wild hopes. Via London, Bór-Komorowski approached Soviet Marshal Rokossovsky by radio with a proposal to coordinate efforts but did not receive an answer.

Whence this change of tactic by Stalin? Firstly, it was no longer possible to hide from the world the scale and horror of the uprising, and the passivity of the Soviet army, which was "not many yards" away from Warsaw. Secondly, Warsaw was already at the end of its strength and was fading, the Germans were prompting the Poles to capitulate, preliminary talks were starting, and a decision had been made to hold a one-hour ceasefire two days in a row to evacuate the civilian population.

Stalin's tactic now seems clear. First he had accused Warsaw of having invented the uprising; the Polish resistance movement was a bluff, and the uprising was a hoax instigated by reactionary criminals. But when the uprising began to die down, and Stalin learned from his agents about the capitulation proposals, he decided to obstruct them by stirring new hopes and new illusions in dying Warsaw, so that it would go on fighting and be totally destroyed by other hands. The more ruins, the more people killed, the easier it would be to take control of Poland afterward. Where Poland was concerned, it was a silent renewal of the Ribbentrop-Molotov Pact.

An episode that has never yet been fully explained is the role at the time of Berling's army. On September 14, Berling's Kościuszko Division—consisting of Polish communists but also of Poles whom

Anders's army had not had time to incorporate in 1942, and who had not joined this division because they held communist views (naturally among the officers there were a good many Russians, transformed into Poles for the purpose)—captured the right bank of the River Vistula along the entire length of the Praga district. On the night of September 14–15 it made an attempt to cross the Vistula; on the nights of 16–17 and then 17–18 as well as on September 19, it continued to try to transport a few battalions across to the left bank, where some of Berling's men were already involved in fierce fighting alongside Warsaw's Home Army soldiers.

This action was improvised, without the involvement of Red Army high command, or even in defiance of its orders. It ended on September 20 with the retreat of these forces under violent fire that was raining down on the Vistula and came at the cost of heavy losses in men killed or drowned. Berling was probably counting on drawing Red Army staff after him or gaining at least the support of the silent Soviet artillery, but he was totally mistaken. According to widespread opinion in Poland, as a result of this spontaneous effort to help dying Warsaw made by General Berling, a Pole, and his staff, the Russians put an end to his postwar political and military career.

Returning to my sister's diary, here are the notes for September.

"September 5: Our street is to be abandoned by the army—white flag. Any moment now the Germans will invade. Only the sick and the old women are staying behind. Bombardment. The whole street is in flames.

"Survivors from the cellar of burning No. 19 are settling on the ground floor of our house in a state of total prostration. There are sacks, pots, and bundles piled up in the indescribable chaos of a destroyed home. I am seeing off the ones who are leaving us. . . . On the asphalt lies a dying boy. His skull is smashed—his dark curly hair is sticky with blood, his eyes are wide open, wheezing, he steadily gasps for air. His whole body is in convulsions. . . . In the evening No. 6 catches fire, then No. 8, then No. 10. The attack is coming from Nowy Świat Street. At dawn Mania hangs up a white pillowcase by way of a white flag, but two hours later, at about six, a new unit arrives with an order to take it down. *They're going to go on fighting. They're building a new barricade.* A very young lieutenant with a sunken gray face … 'Why are you doing this?' I ask in doubt and despair. 'Do you want to destroy the last few people, the last few houses?' 'Help is on its way,' he replies. But there's no hope at all in his eyes or in his petrified features.

"The Red Cross has made an offer to evacuate the population. It is agreed that for two days in a row there will be an hour-long ceasefire to allow the population to leave the city.

"September 7: I wanted to take advantage of the ceasefire hour to get some sleep in the one room that is still intact. The front door has been battered down, the upper floors are empty shells, and the remaining residents are clustered in the cellar and on the ground floor. I'm woken by the sound of footsteps. I leap to my feet.

" 'Who's that?'

" 'Friend,' comes the answer.

"I go out: one is older, the other is very young, still a child, both in camouflage, holding guns. They run through the rooms and creep up to the windows.

" 'What are you doing?' I ask.

" 'Haven't you ladies left? Why not?' he says in surprise.

" 'We haven't been able to,' I reply. 'What about you? It's hopeless.'

" 'Help might come any day now. We must wait.'

" 'Help?' "

The capitulation negotiations were broken off. The American airborne expedition to Warsaw planned to take place before the end of August was subject to constant delay, first because of Stalin's continued refusal to give his consent, and then because of the weather conditions. Not until September 18 did 110 American Liberators fly over Warsaw in broad daylight, making 107 airdrops, only fifteen of which were picked up by the insurgents. What would the sight of this airborne armada have meant to them if it had happened in the first few days of the uprising, rather than on day 49? Perhaps it could have reversed Warsaw's fortunes entirely. In view of the feeble result of this expedition, and despite continued efforts by our representatives in London, the Americans refused to repeat it.

The diary notes for September provide a picture of the uprising as witnessed by a citizen of Warsaw in a district that by September 7 was already occupied by the Germans.

"The houses were burning out, and grenades were going off with a dry crack. The advancing enemy were 'testing' every gateway, every cellar, every nook in the walls. Our house and No. 15 next door were the last 'living' houses on Czacki Street.

"Soon from the rubble of No. 19 we heard voices calling in Russian. So we were being taken by Vlasov's* men. I knew what danger that meant. But my sensibility was so dulled by fever and exhaustion that I felt no fear of what was about to happen. Let it just happen.

"We had already encountered units of this army in the Warsaw vicinity and in Mińsk Mazowiecki. They had been carefully selected according to their ethnicity from the one-hundred-language, multi-racial mass of Russian prisoners. The garrisons operating in Poland were mostly Mongolians.... I also saw dark, hefty Armenians, pale Georgians wearing German uniforms and with swastikas or '*Gott mit uns*' inscribed on their belt buckles. They were kept under very strict discipline, and warned the Polish population that once the German army retreated from Poland, they would run riot, looting and burning everything, they'd been promised...

"With pistols in hand and brightly colored church candles stuck under their belts, breathless and excited, they jumped out of the cellar into the courtyard, tossing grenades into the neighboring gateway. I looked at their faces. They were not Ukrainians, to whom were ascribed the barbaric evacuation of Ochota and the liquidation of the Wola hospital (where all the patients and medical staff were murdered).

---

* These units were mistakenly called "Vlasov's men in Warsaw"; in reality they were not under General Vlasov and did not belong to the Russian Liberation Army. (Also known as the Vlasov army, the RLA was a group of predominantly Russian forces that fought under German command, and was led by Andrei Vlasov, a defected Red Army general. —*Trans.*)

Nor were they Asiatic Mongolians. Very swarthy complexions, black hair... They spoke to each other in a guttural-sounding language... Their eyes were wildly restless, full of lust and fear all at once.

"'Who are you?' I asked.

"'Turkmens, Mohammedans...'

"They herded us down to the basement. Guarded by the Turkmens, we went by the light of candles decorated with small flowers and holy pictures stuck on like decals, tripping over the doorsills and squeezing through gaps in the walls. One or another of them kept skipping up to one of us, threatening us with his pistol and saying in Russian: 'Give us the gold. I'll find it, I'll kill you.'

"With the free hand they searched our pockets, felt our belts and collars... This delayed our march. I saw that a lady named Zofia from No. 19, very old, wounded in the head and arm, had already fallen in the first courtyard. We passed another courtyard and were once again herded across the rubble into a basement.

"'Is it going to be here?'

"But no, the soldier dragged the youngest woman among us into a corner of the cellar. Ever worried about her mother, she clung to her tightly, imploring over and over: 'Together, don't separate us. Together, together.'

"I explained to her what it was about...

"Above us, the rafters were still smoldering. Smoke and a stench of burning. The cellar, into which the soldier finally pushed the three of us together, because we were refusing to be separated, was full of old eiderdowns. Sweat was pouring down our faces... One Turkmen came through, then another. I held the girl's mother in my embrace so that at least she couldn't see... Then suddenly we were left alone. We went up some steps into the courtyard of the Bank of Commerce. On the threshold lay the corpse of an old woman. She had fine, calm features, white hair, and the peace of death, but the position of her half-undressed body prompted hideous assumptions.

"The Turkmens had vanished. We started looking for a way out through large halls filled with rubble, across which Mrs. Krasińska stepped cautiously in her thin shoes, breathing heavily.

"'*Schneller, schneller!*'* a soldier shouted at us.

"'*Sie sehen,*† I said to him. 'We're escorting old and sick people.'

"'Yes, old people,' he said ironically. 'What about the young ones? *Die sind bei den Banditen.*'‡

"'*Warum banditen?*§ We're fighting for our freedom.'

"'*Freiheit?*'¶ he screamed in rage. 'What more do you want? You had everything in excess in Warsaw. You never lacked a thing. *Verfluchte Polaken.*** You all deserve a bullet in the head. *Alle must ihr erschossen werden …*'††

"Our procession headed through a battered-down gate. Some ruins overgrown with grass, a corpse-like odor, and swarms of flies. There were several dozen of us, hauled out of the cellars on Czacki Street. Along the sides of this courtyard stood machine guns. The Germans were sprawling in garden chairs, loading their guns. A wirehaired terrier kept bringing back the helmets they were casually throwing for him, amid bursts of raucous laughter.

"One of our companions, a sickly looking man, took out a small prayer book and calmly started reading out prayers, maybe for the dying … 'When are they going to fire the first series?' I thought. 'Then they'll finish us off as at the Jesuits' church on Rakowiecka Street.' I had no wish to die. I rested my head against Nina's knees. She was sitting up straight against a low ruined wall, slender, calm in her blue dress, never letting go of her mother's hand. She too had been through that cellar, and in her mother's sight too. She had tried to buy the soldier off with a gold bracelet.

"'I don't want gold, I want you,' the savage had said.

"'*Aufmarschieren!*'‡‡

---

*Faster, faster!

†You can see.

‡They're with the bandits.

§Why bandits?

¶Freedom?

**Goddamned Poles.

††You should all be shot.

‡‡March out!

"So they weren't going to shoot us.

"We trailed off in a long row. The remains of barricades, graves under the walls, at the crossroads, and at turns in the walls there were improvised 'Bierstuben' [bars], chairs and small tables gathered in a group. The soldiers were drinking beer and cackling.

"*Die Banditen! Ha, ha ha! Da sind sie, die Banditen!*"*

"At one point a young German came up to Nina. She was walking ahead with her mother, her grace and beauty striking against the background of this series of nightmares, and he accompanied her for a while. He turned out to have said: 'All our auxiliary forces are Vlasov's men. Don't get separated from your group, they're total savages.'

"I was walking almost last, dragging along Mrs. Krasińska (she died a few days later in Pruszkow of a heart attack). Two more old people from our house were trailing along behind us. I heard them being hit and mocked; they couldn't keep up and must have been beaten to death. I didn't look around; any moment the same thing could have happened to us . . .

"Warsaw was going to fight another twenty-six days. With a handful of light weapons, with no food or water, against the entire might of the German army.

"For what? For the right to die with a gun in your hand, rather than in a gas chamber? For the right to be buried under the rubble of your native city, and for its glory? Sixty-four days of freedom at a cost of 200,000 dead?"

I do not intend to write a history of Warsaw's fighting here, its superhuman heroism and the tremendous atrocities inflicted on its body. Anyone in Germany can consult von Krannhals's book *Der Warschauer Aufstand, 1944*, which presents the history of those two months dispassionately and with great honesty. As for the victims, it is almost impossible to establish their number precisely. The figures given by Borkiewicz, citing Pobóg-Malinowski,† appear to be the

---

* The bandits! Ha ha ha! There they are, the bandits!
† Władysław Pobóg-Malinowski was a Home Army officer and leading historian (in exile) of modern Poland in the postwar era. —*Trans.*

most accurate: 22,000 insurgents killed, missing, or heavily wounded; 20,000 insurgents sent to the camps as prisoners of war; up to 50,000 civilians executed, as I have already mentioned; the estimate of total civilian losses ranges from 150,000 to 250,000. A total of 165,000 people physically able to work were transported to the Reich for forced labor, and 60,000 were transported to concentration camps. The destruction of Warsaw began with the air raids of 1939 (throughout the occupation reconstructing or repairing the damaged buildings was forbidden), continued through the annihilation of the ghetto in 1943, and was ultimately completed during the uprising in 1944 and after it.

Even once the fighting was over, on Hitler's direct orders to raze Warsaw to the ground, an order often repeated by Himmler, the destruction of the capital continued, despite the many qualms of the Wehrmacht, headed by General Lütwitz, who tried by various means to avoid carrying out this order or at least to postpone it.

After the uprising, a further 1,417 historic buildings and residential houses were destroyed. Of 987 historic buildings only sixty-four survived; twenty-five churches, the polytechnic, most of the university buildings, 145 schools and fourteen libraries were blown up and burned down. They included the modern Krasiński Library, the basement of which was fireproof, and so throughout the occupation private archives and libraries were stored there, including the most valuable manuscripts. Using special flamethrowers, the Germans burned the entire contents of the underground halls, shelf after shelf. The books incinerated in this way retained their shape, and even some of their color, but crumbled to ashes at the slightest touch.

In a speech made on September 21, 1944,* this is how Himmler described his reaction to the uprising: "When I received news of the uprising in Warsaw I immediately went to see the Führer... Führer, I said, this is an unpleasant moment. But five or six weeks will pass, and then Warsaw, the capital city, the head, the intelligence of this nation of sixteen or seventeen million, will be extinguished, the

*See von Krannhals, *Der Warschauer Aufstand* 1944, p. 309.

capital of the nation that has been blocking our route to the East for seven hundred years, and standing in our way since the First Battle of Tannenberg.* In historical terms, for our children, for everyone who comes after us, and even in our lifetime, the Polish problem will cease to exist."

*Also known as the Battle of Grunwald, 1410 (and thus five hundred years earlier, not seven hundred), was where the alliance of the Kingdom of Poland and the Grand Duchy of Lithuania decisively defeated the Teutonic Knights. —*Trans.*

5. THE END OF THE WAR

THE SITUATION for the Polish soldiers in the West became more and more paradoxical as the war approached its end.

In 1944 there was severe political conflict in London between the commander in chief, General Kazimierz Sosnkowski, and the prime minister, Stanisław Mikołajczyk.

General Sosnkowski, one of the originators of our independence, for years Marshal Piłsudski's closest companion, refused to agree to any political compromise that reduced Poland's territory to the east, and was even more opposed to a settlement that placed Poland's true independence in question.

Prime Minister Mikołajczyk, president of the Polish People's Party (PSL), despite constant resistance on his own part, gave way to ferocious pressure from the Allies, and agreed to talks with Stalin and the Polish communists, organized by Moscow under the name of the Lublin Committee.

Sosnkowski's resignation, forced by the British in September 1944—provoked by an order to the army in which he charged the Allies with responsibility for "Warsaw's agony"—followed in November by the resignation from the government of his adversary, Mikołajczyk, who in defiance of the majority of ministers was becoming more and more committed, ultimately agreeing to the Curzon Line as Poland's border to the east, were stages in the development

Chapter 5 is a summary of events familiar to every Pole, which I have tried to bring together for the foreign reader, following from the chapters on Monte Cassino and the Warsaw Uprising.

of the Polish situation. (Moreover, the idea of the Curzon Line as Poland's eastern border, which provoked these dramatic clashes among the Polish politicians in 1944, had already been accepted by the Allies in the fall of 1943, and in strictest confidentiality, unknown to the Poles, promised to Stalin.)

The renaming of the Lublin Committee in December 1944 as the Polish government under the auspices of the USSR, without any consultation whatsoever with the legal government in London, the revelation of the decisions concerning Poland made at the Tehran and Yalta Conferences—all these pieces of news struck at the Polish soldiers in the West, at the very core of their hopes, their national consciousness, and the very point of their fight.

For these soldiers were still in action on all fronts. In Italy, the Polish Second Corps continued to fight until April 21, 1945. That evening at six, Polish units entered captured Bologna after heavy fighting, in which for the third time they had to fight against the German First Parachute Division, the same one that had defended Monte Cassino. In his order of the day after the capture of Bologna, the commander of the US Fifth Army, General Mark Clark, stressed the role that the Poles had played: "In this battle you have shown a superb fighting spirit, endurance, and combat skills." At Caserta on April 28, the German plenipotentiaries signed the capitulation of the German army in Italy.

The advance of the Red Army into Poland, halted during the Warsaw Uprising and after the fall of Warsaw, was only resumed on January 13, 1945. By then the Germans were only putting up feeble resistance. By the end of January, the Red Army had taken control of Kielce, Warsaw, Częstochowa, Kraków, Katowice, and Królewska Huta.

After the Warsaw Uprising, General Okulicki was appointed to take over from General Bór-Komorowski as commander of the Polish Home Army, by then at the stage of dissolution. He had been a prisoner in the Lubyanka (1939–1941) and was former head of general staff for the army formed in Russia by General Anders (1941–1942), with whom he had twice been received by Stalin. In 1944, parachuted into

Poland, he led the fighting against the Germans to the end, as one of the chiefs and then as commander of the Home Army in the field.

In March 1945 Okulicki received a written invitation to a meeting with General Ivanov, representative of the commanders of the Belarusian front. The aim of the meeting was to discuss and establish conditions for the Home Army and the Polish political parties to emerge from the underground and for cooperation between the Poles in Poland and the Red Army, in close communication with the London government. This letter included the information that a Soviet airplane would be made available to General Okulicki, to representatives of the London government who were in hiding in Poland, and to various others.

It would take too long to list the reasons why once again the Poles believed Soviet promises that turned out, as so many times before, to be a trap. But one fundamental reason was that the Polish resistance leaders who were still in hiding had already been exposed by the British government, which had given their names to the Soviet government, with a warning that arresting them would be regarded by the British government as a "hostile" act. The second reason tipping the scale in favor of the decision to attend the meeting was that in his final telegram Mikołajczyk had encouraged the leaders of his party to reveal their identities.

After a series of discussions by the resistance leaders on their own, and with General Ivanov and his representative, a proposal to leave for London on the Soviet airplane was accepted. Sixteen Poles, including General Okulicki, boarded the plane, but instead of flying to London it took them to Moscow, straight to the Lubyanka. There they were all imprisoned, and after a show trial in Moscow style, were sentenced on June 21, 1946. General Okulicki was given the highest sentence—ten years. Jankowski, the deputy prime minister within Poland, was given eight years, two others were sentenced to five years each, the rest were given lesser sentences, and three were acquitted. No diplomatic notes or complaints were of any use at all. These men vanished from the face of the earth. The explanation only came to light ten years later, when in April 1955, under pressure from Polish émigrés, the British government and the US State Department issued a memorandum in which they "expressed the hope that the Polish activists arrested ten years ago were no longer in any of the Soviet prisons." The Soviet government then announced that Jankowski had died in 1953, two weeks before the end of his sentence, and General Okulicki had died in prison eighteen months after the trial.

On April 5, 1945, the Polish government in London, still recognized by all the Allied nations except for Soviet Russia, learned from the radio and the press that a conference was being convened in San Francisco, with the aim of establishing an international organization for peace and security, and to which the governments of forty-four countries had been invited. The Polish government had not received an invitation to take part in this conference, even though the Polish Army was subordinate to it—the force which since 1939 had been the first to fight and had continued to fight to the very end of the war, on land, at sea, and in the air—and Europe's biggest resistance army was also subordinate to this government.

On May 7, 1945, Germany's capitulation was signed. At the victory parade held in London on May 8, the Polish soldiers, who had taken part in the fighting at Narvik, Tobruk, Monte Cassino, Falaise, and Arnhem, were not present. However, the Polish airmen who defended London were invited but refused to take part in the parade.

On July 6 recognition of the legal government was withdrawn, and the president of Poland, Władysław Raczkiewicz, whom the British king had received at the station in London in 1940 after the collapse of France as president of Britain's only ally in the fight against Hitler, from this time on became a private individual in the eyes of the Allied authorities.

Under pressure from Britain and America, which were concerned about losing face, Stanisław Mikołajczyk, the former prime minister of the London-based government, agreed to join the provisional government, which the Stalinist communists were forming in Poland. In June 1945 Mikołajczyk returned to Poland, where for a short while his presence stirred tremendous hopes: Poland was not going to be abandoned by the West!

The decisions of the Yalta Conference (where Roosevelt, Churchill, and Stalin met), held in February 1945, naturally contained an appeal addressed to the provisional government that was going to be established in Poland to hold free, unobstructed elections on the basis of a secret ballot. All this was expressed in lofty, highly democratic terms—after all, in 1941 these same people had signed the Atlantic Charter, which vetoed any changes of territory not in accordance with the freely expressed wishes of the population, and which recognized "the right of all nations to elect the forms of government under which they want to live."

Mikołajczyk's presence in the government, in which 80 percent of the portfolios were in the hands of communists, did nothing at all to alter the line of action it took. The prisons remained full to the seams with people who had fought for the Home Army, and Mikołajczyk's arrival had provoked an even stronger wave of not just arrests, but the torture and assassinations of PSL activists loyal to him. The elections held in Poland were cynically falsified; Stalin told the organizers of these elections that they need not feel restricted, because Britain and America "aren't going to declare war because of elections in Poland."*

Poland lost 47 percent of the territory it had in 1939 in favor of the Soviet Union and was forced into the bloc of communist states, in the sphere of influence of Soviet Russia, with all the resulting consequences.

The Polish soldier in the West was faced with a choice: return to Poland or emigrate. Naturally, this concerned our corps in Italy. Of the total tally in 1945 of 112,600 private soldiers and officers, 14,217 opted to return. Of the tens of thousands of soldiers who had experienced Soviet Russia, only 310 decided to return. The rest chose to emigrate. Their commander, General Anders, who had led them out of Russia and to victory at Monte Cassino and at Ancona, together with seventy-five other senior Polish Army commanders, was stripped

---

*In the spring of 1947, unable to force through a single one of his basic democratic demands, helpless and himself under threat, Mikołajczyk finally fled abroad.

by the Warsaw government of Polish citizenship, as having acted to the detriment of the Polish state. The soldiers who decided to return to Poland were all accused of espionage on behalf of Britain or America, were subjected to countless interrogations by the Polish security police, imprisoned, and in many cases given long sentences; many of them were also tortured using methods tried and tested in Moscow.

Here I shall close my account of the wartime fortunes and the further history of the comrades with whom I left Russia in 1942, and of the loved ones whom they left behind in Poland. Those of us who decided to go back to Poland ended up in a ruined country, where the flower of society, the soldiers of the Home Army, and ordinary citizens were deported on a large scale to the USSR, and were imprisoned in remote camps or Polish jails that were packed to bursting. The soldiers returning from the West believed they would be protected because since 1939 they had fought on all fronts for Poland. But in the eyes of the new authorities in Poland, that was the main reason for subjecting them to interrogation and persecution. The security police and their reign of terror would remain decisively in control until Stalin's death in 1953. The thaw of 1956 is a new chapter, quite another story, which I shall not tell here.

For those of us who remained in emigration, the years since 1945 have been a time of dispersal all over the world.

We have always called the nineteenth-century migration from Poland "the Great Emigration" because its influence on the country over the next few generations was highly significant and still is to this day, through the creative works produced abroad by our greatest poets, thinkers, and politicians. In those days of a different censorship and different disasters following the 1830 Uprising, that emigration, consisting almost exclusively of men, did not exceed ten thousand! *"Die Sturmvögel der Revolution,"* as they were called in Germany, were received and welcomed with enthusiasm. How can that emigration, including Mickiewicz, Chopin, Słowacki, Krasiński, Norwid, Prince Czartoryski, and Lelewel be compared with today's emigration

---

* "The storm petrels of the revolution."

of tens of thousands, men and women, representing a far wider range of all levels of Polish society? What role will this emigration play, or be able to play, if we compare it with the Great Emigration? For the time being we lack the necessary distance; we must beware of over-estimating the role of the emigration, while also being careful not to minimize its significance too much. Among the many tasks that the emigration can serve, one thing that definitely has meaning, not just for the Poles abroad but for our country, is that the émigré Pole can fully express his thoughts, including those that in Poland nobody is free to write or say. Maybe it is on this point above all that the significance of the emigration will be evaluated one day.

6. THE GERMANS

RELIVING the historical events that I have described in this epilogue, the German world as I see it appeared before my eyes with new force—that is, the German world as seen by a Pole.

Several of my readers have complained that by recalling the past, rather than deleting it from memory, all I am doing is deepening the chasm that separates us from the Germans. But in writing about the past, I wanted to present more than just the bare facts; my aim was to express my belief that, without obscuring or masking the past but by reliving those times, with the distance of the present day, we may be able to liberate ourselves from their shadow.

For one thing, the political attitude of today's Polish government is demagogically and one-sidedly anti-German; the views about Germany expressed by émigré politicians and journalists sometimes, but not always, follow the same line, for fear of appearing to public opinion within Poland less anti-German than it is. Where is the path toward trying to reach agreement? What can people do to this end?—people like the author of these words, who are not politically active, and cannot have any direct influence on current policies, but would welcome a change in the climate of Polish-German relations?

Perhaps they can do more than might at first appear to be the case, by being attentive, by seeking the unembroidered truth, and being open to friendly dialogue, person to person. There may be more people wanting this sort of disinterested dialogue than we think, on one side and the other; a number of them have already established this dialogue, and in time this could alter the political climate. But as far as I am concerned, with regard to the Germans I am *Homo quidam*, I know no more than the average Pole about our mutual Polish-German relations, or about Germany itself. But for that very reason expressing my thoughts and feelings could be of significance, because their source, their point of departure, or of perception, is (to some extent) *typical* for a Pole. So I want to revert to myself, and without recourse to statistics, figures, or volumes of documentation (as I haven't the means), to find a way out through my own conscience, through my own limited personal experience.

"As long as the world is the world, a German will never be a brother to a Pole"—every Pole knows that saying.

It was not the capture of Moscow by the Poles in the seventeenth century but the Battle of Grunwald, and thus a blow inflicted on the Order of Teutonic Knights, that for every Pole is a key date in his history. It is not Ivan the Terrible's *oprichniki*, or even Suvorov's army, but the Teutonic Knights that still embody for us the will to destroy the Polish nation.

Prussian power is the continuation of the Teutonic Knights' power. And then what?

"*Haut doch die Polen, dass sie am Leben verzagen: ich habe alles Mitgefühl für ihre Lage, aber wir können wenn wir bestehen wollen nichts anderes thun, als sie ausrotten, der Wolf kann nichts dafür tot wenn man kann.*"* So wrote the Prussian Bismarck, the great chancellor, to his sister in 1861, and the word he used: *ausrotten* ("exterminate"), is familiar to every Pole, even those who do not speak a word of German.

But who among us—probably almost nobody—knows the testaments of the Hohenzollern, who were well disposed toward Poland, for instance that of the Grand Elector dating from 1667, advising good neighborly relations with the Republic: "*Denn an ihre Conservation und Erhaltung beruhet Eure und Eurer Lande Wohlfart,*" or

---

*"Hit the Poles so hard that they despair of their life; I have full sympathy with their condition, but if we want to survive, we can only exterminate them; the wolf, too, cannot help having been created by God as he is, but people shoot him for it if they can."

of Frederick William I dated 1721, thus already in the age of the partitions: *"Mit der Republik Pohlen ist gut in gute Freundschaft leben und sie ein gut Vertrauen bezeugen."**

The reasoning of some historians (including Bocheński) that neither the historical nor the geographical situation renders antagonism between Poland and Germany *inevitable* is now more alien to Polish consciousness than ever. Nowadays, after Hitler and Himmler, the old cliché "As long as the world is the world . . ." seems to be more of an axiom for many Poles than ever.

Am I free of this cliché? If now, twenty years after the end of the war, I am still surprised by the automatic hostility of my own reaction—one that is not generally encountered among the French anymore—to hearing German tourists talking too loud and too openly in the street, on the train, or even in the Louvre, because they instantly awake dreadful memories in me? How am I to break free of this sort of reaction, which deeply offends and hurts me whenever I sense the least shadow of it in anyone else's attitude toward the Poles? I have been aware of it several times among Jews. Yet who, if not I, should be quicker than others to free myself of such reactions?

My mother was an Austrian, born in the Sudety Mountains. She was the first person to teach me to love Poland. At the age of twelve, during a history lesson, she had declared that she wanted to marry a Pole, because it was an unhappy nation, and then later it came true—she did marry a Pole. Right at the bottom of my childhood memories I can see the twinkling reflection of candles on the piano keys, as at our mother's side, and with her we sang "God Save Poland," and often "Kde domov můj" (Where Is My Home?), the Czech national anthem as well, because as someone born in the Czech lands, my mother felt herself to be half Czech. Thanks to her, alongside Chopin, the German

---

*"Because on its conservation and maintenance depend your and your country's permanent well-being."

"It is good to live on good terms with the Polish Republic and to have complete trust."

I sourced these quotations from Adolf Bocheński's book, *Między Niemcami a Rosją* (Between Germany and Russia), Warsaw, 1937.

composers Schubert, Beethoven, and Schumann were our first musical revelations.

I have heard the German language since childhood. We were taught it in our family home by our beloved old governess, an Austrian from Linz, who even then, contrary to my mother's views, claimed that Austria and Germany were a single entity—our dear governess was passionately *Alldeutsche*.*

I was seven years old when my mother died. She left us a part of her Austrian tradition, as well as the light of her love, ardent Catholicism, and a deeply rooted belief that she was a saint, and that this gave us certain obligations.

My paternal grandmother was descended from German aristocracy that had been settled in Latvia for centuries. As her family had provided Russia with several generations of excellent diplomats, she was devoid of national consciousness. She married a Pole, one of her sisters married a Finn, the other a Russian. She traveled widely around Europe, and as a child had been all the way from Saint Petersburg to Naples in a carriage. Deeply influenced to the day she died by her beloved, extremely pious British governess, she was a committed Protestant.

Always with some needlework in her hand and a lace cap on her snow-white hair, adored by her grandchildren, she was a typical representative of the culture of a certain social sphere in nineteenth-century Europe, where national differences barely existed and seemed unimportant, a sphere that included the author of a book that was famous in the nineteenth century, *Le Récit d'une Soeur*.† This same stratum also included those readers of Stendhal whom he addressed as *ami lecteur*.

Have I ever known a woman who was less inclined to narrow-minded fanaticism, subtler, and to the end of her days more intensely interested in events of world significance, as well as in the old coins

---

*A believer in Pan-Germanism. —*Trans.*

†This book, written by Pauline Craven, née de La Ferronnays, provides a rare depiction of the aura of international society in those times.

that her husband collected, bird nests in her park, or the tame bear cub that went for walks in it? *Je suis cosmopolite*, she used to say, but by blood she was a German. And so there are many reasons for me to be aware of the German world through the filter of all these memories.

My personal history, including life as a student in Saint Petersburg, Russian friendships, Russian literature, Tolstoy and his influence, then Dostoevsky, the experience of the Russian Revolution on the spot, my part in the fighting against the Bolshevik invasion in 1920, and during the last war the camps in Russia, and my role in the formation of the Polish Army there—all these events tied my fortunes, for better or worse, with Russia. Maybe that is why I perceive the Russian world not merely in terms of the harm inflicted on Poland but in all its complex, extremely interwoven, highly specific reality. That is why all absolute judgments of it seem to me so false and even iniquitous.

In comparison with the Russian world, the German one seemed to me almost an abstraction, a faded print.

In 1934, I spent the summer in the remote Eastern Borderlands of what was then Poland, in the mountainous Hutsul region. During one of my expeditions I came upon the remains of some First World War trenches and a small German cemetery among the trees in the absolute middle of nowhere. The few graves were well cared for, and above the entrance there was a carved sign that read: SIE SIND GE-FALLEN WEIL SIE IHRE HEIMAT LIEBTEN.*

I have never forgotten this proof of loyalty and remembrance, those modest German graves, and the laconic message. How close this seemed to me to the German tradition that I had encountered in my childhood.

At this point, Hitler was still a remote figure from a cock-and-bull story, and only in brief moments of awareness did a threat appear to loom over our fate, but it was drowned out by the euphoria of regaining independence, my own work, and an instinctive, irrational optimism, deep-seated within me, with regard to Poland's fortunes.

---

* "They fell because they loved their homeland."

The awakening did not come until 1939, with the outbreak of war, the invasion of Poland, and the further course of events—more and more news of German atrocities and their desire to wipe us from the world map.

Have I ever given any of this deeper thought than purely from the angle of my own country's fate? The Nazis were criminals, the Germans were Nazis—who today can think of the exceptions? I knew that the time would come when one would have to think about the Germans differently; I have always felt and known that thinking of any nation *en bloc* with hostility is morally unacceptable, quite literally a sin.

After the war this thought began to bother me, but from my few encounters with Germans I had not succeeded in forming close enough relations to become reacquainted with contemporary Germany, the Germany of those war and postwar years, from the inside. The stories of more and more friends of mine, Poles and Jews, as they arrived in the West, and new books appearing about the German camps cast increasing light on the German world, giving it a shape, just as the Poles and Jews experienced it during the war within Poland and in the camps—an unbearably cruel shape that at the time seemed nothing but brutal, just as I myself would have experienced it, had I been in Poland in those years. And the shock of it made me think.

In 1950 I went to Berlin, where the Congress for Cultural Freedom was being established. It was my first contact with Germany. At the time, Berlin was still full of ruins and cripples. After triumphant, splendid New York, where I had just been, I was surprised to find that rather than hostile or repugnant, Berlin seemed to me in a way close and familiar. It reminded me of Warsaw; I could sense Poland across the border. A world of ruins, direct contact with people in the streets; the Tiergarten—a few thin trees (I remember the wonderful greenery before the war); the black skeleton of the Reichstag; the flatlands around Berlin amid beautiful forests—"our trees," pines and birches, modest, almost like the ones in Warsaw; cafés by lakes—and many new encounters with Germans, polite conversations with strangers, sometimes effusive, but most often relaxed and friendly in a human way, right through to my encounter with a beggar woman with no legs in a wheelchair; begging in the street at eleven at night, in the rubble of a burned-down house, she asked me the time, explaining that the hour had come for her to go home and sleep.

She seemed to me much closer, and even less tragic in this world of cripples and poverty that surrounded us at the time on all sides, than the crippled beggar woman whom I had seen in New York a couple of weeks earlier, kneeling in Rockefeller Plaza. In a coat that in the Berlin or Warsaw of the day would have been luxurious, a hat patterned with pink flowers, and with a crooked smile ("keep smiling") she was selling pencils, which cost almost nothing there and were just a pretext for begging.

Straight after New York, Berlin, a city of catastrophe and collective poverty, stirred in me the simplest reaction of human community, and I understood that our attitude toward the Germans did not always have to be vindictive. At the time, as a Pole, I kept having ... surprises. A German campaigning for a united Europe told me how amazed he had been when at a prison camp for officers he had come across a Pole who was translating Dante. "It was the first time I learned that there are educated Poles, not just cooks and washerwomen." My chance interlocutors, waiters, porters, and caretakers, sometimes started talking to me in Polish. But they instinctively hid it from the Germans, because they didn't want to be regarded by the Germans as *nur Polen*. (The Swedish family of a friend of mine took in a boy from those times, who was the son of a pastor from eastern Germany. When asked if he had witnessed any executions in his hometown, he thought for a while, and then replied that he had seen people hanged in the square, "*aber es waren nur Polen.*"*)

In 1955 I sailed to South America. The ship was full of Italians, Spaniards, and South Americans. The Italian and Spanish languages prevailed. After a few days I finally noticed quite large percentage of Germans among the passengers.

* "But they were just Poles."

At the very start of our voyage an unpleasant scene occurred in my presence. A sympathetic lady with some small children started up a conversation with an older woman, who after a few pleasantly exchanged remarks suddenly stood up from her seat, and harshly emphasized that she did not wish to have anything whatsoever to do with her interlocutor. Why? Because she was a Jew, and the lady was German! I remember the look of amazement painted on the German woman's benevolent face; she couldn't understand why this cruel injustice had been inflicted on her in her innocence. "What did I do to her?" I saw her asking virtual strangers about the incident, in a state of confusion, and trying to find an answer or an explanation, as if ten years after the war it could not possibly enter her mind that the other woman may have lost her entire family in the gas ovens or the ghettoes.

On the ship I met a professor from the University of Vienna, who was on his way to teach at a college in Brazil. I spent the entire voyage in conversation with him. I owe him my first contact with a German to whom I could say and tell everything. His reaction was never petty or feigned. I told him a lot of things, including a story that I heard in the Soviet camp at Gryazovets from one of my best friends there, Dr. J. Kohn, about a man of whom he had spoken with love and admiration. Dr. Kohn had studied medicine in Lwów; as an army doctor and Polish officer he had ended up in the prisoner-of-war camp. He told me about his mentor, a modest doctor from the small town of Horodenko. It was to this man that he owed his choice of medicine as a career. When the Germans decided to exterminate Horodenko's Jews, they took a few hundred of them into the forest and ordered them to dig their own graves. This doctor was one of the condemned men. While they were digging, suddenly one of the German officers recognized him. Perhaps the doctor had done him a service in the past or had treated him? The officer told him to step out of the line and go home to his family, who were still alive at this point. The doctor refused, preferring to stay there and let himself be shot with the other by the graves they had just dug. What did this mean? How could this gesture help anyone? Those condemned Jews in a forgotten central European town, which hardly anybody in

Western Europe had ever heard of? What significance could the gesture of a poor Jew have within the "complex arithmetic," universal and prophetic, in which even the French writer Drieu la Rochelle,* sensitive and totally disinterested, became entangled? As we sat in deck chairs on the ship, I talked to Professor S. about all this. He assured me, and I believe him, that during the war he knew almost nothing about it. He was a professor at the university in Vienna, while those Jews were being murdered at Horodenko and everywhere else; when very young Poles—almost children—from the camp at Buchenwald were being turned into executioners, by making them tour the villages and cities of Thuringia, carrying a two-arm gallows, on which three people could be hanged from either side; when Poles were being hanged for "betrayal of honor"—in other words for not betraying their comrades who escaped from the camp; when Poles, Jews, Gypsies, and so many others were dying in their hundreds just outside Vienna in Mödling, battered to death with sticks. Mödling was an old gypsum mine, which by the manual labor of prisoners from all over Europe was transformed into a Heinkel jet-plane factory. The laborers had to work up to their knees in water, hauling mud and earth out in wheelbarrows, and the factory worked around the clock on three shifts. There was a stairway down into the quarry but descending and waiting in line in the mud or snow took an hour. The people standing in line froze in the wet snow and died mainly of pneumonia; every few days they were made to do punitive exercises in the courtyard, which involved falling flat in the mud and snow, and a German Gypsy beat the prisoners to death with an iron rod for the slightest disobedience. The usual punishment at the factory was twenty-five blows of a rubber baton. Jarosław Górski, a friend of mine and nowadays an émigré in distant Puerto Ordaz in Venezuela, told me that right before his eyes a Jew was killed because they had found two boiled potatoes in his pocket.

---

*Pierre Drieu La Rochelle was a French novelist and essayist who supported French fascism in the 1930s and collaborated with the Nazis during the occupation of France. —*Trans.*

As the Soviet front approached, those prisoners were herded from there to Mauthausen in the Austrian mountains. Anyone who sat down by the road and hadn't the strength to stand up again was beaten to death on the spot. Of an original two thousand, only six hundred or seven hundred reached their destination. On the way for four days they were not given any food or water but were forced to live on grass and worms. On seeing this procession of ghosts, the local populace turned away in disgust, as if believing that all these people were criminals, murderers, and degenerates. And there in Mauthausen, which was also quite near Vienna, morning, noon, and night, two hundred people at a time were sent to the gas chambers, until ovens were built that killed a thousand at once. The victims' ashes were then sold to Austrian farmers for fertilizer. But as there was never enough of it for these hardworking farmers, they kept asking for more.

We should remember that the *first victims* to be killed at Mauthausen were mainly Austrians from Vienna, people who opposed Hitler.

Among the scenes and facts I told the professor about, there was one incident that might seem trivial in the context of the experiences of those years but perhaps made a very great impression on me because it was personal and symbolic.

In September 1939 the German offensive stopped for a few days on the line of the Vistula and Narew Rivers, on the German-Soviet border originally established by the Molotov-Ribbentrop Pact. At the time, my youngest sister was living at a family property a few dozen miles to the east. The Red Army, which on September 17 struck from the east, had already reached the county where this property was located. It was preceded by news of deportations deep inside Russia, and of the executions of landowners above all. My sister decided to escape to the Kraków area. To get there, she had to make her way across the Narew via a bridge located in Pułtusk, which was already occupied by German troops. In a peasant cart, with her three small children, she reached the river, where she waited to see if the Germans would let her proceed across the bridge.

Still in the euphoria of victory, the German soldiers surrounded the cart. One of them, young and handsome with fair hair, leaned against the side of the cart and started jovially asking my sister questions: "Your husband must be a general, all the Poles are generals... Not in the army? Has a weak heart? Well, of course the Poles are weak, they're afraid to fight, but we all fight; that's why we're victorious."

My sister was in no doubt that her own and her children's lives depended on being allowed to cross this bridge. She waited for the verdict. The answer that came was categorical—they were not allowed to let anyone cross the bridge from east to west.

Among the crowd of soldiers there was a young officer. He said nothing but stared stubbornly at my sister's youngest daughter, seven-year-old Elżbieta, who was sitting on her mother's lap, terrified, with tears in her eyes, moving her lips slightly—she was praying. Maybe he has a small daughter too, maybe he'll save us, maybe he'll be moved by the sight of her, thought my sister. Suddenly this officer came up to the cart. "I haven't the right to let you go across," he said, "but I will do it, if you will make me a promise on oath." ("*Wenn sie mir etwas schwören.*") My sister all but leaned out of the cart. "But of course I will. I'll promise you anything you like." Maybe there was someone he cared about on the other side, was the thought that flashed into her mind; he'll oblige me to take care of them, to help them.

"You must swear to me," he said, still staring at the child, "that you will bring up your children as citizens of the Third Reich, entirely loyal and devoted."

Instead of leaning forward, my sister instinctively recoiled.

"No, that I cannot swear."

"*Zurück!*"*

So my sister was forced to take her children back to the place they had fled from, with the feeling that she was doomed.

It all worked out differently. The Germans did not stop on the Narew but continued their advance, while the Bolsheviks, after a day and a night at the house my sister had left, withdrew beyond the River

---

* "Back you go!"

424 · THE FIGHT

Bug. But this dialogue, which had ended in a verdict likely to condemn a mother and her three children to death, was like a collision between two worlds. However many times I had told this story to Poles, Britons, Jews, or Frenchmen, they had all found the behavior of the German officer monstrous and incomprehensible. None of us had tried to probe the meaning, to discover the root of this sort of conduct. That officer had wanted to help the mother and children, even by overstepping his authority, but had ended up condemning them.

But in this case my interlocutor on the ship, who always reacted in a lively way and usually commented on my stories, was silent. The next day, when all the passengers celebrated crossing the equator, and amid gales of laughter Neptune, in a flaxen wig and paper crown, "christened" some of them by throwing them into the swimming pool, my German professor was sitting in his deck chair, surrounded by books, on the abandoned deck. I sat down beside him. My friend began to speak: "I've thought a lot about what you told me yesterday. Your sister's encounter . . . I didn't know how to reply straightaway. You see . . . the officer, that young German—I want to defend him. He was certainly an idealist. He *believed* in the superiority of his race, he was convinced that not only would it save your sister, but it would *give* her something that he regarded as extremely valuable."

Now I was the one who fell silent. Initially I was shocked. Will it ever be possible to communicate with the Germans, if even the best of them have such a very different reaction to the bare facts from our own?

Then I started telling him everything that I knew from the accounts of direct witnesses about the ways in which his superior race had endeavored to make the Poles happy, and about their methods for annihilating Poles and Jews.

"I swear to you," said the professor, "I knew nothing about any of it." After a long silence he added: "It was only in 1942 that news first reached me of Jews being murdered by the Germans, somewhere in Russia, but we were strictly forbidden to speak of such things, and the information about it was vague and uncertain." So said S., trying his best to remember what he had seen, and to what extent he was to blame for not having been aware of these things. "Yes, I remember that in 1938 a number of synagogues were burned down, and the Jewish stores were destroyed—that I couldn't help knowing about." (He meant *Kristallnacht*). "A young boy, a fan of Hitler and of his racial theories, came running to us at the time, pale and trembling: 'No, this I can't bear,' he said. 'They told us to dress as civilians, pretend to be an enraged crowd, burn and destroy. I'm leaving the Party!'"

"People weren't yet being murdered then," added S., trying to diminish the horror of the facts. "A few days later, the same boy came running to see me, overjoyed: 'It's evident that those orders were only issued by the junior ranks, they came from bad underlings, it was a misunderstanding, today an order came from the senior authorities to stop these practices, so clearly those at the top are against them, Hitler does not condone them,' the young believer told me with relief. And he remained in the Party."

I was finding it hard to listen to my professor. A fan of racial theories? How noble is that?

But then I remembered being on the beach at Sopot in 1936. At the time the place was full of Nordic *Hitlerjugend* types, very fit and very proper, on expeditions. One scene stuck in my memory: a boy of fifteen or sixteen in a uniform was guiding a boy of about six or seven with almost maternal tenderness and care. He seemed to be preparing him for a Party entrance exam, and was lecturing him, as far as I remember, on all the ranks in the navy. The small boy was listening very attentively—evidently the older one had taken on the role of his tutor. The perfect scene. A few years later, if not these same boys, then boys of the same type were beating Jews, driving Poles out of their homes, and kicking the corpses of executed partisans on the streets of Warsaw. And it occurred to me that these more recent memories should not erase my remembrance of that innocent scene. It had happened too.

"One sets out as a volunteer, with the idea of sacrifice, and finds oneself in a war which resembles a war of mercenaries, only with much more cruelty," wrote Simone Weil to Georges Bernanos in 1938, referring to the Spanish Civil War.

My German on the ship told me about these young people: about their *idealism*, about their belief in Hitler, the embodiment of the fatherland, wronged by its evil neighbors. I shall never forget him for making me start to have a sense of this other face of it, abased and poisoned by Hitler.

I can see a connection here with the indignation of the young German woman who was suddenly rejected by the Jewish woman from Israel—the German woman probably felt innocent, not just as an individual but as a German, ever loyal, ever obedient, mystically obedient to authority. She herself may have lost loved ones *mit stolzen Trauer* (with proud mourning) at the front or in the air raids, maybe she still remembered her own surges of love for the Führer. In her mind it would be linked with the memory of her people's heroism, the suffering of her nation; not for a moment was it associated with the hell of the camps and the wrongs inflicted by her nation. Maybe she didn't even believe in them.

The more I watched the Germans on that ship—above all the nice, extremely polite, extremely German women, who on parting wrote sentimental verses in each other's albums, and told how in their wrecked apartments in bombed-out cities they had still managed to place a bunch of flowers on the dinner table for their husbands, and how they had heard amateur quartets playing classical music in the cellars—the more vividly I imagined inhuman scenes of obtuse German cruelty or pathological sadism, as the words of Governor Frank rang in my ears, from a speech he made at a government assembly in the winter of 1941: "We want to have compassion for the German people only, and for nobody else."

In 1939, immediately after the September campaign, the seventeen-year-old son of a famous Polish diplomat arrived at his abandoned family manor house in the Kielce area, wanting to take up residence. The house had been occupied by Bavarians, nice, quiet people from the Landsturm.* They received him politely, refused him the right

---

Landsturm is the German historical term for a reserve force or militia, usually troops of inferior quality. —*Trans.*

to live there, but allowed him to visit his house. To his great surprise, he soon discovered that the Jewish population of the nearest small town was crowded into its capacious cellars. He knew many of these people; in desperation they cried for help, a glass of water, or some food. With hardly anything to eat, they were living under the floor as the nice Bavarians walked around above them. These Landsturm soldiers were Catholics, who donated for Masses to be said for various causes and who took holy communion, as the priest from the local church told him. They "couldn't hear" the screams and groans of the crowd of Jews doomed to die of starvation.

How can one understand, how can one explain this combination of good nature, this *Gemütlichkeit*, and this total indifference, this acceptance? Is it to do with inner censorship? Is it to do with a conscious discipline of *not* making associations, which ultimately leads to an inability to make them?

When one of the women's camps was captured by the Allies, an abandoned photograph album was found; the women who had been imprisoned there could not believe their eyes when in the carefully glued-in pictures they saw touching scenes, in which they recognized the cruelest prison guard of all in her family circle, with her old mother, with a child on her knees, and with a lovely maternal smile on her face. At the camp, this same woman had bullied the women in her charge, and had never been without her crop, with which she lashed them until they bled, sometimes for no reason.

"Man is broad, too broad," wrote Dostoevsky. "I'd make him narrower."

Many other people who survived the camps told me of similar scenes, where as soon as they were outside the wire, their persecutors changed their faces and behavior, cuddling children and stroking kittens—the same people who moments earlier had literally been torturing people, smashing children's skulls by seizing them by the legs and hurling them against a wall. Is it any wonder that as I watched those German women on the ship, refined, musical, and poetic, I kept remembering other scenes and stories, and having suspicions that were cruelly unjust?

The Polish writer Tadeusz Borowski, who survived hell, quite literally, in the German camps, after the war became an ardent, active, committed communist in Poland, because at the time he saw communism as the only possible counterbalance to all the German madness; eventually he was to discover similar distortions and falsifications, and the same injuries to humanity in communism, and killed himself by opening the gas tap in his kitchen. In his raw report of his experiences in the camps, Borowski described a scene he had witnessed. When the people arriving on yet another transport were pulled half-alive from railcars that were packed to bursting, then stripped naked and beaten as they were being led to their death, a young Jewish woman had the strength to seize the revolver from an SS man whose daily task was to herd these people into the gas chambers, and used it to shoot him in the stomach. As he lay there scratching at the earth, the SS man cried: *"Gott, was hab ich getan um so zu leiden?"**

How will a German read these words of mine? Of course I know that not just once but thousands of times, in territory recaptured by Poland and purged of Germans, the Poles committed acts of revenge and crimes including theft and the murder of innocent people. Looking at me, a German might remember those scenes; the question of "who started it" goes back into the past for centuries. But in this instance I am not concerned about the potential for cruelty that lies hidden if not within each human being then certainly within each nation. What I wonder about is the capacity to combine emotions that are mutually exclusive, this double life, and this astonishing sense of innocence. Could it be a specifically German trait? Hitler consciously developed it in the nation and took it to its ultimate consequences, by spreading over time the surprises brought by his decisions, and by raising countless impenetrable barriers, which divided the entire population into strata that were more or less, or not at all initiated into forms and methods of fighting. According to one of Hitler's decrees, nobody had the right to know more than he should— *das niemand mehr erfahren durfte als er musste.*

---

*"O God, what have I done to deserve this suffering?"

Under the influence of S., his descriptions and stories, I started to do some self-analysis. Where is the border between the burden of joint responsibility borne by the Germans for Hitler's deeds, and the burden that each of us has carried and carries within us? Because we have been and are still deaf, because we lack imagination, and prefer the convenience of the idle reasoning that says "it's not my business." Thousands and thousands of Poles, consumed by their own misfortune, by the fight for Poland or simply the fight to survive, watched the extermination of the Jews in Poland with indifference; some were even glad of it. "Hitler, oh yes, he's evil incarnate, but he has done one good thing that we wouldn't have been able to do—he has got rid of Poland's Jews." More than one of us has heard such remarks. Now we know that in the interwar period—when Poland was independent—communists were beaten and tortured at the prison in Łuck (these tortures are mentioned in *Conspiracy of Silence*, an entirely reliable book by Alexander Weissberg-Cybulski). We know that the Polish police specialized in beating the kidneys with rubber batons, just as the specialty of the Hungarian police involved sticking metal pen nibs under the fingernails. I remember that at the time I made an appeal to those at the very top of our police hierarchy on behalf of a communist imprisoned in Łuck. A few months later I received a polite reply, on beautiful paper, to say that the matter was being investigated. Doesn't this give me the capacity to understand the mystery of the German camps, of the extermination of the Jews, or the plans to annihilate the Poles?

In any case, the Germans must *not only* have been blindly obedient to Hitler's orders but also have had a subconscious wish *not to know*, because that would have demanded a moral, *independent* reaction.

"I swear to you, I knew nothing about it," I can still hear S. saying. How many voices like that one have we all heard?

And what about us? What was it like in our country in the years when Hitler was already in power in Germany before 1939? There were the Brest trials, and Bereza Kartuska—luckily the only prison camp in Poland before 1939 where extreme Polish nationalists, Ukrainian nationalists, Jews, communists, and profiteers were sent. The pacification of Ukraine was conducted with great cruelty.* And we all knew about it—there was no conspiracy of silence, and there were voices of protest, including that of the great writer Maria Dąbrowska. But did my own reaction at the time go any further than liberal outrage which involved no personal risk, because we didn't have a Hitler?

Since my long conversations with my German friend, I have not ceased to consider the question of German responsibility, but I no longer find it as simple or as exclusive. In my mind it has become a universal problem that goes far beyond the Germans. Today I am no longer able to think of Germany in isolation. In another form, with another ideology, adapted to its situation, could not any country be taken over by a similar madness?

The automatic disdain of so many Poles for all their neighbors, and even more for the Jews, came from a similar sense of their own superiority or even from a sense of mission. Would not Poland too be capable of yielding—as Germany did—to the sort of hypnotic power exerted by Hitler? Perhaps it would be prevented by the anarchic element that is present in the Polish character but is quite alien to the German psyche, and that would not let a Pole be entirely subjugated, voluntarily, of his own free choice, not just in terms of his deeds but also his thoughts. For in this case it is not thought that shapes a man but a one-track will that shapes thought, and then no part of the brain is capable of free thought.

Of course I do not intend to compare the wrongs committed by Poland with the phenomenon—surely the only one of its kind in

---

*At the Brest trials, held in Warsaw from October 1931 to January 1932, leaders of the Centrolew, a "Center-Left" anti-Sanacja-government political opposition movement were prosecuted on a charge of plotting an anti-government coup.

Bereza Kartuska prison was a detention camp established in 1934 to detain people who were viewed by the Polish state as a "threat to security, peace and social order" without formal charges or trial; initially most detainees were political opponents of the Sanacja regime.

The pacification of Ukraine was the punitive action by police and military in the fall of 1930 in eastern Galicia in response to a wave of acts of sabotage against Polish property in the region. —*Trans.*

history—known as Nazism. There is a difference between Poland's misdeeds and this pyramid of crimes against humanity that could only have arisen as the result of an active, systematic concept, worked out to the tiniest details, and obligatory at the very top, as the result of the systematic, active consent of the nation, the ruthless, blind obedience, and the labor of millions of people, which were the links binding this precise mechanism. No other country has produced so many hundreds and hundreds of engineers, chemists, scholars, and doctors who designed the crematorium ovens, the factories that made soap out of human fat, who gave thousands of people lethal injections of phenol and carried out medical experiments on prisoners, resulting in permanent disability or death; no other country has produced such vast numbers of typists and draughtswomen who urgently typed and retyped chemical formulae for putting thousands of people to death as fast as possible, or under the direction of great scholars and architects drew the plans for buildings designed to accommodate the largest possible number of human beings in order to kill them in the most economical way and in the shortest space of time.

Hitler's magic power and his brilliant sense of when and how to play on the German psyche was not just an accident arising out of nothing, but had its genealogy among the Germans, going back for centuries. Heine wrote about the ancient stony gods that would "rise from the forgotten debris and smash the Gothic cathedrals."

What sort of people would have the courage to refuse to surrender to this mass hypnosis, to stand up to it and wage war against it for years on end, to the death? The word "greatness" applies when we talk of those people's dauntless minds and fearless will.

In the 1950s a group of my Federalist friends invited me to attend a private screening of a movie made for Hitler and on his orders, at the trial in Berlin of those who had taken part in the July assassination attempt, where the prosecutor was Roland Freisler. This movie was discovered in the ruins of Berlin (as far as I know, it was later shown around the world with some other documentary films). I remember that the defendants included von Hassell, who had been the Nazi ambassador to Rome, von Schulenburg, their ambassador to

Moscow, and a series of other top dignitaries and generals. Among all these figures, some of whom I knew by name or function, among all these victorious, decorated men who stood there in dirty shirts holding up their rumpled pants without suspenders and buttons, there was one man whose name I had never heard before and whose role in the attempt on Hitler's life I had no idea of at the time. He was Ulrich Wilhelm Graf Schwerin von Schwanenfeld, a Prussian from Pomerania. He was still a relatively young man, and his face was the picture of calm and concentration, almost absent. When his turn for judgment came, Prosecutor Freisler immediately began to insult him, screaming hideous abuse at him nonstop. I watched Schwerin's focused, distant face, as a hail of curses fell on him, "*Schwein-hund, Schweinhund!*" At one point Freisler fell silent to swallow his saliva, and then we heard Schwerin's voice, speaking calmly, as if to himself: "*Ich habe zu viel Mord in Polen gesehen*" ("I have seen too much murder in Poland").

"*Mord? Mord? Dass nennen sie Mord?*" ("Murder? Murder? You call that murder?") Freisler yelled and screeched.

That was all. But that face of Schwerin's, and that one short remark he uttered told me more about Germany than I ever knew before. Schwerin was executed that same day. To the present I still retain the feeling that not only had I witnessed the condemnation to death of an innocent man, but that from that moment on my attitude to the Germans changed.

The loneliness of the individual amid a hostile crowd, or more than that, dignity recovered. So humanity does exist.

It was many years later that I learned about the role played by Schwerin. In Munich, as early as 1923, he had already seen the danger of Nazism and had fought against it. In 1932 he openly opposed Hitler, before the Reich's presidential elections. In 1935, when one of his friends came back to Germany from Africa, he found that an entire resistance organization had already been formed by Schwerin and his friends. In 1938 they assembled at his house in Mecklenburg—apparently that was when the coup against Hitler's regime was initiated and prepared. But Chamberlain's visit to Germany ruined their plans. On June 20, 1944, Schwerin was found in von Stauffenberg's room in Berlin, from where he was led out in handcuffs to his death. At the time he said: "The only thing we can do for our cause now is to die."

Annedore Leber has published two books consisting of 138 plain biographies of Germans who died in the fight against Hitler.* Each biography is supplied with a photograph. Most of the photographs were taken by the police or in the courtroom. On any person of goodwill, these two books, these short biographies and these faces will have a more profound effect than the most terrifying figures or theoretical dissertations.

Claus Schenk Graf von Stauffenberg, who led the assassination attempt of July 20, 1944, has a profile as if from a Roman medal. If the attempt had succeeded—here I am thinking like a Pole—Warsaw would probably not have been destroyed. This man—whom one of the German generals described as the only genius among his staff officers—a German of that era, on deciding to carry out the coup, said: "Before our God and our conscience, my plan must be carried out, because that man is evil incarnate." He was shot dead on July 20, 1944.

I have been leafing through both books, looking at the portraits and biographies.

Julius Leber, one of the leaders of the north German workers, was a social democrat; delegated in the conspirators' plans to be minister of home affairs in the new Germany, he had already been arrested in 1933. Arrested again in July 1944, he was condemned to death. Before the sentence was carried out on January 6, 1945, he wrote in a message to his friends: "The cost of one's own life is a worthy price to pay for such a good and just cause. We have done what was in our power. It is not our fault that it has turned out this way and not differently."

Michael Kitzelmann, from a peasant family in Thuringia, only in his midtwenties, said to his comrades at the front: "If these criminals

---

Das Gewissen steht auf (The Conscience Awakes), and *Das Gewissen entscheidet* (The Conscience Decides), Mosaik-Verlag, 1956–1957.

are going to be victorious, I would prefer not to live." Tried at the fortress in Orel, he was sentenced to death for "undermining military force." An appeal for mercy was refused. In the same fortress, on a steep bank of the River Oka, the sentence was carried out in 1942.

Twenty-two-year-old Sophie Scholl and her brother Hans were sentenced to death in February 1943 for belonging to the "White Rose," a secret society opposed to Hitler, the aim of which was "to revive the seriously wounded spirit of Germany."

Joseph Wirmer was designated to be justice minister after the coup and would restore justice. Hearing one of Hitler's speeches on the radio in 1933, he said: "I shall be that man's enemy." On September 8, 1944, he stood in a Berlin courtroom, a huge, broad-shouldered, self-contained man, looked at Freisler with a calm gaze and said: "If I am to hang, Prosecutor, it is not I who shall be afraid, but you!" The death sentence was carried out that same day.

The author of this book admits how hard it was for her to select these 138 names from so many whom, for lack of space, she could not include; as she says, those mentioned are just a small number of the German victims of the fight.

The French writer David Rousset, who was a prisoner in Auschwitz, claims that in January 1943 a thousand uniforms were sent for disinfection that had belonged to a thousand German officers who were gassed forty-eight hours earlier.

Eugen Kogon, author of the essential German book about the camps,* who survived seven years in them himself, writes that more than five thousand people from all strata of society were executed after the July coup against Hitler. In a situation where the betrayal of secrets carried the death penalty, these figures acquired at great risk can only represent a small percentage of the victims of the plot. Nowadays, twenty years after the war, do the Germans themselves know how many there were?

---

*Der SS-Staat. Das System der deutschen Konzentrationslager, published in English as The Theory and Practice of Hell, New York, 1950, translated by Heinz Norden. —Trans.

At the above-mentioned trial, Prosecutor Freisler thundered at the condemned Helmuth James Graf von Moltke: "Herr Graf, we National Socialists have one thing in common with Christianity, and one thing alone—we demand the whole man."

The fight against Nazism also demanded the whole man. It was not just Wotan and Thor who shaped the mold of German consciousness and subconsciousness.

Many years before the catastrophe the French critic Charles du Bos wrote: "I believe that if everything deserted mankind, the music of Bach would be eternal; if the world were swept away by a great cataclysm, one cannot begin to imagine that the music of Bach would also be engulfed by it."

In Germany Bach was, and still is, not just the sustenance of the elite but the daily bread of innumerable masses; people listened to his music amid the apocalypse of bombardment, amid corpses and charred ruins, and it restored them to life.

And suddenly, as I look at the photographs in Annedore Leber's two volumes—the faces of those exterminated by Hitler—as I think of the millions of German victims, it strikes me that anyone who identifies Nazism with Germany, with Germany as a whole, is mean-spirited.

APPENDIX
Wicio's Story

Translator's note: The following piece of text was found in Józef Czapski's archive at the National Museum in Kraków in a file containing various pieces of material that he did not include in the first edition of *Inhuman Land*. It was added to the most recent Polish edition (Wydawnictwo Znak, Kraków, 2017), edited and with a commentary by Janusz S. Nowak. Czapski heard this story in the Starobilsk prisoner-of-war camp from a fellow prisoner, Captain Witold (Wicio) Kaczkowski. It describes the fate of his uncle, a landowner from near Łódź, who in 1915 was innocently arrested by the Germans for espionage. The underlinings are Czapski's own.

On September 2 [1941] we left Gryazovets. Thus we had been in captivity for almost two years.

Before the war it had once occurred to me with mild regret that I had never had the experience of being in prison, so I didn't know what it was like to endure such physical and moral limitation.

Here, in Starobilsk, as I was out walking in the twilight I saw the dark major's block, its windows dark in the nighttime, I realized that this was it—this was exactly what I had wanted, the experience of being a prisoner.

Nevertheless, this was not a prison; being in the camp—where we could move about within a few hundred square meters, where we were able to commune with a large number of comrades, and where we had the right to spend time outside each day—was of course incomparably easier than being in prison.

After the tragedy of April 1940, when most of our fellows were murdered, only those who endured this year together in the cramped conditions of the crowded bunks, as we shared the same miseries and joys behind the wire, can know the true meaning of fellowship and friendship in such circumstances. Larger and smaller groups form— out of seemingly comical patriotism felt in the barracks or on the bunks—but it's an expression of the hunger of the environment, the hunger for fresh air among people deprived of their loved ones, with almost no news from them, and so every time these groups or teams are split apart it's very painful.

After the breakup of Starobilsk—when as a group of seventy-nine we were transferred via Pavlishchev Bor to Gryazovets—from 1940 onward we ended up in what were probably the best conditions for any Polish POWs in Soviet Russia.

We were fed on three kinds of buckwheat cooked with suet, we had rations of bread and rations of sugar, and we had the opportunity to correspond once a month.

The monastery where the majority lived and the two cottages where the seniors lived were separated from each other by a little valley, with a skinny stream flowing down it—thick grass and tall trees grew there—birches and poplars?

Anyone who had time off (not everyone was taken to work every day) spent all day in the summer on the grass, and in winter on the bunk, or even in bed, because there were beds in the cottages.

It was dark, and there were bedbugs, but in a pinch one could do a bit of work, study, or read.

The most agonizing thing was a feeling which as soon as one was released one automatically forgot—the sense of being totally unsure if we would ever see anything again in our lives apart from the wire fences and this alien, hostile world. Each man lived on hope, each man needed to hope for a change of situation. Each optimistic hint smuggled through in cards from our relatives—each prophecy was passed around with faith, everything served as fuel for our hopes, but in fact that very feeling, that sense of being buried alive, was cruel, and it was unlikely that we'd ever get beyond the wire, unless to get

A drawing of Witold (Wicio) Kaczkowski while reading a book at either the Starobilsk or the Gryazovets camp. Czapski recorded Kaczkowski's tale in "Wicio's Story." The drawing is from the first, now missing volume of the diary. A reproduced manuscript of the text was found in Czapski's archive.

a bullet in the back of the skull, if out of the fifteen thousand who had been in Starobilsk, Kozelsk, and Ostashkov there were only about four hundred of us left in Gryazovets at that time.

I was never as clearly aware of this as on the day in Gryazovets when one of our comrades told us about the fate of his paternal uncle.

I had met Captain K. on the journey from Starobilsk to Pavlishchev Bor—on the very worst shelves in the stifling prison train. He was reticent, his hearing was poor, and he had trouble communicating. He had widely set, strikingly bright blue eyes and a tired, middle-aged face with an unhealthy complexion, and was one of a small number who wore a four-cornered hat.

While we were in the prison train he had a heart attack, so he had to spend the first few days at Pavlishchev Bor in the hospital.

In our cottage at Gryazovets, where we lived in luxury—because we slept in beds, seven of us in a small room—Captain K. was my neighbor.

And here for quite a time he kept a polite distance from the rest of us; a few months went by before we had grown used to each other and actually did make friends. He was a landowner from near Łódź, cultured, an old-school National Democrat—with very distinct political views dating from a certain era, alien to my own. He was fiercely independent in his views and in his attitude—he never resorted to opinions aimed at winning him greater sympathy but always spoke his mind, and for hours and hours on end he would walk to and fro along the only road that cut across our camp. In the very coldest weather he would wrap himself in a shawl, put on a padded jacket and his green four-cornered hat, and keep on and on walking.

Once I suddenly came upon him in total darkness. That night the moon was shining. He had his hands folded, and he was kneeling down—this was at the start of our time in Gryazovets, the period when Paris fell, and France was defeated, such a patent victory for the world of antidemocratic states that for some infected by communism the possibility of victory in the future for anything other than fascism or communism seemed downright comical.

Nowadays no censor would let through the epithets in which

our *politruki*, lecturers etc. showered not just France but perhaps even more so Britain, whose fall they were anticipating with undisguised joy.

At this point we no longer had the right to write letters home—they had taken it away from us when we left Starobilsk, and only restored it in late fall.

I shall never forget that figure, that austere, refined gentleman, broken by pain, kneeling in the darkness to pray.

Much later on, in that soft, cold, unaffected voice of his he told us about the strange fate of his uncle in the other war. It stuck in my memory and became for me a symbol of the strange fate of every Polish generation; in the light of the fantastical fortunes of this Polish individual, our own fate seemed less full of acrimony.

Our consolations and hopes seemed insignificant, if such a fate could befall a man during that last, still civilized war.

How many hundreds of thousands have a similar fate of permanent perdition ahead of them today.

"My uncle was a landowner. He had an estate on the Warta River, a wife, and two small children; he was a national activist, respected in the district." He didn't want to leave the estate when the Germans invaded. He hid in the cellar and only emerged when the Germans drove out the Russians. When he came out he was arrested by the Germans, suspected of espionage, and sent to a camp in Kalisz. From there he wrote to his wife in 1915. Then all trace of him vanished.

The war ended, the POWs returned, but Mr. K. did not. His wife made efforts to find him, and even went to Germany, but all trace of him had disappeared.

The children grew up. The daughter went into a convent—there was no news of her father, and his wife, permanently in mourning, did not sit praying at the small estate on the Warta; she couldn't delude herself that her husband was alive and would return!

One evening in 1935, and thus twenty years later, a strange man arrived at the manor, dressed like a beggar. He asked if he could see the "young lady." He knew her pet name. When it was explained to him that the young lady was not there but had gone to a convent, after much hesitation he finally agreed to talk to the mother, and to tell her why he had come to see the young lady.

The strange man informed the wife that her husband was alive!, that he was in French Guyana, and that he was asking to be rescued. And this is the story he told—he himself had been jailed in France and exiled to Guyana by the French government. Apparently it was the custom in Guyana that anyone who escaped by swimming into the sea and was fished out by a passing British ship was not handed over to the French authorities but taken to the nearest port where he wanted to stay, and there set free.

In Guyana, the strange "beggar" had still been full of strength and had jumped into the sea—a British ship had fished him out and cast him up on the shore in Portugal.

Before jumping into the sea, he had worked and lived with an old man, who had already been in Guyana for many years, and who told him to go and see his family and tell them his strange story.

And so, according to the newcomer's account, Mr. K. had been transported from Kalisz to a POW camp in Bavaria; he had escaped from it and stolen his way across the borders into Italy. Here he had suffered the typical fate of a fugitive. He had no documents, of course, so to be on the safe side the Italians had sent him to the Aeolian Islands along with a group of Austrian prisoners. There he had met a Polish doctor who, in an effort to help him, had given him the passport of a deceased Polish prisoner whose name was Pająk.

Equipped with this other man's passport, K. tried his luck again. He escaped from the islands in a small boat, was fished out by a ship, and reached Marseille. At this point the whole story became complicated and confused.

There, for unknown reasons, he was sentenced to life imprisonment and deported to Guyana. All this was fantastical, but the details the stranger provided about the lost husband and father, and the things he knew about the entire family that he'd heard from the prisoner in Guyana were too authentic for the family to be in any doubt. The task in hand was to save K. at any cost, an innocent man who had spent twenty years as a prisoner.

An adult by now, his son set off for Paris with special letters from Polish Foreign Minister Józef Beck to the Quai d'Orsay, requesting the help of the highest authorities.

The top French lawyers took the matter in hand. They managed to confirm the following: In 1917 a Russian division had revolted on the French front. Without investigating the individual differences very closely, the French had shot a number of people and had exiled some large groups of soldiers to Guyana. They managed to confirm that there had indeed been a man called Pająk in one of the groups destined for deportation.

A letter was sent to Guyana to ask if among the prisoners the man called Pająk was still alive. The administration replied to say that there had never been any prisoner of that name, and that it must be a misunderstanding or a mistake. The family had failed to find out any more. Maybe he was dead, or maybe the French police was reluctant to admit that it had kept an innocent man in prison for twenty years in the harshest exile, from where POWs from Russian camps had no correspondence rights.

Wicio told us the whole story calmly, in a soft and even tone. I remember how much the story shook me at the time. The old man, who spent hours pacing the prison courtyard in Guyana—how similar he was to the man telling the story, who even in the coldest weather had to walk to and fro at a steady pace along the one road linking the exit gate and the main monastery building.

In fact at the time everything implied that we too would never see the world beyond the prison wires again.

Józef Czapski testifying to the United States House Select Committee to Conduct an Investigation of the Facts, Evidence, and Circumstances of the Katyń Forest Massacre. Frankfurt, April 23, 1952: "First of all, there is no doubt in my mind that these men were murdered by the Soviets. Secondly, we keep forgetting that Russia is the most centralized country in the world whenever it comes to issuing orders or directives or policy. Therefore, the full responsibility for this crime does not rest with some NKVD sadist; the full responsibility rests with Beria and Stalin." (Quoted in the movie recorded during the hearing.)

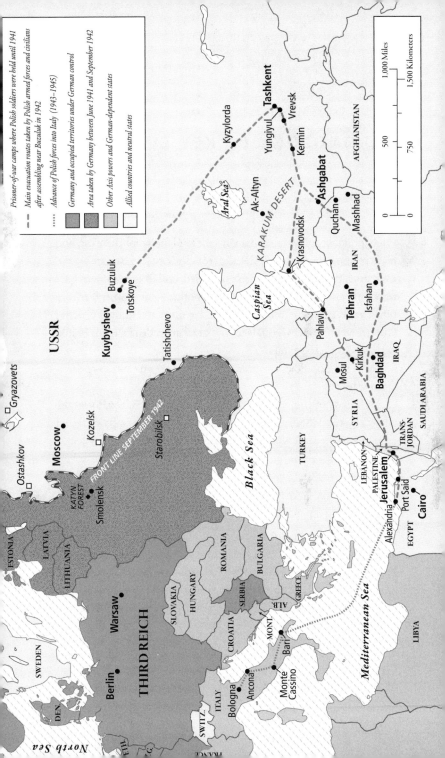

Prisoner-of-war camps where Polish soldiers were held until 1941

Main evacuation routes taken by Polish armed forces and civilians after assembling near Buzuluk in 1942

Advance of Polish forces into Italy (1943–1945)

Germany and occupied territories under German control

Area taken by Germany between June 1941 and September 1942

Other Axis powers and German-dependent states

Allied countries and neutral states

1,000 Miles

1,500 Kilometers

500

750

0

0

AFGHANISTAN

Tashkent

Yungiyul   Vrevsk

Kyzylorda

Kermin

Ak-Altyn   **Ashgabat**

Aral Sea   Quchan   Mashhad

KARAKUM DESERT   Krasnovodsk   **IRAN**

Caspian Sea   **Tehran**

Pahlavi   Isfahan

USSR

Buzuluk   Totskoye

Kuybyshev

Kirkuk   **IRAQ**

Tatishchevo   Mosul   **Baghdad**

Gryazovets   **SYRIA**   SAUDI ARABIA

Ostashkov   **Moscow**   **TRANS-JORDAN**

Kozelsk   Starobilsk   **LEBANON**

FRONT LINE SEPTEMBER 1942   **PALESTINE**   **Jerusalem**

KATYN FOREST   Port Said

Smolensk   Alexandria   **Cairo**

Black Sea   **EGYPT**

TURKEY

ESTONIA   **LIBYA**

LATVIA

LITHUANIA   ROMANIA

Mediterranean Sea

THIRD REICH   HUNGARY   BULGARIA

Warsaw   SLOVAKIA   SERBIA   GREECE   ALB.

CROATIA   MONT.

Berlin   Bari

SWEDEN   ITALY   Ancona

DEN.   Bologna   Monte Cassino

SWITZ.

North Sea   FRANCE

CHRONOLOGY OF KEY EVENTS

1939

On September 1, Nazi Germany invades Poland from the west, and on September 17 the USSR invades from the east. Resistance is soon overcome, the country is entirely occupied, and its government goes into exile abroad. The Germans incorporate some Polish territory into the Reich and from the remainder form a colonial "General Government," under German administration headed by Hans Frank, with Kraków as its capital.

Some 230,000 Poles are interned in Soviet prison camps as prisoners of war.

Hundreds of thousands of Poles from the eastern territories occupied by the USSR are deported to Soviet labor camps scattered throughout Central Asia, Siberia, and the Far East.

1940

On March 5, the Soviet Politburo takes a decision to execute the Polish prisoners held in camps at Kozelsk, Starobilsk, and Ostashkov in secret. Thousands of Polish officers imprisoned at Kozelsk are murdered and buried in pits in Katyn forest near Smolensk, and the rest are killed at other sites. Others are sent to labor camps in Kolyma. The name "Katyn" has come to signify the massacre at various sites of some 22,000 Polish prisoners, including officers, policemen, and others.

1941

On June 22, Germany launches Operation Barbarossa, the invasion of the USSR. On July 30, the Sikorski-Maisky Agreement is signed, forming an alliance between Poland and the USSR. Shortly after, under a declared "amnesty," all exiled Poles are released from Soviet labor camps. They start traveling to Buzuluk, where a Polish army is to be formed.

1942

Under the command of General Władysław Anders, the new army travels through the Middle East.

In the spring and summer, approximately 78,600 Polish soldiers and tens of thousands of Polish civilians leave the USSR and enter Iran.

1943

The Polish Second Corps is created from various units fighting alongside the Allies in all theatres of war, and will play an important role in the Italian campaign.

1944

In May, the Polish Second Corps fights with distinction at the Battle of Monte Cassino.

In August the Warsaw Uprising begins but is entirely crushed by September 27. The Red Army lingers on the far side of the River Vistula while the Germans destroy the city. By the end of the year the Soviets have installed a communist government in Poland.

1945

In February at the Yalta Conference, Stalin, Roosevelt, and Churchill agree on the postwar reorganization of Europe. The Polish eastern border will follow the Curzon Line, effectively allowing the USSR to keep all the Polish territory that it had annexed in 1939. To compensate, Poland is given formerly German territory to the west.

After the war ends, many demobilized Polish soldiers and other Polish exiles settle in Great Britain.

OTHER NEW YORK REVIEW CLASSICS

For a complete list of titles, visit www.nyrb.com or write to:
Catalog Requests, NYRB, 435 Hudson Street, New York, NY 10014

J.R. ACKERLEY My Dog Tulip*
J.R. ACKERLEY My Father and Myself*
HENRY ADAMS The Jeffersonian Transformation
RENATA ADLER Pitch Dark*
RENATA ADLER Speedboat*
AESCHYLUS Prometheus Bound; translated by Joel Agee*
ROBERT AICKMAN Compulsory Games*
LEOPOLDO ALAS His Only Son *with* Doña Berta*
CÉLESTE ALBARET Monsieur Proust
DANTE ALIGHIERI The Inferno
JEAN AMÉRY Charles Bovary, Country Doctor*
KINGSLEY AMIS The Alteration*
KINGSLEY AMIS Ending Up*
KINGSLEY AMIS Girl, 20*
KINGSLEY AMIS The Green Man*
KINGSLEY AMIS Lucky Jim*
ROBERTO ARLT The Seven Madmen*
U.R. ANANTHAMURTHY Samskara: A Rite for a Dead Man*
IVO ANDRIĆ Omer Pasha Latas*
WILLIAM ATTAWAY Blood on the Forge
W.H. AUDEN (EDITOR) The Living Thoughts of Kierkegaard
W.H. AUDEN W. H. Auden's Book of Light Verse
ERICH AUERBACH Dante: Poet of the Secular World
EVE BABITZ Eve's Hollywood*
EVE BABITZ Slow Days, Fast Company: The World, the Flesh, and L.A.*
DOROTHY BAKER Cassandra at the Wedding*
DOROTHY BAKER Young Man with a Horn*
J.A. BAKER The Peregrine
S. JOSEPHINE BAKER Fighting for Life*
HONORÉ DE BALZAC The Human Comedy: Selected Stories*
HONORÉ DE BALZAC The Memoirs of Two Young Wives*
HONORÉ DE BALZAC The Unknown Masterpiece *and* Gambara*
VICKI BAUM Grand Hotel*
SYBILLE BEDFORD A Favorite of the Gods *and* A Compass Error*
SYBILLE BEDFORD Jigsaw*
SYBILLE BEDFORD A Legacy*
SYBILLE BEDFORD A Visit to Don Otavio: A Mexican Journey*
MAX BEERBOHM The Prince of Minor Writers: The Selected Essays of Max Beerbohm*
MAX BEERBOHM Seven Men
STEPHEN BENATAR Wish Her Safe at Home*
FRANS G. BENGTSSON The Long Ships*
ALEXANDER BERKMAN Prison Memoirs of an Anarchist
GEORGES BERNANOS Mouchette
MIRON BIAŁOSZEWSKI A Memoir of the Warsaw Uprising*
ADOLFO BIOY CASARES The Invention of Morel
PAUL BLACKBURN (TRANSLATOR) Proensa*
CAROLINE BLACKWOOD Great Granny Webster*
LESLEY BLANCH Journey into the Mind's Eye: Fragments of an Autobiography*

* *Also available as an electronic book.*

CHARLES DUFF A Handbook on Hanging
BRUCE DUFFY The World As I Found It*
DAPHNE DU MAURIER Don't Look Now: Stories
ELAINE DUNDY The Dud Avocado*
G.B. EDWARDS The Book of Ebenezer Le Page*
JOHN EHLE The Land Breakers*
MARCELLUS EMANTS A Posthumous Confession
EURIPIDES Grief Lessons: Four Plays; translated by Anne Carson
J.G. FARRELL Troubles*
J.G. FARRELL The Siege of Krishnapur*
J.G. FARRELL The Singapore Grip*
ELIZA FAY Original Letters from India
KENNETH FEARING The Big Clock
FÉLIX FÉNÉON Novels in Three Lines*
M.I. FINLEY The World of Odysseus
THOMAS FLANAGAN The Year of the French*
BENJAMIN FONDANE Existential Monday: Philosophical Essays*
SANFORD FRIEDMAN Conversations with Beethoven*
MARC FUMAROLI When the World Spoke French
CARLO EMILIO GADDA That Awful Mess on the Via Merulana
BENITO PÉREZ GÁLDOS Tristana*
MAVIS GALLANT The Cost of Living: Early and Uncollected Stories*
MAVIS GALLANT Paris Stories*
MAVIS GALLANT A Fairly Good Time *with* Green Water, Green Sky*
MAVIS GALLANT Varieties of Exile*
GABRIEL GARCÍA MÁRQUEZ Clandestine in Chile: The Adventures of Miguel Littín
LEONARD GARDNER Fat City*
WILLIAM H. GASS In the Heart of the Heart of the Country: And Other Stories*
WILLIAM H. GASS On Being Blue: A Philosophical Inquiry*
THÉOPHILE GAUTIER My Fantoms
GE FEI The Invisibility Cloak
JEAN GENET Prisoner of Love
ÉLISABETH GILLE The Mirador: Dreamed Memories of Irène Némirovsky by Her Daughter*
NATALIA GINZBURG Family Lexicon*
JEAN GIONO Hill*
JEAN GIONO Melville: A Novel*
JOHN GLASSCO Memoirs of Montparnasse*
P.V. GLOB The Bog People: Iron-Age Man Preserved
NIKOLAI GOGOL Dead Souls*
ALICE GOODMAN History Is Our Mother: Three Libretti*
PAUL GOODMAN Growing Up Absurd: Problems of Youth in the Organized Society*
A.C. GRAHAM Poems of the Late T'ang
JULIEN GRACQ Balcony in the Forest*
HENRY GREEN Back*
HENRY GREEN Caught*
HENRY GREEN Doting*
HENRY GREEN Living*
HENRY GREEN Loving*
HENRY GREEN Nothing*
HENRY GREEN Party Going*
HANS HERBERT GRIMM Schlump*
EMMETT GROGAN Ringolevio: A Life Played for Keeps
VASILY GROSSMAN An Armenian Sketchbook*

VASILY GROSSMAN Everything Flows*
VASILY GROSSMAN Life and Fate*
VASILY GROSSMAN The Road*
LOUIS GUILLOUX Blood Dark*
PATRICK HAMILTON The Slaves of Solitude*
PETER HANDKE Short Letter, Long Farewell
THORKILD HANSEN Arabia Felix: The Danish Expedition of 1761–1767*
ELIZABETH HARDWICK The Collected Essays of Elizabeth Hardwick*
ELIZABETH HARDWICK The New York Stories of Elizabeth Hardwick*
ELIZABETH HARDWICK Sleepless Nights*
L.P. HARTLEY The Go-Between*
ALFRED HAYES In Love*
PAUL HAZARD The Crisis of the European Mind: 1680–1715*
ALICE HERDAN-ZUCKMAYER The Farm in the Green Mountains*
WOLFGANG HERRNDORF Sand*
YOEL HOFFMANN The Sound of the One Hand: 281 Zen Koans with Answers*
HUGO VON HOFMANNSTHAL The Lord Chandos Letter*
JAMES HOGG The Private Memoirs and Confessions of a Justified Sinner
RICHARD HOLMES Shelley: The Pursuit*
ALISTAIR HORNE A Savage War of Peace: Algeria 1954–1962*
GEOFFREY HOUSEHOLD Rogue Male*
BOHUMIL HRABAL Dancing Lessons for the Advanced in Age*
BOHUMIL HRABAL The Little Town Where Time Stood Still*
DOROTHY B. HUGHES In a Lonely Place*
RICHARD HUGHES A High Wind in Jamaica*
RICHARD HUGHES In Hazard*
RICHARD HUGHES The Fox in the Attic (The Human Predicament, Vol. 1)*
RICHARD HUGHES The Wooden Shepherdess (The Human Predicament, Vol. 2)*
INTIZAR HUSAIN Basti*
YASUSHI INOUE Tun-huang*
HENRY JAMES The New York Stories of Henry James*
TOVE JANSSON The Summer Book*
TOVE JANSSON The Woman Who Borrowed Memories: Selected Stories*
RANDALL JARRELL (EDITOR) Randall Jarrell's Book of Stories
UWE JOHNSON Anniversaries*
DAVID JONES In Parenthesis
JOSEPH JOUBERT The Notebooks of Joseph Joubert; translated by Paul Auster
KABIR Songs of Kabir; translated by Arvind Krishna Mehrotra*
FRIGYES KARINTHY A Journey Round My Skull
ERICH KÄSTNER Going to the Dogs: The Story of a Moralist*
HELEN KELLER The World I Live In
YASHAR KEMAL Memed, My Hawk
YASHAR KEMAL They Burn the Thistles
WALTER KEMPOWSKI All for Nothing
MURRAY KEMPTON Part of Our Time: Some Ruins and Monuments of the Thirties*
ARUN KOLATKAR Jejuri
DEZSŐ KOSZTOLÁNYI Skylark*
TOM KRISTENSEN Havoc*
GYULA KRÚDY The Adventures of Sindbad*
SIGIZMUND KRZHIZHANOVSKY Autobiography of a Corpse*
SIGIZMUND KRZHIZHANOVSKY The Return of Munchausen
K'UNG SHANG-JEN The Peach Blossom Fan*
GERT LEDIG The Stalin Front*